Social Studies and the Elementary School Child

THIRD EDITION

GEORGE W. MAXIM

West Chester University

MERRILL PUBLISHING COMPANY

A Bell & Howell Information Company

Columbus ▪ Toronto ▪ London ▪ Melbourne

Cover Photo: © Merrill/Bruce Johnson. Second and third grade
students visit the Ohio Village, the Ohio Historical
Society's replica of a nineteenth-century town.

Published by Merrill Publishing Company
A Bell & Howell Information Company
Columbus, Ohio 43216

This book was set in Serifa.

Administrative Editor: Jeff Johnston
Production Editor: Molly Kyle
Cover Designer: Cathy Watterson
Photos: pp. 17, 80, 98, CEM/Bruce Johnson; pp. 156, 337,
CEM/Kevin Fitzsimons; pp. 174, Pat McKay; pp. 248, CEM/
Dan Unkefer.

Library of Congress Catalog Card Number: 86-61673
International Standard Book Number: 0-675-20707-x

Printed in the United States of America
5 6 7 8 9—91 90

To Michael and Jeffrey

Into my heart's treasury
You have slipped memories more precious than gold.

Preface

Like the second edition of *Social Studies and the Elementary School Child*, this third edition is directed toward prospective teachers who plan careers in elementary education. It is designed to influence professional growth and caring by drawing from several major sources: sound research and theory, personal classroom visitations, and my own teaching experience.

Many changes were made for this new edition. Two new chapters have been added. Chapter 2 focuses on the personal and professional characteristics of good social studies teachers, and Chapter 10 addresses the valuable contributions of the arts to the social studies program. You will also find new or expanded discussions of alternative teaching styles, closed-ended and open-ended inquiry, directed learning, classroom socialization, action learning, computers, and grouping children for social studies instruction. I have also attempted to convince teachers of the critical importance of *teaching* toward the levels of Bloom's Taxonomy. As Dolores Durkin notes, too much time is spent *testing* those levels with uncreative, routine questions without leading children through the thought processes necessary to produce meaningful responses.

Finally, I have redesigned this edition as a developmental approach to social studies instruction. Each chapter presents its recommendations in a developmental framework so that, for example, even kindergarten teachers will understand and appreciate their role in providing the kinds of experiences that allow upper-elementary students to use the process of inquiry successfully. There are specific examples, vignettes, and practical suggestions throughout the text.

As a teacher, your classroom practices should help prepare children to face the challenges of today's world and the unique conditions of the future. You must become a concerned decision maker and a master of the techniques for guiding children in the social studies. As you use this text, you will come to realize that there is no single correct way to teach social studies. You will be asked to consider old theories and new ones. Though you may be tempted to look more favorably on new theories because of their freshness, it is important to examine each option carefully to choose the one that is likely to produce the desirable result. Even the most innovative teaching technique can make the classroom dull and lifeless if it is not suitable for the children. You will also need to adjust or abandon techniques that bore or frustrate children or produce insignificant results. This text is designed as a sourcebook and guide to help you interpret and apply different teaching options.

The importance of alternative teaching styles (e.g., textbook, inquiry, learning centers) and the role of the teacher as decision maker form the central themes of the third edition of *Social Studies and the Elementary School Child*, designed for both preservice and inservice teachers.

Writing a book is never an individual accomplishment. An author can never take complete responsibility for the finished product. This is especially true in my case. Many individuals have made valuable contributions to this book.

This third edition reflects the benefit of valuable comments from the many readers and users of the second edition, who have offered specific ideas and asked challenging questions. That was one of the most exciting parts of the revision process. Readers and users have contributed to my growth as a professional.

My deepest appreciation goes to my wife, Libby. Her patience was certainly pushed to the breaking point a number of times, but she never let me know. Her understanding and encouragement sustained me through many long hours of writing. Without her help, I would never have been able to finish the book. My sons, Michael and Jeffrey, also contributed, although they did not know it. Their cheerfulness and affection picked up my spirits whenever the "writing day blues" began to descend.

I also wish to thank Molly Kyle, my production editor at Merrill, for her help.

Terri Dero, typist of the manuscript, was tireless in preparing material for the project and always cooperative. My colleagues at West Chester University warrant special thanks for their support and recommendations along the way: Kenneth L. Perrin, President; Shirley Walters, Assistant Dean of the School of Education; Joan Hasselquist, Chairperson of the Department of Childhood Studies and Reading; and the others involved in teaching elementary school social studies methods—A. Scott Dunlap and E. Riley Holman.

Last, I would like to thank the reviewers of the manuscript for their excellent suggestions: Helen Darrow, Western Washington University; Vernon Schumacher, University of Wisconsin, Whitewater; Joan Breiter, Iowa State University; Robert Brown, Atlantic University; John Kelly, University of Bridgeport; Verlie Ward, Walla Walla College; M. S. J. Greek, Stetson University; Dennis Strasser, Kutztown University; Robert Lee, Fitchburg State College; Glen Kinzie, University of Southern Indiana; Michael Dianna, Millersville University; John Wilson, Wichita State University; Richard Needham, University of Northern Colorado; Ronald Wheeler, College of William and Mary; Grover Baldwin, Pittsburg State University; Ronald Sterling, University of Cincinnati; Robert Otto, Western Kentucky University; Nell Nicholson, Alabama A&M University; Robert Cornish, University of Arkansas; Marjorie Souers, Indiana University-Purdue University; Joan Moyer, Arizona State University; Tom Rosebrough, Trevecca College; Lon Kellenberger, California State College, Bakersfield; Donald Kelly, University of New Mexico; David Thatcher, Sonoma State University; Thomas McGowan, Indiana State University; Thomas Turner, University of Tennessee; Margaret Laughlin, University of Wisconsin, Green Bay; Jeanette Parker, University of Southwestern Louisiana; and Mary Nan Aldridge, University of Northern Iowa.

Contents

5 ACTIVITY-BASED INSTRUCTION: THE INQUIRY PROCESS 153

6 LEARNING CENTERS   199

Introducing Social Studies Education

KEY CONCEPTS

- ☐ *Understanding how social studies education evolved into what it is today*
- ☐ *Becoming aware of some contemporary trends in the social studies field*
- ☐ *Identifying major objectives of social studies programs in the elementary school*
- ☐ *Differentiating among more and less desirable instructional practices in social studies education*

All education springs from some image of the future. If the image of the future held by a society is grossly inaccurate, its educational system will betray its youth.[1]

Preparing children for the future has always been a major goal of education. And, until about twenty years ago, the future was generally stable and predictable. Elementary school curricula could concentrate on specific subject matter and skills, because the world of the future could be expected to demand little more from its citizens than the world of that day. This condition no longer exists; the future some people predict for our children borders on what others consider science fiction. The current "knowledge explosion" foretells only one thing for certain: elementary school children will experience many changes in the world during their lifetimes. Arthur W. Combs describes a world in the midst of a knowledge explosion.

Few of us really comprehend the extent of the increase in available information. Here are a few statistics provided by futurists: Ninety percent of all the scientists who have ever lived are alive today. Technical information doubles every ten years. There are 100,000 technical journals available now, and the number doubles every 15 years. . . . Futurists tell us this is only the beginning. The explosion will continue at even faster rates in the years to come.[2]

Almost everyone is aware of the rapid change surrounding us, but few can envision its full significance to future goals of education. To further complicate matters, rapid change is not the only factor to consider in educating our youth; we must also be concerned about adult-child interactions. Lloyd DeMause, in comparing the influences of technology and adult-child relationships, suggests that:

The major dynamic in historical change is ultimately neither technology nor economics. More important are the changes in personality that grow from differences between generations in the quality of the relationships between [adult] and child.[3]

Elementary school curricula, then, are products of the sophisticated interrelationships of two major factors: (1) the conditions of society and how its citizens perceive the needs of the future, and (2) the quality of adult-child relationships. Certainly, *each* of these dynamics is an important catalyst for educational change and particularly influences what is presently recommended as desirable teaching in the social studies. To better understand those recommendations for social studies instruction and how we arrived at them, let us explore the traditional practices of the past and how the two dynamics for change influenced our current state of affairs.

SOCIAL STUDIES INSTRUCTION AND ATTITUDES TOWARD CHILDREN

George Santayana has said that a nation that does not remember its history is doomed to repeat it. Surely he was referring to a nation's failures rather than its successes, but his words remind us of the importance of examining how and why things were done in the past—whether on a national scope or at a more limited level such as social studies instruction. To convince people of the value of examining past practices in social studies instruction, I often relate this popular old tale to make my point.

> There is an old story that bears retelling because it illustrates so well how easily things can go on being accepted without ever being questioned.
>
> When Bismarck was the Prussian ambassador to the court of Alexander II in the early 1860s, he looked out a window and saw a sentry on duty in the middle of the vast lawn.
>
> He asked the Czar why the man was there. The Czar asked his aide-de-camp. The aide didn't know. The general in charge of the troops was summoned.
>
> In answer to the question the general replied, "I beg to inform his majesty that it is in accordance with ancient custom."
>
> "What was the origin of that custom?" interrupted Bismarck.
>
> "I don't recall at present," answered the general.
>
> "Investigate and report the result," ordered Alexander.
>
> The investigation took three days. It revealed that the sentry was posted there by an order put on the books 80 years before. The custom had begun one morning in the spring of 1780. Catherine the Great looked out on the lawn and saw the first flower thrusting above the frozen soil. She ordered the sentry posted to prevent anyone's picking the flower, and in 1860 there was still a sentry on the lawn. The sentry was a memorial to custom, habit, or just to everyone's saying, "But we've always done it that way."
>
> And so it is today. Far too few ask, "Why?" When told that something can't be changed, far too few ask, "Why not? Why can't we find a new or better way? How can it be done more easily and effectively? What is worth saving?"

After telling the story of the flower, I ask my students to interpret its implied message. I ask you to do the same. Stop reading and jot down some of your own immediate impressions. These comments are representative of my students' responses:

> The flower was guarded every year and people didn't really know why. Even though it was a ridiculous idea, no one suggested a change for over eighty years. I hate to think what would happen to social studies education if everyone in our field refused to examine what we're doing and why we're doing it.
>
> The people really didn't suggest change because they didn't know why the practice of guarding the flower was started in the first place. If they had tried to find out earlier, the dumb custom wouldn't have been around so long. I guess that's why it's important to examine the history of social

studies, too, so we wouldn't lock ourselves blindly into past practices merely because that's the way it was always done.

Yes, all you've said is true. But, if the custom was a good one, it would have been interesting to see how *it* was started, too. I can think of a couple of old customs that are parts of our lives, such as celebrating holidays like Groundhog Day or Valentine's Day, and I have no idea how they got started. They're something we do automatically every year and enjoy, but don't even realize how they began. It would be interesting to find out. I guess the same is true for social studies education—it would be interesting to see how some of our good practices also got their start in the past. How and why did they happen?

If we didn't know what happened in the past, how would we be convinced that what we consider innovative today is really new?

Most of us do not think of history in these terms. We often associate history with memorizing an endless flow of events from the past, such as the dates of battles or the names and order of presidents. The "living spirit" of history, however, should transcend facts and become transformed into experience. Such an approach does not eliminate facts but goes beyond them by introducing significant events into our lives and encouraging us to reflect upon their meanings.

So, do not read this book for the purpose of storing a conglomeration of facts for recall on a quiz. Instead, look at it the way the general in the story searched for the reason that the flower was so closely guarded for generations. Investigate the past to explain what we are doing now in social studies education and examine the present to understand its historical significance for the future. As you do so, consider these questions to guide your reading: What was it like to be a child during particular historical eras? How did the prevailing view of children affect their schooling?

Earliest Schooling in America

When we review historical accounts of childhood, we readily see that treatment of children was as primitive in comparison to contemporary views of childhood as the original abacus is to the computer. The history of childhood could be considered a nightmare; the farther back we go, the more likely were children to have been killed at birth, abandoned, beaten, sexually abused, or mistreated. It would be easy to discount this treatment of children because of society's general conditions—poor housing, lack of food, medical ignorance, and inadequate health care—but the resentment and hostility toward young children was often worse than the treatment of animals. In fact, societies for the prevention of cruelty to animals sprang up earlier in England and the United States than did societies for the prevention of cruelty to children.

We know little about the treatment of children in America during the colonial period, but since the Europeans who settled in the colonies brought their ideas of child rearing with them, we can assume that colonial practices were much like those in Europe, where children at about the age of three or four—who had not been abandoned, sold, neglected, or killed during infancy—became full-fledged members of adult society. The awareness of what distinguished children from adults was lacking, so "as soon as the child could live without the constant solicitude of his mother, his nanny, or his cradle-rocker, he belonged to adult society."[4] Not knowing why this "adult" acted in ways so foreign to adulthood (running, jumping, laughing, squealing), parents often found young children difficult to care for. Their actions were interpreted as "demonlike"; if allowed to continue, their behavior would make them susceptible to "the power of the devil." To keep children in line, adults regularly terrorized them in a variety of ways. Adults often administered opium and liquor to keep children from crying and tied them to chairs to keep them from crawling. Even into the nineteenth century, strings were attached to children's clothes to control their movements the way a marionette is controlled. By today's standards, acts of discipline would be described as child abuse. Beatings were administered with whips, shovels, canes, and rods. Such "discipline" was widely advocated through the nineteenth century (when it gradually began to go out of style), as century after century of battered children grew up into adulthood and battered their own.

As beatings slowly began to decrease, other forms of punishment had to be found to control children. Shutting children in dark closets or drawers for hours was popular; another method was to threaten children with hideous masks, with "ghosts" who would steal bad children and suck their blood, or with "devils" who would take the children away to Hell, where they would live forever in a red hot oven. Some parents went as far as taking their children to the gallows and forcing them to view executions and rotting corpses. This experience was intended to serve as a lesson of what would happen to children whose behavior wandered from acceptable standards. Children's behavior toward adults was of such concern that the Massachusetts Colony had a "filial disobedience law"—young people who did not obey elders could be put to death. Children were thus totally subservient to adults, but were expected to exhibit adult characteristics. For example, children dressed as adults, worked with adults in tasks around the home and in the fields, drank with adults, and even participated freely in sexual activities. Children could be everything an adult could be; they were husbands or wives, field or factory workers, and kings or queens.

RELIGIOUS INFLUENCES. Why was the period we now know as "childhood" viewed so heartlessly? A logical explanation might be found in the prevailing religious beliefs. Confused about why their miniature adults preferred to run, jump, squeal, and laugh rather than exhibit acceptable adult behaviors, people turned to their religious doctrines for answers. Interpretations of the Bible led them to believe that such giddy, strange behaviors were tied to the concept of *native depravity.* "*Native depravity* is certainly the source of all moral evil in the conduct of mankind. . .hence it will be easy to trace the follies of youth. . .to the impurities of the heart, which is declared by the highest authority to be 'Deceitful above all things, and desparately wicked'."[5]

Youngsters, then, were considered to be under the influence of the devil, and their childlike behaviors (as we know them today) were "demonlike" and "wicked." The purpose of schooling was to eradicate this native depravity by turning the children into "saints," since "saints were wiser than other people because they knew

God. In one way or another everything done in the schools tied into the overall purpose which was the development of saints."[6] These educational aims were important enough to be legislated; for example, the Massachusetts law of 1647, commonly referred to as the "Old Satan Deluder Act," required teaching the scriptures as a deterrent to the devil's cunning.

For the children who attended school, their six-day school week began at seven in the morning and ended as late as five in the afternoon, a purposely long time to make sure attendance at school would not "soften" the children. Because the children were viewed as wicked, the curriculum centered around the teaching of morality and religion.

SCHOOLING.   To further develop our picture of colonial schooling, imagine a stern-faced schoolmaster (women were not considered strong enough to handle large groups of children) standing in front of rows of children seated stiffly on wooden benches. Children were required to memorize the Lord's Prayer as well as passages from the Bible, such as "He that spareth his rod hateth his son: but he that loveth him chasteneth him betimes" (Proverbs 13:24). Religious views of childhood were also reflected in the children's reading books, as in these examples from the presentation of the alphabet in the *New England Primer*:

A   In *Adam's* Fall
        We sinned all.
F   The idle *Fool*
        Is whipt at school.
J   *Job* feels the Rod
        Yet blesses GOD.
R   *Rachel* doth mourn
        For her first born.

Paul Leicester Ford describes the *New England Primer* as "prose as bare of beauty as the whitewash of their churches, with poetry as rough and stern as their storm-torn coast, with pictures as crude and unfinished as their own glacial-smoothed boulders, between stiff oak covers which symbolized the contents."[7] Children were educated in this way until they "attained that happy state . . . when they were afraid they would 'go to hell,' and were stirred up dreadfully to seek God!"[8] So, our first idea of schooling dealt with religious and moral training, using tales, stories, and mythology to transmit cultural values to a new nation—an area of the curriculum we now call social studies. This pattern of schooling remained dominant until the late 1700s when new social conditions helped to create change.

Revolutionary America and Developing Patriotism

The colonial schools changed little through the late 1700s because society was convinced that it was adequately addressing its major concerns of moral development and religious training. With the major upheaval of the Revolutionary War, however, an emerging nation's struggle for independence was won and new social concerns surfaced. The immediate need to develop patriotic citizens for a growing new republic joined with the importance previously accorded to religious and moral training in emerging national goals of loyalty, unity, and citizenship. As a result, teachers were compelled to supplement religious subject matter with that which would cultivate "loyal citizens."

EDUCATION. This situation presented a monumental challenge for the schools. Before this new emphasis on loyalty to country, teachers were able to achieve their objectives with formal lectures and teachings from the Hornbook, Catechism, Psalter, and Bible. As religious sentiment began to wane somewhat and the nation became concerned about separation of church and state, schools needed materials that stressed American virtues of courage, honesty, truth, and obedience. The materials were difficult to obtain, but teachers were able to find a limited number of books that emphasized patriotism and read appropriate selections to the children. "The Power of Kindness" is a sample of the reading materials the schools used after the Revolutionary War.

THE POWER OF KINDNESS

William Penn, the founder of Philadelphia, always treated the Indians with justice and kindness. The founders of other colonies have too often trampled on the rights of the natives, and seized their lands by force; but this was not the method of Penn. He bought their lands, and paid for them. He made a treaty with the Indians, and faithfully kept it. He always treated them as *men*.

After his first purchase was made, Penn became desirous of obtaining another portion of their lands, and offered to buy it. They returned for answer that they had no wish to sell the spot where their fathers were buried; but to please their father Onas, as they named Penn, they said they would sell him a part of it.

A bargain was accordingly concluded, that, in return for a certain amount of English goods, Penn should have as much land as a young man could travel round in one day.

On the whole, however, teachers relied almost completely upon lecture and recitation because of the absence of books and other supplies. Paper was scarce, because it was not until the late 1860s that an efficient system of making paper from wood pulp replaced making paper from rags. There were no chalkboards, maps, writing tablets, pencils, or other visual aids we take for granted today. Early teaching of geography and history did appear to some extent in the elementary school, however. Jedediah Morse started this trend by writing the first social studies text produced in America; his *American Universal Geography* was published in 1784. Nathaniel Dwight followed with *A Short but Comprehensive System of the Geography of the World* in 1795 and William C. Woodbridge added *Rudiments of Geography* in 1821. Geography became an extremely popular subject in the elementary schools as teachers openly welcomed the presence of these new teaching materials.

Although the *content* of instruction changed during the late 1700s and early 1800s, *methodology* remained much the same. Despite its removal from a religious context, morality maintained a primary place in the curriculum. The story of William Penn was, of course, intended to instill patriotic pride, but its content was also designed to serve as a model for adult behavior. Similarly, stories of George Washington and the cherry tree and other exemplary experiences of the country's leaders slowly replaced the use of stories from the Bible. But the teaching of morality was not limited to stories alone. Strict teacher discipline, forceful leadership, memorization, and the puritanical guidance of the colonial era of social studies instruction were commonly utilized in an attempt to produce citizens who were as unwavering in their allegience to a new nation as they were in their approach to learning. And, because childhood was still not recognized as a separate stage of human development, children were still viewed as miniature adults and treated much as they had been in earlier years.

THE NINETEENTH CENTURY

After the new nation was organized, people began to move into the southern and western territories as new lands were gained through annexation, purchase, or cessation from other countries. As a result, twenty new states were added to the nation by 1870 and the population more than doubled. The growing nation encountered a need for new and better ways to produce goods and services, which led to pursuits such as coal, iron, and gold mining; cattle raising; railroad construction; and clothing and sheltering businesses. Until this time, skilled workers had made things one at a time by hand, but complicated new machines soon replaced simple hand tools, initiating the Industrial Revolution. The Industrial Revolution actually began as early as 1790 when a British immigrant, Samuel Slater, built a weaving mill in Rhode Island. Factories subsequently sprang up all over the United States, and Slater became known as the "Father of the American Factory System." There were several reasons for the rapid industrial growth. Railroads made it possible to ship raw materials and finished goods easily across the country. New natural resources such as coal and iron were discovered, along with new sources of power such as steam, oil and, later, electricity. Factories made more and better goods as a result of these advances. Into the 1800s, the United States government favored rapid business growth through a policy of *laissez-faire*, meaning that government stayed away from business and did not attempt to control it. This policy soon led to great disagreements and political schisms as the nation's agrarian life clashed with the new directions of industrialization and capitalism.

In addition to the issues of industrialization, the nation became further divided by disagreements about slavery. Some people, especially Southerners, were willing to accept the spread of slavery, while others, primarily Northerners, wished to control or abolish it. This burning disagreement boiled over in 1860 when four men, each with differing views of slavery, ran for the Presidency. Abraham Lincoln won the election, but his plan to accept slavery where it already existed and to refuse to let it spread into new territories angered every slave state. By 1861, seven slave states seceded from the Union and formed their own country, the Confederate States of America. They drew up a constitution and chose Jefferson Davis as President. On

April 14, 1861, the Confederate Army captured Fort Sumter in South Carolina and the Civil War had begun. Death and destruction were an inevitable part of this Civil War, and the scars resulting from its battles festered through generations.

Social Studies Curriculum

In the years before, during, and immediately after the Civil War, social and economic forces brought major changes in the social studies curriculum. Religious groups lost even more power than they did during the era following the Revolutionary War, but the religious motive in education continued to be channeled into the constantly pervasive goal of "moral and character development." Although many argued that this goal could best be achieved through religious teachings, the concern for the constitutional ideal of separation between church and state impeded training in any particular religious faith. But by far the greatest educational ramification of industrialization and the Civil War was an increasing concern for the treatment of *citizenship* in the elementary school curriculum. It seemed logical at the time that the thousands of factory workers coming from Europe, as well as the numbers of citizens alienated by the events of the Civil War, would benefit from a program that stressed moral and character training along with patriotic loyalty and responsibility. As a result, new history and geography texts were produced for the purpose of imparting information and exerting a significant moral influence. Samuel Goodrich, who wrote elementary texts under the name of Peter Parley, published *A History of the United States*, and Noah Webster published another history book—both books contained detailed accounts of significant historical events as well as the *Constitution of the United States*. Thus, civics, or the study of government, was added to the elementary school curriculum, but primarily in association with the study of history and geography. Together these three areas surfaced during the 1800s as the three major social sciences in the curriculum that would dominate instruction for some time. History and geography maintained the greatest popularity; over one hundred textbooks in those disciplines had been published by the late nineteenth century. These texts employed a drill-type, question-and-answer format that stressed memorization of facts and details. Samuel Goodrich's pictorial version of *Parley's Common School History of the World*, for example, boasted that, "a pupil may commit the whole volume to memory during a winter's schooling."[9] The book began with Biblical creation and closed with the American and French Revolutions. Patriotism continued to create a fervor almost as great as religious materials had inspired in earlier years, but the fervor resulted only in formal, abstract, and uninspired instruction. Information was to be "learned by heart and, when forgotten, learned again," until children stored an accumulation of facts considered appropriate for patriotic citizens. This statement by two historians at the turn of the twentieth century illustrates the characteristics of educational methodology at the time:

> In its effect on the mind, American history is distinctly to be commended. The principal reasons for the study of history are that it trains the memory, is a steady practice in the use of materials, exercises the judgment and sets before the students' minds a high standard of character. In all these respects, American

history is inferior to that of no other country. The events which are studied and should be kept in memory are interesting in themselves and important for the world development.[10]

This feeling about the role of history did not change with the turn of the twentieth century, for even into the 1920s, one educator said, "Drill thoroughly on the emphasized points. Decide what is important and then assure yourself that your students will carry it with them to their grave."[11]

Morality

Aside from using these strict, formal teaching methods to develop good citizens, teachers were expected to serve as models of moral behavior implicit in the writings of the Old and New Testaments. Parents insisted that teachers live by the moral codes held by the community and controlled the teachers' lives to ensure that they would exhibit appropriate moral values for their children to emulate. These were some of the behaviors expected of teachers in 1872:

Teachers each day will fill lamps, clean chimneys.

Each teacher will bring a bucket of water and a scuttle of coal for the day's sessions.

Make your pens carefully. You may whittle nibs to the individual taste of the pupils.

Men teachers may take one evening each week for courting purposes, or two evenings a week if they go to church regularly.

After ten hours in school, teachers may spend the remaining time reading the Bible or other good books.

Women teachers who marry or engage in unseemly conduct will be dismissed.

Every teacher should lay aside from each pay a goodly sum of his earnings for his benefit during his declining years so that he will not become a burden on society.

Any teacher who smokes, uses liquor in any form, frequents pool or public halls, or gets shaved in a barber shop will give good reason to suspect his worth, intentions, integrity and honesty.

Be home between the hours of 8 a.m. and 6 p.m. unless attending a school function.

Do not leave town at any time without permission of the school board.

Women should not get into a carriage with any man except her father or brother.

Do not dress in bright colors.

Women do not wear any dress more than two inches above the ankle.

> The teacher who performs his labor faithfully and without fault for five years will be given an increase of twenty-five cents per week in his pay, providing the Board of Education approves. [Source unknown]

EUROPEAN INFLUENCES

Around the turn of the century, millions of additional people, with dreams of finding a better life, left their homelands to come to the United States. These immigrants came for many reasons: to settle the wilderness; to farm and mine the land; and to work in the factories. This last reason caused a technological transformation the nation had never before experienced. With the advent of specialization of labor by 1918, workers created a host of new inventions that were unknown fifty years earlier: automobiles, telephones, refrigeration, electric lights, skyscrapers, and elevators, to mention only a few. As more and more factories were built to produce these goods and services, workers were desperately needed; consequently, immigration, especially from Western European nations, increased. The influx of people with diverse ideas forced curricular and methodological changes that might not otherwise have occurred.

Because educational ideas were based upon prevailing concepts of childhood, most education centered on memorization. The concepts of miniature adulthood and innate badness dictated that adults firmly control the child's environment through strict discipline and highly formalized instructional techniques. Those ideas changed, however, as educational theories from Europe filtered into America along with the immigrants searching for new opportunities. The European ideas, stemming mainly from the writings of Rousseau, Pestalozzi, Froebel, and Herbart, contradicted memorization techniques and promoted development of children's intellectual powers through activities, concrete experiences, and sensory impressions. These educational innovations were based on a much different view of childhood than that of native depravity or innate badness. Describing childhood as a period of goodness or innocence, the European educators gained their support from writers such as Rousseau, who described the nature of childhood in *Emile*:

> God makes all things good; man meddles with them and they become evil. He forces one soil to yield the products of another, one tree to bear another's fruit. He confuses and confounds time, place, and natural condition. He mutilates his dog, his horse, and his slave. He destroys and defaces all things; he loves all that is deformed and monstrous; he will have nothing as nature made it, not even man himself, who must learn his paces like a saddlehorse, and be shaped to his master's taste like the trees in his garden.[12]

Such sympathetic descriptions of childhood stirred European educators to create innovative strategies that centered on active involvement—doing, experiencing, and manipulating. As might be expected, the movement from rote memorization to activity learning was difficult in a country entrenched as the United States was in its traditional teaching practices. After all, wasn't a "good citizen" one whose moral character was shaped by the tenacious discipline of a formalized curriculum and whose mind was sharpened through drill and repetition? Something significant was required to change this attitude, and that stimulus came from American historians.

History in the Curriculum

History was far and away the most dominant academic discipline into the early twentieth century. Organized in 1884, the American Historical Association was one of the first committees to make recommendations for elementary school programs and, of course, established a dominant position for history in the curriculum. Other major educational committees, such as those of the National Education Association, also bore the mark of historians. These groups' recommendations stressed the teaching of history through mental discipline, based on the belief that the mind was a muscle that could be developed most effectively through rigorous exercise. The more difficult and voluminous the material to be learned, the more the mind was exercised. In 1916, though, the National Education Association (NEA) broke with tradition and assembled a curriculum-study committee comprised of scholars who were not primarily historians. Its purpose was to study programs in elementary school education and make recommendations for change. One influential historian on the committee, James Harvey Robinson, convinced the other committee members that the actual character of history was not compatible to the mental disciplinary approaches of the past. He made a resounding plea for reform in his revolutionary book *The New History*:

> The one thing that [history] ought to do, and has not yet effectively done, is to help us to understand ourselves and our fellows and the problems and prospects of mankind. It is this most significant form of history's usefulness that has been most commonly neglected. . . .It is high time we set to work boldly. . .to bring our education into the closest possible relation with the actual life and future duties of. . .those who fill our public schools.[13]

Goals of Education

The NEA committee sought for the first time to define the overall goal of education and then, more specifically, to identify the role of individual curricular areas in preparing children for the future. The committee defined the overall goal of schooling as the cultivation of *good citizenship*, but moved sharply away from the popular teaching recommendations of the time and, instead, urged teachers to instruct much as James Harvey Robinson did—by involving children in classroom opportunities that presented the problems, conflicts, and dilemmas of citizens rather than forcing them to memorize endless facts. This 1916 report had a tremendous impact on the public schools, but because of a reluctance to change things that had lasted so long, it was not met with enthusiasm or anticipation by educators entrenched in time-honored methods. The battle lines were drawn, and each group sought to defend its position. They did so primarily with information gathered from the emerging scientific child-study movement.

CHANGING VIEWS OF CHILDHOOD

Views of childhood remained fairly static until the early twentieth century, when changes emerged in staccato fashion. With impetus from scholars in other fields who had developed popularly endorsed methods of *scientific study* in their disciplines, child-study advocates sought ways to uncover verifiable information about children that would explain their behaviors and patterns of development. They attempted to apply the techniques of *physical scientists* (biologists, physicists, chemists) who learned to use controlled methods of observation and experimentation to explain how, for example, a caterpillar becomes a butterfly. The physical scientists discovered that explaining natural phenomena through their "scientific method" provided much more truthful information than information uncovered through the previously popular technique of "introspection." Before application of the scientific method, humankind received its explanations of natural phenomena not from direct observational study but from highly respected individuals who pondered certain problems and offered their personal interpretations for others to accept. By the turn of the twentieth century, however, physical phenomena were explained more accurately with information gathered through scientific study, although phenomena such as human growth and development were still subject to introspective explanations such as those offered by Rousseau, Pestalozzi, Froebel, and others. Discontented with this situation, educators in the United States clamored for scientifically supported information about young children so they could build their educational reforms upon an accurate, solid foundation of knowledge. Thus emerged a field of formal study dealing with people—a new *social science* referred to as *developmental psychology*.

Developmental Psychology

Undoubtedly, the scientific study of childhood was given its greatest impetus by G. Stanley Hall who had, by 1890, become the most respected psychological researcher of his time. Hall used a *questionnaire* technique to collect his data. With questionnaires, Hall could collect a great deal of information from adults and children in a short time. For instance, in one of his earliest studies, Hall solicited the cooperation of kindergarten teachers in the Boston area to answer questions about matters of nature. After tabulating his data and finding the percentage of children who were uninformed about such things as growing apples, for example, Hall would recommend frequent trips to the country to experience natural phenomena first-hand.

Most of G. Stanley Hall's writings intended to show that childhood is a separate stage of human life during which individuals have different characteristics and needs than do adults and that schools could better serve children if their practices were based upon an understanding of *child development*. Because Hall subscribed to Darwin's controversial theory of evolution, his theories of child development were strongly influenced by Darwin. He often wrote that children's development parallels the evolution of the human race, calling his theory the *Law of Recapitulation*: "This law declares that the individual, in his development, passes through stages similar to those through which the race has passed, and in the same order."[14]

Hall saw this development as instinctual and proceeding through a *hereditarily predetermined* sequence of unfolding stages. He thus explained the infant's grasping reflex as an extension of the branch-grasping days of his ancestors, the monkeys. The child's love for climbing trees was related to the caveman era and cowboy play to frontier times. Despite the primitiveness of these ideas compared to contemporary thought, Hall provided a great deal of impetus for further research into childhood and for applying knowledge about children to the design of teaching practices.

ARNOLD GESELL.   One of the most prominent specialists to be influenced by Hall's work was Arnold Gesell. Following the pattern of other social scientists during his time, Gesell was interested in *normative data*, or information detailing patterns of "normal" behavior and growth.

Studying children up to the age of ten, Gesell's work concentrated on describing the changes in language, motor development, visual skills, social relations, and personal growth as children grew from infancy. He and his colleagues, primarily Frances Ilg and Louise Bates Ames, meticulously gathered data from large groups of children by observing and measuring physical and behavioral characteristics. These voluminous, detailed observations were averaged for each age to create a composite picture of a normal infant, a normal two-year-old , a normal four-year-old, and so on. For example, Gesell described advances in children's large motor performance from the hesitant, tottering movements of a two-year-old through the fluid movements of a ten-year-old.[15] He also described small motor skills: four-year-olds can button their own clothing and, at times, tie their own shoelaces. The two-year-old is capable of copying vertical lines, while the three-year-old becomes skilled at reproducing a horizontal line or a circle. By five years, the child should be able to draw a cross, square, diamond, and triangle. Thus, from Gesell, we learned that infants first gain control over large muscles and then refine their motor skills so they can direct smaller, more precise movements.

Publishing books and articles replete with such information, Gesell and his colleagues became a driving force in child development by 1930. Mothers became especially attracted to their works as they searched through his descriptions for standards by which they could compare their children with others. For the first time, "keeping up with the Joneses" became a parental compulsion as every parent wanted his or her baby to be the best. Gordon described Gesell's impact at the time:

> You were supposed to buy Gesell, which was the standard 'bible' and had a maturational orientation. If you had a two-year-old, you turned to the right page in Gesell and checked out your child. If he or she were behaving like a two-year-old, you sighed with relief; if the child was behaving like a one-year-old, you locked the child in the back room. But you did not do anything about it.[16]

The reason parents "did not do anything about it" has to do with the second part of Gesell's work—the theory. For, besides the normative data he organized, Gesell also presented his ideas of *why* and *how* children grow as they do. What determined growth? According to Gesell, *maturation* was the necessary condition of developmental change; that is, children grow as their hereditary composition (genetic factors) directs. Gesell explained to parents and teachers that "the total ground plan is beyond your control. It is too complex and mysterious to be altogether entrusted to human hands. So nature takes over most of the task, and simply invites your assistance."[17] Gesell thus viewed age as the major influence over developmental change. For instance, the two-year-olds he studied were somewhat boisterous. Gesell not only described their unruly behaviors in great detail, but also assumed that the single reason they acted that way was *because* they were two. Such impressions led to stereotyped labels for certain ages, such as the "Terrible Twos." Gesell even conducted studies to demonstrate that certain developmental skills were controlled entirely by genetics. For instance, Gesell and Thompson found that giving children special practice in skills such as climbing stairs had minimal effect on their stair-climbing ability.[18] Notice how closely Gesell's ideas reflect Rousseau's thoughts of the child as a product of natural unfolding. Gesell, like Rousseau, says that "Nature" is the most influential ingredient in the child's development. Gesell's thinking attained legendary proportions, and he established a powerful following until his retirement from Yale in 1948. His followers keep Gesell's work alive today at the Gesell Institute in New Haven, Connecticut.

Progressive Education

Armed with this wealth of new information about the uniqueness of the period of life called childhood, educators initiated plans to suit schooling to the particular needs and interests of children at different stages of life. Chief among this group was John Dewey, who challenged formalized teaching strategies by offering creative ideas that called for democratic teachers in informal learning environments. Dewey believed the curriculum should be built around the needs and interests of children rather than upon considerations of subject matter only.

DEWEY'S LEARNING PROJECTS.   Suddenly, real objects and special projects replaced the traditional technique of teaching lessons from books. Games, field trips, conversations, art projects, classroom visitors, and other innovations characterized the "progressive" movement. The overall aim of progressive schooling was social competency, designed to be achieved through cooperative group projects and activities. It was through these cooperative projects, rather than through drill and memorization, that children also learned subject matter.

Dewey's projects were arranged so that traditional subject matter designations, such as spelling, reading, and history, were dropped, but the associated content or experiences were integrated into a total experience designed to solve problems.

The simultaneous learning could occur in any of these four different types of learning experiences:

1. *Producer's project*—making a model or a drawing
2. *Consumer's project*—examining someone else's product, such as a statue from Greece during a museum trip
3. *Problem project*—solving a problem or difficulty, such as "how to encourage birds to stay for the winter" by building a birdhouse and feeder
4. *Drill or specific learning project*—learning facts and skills only when the need arises, such as learning spelling words related to the study of "Our Colonial Heritage"

Projects, then, served as a means to relate everything to a core topic or theme of interest. A teacher might, for instance, select birds as the central topic of the month and read a bird story. All subsequent learning that month would involve the study of birds—birds throughout history, the geographical distribution of birds, spelling words related to birds, writing compositions about birds, drawing pictures of birds, singing songs about birds, and solving arithmetic problems related to sizes of birds, migration patterns, and so on. Such instructional techniques eventually resulted in replacing traditional subjects with new organizations of content and activities more closely attuned to the emerging principles of child development. As Martin S. Dworkin explained, "In education, [Dewey] brought . . . a romantic emphasis upon the needs and interests of the child, in the tradition of Rousseau, Pestalozzi, and Froebel—but now colored and given scientific authority by the new psychology of learning and behavior."[19] Dewey's impact was so great that the famed 1916 NEA Committee recommended that schools immediately focus on problems growing out of the needs and interests of youth rather than on teaching isolated facts.

DEWEY'S INFLUENCE ON SOCIAL STUDIES.   Social studies educators, especially Lucy Sprague Mitchell and Caroline Pratt, were quick to adopt Dewey's philosophy of education. Mitchell's "Here and Now" program and Pratt's "Object Orientation" were offered as alternatives to the historically popular technique of memorizing social studies facts about events, people, or places that children had never experienced. Mitchell and Pratt proposed that the first step in social studies education was to help young children experience things for themselves. Mitchell's "Here and Now" philosophy, for example, stressed that giving the child anything outside the realm of direct experience was a waste of time. She recommended first-hand experiences for children—field trips, resource persons, and contacts with real things—believing that even into the elementary grades, the young child is "absorbed in developing a technique of observation and control of his immediate surroundings" and that "for the child the familiar is the interesting."[20]

Caroline Pratt suggested that the real function of social studies education was to provide the child with practical experiences that integrated all the subjects taught in school.[21] In effect, social studies was seen as a "real life" experience that bond-

Social studies teachers have long been advised to begin instruction with direct personal experiences that provide the foundation for abstract learning.

ed together all other curricular areas in a purposeful way. Pratt explained that through useful social activity and positive emotional support, children could build a foundation of practical skills that would serve them throughout life.

Despite the promise of these new educational practices, the schools soon reverted to teacher-centeredness. Why were we so resistant to educational change? Perhaps it was because of the tendency to resist what is new and different and hang onto what is comfortable. How much simpler it is to do what was done last year than to work hard to try something different! Another reason for the swift demise of the early child-centered social studies programs was that some teachers misinterpreted what was meant by ''child-centeredness'' and carried *permissiveness* to an extreme, often allowing children to wander aimlessly throughout the classroom all day. Because obvious learning needs were often ignored and subject matter lacked continuity from one grade level to the next, this new plan of instruction faded from the educational scene.

BEHAVIORISM.   Educators then reached back to the historically familiar tradition of mental discipline. But with the clamor to support teaching methodology with scientific evidence, educators were forced to produce theories to bolster their beliefs, which they found in a new school of psychology—behaviorism. A pioneer of behaviorism, John B. Watson, described children's brains as pliable; he claimed that, from infancy, their behaviors and skills could be molded and shaped like a lump of clay. Because of this malleability, Watson said that by carefully controlling the environment, teachers could make children anything they wanted them to be:

> Give me a dozen healthy infants, well-formed, and my own specified world to bring them up in and I'll guarantee to take any one at random and train him to become any type of specialist I might select—doctor, lawyer, artist, merchant, chief and, yes, even beggarman and thief, regardless of his talents, penchants, tendencies, abilities, vocations, and race of his ancestors. . . .Please note that when this experiment is made I am to be allowed to specify the way the children are to be brought up and the type of world they have to live in.[22]

By what power could such an accomplishment take place? Behaviorists defined learning as comprising two major components: (1) *the law of effect*, which purports that those behaviors leading to satisfying consequences tend to be repeated under like circumstances; and (2) *the law of exercise*, which presumes that learning is strengthened with repeated practice provided that the learner experiences satisfaction rather than annoyance with the learning activity. From these theories and Watson's came the strength needed to support the use of *associative learning*. Associative learning can best be described as pairing a stimulus with a response and satisfying the learner when he makes a correct connection by rewarding him verbally ("you're correct") or materially (a gold star). Names, dates, and events ("Columbus discovered America in 1492") were repeated over and over until students developed a "mental reflex" so effective that, when presented with the question "Columbus discovered America in the year _____ " on a test, they would automatically respond "1492." This was considered an important skill during the first half of the century, because it was through tests that educators measured learning, and through drill-type activities that students were best prepared for tests.

Enamored with the idea of using tests as a source of scientific evidence for growth in learning, a major segment of public schooling refused to alter the traditional role of teachers as stern disciplinarians and as extractors of uniform knowledge. Now basking in scientific support, educators continued to operate with a conviction that the "best" citizen was the most knowledgeable citizen.

Despite losses in the struggle to significantly alter teaching methodology, progressive educators did affect the range of elementary school social studies content. For example, before 1916, children studied separate *social science* subjects such as history, geography, and civics. But in 1916, the term *social studies* was introduced as a convenient title to refer to several social sciences that should be integrated for instructional purposes. Instead of learning only geography in grade five, children would receive instruction in a synthesized format that might cover *The United States* for the entire year. The curriculum would include subject matter not only from geography, but also from history, civics, or even economics and sociology.

PAUL R. HANNA.   Another educational theorist along the lines of Gesell and Dewey was Paul R. Hanna, who influenced content selection and distribution in the social studies. Reasoning that children progress through developmental stages of social awareness and that social studies programs should be based on a knowledge of those stages, Hanna proposed a sequence of instruction called the *Expanding Environment Approach*. This approach began with social contacts the child most often experienced (usually the home) and gradually expanded through the school, neighborhood, community, and so on as the child gained maturity and experience. Hanna influenced the selection and grade-level ordering of social studies content more than any single factor up to this time.[23] Hanna's plan, adopted by school districts and textbook publishers throughout the country, followed this sequence:

Grade 1: Home, Family, School

Grade 2: Neighborhood, Neighborhood Helpers

Grade 3: Community, Community Helpers

Grade 4: The State, The Region

Grade 5: The United States or North and South America

Grade 6: North and South America or The World

Grade 7: World Geography (the Western World)

Grade 8: History of the United States

Grade 9: Civics (Political Science)

Grade 10: World History (the Western World)

Grade 11: History of the United States

Grade 12: Problems of Democracy

Even though Hanna's curriculum model advocated combining the several social sciences in elementary school, the separate social sciences (especially history) dominated secondary school programs into the 1950s. (Notice how Hanna's topics for grades seven through twelve reflect that trend.) And, although many teachers continued to emphasize the acquisition of knowledge with textbook-centered instruction throughout each grade level up to the mid-1960s, most supplemented their teaching strategies with field trips, examination of real objects, and a variety of other group or individual activities to stimulate and enhance learning. This pattern of activity-enriched instruction was particularly popular from kindergarten through grade six, but gradually became less and less frequent into the later elementary grades. Supplemental activities came to be treated more like ''icing on the cake'' than as an essential part of the learning process.

AN ERA OF TURMOIL

The period between 1940 and 1960 was characterized by bitter philosophical battles. On one hand, several educators led a movement to integrate the social sciences into a sophisticated social studies program; on the other, proponents of the separate social sciences contended that each provided the most reliable means of providing the facts and principles required of good citizenship. Scholars from various blue-ribbon committees and commissions battled over this issue and debated its positive and negative influences on the school curriculum. The schools were hopelessly confused by conflicting recommendations from a variety of sources. Uneasiness with this chaos led a number of researchers to study its effects on students' social studies achievement. Overwhelmingly, the research found that American youth, even into the college years, were shockingly uninformed about basic historical information, such as the name of the U.S. President during the Civil War. The findings created a nationwide furor. Social studies programs were branded ineffective and a new call arose for social studies reform.

Critics blamed the "fads and frills" of the progressive social studies programs for such failures, but in fact, progressive programs were rarely practiced by this time. Most social studies programs were content-centered and expository in nature. Even so, groups clamored for educational reform and collected data to support a return to rigorous methodologies and separate academic disciplines, which amounted to "back to history"—a plea given immediate credibility when supported by Edgar B. Wesley, dean of social studies educators. Wesley said that "at any one level [of schooling] much may be taught, less will be learned, and a great deal will be subsequently forgotten. Educational realism demands that any subject be taught again and again until the cumulative effects become significant and enduring."[24] The historians rejoiced at Wesley's message: teach history again and again! Growing sentiment caused a major back-to-history movement highlighted by factual historical study replete with lists of people, places, dates, and events to be memorized.

Two major events supported the back-to-history movement: World War II and the Korean Conflict.

Effects of World War II

Before World War II, American school children were exposed almost exclusively to Western culture. According to Kenworthy, "They studied European history, European languages, European art and music, and European literature. Such an education was probably sufficient in the days when most of today's adults went to school."[25] This type of education caused unexpected difficulties during and after World War II, however, when many Americans displayed unsophisticated reactions to the mannerisms of strange and exotic cultures.

With other distressing signals of the dearth of knowledge about other peoples of the world, American educators recommended introducing international concepts early in the social studies program. The goal was to develop an international understanding that would remove the attitudinal barriers that had prevented cooperation among the nations of the world.

The second major force boiled over in the 1950s during the aftermath of the Korean Conflict. Distressed that great numbers of American soldiers were sympathetic to Communist lines during that war, government officials became particularly sensitive to the spread of Marxism in the United States. The McCarthy hearings stirred the public's interest and helped highlight critics' descriptions of what was wrong with the social studies. Almost immediately, school districts required courses in United States government to supplement the many history courses and demanded that social studies programs do all but transform our uninformed, "antidemocratic" young citizens into junior historians. From this reaction was born the "New Social Studies" of the 1960s.

Confusion of the 1960s

By 1960, the mission of social studies education had become so clouded and confused that some critics wondered whether it would ever recover:

> Whatever social studies was, or purported to be, it was judged by many to be soft and ineffective, if not outright dangerous. Social studies had been shown to be grossly ineffective in teaching substantive content and in influencing positive attitudes; and it was based on a curriculum that had not changed appreciably in over fifty years.[26]

Hopelessness, impotence, defeat, confusion—a sad state for a subject area that would soon be asked to respond to the impending torment and violence of the 1960s. Frustration led to cries of: "But we've tried it all! What do we do now?"

JEROME BRUNER. The answer seemed to rest on a short passage from Jerome Bruner's influential book, *The Process of Education*, written in the aftermath of the successful Russian launch of Sputnik I in 1957. Americans, afraid of losing the technology race to the Russians, questioned the quality of education provided to our children, especially in science and mathematics. So, in 1959, the National Academy of Sciences sponsored a conference of leading educators in Woods Hole, Massachusetts, to determine how science and math programs could be improved. Jerome Bruner chaired that conference and reported the group's recommendations in a book so popular that it became required reading in nearly all graduate courses for the next decade. One of its strongest recommendations was that science be taught in the primary grades (elementary science had previously been mostly nature study) and that some math concepts traditionally taught in the intermediate grades be moved back into the primary grades. To support this idea, Bruner wrote: "We begin with the hypothesis that any subject can be taught effectively in some intellectually honest form to any child at any stage of development."[27] The statement was originally intended only to provide philosophical motivation for restructuring science and math curricula so that even kindergarten youngsters would be exposed to rudimentary concepts. Misinterpreting Bruner's intent, some educators attempted to teach complex concepts to youngsters without first translating them into "some intellectually honest form." For instance, two- and three-year-olds were formally taught to read and write and first graders were asked to deal with fundamentals of algebra in ways far beyond their years. Social science educators did not hesitate to jump on the bandwagon. If the knowledge and skills of the social sciences could be taught even to primary grade youngsters, they reasoned, why should the elementary schools waste their time with that "mishmash" called the social studies?

Social scientists thus quickly embarked on a movement to reform the social studies once again. This time, though, they were armed with the support of Bruner's blockbuster statement. Nearly all social science professional groups established curriculum study committees, but the most active attempts at curriculum reform came from the Office of Education, which funded *Project Social Studies* in 1962. With these funds, research centers were established throughout the country in our most ambitious effort to reform the social studies. The research objectives were to:

1. Bring together educators, social scientists, and educational psychologists as teams of experts to reexamine the direction and nature of existing social studies programs at all grade levels
2. Create innovative instructional materials and teaching techniques based on contemporary learning theories and research findings
3. Field-test, improve, and reevaluate proposed directions for change
4. Disseminate information, products, and ideas related to the new approach

Eventually, the Office of Education funded more than 50 projects, some of which had greater success than others. Some projects reflected the trend toward integrating the social sciences; others were organized around a single social science. Some included exciting materials such as slides, tapes, artifacts, models, simulations, and photographs, while others offered only teachers' guides. Whatever the final package, however, all programs echoed a renewed message from the early part of this century: *activity learning.*

JEAN PIAGET. The programs of the Project Social Studies centers derived their greatest philosophical support from the works of two educational philosophers, Jean Piaget and Jerome Bruner. Piaget provided a general theory of learning that significantly influenced the development of new social studies programs. His definition of the learning process is too comprehensive to detail here, but an explanation of one component helps to identify Piaget's impact on contemporary social studies instruction. Piaget viewed the growth of intelligence as an ascent of a flight of stairs, each stair representing a balanced state of *equilibrium*. He used this term from physics to describe an inner drive to seek a balance between what is already known and what is yet to be understood. As individuals find that "balance," they reach a new level of equilibrium (intelligence). This movement from one level or stair to the next is called *adaptation*, a combination of the two processes of assimilation and accommodation. *Assimilation* is the process of dealing with the environment in terms of current mental structures. *Accommodation* is the process of changing existing structures when those structures do not allow us to deal effectively with the environment. This example illustrates the process of adaptation.

> Suppose that a first-grade teacher wished to develop the idea that all cultures rely on a system of language, but that some cultures use different forms of language. She gathered the children together, seated them comfortably on the floor, and asked one child to stand alone in a corner of the classroom. She then asked the others to think about ways they might be able to direct the

lone child to walk from the corner of the classroom to where they were seated. The children offered obvious solutions by using their voices or printing a command on a large sheet of paper (*assimilation*). To extend the lesson, the teacher brought the children's attention to a drum, explaining that the drum is one of the oldest ways of communicating. She told the children they were to use the drum to tap messages to the child in the corner, each message identifying a different way to move from the corner to their circle: walking, running, dancing, and so on. The children had participated in rhythm and movement activities in kindergarten and first grade, and they needed to apply those experiences to this new problem (*accommodation*). Taking turns, the children tapped out fast rhythms to stimulate running, slower rhythms to encourage marching, skipping, galloping, and other movements. The children learned through this direct experience that drums can talk to them without using words (*adaptation*).

The simultaneous processes of assimilation and accommodation, then, are *adaptation*. Equilibrium is achieved as the child adapts and moves from one level of understanding to a higher level. Can you think of a way to extend the sample lesson so the children will experience growth to a higher level of understanding about communication?

In all his writings, Piaget stressed the importance of activity, exploration, and direct experience as necessary ingredients of effective learning. From Piaget's viewpoint, then, the goal of education would be to stimulate children's curiosity, for the more curious they are, the more they will explore, the more discoveries they will make, and the more knowledge they will gain. And the more knowledge they have, the more advanced the nature of their curiosity will be, and the more mature their systems of exploration.

The New Social Studies

Piaget's ideas regarding acquisition of knowledge received overwhelming acclaim from the 1960s onward and were used as philosophical support for most new elementary social studies programs. These programs became known as *inquiry, problem solving,* or *discovery* programs, their names reflecting children's active involvement in discovering solutions to problems. One of the most influential educators to specifically apply Piaget's basic ideas of knowledge acquisition to the creation of activity-oriented models of elementary social studies instruction was Jerome Bruner. Examining Piaget's tenets, he said that quality social studies instruction should reflect these characteristics:

1. A "match" must be found between what children already know and the new learnings to which they will be exposed.
2. Children must be actively engaged in the exploration of social studies data.
3. The goal of social studies instruction should be to use information rather than to store it.

These ideas were effectively transferred to program development when Bruner assumed leadership of an innovative elementary school social studies project under production at Harvard University. That program, *Man: A Course of Study*, departed significantly from traditional programs in many ways.

MAN: A COURSE OF STUDY.   *Man: A Course of Study* (MACOS) was conceived in 1962 at Dedham, Massachusetts, when a group of forty-five educators and scholars led by Douglas Oliver met in an effort to improve social studies on a K–12 basis. Jerome Bruner succeeded Oliver in 1964 and applied his theories of instruction to the materials the group had already gathered. By the end of his year's work, Bruner had led the group in the completion of MACOS, but only for implementation at a single grade level (fifth). Eventually the program became used throughout the upper elementary grades and into the middle school.

Bruner summarizes the major emphasis of MACOS—humanness—in three questions:

What is human about human beings?

How did they get that way?

How can they be made more so?

The developers of MACOS sought to actively engage children in studying the uniqueness of humanity through a wide variety of activities dealing with animal behavior and the Netsilik Eskimo culture. Children are encouraged to question the fundamental nature of humanity by way of animal contrasts. The program is divided into four phases. The first phase deals with the life cycle of the salmon. By exploring the behaviors of this species, children learn that some beings must survive without parental protection: the young salmon, for example, manages to swim and eat, protect itself, and, if it lives long enough, even finds its birthplace, where a new generation begins the same cycle. The young salmon is considered important to the study of humanity when it is compared to human babies: "If salmon of the Pacific can survive without parents, why are human beings born so helpless?" This question, and others related to it, is the central core of the salmon unit.

The second phase deals with the behavior patterns of herring gulls. Here, the children extend their understandings of parenthood by examining a species whose basic family patterns are much like those of humans: two parents mate and produce a small number of dependent offspring in need of parental care. The young are born relatively helpless, relying on an instinctive pecking behavior that allows them to open their parents' beaks to obtain regurgitated meals. This herring gull study illustrates how learning helps us adapt to our environment and how all behavior must be understood in terms of requirements for survival.

The third phase involves *baboons*. The children extend their knowledge of humanness by learning about the rudimentary group social structure of baboon troop members. Infant care, food gathering, defense systems against predators, and communication are studied as mechanisms leading toward social behavior. Children are encouraged throughout to ask questions about dominance, aggression, sharing, territoriality, exchange, and various other intergroup behaviors. These questions offer a contrast for studying the child rearing and social behavior of humanity.

4.
Netsilik
Eskimos

The final phase is an investigation of culture. Here the children study the Net-silik Eskimos for the meaning of humanness by examining similarities and differences among themselves and a group of people whose lives appear to be much different. The structure of family, its members' behavior, the ways it survives, and its values and beliefs are studied in an attempt to understand "culture."

The entire course contains about sixty lessons. Each involves the child as an active inquirer and problem solver, thus giving the child opportunities to gather and organize data in ways similar to social scientists. Children are led to hypothesize, observe, collect data, and form conclusions as they actively explore a wealth of classroom materials. A set of classroom materials includes twenty-two student book-lets, five filmstrips, twenty-one films, three educational games, twenty-three maps, posters, and photomurals, two records, observational materials, and comprehensive teacher's guides containing background information and suggested lesson plans.

MACOS, departing significantly from traditional social studies offerings, was perhaps the most controversial program of its time. Its supporters defended MACOS with these arguments:

It gave children a respect for their problem-solving and reasoning powers.

It provided children with abilities to think critically about human conditions.

It made children more tolerant of value systems different from their own.

Children with poor academic backgrounds gained as much learning as did those whose beginning background was much stronger.

Children were eager to study the topics and developed greater interest in social studies.

CONTROVERSY.   Educators who did not embrace the MACOS approach more or less echoed the feelings of a teacher who used the program, Mrs. Sheilah Camp-bell Burgers. Mrs. Burgers's objections were made public by columnist James J. Kil-patrick in a biting editorial:

A Teacher's View: MACOS Controversy*

Controversy continues over "Man: A Course of Study," the fifth-grade social studies program subsidized and promoted by the National Science Founda-tion. Some parents love "MACOS." Others denounce it. Some taxpayers de-fend the expenditure. Others resent it. There seems to be no middle ground.

Mrs. Sheilah Campbell Burgers taught this course of study for one year in the public schools of Sheffield, Mass. Her personal experience carries a ring of bell-like conviction.

After one year with MACOS, she writes, "I refused to teach it again." Let me yield the floor to Mrs. Burgers.

"After having read nine teachers' manuals and 31 books, after having seen the 21 course films several times, and after having worked with 75 fifth-graders, I felt that MACOS not only restricted academic freedom but also inhibited the

---

*A CONSERVATIVE VIEW by James J. Kilpatrick. COPYRIGHT 1975 UNIVERSAL PRESS SYNDICATE. Reprinted with permission. All rights reserved.

development of my students by presenting a negative, one-sided and dishonest picture of man. In short, MACOS is a brainwash—clever, well-executed and lethal.

"The method of teaching is inquiry. The teacher asks questions; the student finds answers. This has been a valid method since Socrates, but Jerome Bruner and his friends have developed a new twist. The teacher is not permitted to initiate the questions; all questions come from manuals—and manuals must be followed exactly. All answers are found in course books and films. Outside sources cannot be used because material concerning the course content (the social structure of the herring gull, salmon, baboon and the Netsilik Eskimo) is understandably nonexistent at the fifth-grade level. Input and output are thereby totally controlled.

"Books cannot leave the classroom. Except for projects, homework is discouraged. Manuals are kept at school for professional use only. Adult intervention, therefore, is minimal.

"How are the children controlled? Bruner knows psychology well. Children are at their most passive, and therefore most receptive, at 10 and 11. They like films, games, role-playing; they like animals and they not only empathize, they identify with them. In a matter of days they speak fluent baboon. They readily learn that the physically strong survive at the expense of the weak. And if they do not learn this from hours of filmed violence, which ranges from the mating rites of herring gulls to the drinking of fresh caribou blood by the Eskimos, they learn by role-playing and games.

"Hunt the Seal is a simulation game; it takes a week to play. The victor must procure enough seals to insure his own survival. He can do this only by 'starving' his co-players. The price of survival is killing; the lesson is re-enforced by the story of the old woman who was left on the ice to die because she could not contribute to her society.

"The book word for this is 'senilicide,' a tough word for fifth-graders, but they got it. They approved and defended abandonment of the old woman. At this point I deviated from the manual and asked one of the children what he would call this act in terms of his own culture. He gulped and answered, 'murder.' (I was reprimanded for infusing irrelevant questions into the program.)

"Defenders of MACOS insist that the teaching materials give children an opportunity to compare different life styles, to become tolerant of other moral values. The defenders never mention that ten-year-olds have not studied Western civilization, and have no formal training in the history, technology or social structure of their own world. The only moral values children in MACOS are taught are the moral values of a primitive, nearly extinct tribe—and those of the baboon.

"In terms of tax dollars, the price for MACOS, thus far, is $6.5 million. What is the price in terms of the child of the future?"[28]

Despite the controversy surrounding MACOS, other new programs that represented significant departures from earlier programs were received with varying degrees of acceptance. The dynamic social evolution of the mid-1960s and 1970s added an impetus for deeper scrutiny of social studies practices. The 1960s opened with optimism and altruism reflected by the "New Frontier," the Peace Corps, and the War on Poverty, but closed in bitterness and torment. National leaders—John F. Kennedy, Robert Kennedy, and Martin Luther King, Jr.—were assassinated, and the Civil Rights Movement climaxed with death and destruction in many metropolitan areas. Impatience and frustration with the Vietnam War resulted in riots on city streets and college campuses. Watergate and other dishonesty in government surfaced. Use of illegal drugs, as well as the emergence of sensitive issues such as abortion, women's rights, teacher strikes, runaway inflation, nuclear war, and a host of other volatile issues gave strong indication that the "American Dream" was slipping away.

CONTEMPORARY TRENDS

Leaps in technology and the information explosion added to society's disquiet, causing critics to indict the schools for failing to initiate meaningful change for more than fifty years. As a result, social studies educators reemphasized the recommendations of the Piagetian social studies of the early 1960s:

1. To broaden instructional goals to include teaching toward examination of values as well as toward development of knowledge and skills.
2. To teach toward development of concepts rather than memorization of facts and details.
3. To support action learning, giving children opportunities to think, inquire, and solve problems.
4. To synthesize the several major social sciences into one program called the social studies.
5. To realize that conflicting issues of a contemporary society need to be addressed objectively.

Broadening Instructional Goals

The time-honored overall goal for social studies education has been to perpetuate our culture through instructional programs that would develop "good citizens." Throughout the years, this goal was addressed in many ways as generations pondered the questions, "What do we expect of children growing into our culture? What understandings, skills, or values should a child amass to become a fully assimilated, productive member of society?" Those questions have been difficult to answer conclusively, partly because our democratic society is built upon the ideals of liberty and freedom of choice—beliefs that have opened up alternative directions to follow in all areas of life, including schooling. As a result, old practices are systematically replaced by new ones; each generation heralds innovations that sometimes conflict with old techniques and values and with each other. Such a state of affairs arouses uneasiness in some educators, but the opportunity for criticism and change lies at the heart of a democracy. Freedom to alter education to meet a culture's changing expectations offers a major contrast to static, totalitarian governments that insist upon a singular, systematic, and persistent educational program to indoctrinate its youth to its particular way of life.

Fluidity is especially important in an era when informational and technological changes occur literally overnight. Uncertainty about what next month will bring, let alone what lies ten years away, makes mere coverage of subject matter alone no longer acceptable as the answer for developing effective citizenry. But what *is* needed?

David Mathews points out that social studies educators offer at least four ways to achieve the goal of "good citizenship":

1. *Civic literacy*—teaching the great issues of the day: the perils of the nuclear age and the dilemmas of social welfare, for example, as well as the mechanics of the political system
2. *Civic values*—developing a sense of social responsibility
3. *Civic skills*—promoting leadership skills that will enhance active participation in society
4. *Civics by indirection*—helping learners reason, or process information through a critical, reflective inquiry approach.[29]

Mathews recognizes the merits of each approach, but adds another necessary component for today's students: *civic intelligence*. Civic intelligence goes beyond civic literacy, values, and skills, a capacity to discover both what the facts are *and* what those facts mean to *others*. Civic intelligence allows us to understand issues from perspectives different from our own. Such a view grew from the concern many individuals have today about what Arthur Levine labeled "meism": an attitude that public policy and social issues are of almost no interest except in how they affect one individually.[30] In the extreme, according to Levine, this attitude robs people of the ability to work together toward a common solution and could be the classic prescription for poisoning a democratic society. Not understanding their personal connectedness to the larger world around them would produce what the Greeks called "idiots." They used the term not to label someone of low intelligence, but to describe people whose understanding was bounded by their own private worlds. The traditional lecture or read/recite/test format of instruction cannot provide all that is needed to address the goal of *civic intelligence*. It has its place if used well, but we need to recognize that active learning and participation in decision making must also be components of a developmental curriculum.

In 1979 the National Council for the Social Studies joined eleven other professional organizations in addressing the issue of civic intelligence by outlining a series of multiple objectives considered essential to effective citizenship.

Their recommendations were stated in terms of "Essentials of Exemplary Social Studies Programs" with goals designed to link knowledge and skills with an understanding of and commitment to democratic values. Throughout the NCSS statement we find references to the four trends enumerated earlier: (1) teaching toward development of concepts, (2) supporting action learning, (3) synthesizing the major social sciences, and (4) addressing conflicting issues of a contemporary society.

Citizen participation in public life is essential to the health of our democratic system. Effective social studies programs help prepare young people who can identify, understand and work to solve the problems that face our increasingly diverse nation and interdependent world.

Knowledge

Students need knowledge of the world at large and the world at hand, the world of individuals and the world of institutions, the world past, the world present and future. An exemplary social studies curriculum links information presented in the classroom with experiences gained by students through social and civic observation, analysis and participation.

Classroom instruction which relates content to information drawn from the media and from experience focuses on the following areas of knowledge:

History and culture of our nation and the world.

Geography—physical, political, cultural and economic.

Government—theories, systems, structures and processes.

Economics—theories, systems, structures and processes.

Social institutions—the individual, the group, the community and the society.

Intergroup and interpersonal relationships.

Worldwide relationships of all sorts between and among nations, races, cultures and institutions.

From this knowledge base, exemplary programs teach skills, concepts and generalizations that can help students understand the sweep of human affairs and ways of managing conflict consistent with democratic procedures.

Democratic Beliefs

Fundamental beliefs drawn from the Declaration of Independence and the United States Constitution with its Bill of Rights form the basic principles of our democratic constitutional order. Exemplary school programs do not indoctrinate students to accept these ideas blindly, but present knowledge about their historical derivation and contemporary application essential to understanding our society and its institutions. Not only should such ideas be discussed as they relate to the curriculum and to current affairs, they should also be mirrored by teachers in their classrooms and embodied in the school's daily operations.

These democratic beliefs depend upon such practices as due process, equal protection and civic participation, and are rooted in the concepts of:

Justice

Equality

Responsibility

Freedom

Diversity

Privacy

Thinking Skills

It is important that students connect knowledge with beliefs and action. To do that, thinking skills can be developed through constant systematic practice throughout the years of formal schooling. Fundamental to the goals of social studies education are those skills which help assure rational behavior in social settings.

In addition to strengthening reading and computation, there is a wide variety of thinking skills essential to the social studies which can be grouped into four major categories:

Data Gathering Skills.   Learning to:

Acquire information by observation

Locate information from a variety of sources

Compile, organize, and evaluate information

Extract and interpret information

Communicate orally and in writing

Intellectual Skills.   Learning to:

Compare things, ideas, events, and situations on the basis of similarities and differences

Classify or group items in categories

Ask appropriate and searching questions

Draw conclusions or inferences from evidence

Arrive at general ideas

Make sensible predictions from generalizations

Decision Making Skills.   Learning to:

Consider alternative solutions

Consider the consequences of each solution

Make decisions and justify them in relationship to democratic principles

Act, based on those decisions

Interpersonal Skills.   Learning to:

See things from the point of view of others

Understand one's own beliefs, feelings, abilities, and shortcomings and how they affect relations with others

Use group generalizations without stereotyping and arbitrarily classifying individuals

Recognize value in individuals different from one's self and groups different from one's own

Work effectively with others as a group member

Give and receive constructive criticism

Accept responsibility and respect the rights and property of others

Participation Skills

As a civic participant, the individual uses the knowledge, beliefs, and skills learned in the school, the social studies classroom, the community, and the family as the basis for action.

Connecting the classroom with the community provides many opportunities for students to learn the basic skills of participation, from observation to advocacy. To teach participation, social studies programs need to emphasize the following kinds of skills:

Work effectively in groups—organizing, planning, making decisions, taking action

Form coalitions of interest with other groups

Persuade, compromise, bargain

Practice patience and perseverance in working for one's goal

Develop experience in cross-cultural situations[31]

DEVELOPING KNOWLEDGE. It would be futile to dispute the belief that informed citizens are better citizens or that responsible citizenship requires functional knowledge. For that reason, schools have traditionally been charged with transmitting knowledge to the young. Social studies knowledge centers on the traditional sources for knowledge—the social sciences. They are and should remain important sources. The main issue in considering knowledge from the social sciences is not the *source*, however, but the *purpose* for which it is chosen—how it meets the "needs" of students and society as those needs change with time. Social studies content should be dynamic and flexible, and should vary continually as needs change. We must also keep in mind the broad function of knowledge: to provide a reservoir of data which, when organized to develop higher-order thinking skills (formation of concepts), children can use to function rationally. Children must be able to associate knowledge with action.

DEVELOPING DEMOCRATIC BELIEFS. Jeane J. Kirkpatrick, former representative to the United Nations, has said, "If democratic government is to survive, schools should teach democratic values."[32] The NCSS certainly supports Kirkpatrick's belief, and goes so far as to identify certain core beliefs of our democracy that schools should aim to teach. "Teach," in the spirit of the NCSS statement, does not mean to *indoctrinate*, but to introduce children to democratic values and help them weigh them against alternatives.

In the past, social studies was considered the school subject primarily responsible for helping children develop values; until only about twenty years ago, the major teaching technique was called *inculcating* or *fostering*. A set of values was identified as ideals for society, and the school's role was to "indoctrinate" youngsters by training them to accept specified ways of behaving or to assume particular positions on social issues without question. This poem, "Work," by Eliza Cook, extolled the work ethic:

Work, work, my boy, be not afraid;
  Look labor boldly in the face
Take up the hammer or the spade,
  And blush not for your humble place.

There's glory in the shuttle's song;
  There's triumph in the anvil's stroke;
There's merit in the brave and strong
  Who dig the mine or fell the oak.[33]

Because school children tend to be open in sharing their ideas and feelings, the elementary grades are a logical time to start values education.

Critics attacked this role for our schools, claiming that indoctrination was not only an ineffectual technique but also one that went against the grain of a democratic society. They pointed out, particularly, the conflicting values of various groups; for example, what attitudes would you most likely hear if you asked a Catholic priest about the desirability of abortion? A women's rights group? The schools can help children recognize that a free, democratic society offers many choices each of which is legitimate in terms of a particular culture or social group. Schools can encourage children to examine the conflicting values that underlie social issues and to evaluate the respective positions carefully so as to make meaningful personal decisions.

DEVELOPING THINKING SKILLS.   Thinking skills have long been considered important in education, but how to teach them has been a subject of disagreement. Social studies programs historically defined thinking as an ability to acquire a great deal of knowledge through intellectually demanding subjects such as history. The NCSS statement, however, supported by a great deal of research on thinking processes, takes the position that thinking skills are hierarchical in nature and can be taught systematically within the social studies program. It is important to know the thinking skills described in the NCSS statement, for different teaching strategies are required for each. As Taba et al. offer:

> Students can learn a specific date such as the discovery of America by means of straightforward presentation and recall of information, but learning to conceptualize or make warranted inferences from data requires frequent practice over an extended period of time. Attitudes and feelings are not changed by studying facts alone; they are changed through participating in experiences, real or vicarious, which have an emotional impact.[34]

Thinking skills objectives can be accomplished only by knowing the nature of the skills emphasized in the curriculum and the recommended strategies for implementing those skills. Keller points out, however, that "Most social studies teachers do not consciously teach . . . social studies skills. To teach skills successfully, the teacher must identify the components of general skills."[35]

DEVELOPING PARTICIPATION SKILLS. The most fundamental purpose of education is to reflect upon what is important after thoughtful consideration of issues, to commit oneself to a standard or ideal, and to act upon those standards or ideals in one's life. Mature adulthood in a democratic society is an achievement—a synthesis of all the components of a strong educational program that stimulates individuals to commit themselves to strong civic responsibility. It is the ultimate outcome of providing real instruction in how to think for oneself and how to learn for oneself.

Teaching Concept Formation

Social studies education presents many opportunities for children to acquire the knowledge they need for competent participation in society, but that knowledge should not be chosen as an end in itself. Modern social studies programs must select knowledge for the purpose of developing higher-order thinking skills, including the formation of meaningful concepts. Often used synonymously with *idea*, a *concept* is an idea represented by a word label. The word "horse," for example, stands for the idea of an animal, an idea determined by all the special attributes we attach to the animal through our experiences. Repeated experiences with horses in a variety of settings help us deepen our understanding so that we may properly classify any new information under that word label.

The *process* of concept formation in young children begins with developing an ability to recognize and classify information so that distinctive characteristics of things can be efficiently organized with word labels. Just as children begin to conceptualize "horseness," so do older learners carry out the process when they study abstract concepts such as "culture": how people eat, the kinds of houses they live in, how they earn a living, what language they speak, religion, clothing. Carefully and deliberately, children should be led to observe and differentiate the elements of various cultures so they can categorize objects with shared attributes into groups.

Since concepts are efficient, convenient ways to organize knowledge, it seems logical that newer social studies programs should be developed within conceptual frameworks. These programs operated on the premise that concepts would act as central organizers of content and learning experiences would be developed sequentially from grade to grade, leading to eventual meaningful mastery of the whole. A concept such as "specialization" might be chosen as one central concept organizer. Its study would be initiated during first grade, with the children examining the specialized roles of family members, for example, a parent's specialized responsibilities of going to work, caring for the home, or providing clothing, food, and shelter for the family. A child's specialized responsibilities might include caring for a pet, clean-

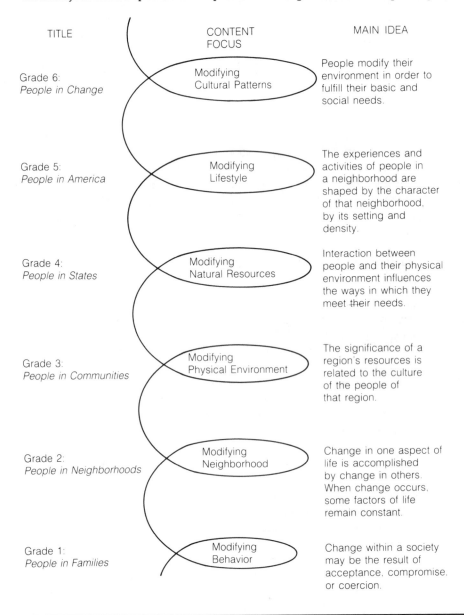

TITLE	CONTENT FOCUS	MAIN IDEA
Grade 6: *People in Change*	Modifying Cultural Patterns	People modify their environment in order to fulfill their basic and social needs.
Grade 5: *People in America*	Modifying Lifestyle	The experiences and activities of people in a neighborhood are shaped by the character of that neighborhood, by its setting and density.
Grade 4: *People in States*	Modifying Natural Resources	Interaction between people and their physical environment influences the ways in which they meet their needs.
Grade 3: *People in Communities*	Modifying Physical Environment	The significance of a region's resources is related to the culture of the people of that region.
Grade 2: *People in Neighborhoods*	Modifying Neighborhood	Change in one aspect of life is accomplished by change in others. When change occurs, some factors of life remain constant.
Grade 1: *People in Families*	Modifying Behavior	Change within a society may be the result of acceptance, compromise, or coercion.

FIGURE 1–1

Spiral Development of a Key Concept *(Adapted from "This is TABA" [advertising brochure], Addison-Wesley)*

ing her room, or going to school. In second grade, specialization would be examined within the context of the community, deepening the concept. In the same way, this and related concepts might serve as organizers for content selection through grade twelve, with the goal that the child not only master the content but also develop frameworks for categorizing new information as the individual moves into adulthood.

Programs organized this way are often referred to as *spiral curricula,* meaning that concepts are developed in different contexts and through increasing degrees of complexity as the child moves through the grades. Figure 1–1 illustrates how the concept of "modification" weaves its way through an elementary school social studies program and increases in depth as it progresses through grade six.

Ten additional key concepts of the Taba program similarly appear as separate threads of continuity throughout the program. They may not receive equal emphasis in any one year, but in the total program, each concept is developed consistently. This *spiral approach* to concept presentation is the most popular method of organizing social studies content.

There is consensus that the conceptual approach, or spiral curriculum, meets the needs of a contemporary social studies program, but there is considerable disagreement over which of the many concepts from the social sciences should be chosen. To highlight this dilemma, Table 1–1 lists concepts from two popular ele-

TABLE 1–1

Conceptual Organization of Two Popular Elementary School Social Studies Programs

Holt Databank*		Taba
Kindergarten	*Level Four*	*All Grades*
self	culture	Causality
family	tradition	Conflict
school	society	Cultural Change
groups	minorities	Differences
		Institutions
Level One	*Level Five*	Interdependence
people	immigration	Modification
earth	nation	Power
roles	rules and laws	Societal Control
seasons	values	Tradition
		Values
Level Two	*Level Six*	
communication	supply and demand	
community	material culture	
specialization	culture change	
land use	poverty	
Level Three		
cityness		
suburbs		
megalopolis		
population		

*This is only a sampling of the concepts in the Holt Databank program.

mentary school programs. Notice that the Holt Databank Program contains more than twenty concepts, while the Taba program identifies only eleven, and that neither program contains a concept listed by the other. Most new programs, although they do not agree on specific concepts, are fashioned this way.

The concepts for both programs in Table 1–1 can be separated into two distinct categories. For example, concepts relating to *real people, places,* or *things* were labeled "school," "seasons," "institutions," and so on. Other concepts relating to more abstract ideas associated with *behaviors* or *feelings* were labeled "values," "power," "conflict," and so on. Of course, children more easily understand concepts that deal with real things than those that deal with abstract ideas. Regardless of the type of concept, however, newer social studies programs have operated on the premise that social studies concepts cannot be fully developed if presented only in a single unit of study or even at only one grade level. The concepts must be viewed as threads that appear over and over again throughout the grades in a spiral, beginning at a small level early in the grades and moving to a fuller, higher level at each succeeding grade level. As the children's experiences broaden and their intellectual capacities mature, they are given repeated opportunities in a variety of contexts to develop an increasingly sophisticated understanding of key concepts.

The selection of concepts and their supporting subject matter is commonly referred to as the *scope,* or the "what," of the social studies curriculum. Curriculum planners and teachers cannot effectively plan a social studies program by identifying only the scope, however, for they must also decide when the various components are to appear. The arrangement of content is referred to as the *sequence* of the social studies curriculum, identifying the point at which specific learnings are expected to occur. Descriptions of social studies programs usually use these two terms concurrently, as in the *scope* and *sequence* of the program.

Although many variations had been suggested over the years, the last nationally significant elementary school scope and sequence pattern before the 1980s was Paul Hanna's "Expanding Environment" approach of the 1930s. In 1983 the National Council for the Social Studies created a task force to study the suitability of existing organizational plans for today's youth. Chaired by John Jarolimek, the task force made this statement:

> The Task Force does not recommend that a social studies sequence rely *solely* on the expanding environment principle. The life space of today's children is greatly affected by modern methods of communication and transportation. Who would claim that the life space of a six-year-old is the local environment when each evening the child views television accounts of events *in progress* from anywhere in the world? Therefore, the social studies curriculum should not move sequentially from topics that are near at hand to those that are far away for the purpose of expanding the environment. The purpose of extending content outward, away from a self-centric focus, is to illustrate how people and places interact; how people of different areas depend on each other; how people are part of interlocking networks that sustain the life of modern societies; and how people and places everywhere fit into a global community.[36]

Based on this rationale, the Task Force outlined recommendations for selection and placement of social studies content in the elementary schools. Although similar to Hanna's, this scope and sequence pattern departs from that model in significant ways:

It assumes that critical thinking is a major outcome of learning

It assumes that subject matter at *each* grade level will reflect a global perspective

It assumes that teachers throughout the grades will share in teaching, extending, and refining concepts in a developmental manner.

These are the broad curriculum recommendations of the task force:

Kindergarten—Awareness of Self in a Social Setting
Providing socialization experiences that help children bridge their home life with the group life of school

Grade 1—The Individual in Primary Social Groups: Understanding School and Family Life
Continuing the socialization process begun in kindergarten, but extending to studies of families (variations in the ways families live; the need for rules and laws)

Grade 2—Meeting Basic Needs in Nearby Social Groups: The Neighborhood
Studying social functions such as education, production, consumption, communication, and transportation in a neighborhood setting

Grade 3—Sharing Earth-Space with Others: The Community
Focusing on the community in a global setting, stressing social functions such as production, transportation, communication, distribution, and government

Grade 4—Human Life in Varied Environments: The Region
Emphasizing the region, an area of the earth defined for a specific reason; the home state is studied as a political region where state regulations require it

Grade 5—People of the Americas: The United States and Its Close Neighbors
Centering on the development of the United States as a nation in the Western Hemisphere, with particular emphasis on developing affective attachments to the principles on which the nation was founded; Canada and Mexico also studied

Grade 6—People and Cultures: The Eastern Hemisphere
Focusing on selected people and cultures of the Eastern Hemisphere, directed toward an understanding and appreciation of other people through development of such concepts as language, technology, institutions, and belief systems

Grade 7—A Changing World of Many Nations: A Global View
Providing an opportunity to broaden the concept of humanity within a global context; focus is on the world as the home of many different people who strive to deal with the forces that shape their lives

Grade 8—Building a Strong and Free Nation: The United States
Studying the "epic of America," the development of the United States as a strong and free nation; emphasis is on social history and economic development, including cultural and aesthetic dimensions of the American experience

Supporting Action Learning

Today's emphasis on action learning has developed from the philosophy of John Dewey. Rediscovered after a hiatus of nearly fifty years, Dewey's ideas of action learning and problem solving have stimulated innovative teaching practices centering on individual interests, manipulation of objects, and experimentation. Dewey's ideas, although important in themselves, were modernized and given contemporary philosophical support by the work of Jean Piaget, who also believed social studies instruction should continually stimulate children's curiosity.

This demand on social studies instruction is especially critical for today's child. Our educational system, unable to accurately predict the knowledge or behaviors desirable in an uncertain future, must concentrate on producing individuals who are able to solve problems that cannot be foreseen. It has been said that of all the learning elementary school children acquire today that will be useful in the future, *problem solving* is the most important. Arthur W. Combs emphasizes the "essential" nature of problem solving:

> It is impossible to be certain that any specific subject matter will be essential to cope with life even in the very near future. With respect to skills, reading, writing, and arithmetic . . . seem likely to be significant requirements for successful functioning for some time to come. But even these can no longer be regarded as vital for *every* student. Television and radio have made it possible for many citizens to get along quite adequately in modern society with very little reading. The typewriter and telephone have done the same for writing, and calculators are increasingly employed by everyone. . . . Only the process aspects of curriculum meet the criterion "essential" to prepare youth adequately for the world they will inherit.[37]

If schools accept that teaching problem-solving skills is a primary goal of instruction, then the curriculum must become increasingly involved with the real environment so that students are able to utilize primary sources of data. Children must become aware of the phenomena around them. The "geographer" bends down to allow sand to sift through her fingers. The "economist" plans a portion of his allowance for the school fair. The "political scientist" petitions the principal for a new piece of playground equipment. The "historian" listens in awe as a grandfather describes his childhood. Each investigator has a unique focus, but all have one thing in common—a realization that the world is a fascinating place.

A good social studies classroom encourages inquisitive minds. It inspires children to examine their world and prods them to collect evidence as do social scientists. Activity learning and problem-solving lessons are difficult to prepare, but they have large rewards. Children not only learn the subject matter, they also learn to think for themselves. As a result, teachers usually have more enthusiastic students. Read these two comments from sixth-grade youngsters who were asked to tell about their social studies program:

> We had fun the other day. We were studying dinosaurs and the teacher asked us to bring in bones we had left over from our dinner at home. We brushed them clean with a stiff scrubber, boiled them in vinegar water, soaked them in bleach and water to make them white, and put them in a big box we called the "Boneyard." We were put in groups then and each group could choose any bones they wanted. We glued and wired them together in the shape of the dinosaur we were supposed to find out about. We had to give the dinosaurs their real, scientific name and display an information card next to our model. Our teacher called us "paleontologists"—it was great!

> I didn't like studying about laws. The teacher talked about it a lot and we just sat there. Then she asked us to read in our books and do a worksheet. Social studies is so boring. Every day when social studies comes you know you're just going to have to sit there and do the same stuff.

Project methods, inquiry, problem solving—whatever term you choose to describe the type of instruction that appeals to the first youngster—all have one important characteristic in common: children engage in gathering evidence to answer problems. Without doubt, action-oriented methods are valuable teaching strategies and belong in your repertoire; perhaps not for exclusive use in your program, but as a valuable accompaniment to other recommended instruction strategies.

Synthesizing the Major Social Sciences

Social studies educators have long argued over an exact definition of the term *social studies*. After its introduction in 1916 by the National Education Association, the term was broadly defined as all subject matter dealing with human society. That definition was never popularly accepted, and a great deal of effort has been spent on a definition since then. At first, "social studies" became more or less a synonym for the three areas that dominated instruction at that time: history, geography, and political science. But, as new disciplines such as sociology, economics, and anthropology began to develop and enter school curricula, the need for a comprehensive "social studies" program was stressed. Even today, we have no single acceptable definition for the *social studies* and appear to be in even more disagreement than we were in 1916. Joyce and Alleman-Brooks, for example, asked authors and co-authors of professional textbooks on the teaching of elementary and middle school social studies to define this subject.[38] The respondents' definitions were polarized, ranging from active, inquiry-centered emphasis to knowledge-centered emphasis. One wrote "Social studies is the integration of thinking, feeling, and acting within one's life as one relates to self, others and the environment." Another wrote, "Social studies is knowledge about social, political, cultural, economic, and environmental phenomena." An interesting facet of the Joyce/Alleman-Brooks study is that respondents who coauthored a professional text did not always agree on a definition of the social studies. One author wrote, "Social studies is the familiarization of the world in terms of past and present social and physical phenomena that affect the planet's inhabitants," while the coauthor of the same text wrote, "Social studies is a skill-combined multidisciplinary field drawing upon the social sciences and related areas with a major focus on contemporary problems vital to children, youth, and society." The magnitude of this identity problem was of great concern to Edgar B. Wesley:

> The phrase, "social studies" has been defined as social science, as social service, as socialism, as radical left-wing thinking, as social reform, as antihistory, as a unification of social subjects, as a field, as a federation, as an integrated curriculum, as prochild reform, as curriculum innovation. Elements of truth may be found in each of these concepts. No other subject has suffered such divisive doctrines. While other areas may involve combinations of various disciplines, none of them leads to the confusion that exists in the social studies.[39]

FIGURE 1–2

What to Include in the Social Studies Curriculum? (Source: National Council for the Social Studies)

Arthur Bestor commented on the continuing turmoil, "This label (social studies) has itself contributed so greatly to educational confusion and stultification that it ought to be abandoned forthwith."[40] (See Figure 1–2.) To offer my own definition of today's social studies does no more than add waves to the water, but without it this book would lack meaningful focus. Based on popular thinking, a satisfactory definition might be: *the application of concepts, generalizations, and methods of inquiry associated with the various social sciences for the purpose of helping children learn to understand themselves, other people, their environment, and how each of these ingredients interacts with one another.*

We have discussed the importance of inquiry, concepts, and generalizations as components of a contemporary social studies program; now let us examine the characteristics of each social science that contributes to the content structure of this subject. Each of the social sciences views society from a different perspective and uses its unique body of knowledge to explain the human condition. The social studies program synthesizes these separate, unique viewpoints into one interdisciplinary subject consisting of selected concepts and generalizations from history, geography, political science, economics, sociology, and anthropology (Figure 1–3).

The result of the quest to discover structures of the social sciences was the generation of a large number of alternative choices for concepts and generalizations

FIGURE 1–3

Characteristics of the Social Sciences that Contribute to Contemporary Social Studies Programs

for inclusion in school programs. You saw two of those lists in Table 1–1. State school laws also reflected a concern for utilizing concepts and generalizations from the social sciences in their curriculum requirements, as in this section of the Pennsylvania school code:

> A planned course in the social studies shall be taught in each year of the elementary school. The content of this program shall include anthropology, economics, geography, history, political science and sociology. These may be combined into one general area known as social studies.[41]

Addressing Society's Conflicting Issues

Not all educators believe that content drawn from the social sciences should be the exclusive vehicle by which children are guided toward the overall objective of the social studies—*effective citizenship.* These individuals advocate an expanded view of the social studies, one that emphasizes an awareness of contemporary concerns, such as ecology, and the methods by which people make decisions regarding those concerns. The real test of a sound social studies program, they argue, is how well children apply their learning to intelligent participation in the reality of out-of-school society. A National Council for the Social Studies Task Force emphasized these ideas in a position statement regarding inclusion of social issues in the "new" social studies curriculum:

> Broadly based social issues do not respect the boundaries of the academic disciplines. The notion that the disciplines must always be studied in their pure form or that social studies content should be drawn only from the social sciences is insufficient for a curriculum intended to demonstrate the relationship between knowledge and rationally based social participation. It is true that the social sciences can make a marked contribution to clarifying the basic issues which continue to require social attention. But the efforts of social scientists to develop an understanding of human behavior through research are not necessarily related to society's persistent problems and are seldom intended to arrive at the resolution of value conflicts or the formulation of public policy. In short, one can "do" social science outside the context of the social problems which constitute the major concern of the social studies curriculum. Thus, while there could be no social studies without the social sciences, social studies is something more than the sum of the social sciences.[42]

Contemporary programs, then, call for applying knowledge in the social arena— *social participation.* These programs should develop individuals who will say: "I'm part of what's going on and I'm going to do something about it."

Of course, children cannot be socially active unless they are aware of the major issues that face contemporary society. You must help and encourage children to identify those issues and engage them in decision-making activities. Some state curriculum guidelines address this concern by recommending the addition of *special topics* to the regular social science based program. Recall that the Pennsylvania Curriculum Guidelines decree that all public and private schools in Pennsylvania offer a social studies program based upon content drawn from the six social sciences.

Recognizing the importance of including topics of contemporary significance, however, the document specifies:

> *Racial and Ethnic Group History:* In each course in the history of the United States and of Pennsylvania taught in the elementary and secondary schools of the Commonwealth, there shall be included the major contributions made by Negroes and other racial and ethnic groups in the development of the United States and the Commonwealth of Pennsylvania.
>
> The inclusion of minorities in the curriculum recognizes that America is a pluralistic society made up of many ethnic and cultural groups which have contributed to our quality and strength. Since there is a discouraging lack of evidence that man has become more sensitive and more accepting of human differences and since ours is an increasingly mobile society in which children will inevitably live and work in multigroup situations, education must provide *all* children with the competencies and skills required for a productive life in today's society. The fact that this is a responsibility of the total school program does not excuse the social studies area from its special role of leadership.[43]

Newer thrusts in the curriculum also include, besides study of the contributions of racial and ethnic groups, topics such as environmental issues, citizenship education, consumer education, career education, and "worldmindedness."

PLANNING FOR THE FUTURE

New trends in social studies programming have brought about significant changes. Materials have become more sophisticated, teaching strategies more complex, and the children more involved. Despite the positive nature of these changes, social studies educators have continually reevaluated the state of instruction in our schools and offered suggestions for the continued revitalization of social studies programs and methods of instruction. Their questions and concerns led to the development of many self-study programs. The most recent work in this area is being done by Project SPAN (a loose acronym for "Social Studies/Social Science Education: Priorities, Practices, and Needs"). This project was funded by the National Science Foundation (NSF) in 1978 for purposes similar to those of Project Social Studies during the 1960s:

1. To assess the current state of social studies education
2. To identify needs in the field
3. To recommend actions and directions for the future

The results of Project SPAN* were published in 1980 and the conclusions were somewhat startling.[44] The project pointed out, for example, that despite all the in-

---

*For more information on the current state of the social studies and on Project SPAN's suggestions for educational reform, write to this address: Publications Department, Social Science Education Consortium, 855 Broadway, Boulder, CO 80302.

novative suggestions of the "New Social Studies" era, little has changed since the 1950s. Positive changes include significant improvement in textbooks and a somewhat wider use of creative teaching methods, but six major problems were identified:

> Student learning: too many students fail to learn important social studies knowledge, skills, and attitudes and do not like or value social studies
>
> Teacher instruction: instruction in social studies is generally characterized by lack of variety in teaching methods and evaluation practices, limited kinds of learning experiences, and inattention to the implications of educational research
>
> Curriculum: the present social studies curriculum does not contribute as much as it could to learning that is useful for helping students understand and participate more effectively in the current and future social world
>
> Profession: the social studies profession is characterized by a lack of constructive interaction among the various participants, by limited opportunities for personal growth for teachers, and by confusion about the role of social studies in the education of young people
>
> Culture of school: the culture and organization of the school focus much of the energy of teachers and administrators on matters of management and control rather than on teaching and learning
>
> Public awareness: the public does not fully understand or appreciate the importance of social studies.[45]

These six problems are not new, and their continued existence only adds to the frustration of trying to develop a sense of direction, identity, and worth. Working with this realization, Project SPAN offered a number of recommendations to address the problems, but their major suggestion for reform mainly restates the trends described in this chapter. SPAN did emphasize one additional point: flexible and creative teachers are the key to productive change. For instance, the first principle to emerge from SPAN's analysis of the 1980s was this: "Teachers are the key to success and improvement in social studies. This is an overwhelming conclusion of the NSF researchers, and one cited by many other analysts. Teachers occupy a central position in curriculum, instruction, the culture of the school, and their profession; their concerns, ideas, and energy must be integrally involved in any effort to improve social studies teaching and learning." Only time can tell us the specific solutions for meeting the challenges of the 1980s, but we can readily anticipate one important implication of Project SPAN's work—contemporary change must be initiated and implemented by energetic, innovative, and concerned teachers who are convinced of the value of the social studies in children's lives.

SUMMARY

Every society prepares its young members to assume expected behaviors and values through some form of education. Through whatever educative process it chooses, the social group insures its perpetuation by teaching the basic skills such as language and computation, passing on the heritage and traditions of the group, interpreting the legal and political system, communicating the accepted values and morals of the society, and establishing feelings of loyalty and unity toward the group. For some groups, presently and in the past, this educative process was somewhat stable and predictable—society's conditions changed little from generation to generation. In today's world, however, inducting children into a society as complex as that of the modern United States is an enormous task.

Until the 1960s, social studies education was charged with that task. At the same time, it was characterized primarily as a body of knowledge to be learned through drill and recitation. Disconcerting social events of the 1960s, however, along with innovative views of the learning process as proposed by individuals such as Piaget and Bruner, enlightened educators to the need for change from that static, unimaginative approach to social induction. Resulting changes seem to fall into these areas: (1) broadening instructional goals to include examination of values as well as development of knowledge and skills; (2) teaching concept development rather than memorization of facts and details; (3) supporting action learning, giving children opportunities to think, inquire, and solve problems; (4) synthesizing the several major social sciences into one program called the social studies; and (5) realizing that conflicting issues of a contemporary society must be addressed objectively.

ENDNOTES

1. Alvin Toffler, *Learning for Tomorrow: The Role of the Future in Education* (New York: Vintage Books, 1974).

2. Arthur W. Combs, "What the Future Demands of Education," *Phi Delta Kappan,* 62, no. 5 (January 1981): 369–372.

3. Lloyd DeMause, "Our Forebears Made Childhood a Nightmare," *Psychology Today,* 8, no. 11 (April 1975): 85.

4. Philip Aries, *Centuries of Childhood* (New York: Vantage Books, 1962), p. 128.

5. William Kessen, *The Child* (New York: John Wiley, 1965), pp. 37–38.

6. Paul Leicester Ford, *The New England Primer: A History of its Origin and Development* (New York: Dodd, Mead, 1979), p. 1.

7. Ford, *The New England Primer,* p. 1.

8. Ford, *The New England Primer,* p. 1.

9. Alexander Frazier, *Values, Curriculum, and the Elementary School* (Boston: Houghton Mifflin, 1980), p. 193.

10. Edward Channing and Albert Bushnell Hart, *Guide to the Study of American History* (Boston: Ginn and Company, 1903), p. 1.

11. Francis M. Moorehouse, "Syllabus for Ninth Grade Study of American History," Part III, Report of the Committee on History and Citizenship Education, *The Historical Outlook* (April 1921), p. 119.

12. Jean Jacques Rousseau, *Emile, or a Treatise on Education* (B. Foxley, trans.) London: Dent, 1911, p. 5. The first French edition was published in 1762.

13. James Harvey Robinson, *The New History* (New York: The Macmillan Company, 1912), pp. 17–18, 134.

14. Stanley G. Hall, *The Psychology of Adolescence* (New York: D. Appleton and Company, 1904), p. 8.

15. Arnold Gesell, *The Mental Growth of the Pre-School Child* (New York: Macmillan, 1925).

16. Ira J. Gordon, "Parenting, Teaching, and Child Development," *Young Children,* 31, no. 3 (March 1976): 173.

17. Arnold Gesell and Frances L. Ilg, *The Child From Five to Ten* (New York: Harper, 1946), p. 6

18. Arnold Gesell and Helen Thompson, *The Psychology of Early Growth* (New York: Macmillan, 1938), p. 27.

19. Martin S. Dvorkin, *Dewey on Education: Selections, with an Introduction and Notes* (New York: Teachers College Bureau of Publications, 1959), p. 9.

20. Lucy Sprague Mitchell, *Young Geographers* (New York: John Day, 1934).

21. Caroline Pratt, *Experimental Practice in City and Country Schools* (New York: Dutton, 1924).

22. John B. Watson, *Behaviorism* (Chicago: University of Chicago Press, 1925), p. 82.

23. Paul R. Hanna, "Generalizations and Universal Values: Their Implications for the Social Studies Program," *Social Studies in the Elementary School.* Fifty-sixth Yearbook, National Society for the Study of Education, Part II (Chicago: University of Chicago Press, 1957), pp. 27–47.

24. Edgar Wesley, in Ronald D. Barr, James L. Barth and Samuel S. Shermis, *Defining the Social Studies* (Washington, DC: National Council for the Social Studies, 1977), p. 40.

25. Leonard S. Kenworthy, *Social Studies for the Seventies,* 2nd ed. (New York: John Wiley, 1973), p. 64.

26. Robert D. Barr, James L. Barth, and Samuel S. Shermis, *Defining the Social Studies* (Washington, DC: National Council for the Social Studies, 1977), p. 42.

27. Jerome S. Bruner, *The Process of Education* (Cambridge, MA: Harvard University Press, 1960), p. 33.

28. Reprinted by permission of Universal Press Syndicate.

29. David Mathews, "Civic Intelligence," *Social Education,* 49, no. 8 (November/December 1985):678–681.

30. Arthur Levine, in David Mathews, "Civic Intelligence," p. 679.

31. "Essentials of the Social Studies," *Social Education,* 45, no. 3 (March 1981): 163–164.

32. Jeane J. Kirkpatrick, "The Teaching of Democratic Values," *American Education,* Spring 1979.

33. Eliza Cook, "Work," in *McGuffey's Fifth Eclectic Reader* (New York: The New American Library, 1879), p. 71.

34. Hilda Taba, et al., *A Teacher's Handbook to Elementary Social Studies* (Reading, MA: Addison-Wesley, 1971), pp. 14–15.

35. Clair W. Keller, *Involving Students in the New Social Studies* (Boston: Little, Brown, 1974), p. 13.

36. Task Force on Scope and Sequence, "In Search for a Scope and Sequence for Social Studies," *Social Education,* 48, no. 4 (April 1984): 252–253.

37. Arthur W. Combs, "What the Future Demands of Education," *Phi Delta Kappan,* 62, no. 5 (January 1981): 369–372.

38. William W. Joyce and Janet Alleman-Brooks, "Resolving the Identity Crisis in Elementary and Middle School Social Studies," unpublished paper, Michigan State University, pp. 20–21.

39. Edgar B. Wesley, Foreword to R.D. Barr and S. S. Shermis, *The Nature of the Social Studies* (Palm Springs, CA: ETC Publications, 1978), p. iv.

40. Arthur Bestor, *Restoration of Learning* (New York: Alfred A. Knopf, 1955), p. 126.

41. Pennsylvania Dept. of Education, *Social Studies Curriculum Requirements in Pennsylvania* (October 1971), Section 7–2111, j. of General Curriculum Regulations.

42. Gary Manson et al., *Social Studies Curriculum Guidelines* (Washington, DC. National Council for the Social Studies, 1971), p. 9.

43. Pennsylvania Dept. of Education, *Social Studies Curriculum Requirements in Pennsylvania* (October 1971), Section 7–151 of General Curriculum Regulations.

44. Irving Morrissett, Sharryl Hawke, and Douglas P. Superka, "Six Problems for Social Studies in the 1980s," *Social Education*, 44, no. 7 (November-December 1980): 561–69.

45. Morrissett, Hawke, and Superka, "Six Problems for Social Studies in the 1980s."

Becoming a Social Studies Teacher

KEY CONCEPTS

- ☐ *Identifying the professional competencies and ethical standards shared by good elementary school social studies teachers*
- ☐ *Understanding how children's backgrounds and experiences influence social studies instruction*
- ☐ *Appreciating the need to use a variety of strategies and techniques in the social studies program*
- ☐ *Describing the content and methods of investigation associated with the major social sciences that comprise the elementary school social studies program*

> "When I die, I hope it will be my good fortune to go where Miss Blake will meet me and lead me to my seat."
>
> –Bernard M. Baruch

As you can see from this quotation, Bernard Baruch's teacher obviously made a significant impact on his life. Like Baruch, we all hold precious memories of a caring teacher who made some aspect of school exceptional for us, too. It may be that your own "Miss Blake" influenced you to choose teaching as a career. Through their actions and attitudes, these memorable professionals exhibit the qualities of superior teachers. A group of confident, happy, active children reflects the masterful touch of a Miss Blake, someone who is able to pull together all the essential qualities of an educational program so that every child's special interests and needs are met through a wide range of stimulating learning experiences.

Despite the problems that face social studies education, there are examples of superb teaching everywhere. Many programs are excellent, built by teachers who have a sound knowledge of why they are teaching, whom they are teaching, what they are teaching, and how they are teaching.

Becoming a teacher is a momentous goal and a rewarding one. Special people work with children—they understand the long-range implications of their work not only as it affects children but also as it affects families, communities, and even the nation or world. That responsibility cannot be taken lightly, and the purpose of this text is to help you develop strategies and attitudes appropriate for establishing positive classroom practices. To achieve this goal, this book will fuse personal and professional components of teaching to show that teaching is done *with* children rather than *to* them.

The book combines theory with practice, but as with problem solvers at any level of schooling, you must not only decide upon personally appealing teaching methodologies but also back up your selection with sound knowledge of the theory that supports your choice. This ability will help you become a true professional—someone who can combine *knowledge about child development* with a mastery of *teaching techniques*, including ways to stimulate enthusiasm and help children acquire skills, concepts, and attitudes. Acquiring these abilities is neither accidental nor a "natural phenomenon." You've probably heard of some amazingly effective "untrained adults" who are referred to as "natural teachers." Some people believe these so-called natural teachers would, in a classroom teaching situation, experience the same level of success as a trained teacher. That notion is comparable to expecting someone to defend clients in court or perform delicate surgery without specialized training in those fields. You must master a body of knowledge and a specialized range of skills, because you will hold a critical place in the lives of young children. You will be a *professional*.

CHARACTERISTICS OF GOOD TEACHERS

There are many ideas about what constitutes a good social studies teacher. Despite the volumes of literature identifying all the categories and subcategories of effective teaching, I like to think that good teachers are distinguished by these three criteria:

Good teachers are fine people. They have a positive view of others. They do not seem prone to suspect others of ulterior motives. They do not have a neurotic need for power. They are not dominated by anxieties that affect interpersonal relationships. They have the ability to see things from another's point of view. They have a fondness and respect for children.

Good teachers are flexible. They are not fixed on a single approach to education. They understand the multiple needs of their students. They are able to move to what they must do to meet the needs at the moment. They have a favorable view of democratic classroom procedures. They see students as individuals capable of doing things for themselves.

Good teachers know what they are teaching. They realize they cannot help children only by being child-centered, but must be knowledgeable. They must be broadly educated and well-informed. "Professional education" in a teacher preparation program alone will not guarantee a successful teaching career. Your liberal arts or general studies background is an important part of your training. You must understand and respect the knowledge in the field you teach, for young children are motivated to learn not only by respect for their teacher's level of knowledge about the world but also by her thirst to find out more.

The most important ingredient of a successful social studies program is a good teacher. The physical setting is important, but the teacher's skills and enthusiasm are more important. The teacher's personality, attitude, and behavior determine the tone of the environment and make a lasting impact on the children, on their families, and, indirectly, on society in general. Few individuals are more important in the lives of young children than their parents, close relatives, and teachers. Teachers are admired and imitated; they are expected to display courage, cleanliness, honesty, open-mindedness, generosity, faithfulness, sensitivity, tact, and other qualities. Teachers should be among the finest people we can imagine.

Teachers cannot expect to function in a professional environment unless they can get along with others and respect the children with whom they work. You can gain a sense of the qualities you will bring to the teaching profession by reviewing this list of characteristics to see which ones apply to you:

- I love young children.
- I know youngsters are active, so I eat and sleep well and exercise to stay physically fit.

- I observe young children so I can evaluate their levels of maturity and plan accordingly.
- I get along well with people.
- I am a hard worker.
- I am willing to put in extra time to complete a job.
- I am punctual and dependable.
- I can keep secrets regarding confidential matters.
- I admit mistakes and work hard to correct them.
- I observe the rules of the groups to which I belong.
- I leave my problems at home and do not let them affect my work.
- I ignore rumors and refuse to gossip.
- I am well-groomed and neat.
- I keep my work area in order.
- I use supplies and equipment as carefully as if I purchased them myself.
- I take pride in my work.
- I follow directions and respect the leadership of others.
- I have a good sense of humor; I can laugh with others.
- I am flexible; I can vary my approach if the situation calls for it.
- I am curious and want to explore new ideas for working with young children.

Much can be said about each item on this list, but the first item especially deserves elaboration: "I love young children." As a matter of fact, a recent survey of beginning teachers by Mary Harbaugh indicated that 90 percent of new teachers chose their profession because they love children and believe that teaching is important and honorable.[1] Once, though, while I was discussing this feature with a group of graduate students, one raised her hand and commented somewhat forcefully, "We've been talking about loving children for some time now and, frankly, I'm getting tired of it. I don't think you can *love* all your children. I love my husband, my parents, and my own youngsters at home, but I don't love the children I teach. Sure, I have a close attachment to them or I wouldn't be teaching, but I don't *love* them." Naturally, this unexpected reaction created a great deal of discussion. The class attempted to convince the skeptic that *love* certainly was a way to describe the feelings of a teacher toward the children in his or her care. Finally, someone said, "There are many different kinds of love among people, and the love for your spouse or parents is much different than the love of a teacher for her children." This statement was enlarged upon when the class brought me a special item for our next session. Figure 2–1 illustrates the kind of caring teachers communicate to their students. The strong tie between teacher and child is close to that between parent and child. Can you add examples of the ways teachers show love for their students?

In your career, you will become trusted by parents, colleagues, and the community as someone who makes a significant positive contribution to the growth and

LOVE IN A CLASSROOM IS—

A teacher who cleans your scraped knee.

When your teacher hugs you at a special moment.

A teacher who sits next to you and says something especially meant for you!

A teacher who *really* listens!

. . . CARING. SHARING. TOUCHING. FEELING. HELPING. ACCEPTING. UNDERSTANDING.

FIGURE 2–1

How Teachers Show Love for Their Students

development of young children. You must prepare for this responsibility by examining and reexamining your personal and professional characteristics as you progress through your training so that you can enter the profession as a confident, responsible, happy person, willing and able to develop a unique leadership style.

HIERARCHY OF NEEDS. Maslow's theory of *needs* emphasizes the importance of an understanding, caring teacher. As shown in Figure 2–2, a hierarchy of needs evolves from infancy through adulthood in all human beings.[2] Maslow contends that if basic *physiological needs* (oxygen, food, warmth, and other factors necessary to maintain life) are not met, children will not strive to attain the subsequent needs. So, before we can expect children to be motivated to learn (the uppermost need), we must be careful to first meet the subsidiary needs. The needs as Maslow describes them are:

Physiological needs—oxygen, food, warmth, rest, activity, and other essentials necessary to maintain life

Safety needs—routine, rhythm, and order in life, and protection from danger situations

Love and belonging needs—desire for affectionate relationships with people and for acceptance in a group

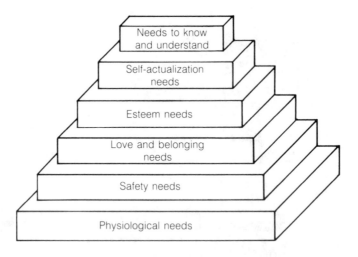

FIGURE 2–2
Maslow's Hierarchy of Needs

Esteem needs—receiving recognition as a worthwhile individual, developing confidence and a sense of worth

Self-actualization needs—striving to fulfill one's potential and satisfaction with what one has chosen to become in life

Needs to know and understand—curiosity, exploration, and the desire for further knowledge; systematizing, organizing, and analyzing information

Maslow's ideas have important educational implications. If, for example, you want your children to participate in social studies learning activities but their needs for *love* or *esteem* have not been satisfied, you may be disappointed in their response to you and the learning task. Children who are consistently subjected to harsh treatment from their teacher find it difficult to focus on intellectually challenging tasks; instead, they are "energized" (motivated) to satisfy the stronger needs for love and acceptance. Children come to school searching for someone who will love them, and, likewise, for someone who will accept their love in return. Do not expect such love to be the same as family love, but a mutual feeling of care and respect necessary for a sound educational program to flourish.

INDIVIDUAL DIFFERENCES. Besides respecting children's basic needs, good teachers are aware of individual differences among the youngsters in their classrooms and are able to make instructional decisions that have the greatest possibility of successful learning for all. Sometimes, though, the differences among children are so great, even in one classroom, that it often seems the only thing in common among a group of twenty-five youngsters is their assignment to the same teacher. What are some ways youngsters differ from one another? A typical class of fourth-graders might differ in these ways:

Self-Confidence	Sex	Achievement Levels
Enthusiasm	Age	Interests
Motivation	Weight	Values Orientations
Social Adjustment	Race	Intelligence Levels
Self-Perception	Height	Ethnic Backgrounds
Behavior	Creativity	Socioeconomic Class
Life Experiences	Learning Modalities	Physical Health
Reading Levels	Emotional Factors	Personality

Children differ from the time they come into the world and gradually become more unique as the environment and genetic factors combine to form individuals who vary in physical, creative, emotional, and behavioral characteristics as well as in intellectual potential, social attitudes, interests, and special talents. They differ, also, in their ways of learning. No single system of instruction (including the use of a single textbook) can possibly do justice to all these differences. But the differences among children are normal, and those differences contribute to the challenge we all face as teachers.

What does this all mean? Calvin W. Taylor suggests that teachers view all children as talented; that is, each can be above average in at least one of the many important intellectual talents we can now measure.[3] Furthermore, with major adjustments in our teaching styles, children can use their multiple talents to acquire knowledge in the social studies classroom. In fact, Taylor says they can exercise and develop every one of the known intellectual talents as they ponder and process knowledge in the social studies.

Taylor suggests grouping intellectual talents as in Figure 2–3. The grouping is based on world-of-school needs, specifying *academic talents* and six other extremely important types that are especially significant in the social studies classroom: productive thinking, planning, communicating, forecasting, decision making, and human relations.

Let us assume that the child named Kathy is toward the bottom of the academic totem pole because she consistently obtains lower grades than her classmates and performs below average on achievement tests. When we begin to examine other talents, however, we also find that she had some trouble in activities where productive thinking was required. Extending Kathy's profile by following the line in Figure 2–3, we see that her ability to make sound decisions is high, especially in judging which information is valuable and which should be discarded. Kathy also displayed strong skill in communicating her decisions to others. Choose any of the other hypothetical children and plot the pattern of talents. Each, like Kathy, will certainly have at least one talent strength and some weakness.

According to Taylor, talent searches should occur in the classroom, and children can experience greater success if they are encouraged to use multiple talents rather than any single type. Multiple talent teaching requires the selection of activities that work across a greater number of children's talents than was ever before possible

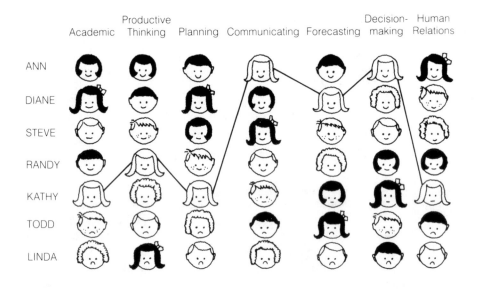

FIGURE 2–3

Multiple-talent Totem Pole (Adapted from Calvin W. Taylor, "Be Talent Developers. . .as Well as Knowledge Dispensers," Today's Education 57, no. 9 (December 1968): 69. Reprinted with permission.)

with the sole use of a single social studies textbook. Of course, academic talent is valued, but we must augment the emphasis on this single talent with activities that encourage creative talent, decision-making talent, and all the rest.

The implication is that you must develop a personalized teaching style while being aware of and responsive to the needs of each individual. Regardless of style, whether a strict no-nonsense approach or a highly personal, informal one, you must constantly search for self-improvement by combining your knowledge of teaching practices with your understanding of the uniqueness of each child in your classroom.

Flexibility

The second ingredient of good teachers, that of *flexibility*, is probably the most widely discussed characteristic in educational literature. Flexible teachers are able to examine teaching strategies and materials and choose what is most appropriate for any given situation, not because they are "cute" or "gimmicky" but because they will probably make the greatest contribution toward the success of any learning episode. There are many methods for teaching social studies, but some are more appropriate for elementary school children. Not all contemporary methods are new, radical, or revolutionary; most are adaptations of older, standard methods. Regardless, the crux of successful teaching lies in the fact that *any* single method of instruction should be used sparingly with elementary school children. And the younger the children, the greater the methodological variety should be. Here are some general guidelines to consider as you begin to choose methods through which you will teach social studies:

Smiling, accepting, and sharing are signs of a teacher's affection for her students.

Sometimes you will lecture to your children, but rarely; the younger the child, the less you talk.

Sometimes you will hold discussion sessions with the entire class, using good questioning and discussion techniques.

Sometimes you will lead whole-group learning experiences from the textbook or another common source of information—such experiences offer balance and proportion to the program.

Sometimes you will encourage the children to work together in committees—the children learn a great deal from each other.

Sometimes you will choose books, movies, slides, tapes, filmstrips, recorders, pictures, bulletin boards, and other learning aids—variety of materials is essential.

Sometimes you will encourage children to solve problems and search for answers to their own questions—an independent quest for information is a lifelong necessity.

Sometimes children will work alone—meeting personal interests and needs must assume high priority in all classrooms.

ADAPTING METHODS.   From what special social studies teaching methods are you able to choose? Figure 2–4 illustrates the general categories of teaching methods in the social studies. It is organized as a continuum ranging from teacher-centered to child-centered methods. Because variety is a way of life for elementary school teachers, you will need to develop competencies at each point on the continuum. You must know how to deliver a worthwhile lecture as well as how to encourage children to pursue topics of interest independently. The strongest emphasis in your program, especially for the primary-grade child, however, should be on an activity, child-centered approach. Your concern is to take the children to the action or bring the action to them. You must look for and design learning experiences in which the children become actively involved—digging, making, selling, buying, building, interviewing, polling, painting, cooking, and so on. You will also rely on textbooks, workbooks, and the like, but you must get elementary school children up and around. Make sure they are busy participating. Doing comes first—it is an essential ingredient for the success of any social studies program. Inherent in any learning activity or teaching methodology, however, is the fact that teachers must provide for a meaningful intake of information. Whether controlling that intake through a lecture, by asking children to read specific pages in the text, or by allowing children to uncover their own data by interviewing school personnel during a unit on careers, the teacher must be aware not only of the materials available but also of acceptable techniques for using them.

We will discuss some basic principles to follow in planning successful social studies lessons along each point of the continuum, but we will not eliminate personal creativity from the teaching process. You will need to adapt these principles to your personal teaching style. All good teachers succeed in different ways; two

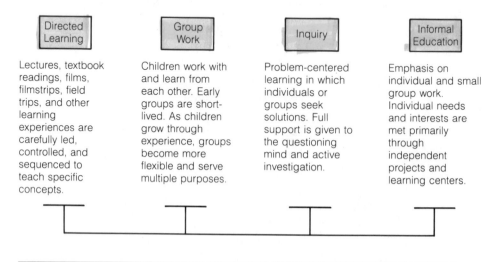

Directed Learning	Group Work	Inquiry	Informal Education
Lectures, textbook readings, films, filmstrips, field trips, and other learning experiences are carefully led, controlled, and sequenced to teach specific concepts.	Children work with and learn from each other. Early groups are short-lived. As children grow through experience, groups become more flexible and serve multiple purposes.	Problem-centered learning in which individuals or groups seek solutions. Full support is given to the questioning mind and active investigation.	Emphasis on individual and small group work. Individual needs and interests are met primarily through independent projects and learning centers.

FIGURE 2–4

Continuum of Teaching Methodologies Common to Elementary Social Studies Classrooms

different teachers may use similar teaching practices, but their personalities influence their approaches to such a degree that, if both taught the same content, each lesson would appear vastly different. Reissman suggests that instead of trying to develop a hypothetical model of the ideal teacher, we strive instead to think about developing individual teaching styles, with each style matching the teacher's personality.[4] Successful teachers are those who develop their own repertoires. They adapt teaching recommendations to fit their personalities. Albert Cullum recognized early in his career the need to act naturally: "When I first began teaching, there was Al Cullum the teacher and Al Cullum the person. I soon discovered that this split personality was not a healthy one for the children nor for me."[5] Teachers behave in different ways while fulfilling their professional responsibilities. They may appear to be a stern commander or a concerned helper and guide, but their success comes from allowing their true personalities to emerge while they use any of the acceptable teaching methodologies of the social studies.

Knowledgeability

The teacher's knowledge of the subject matter she is expected to teach is the third major factor that affects the success of the social studies curriculum. *Academic specialization*, or the in-depth study of subjects a teacher candidate may teach in an elementary school, is a primary concern among critics of teacher preparation. Command of subject matter is easier for high school teachers, who teach within their areas of specialization. By contrast, an elementary school teacher is an entire faculty—she teaches reading, the language arts, literature, mathematics, physical sciences, biological sciences, social sciences, art, music, health, and physical education. Because their responsibility is so broad, it is impossible for elementary school teachers to acquire the equivalent of an academic major in each field. But teachers of the elementary social studies do need information at their fingertips. They must anticipate children's questions before providing a learning experience and become familiar enough with the content to explain important information accurately, not by guessing or fabricating. Your scholarship should be broad to help you supply information to your children, but you must also consistently communicate your *spirit* for learning. It is acceptable to say, "That's an interesting question; let's look it up," but try not to let that happen too often. Children may begin to question your competence if you consistently give them the impression of not knowing. So, read books, examine encyclopedias, talk to specialists in a field, and check other sources of information before you plan to teach something. Those who know a subject well have little difficulty arousing children's enthusiasm for learning.

As you leave your teacher preparation program, you cannot be expected to be in total command of all the content you are expected to teach, but you should be aware of the nature of knowledge, the structure of the discipline, and the relationships among the disciplines you teach. To that end, let us examine the disciplines that make up the social studies program and determine what they have to offer the elementary school curriculum.

DISCIPLINES OF THE SOCIAL STUDIES

History

History is the study through a chronological framework of what has happened to humanity in the past. Historians study the human condition by gathering and evaluating relevant traces of people, places, and things past. Historical sources include physical remains and oral or written records of the past.

PHYSICAL REMAINS.   Physical remains include artifacts, relics, and other "accidental survivors" of the past. By critically examining these sources, the historian is able to partially reconstruct the story of human life. I like to use the term "accidental survivors" because few historical artifacts or relics were planned to be preserved to describe a way of life to people in the future. Take a coin for example. What do you think historians could learn from a coin? Suppose a recently unearthed coin had a figure of a person on one side and a series of fish on the other, along with some words that could not be read. What could we tell about the people who used the coin? Ponder that question for a moment, then compare your ideas to these:

1. The people were advanced enough to use a monetary system.
2. They were advanced enough to use metal.
3. Their clothing and hairstyles can tell us something about their lifestyle.
4. The fish indicate something about their economy.
5. A stamped date would tell us how old the civilization was.

ORAL OR WRITTEN RECORDS.   In addition to examining artifacts and relics, historians study oral or written records. Historians put the most trust in primary witnesses who were close to an event and able to offer oral accounts. Suppose you attended the launching of a revolutionary new space vehicle. In the future, historians would most likely believe your account of that event rather than someone who heard about it from another (secondary witness). People who listen to the Super Bowl on radio every year and hear the announcer describe the action are secondary witnesses to the event. Written records in the form of diaries, wills, mortgages, government records, newspapers, magazines, and so on are witnesses for the historian to draw on. No source of information is insignificant to historians until they examine it and evaluate its usefulness. How many American colonial housewives thought their shopping lists or cooking utensils would be used by historians as evidence to explain colonial life, businesses, and activities in the home?

Regardless of the source, validity and authenticity must be checked. Much as detectives prepare a criminal case for court, historians must carefully gather information from more than one source and decide what is truthful. The historian's final responsibility is to write about the information without showing personal bias. This is perhaps the ultimate challenge, because historians see various meanings in the facts they uncover. For example, sometimes historians from different regions write conflicting accounts of an event. How might a Southerner's account of slavery differ from a Northerner's? An English account of the American Revolution from an American? In addition, historians often try to write about things they think will interest their readers, thereby choosing to report only the facts they believe to be of interest to the general population at the time. The Watergate activities of the 1970s, for example, provoked several conflicting accounts ranging from Richard Nixon's memoirs to those of legal prosecutors. In summary, the role of the historian is to:

Carefully search for facts

Use a variety of sources for evidence

Judge the evidence for accuracy

Write about the facts without showing personal bias

You will want to teach history in a way that allows children to investigate as historians. Provide situations where they can examine historical materials firsthand. Bring artifacts to the classroom, invite guest speakers to demonstrate items from the past, visit museums and historical sites to examine original written materials, compare written accounts of historical events to detect personal biases. Encourage children to make their own hypotheses about what they observe and give them opportunities to test their guesses. They should use the historian's methods of investigation to study a variety of local, regional, state, national, or international topics.

Geography

Imagine that you are blindfolded and taken to a faraway land. As you look around after your blindfold is removed, everything appears new to you. You might ask yourself these questions: Where is this place? Do people live here? If so, where? How many people are there? How do the people make a living? What kind of climate does this place have? How can I survive? How will I get food and clothing? How will I find shelter or build a home?

Your answers reflect the kind of information geographers seek as they study people and the places people live. Geographers contribute to the study of human beings by investigating conditions of areas of the world and describing how physical and cultural forces influenced these conditions. Physical forces include *place location* and *regions;* cultural forces include *population growth* and *distribution.*

PLACE LOCATION.   We all have been asked at one time or another for directions to a place a stranger may be trying to find in our community. Careful thought goes into our directions, which might sound something like this:

It's very easy to find. Go south on High Street until you pass three traffic signals. On the street past the third signal—Walnut Street—turn right. You will first pass a hospital and then a small park. Continue on Walnut Street until you see the Blue Chip Garment Factory. The Granite Hill Mall is two blocks beyond the factory on Walnut in front of a natural mountain formed by stone.

Your directions said a great deal about the location of the mall as you described the physical features of the immediate area. The mall was not developed there haphazardly—its location required a great deal of study. What questions did the mall planners need to answer? "Is there enough space for parking? Is there easy access for automobile traffic? Is the site attractive?"

Geographers ask similar questions when they study neighborhoods, communities, and other locations. "Is the climate comfortable? Are there adequate sources of transportation? How would people earn a living? Geographers use answers to questions like these to organize information to describe characteristics of places.

REGIONS.   In addition to studying locations of places, geographers collect data to discover major similarities and differences among various locations. On the basis of these discoveries, they categorize similar places into *regions*. Groupings of states— the Northeastern States, the Far West, the Southwest—are referred to as regions. Sometimes geographers group locations because of common physical features; at other times they group places because of common crops (Iowa, Nebraska, and Kansas as wheat growing areas), the shape of the land (Kansas and Nebraska as plains regions), the goods they produce (Pennsylvania and West Virginia as coal-producing regions), the climate (Alabama, Louisiana, and Florida have almost the same climate), or natural vegetation (Washington and Oregon as tree-growing states). Geographers, then, organize and group the facts they discover about places into regional descriptions. Regional studies help children understand the likenesses or differences of parts of the world and how they affect people's lives.

POPULATION GROWTH.   Geographers also describe characteristics of the world's *population*. Two major geographical concepts are population *growth* and *distribution*. Geographers are interested not only in the numbers of people in any specific location, but the way those numbers change over a period of time and why those changes occur. For example, the 1980 census figures showed the greatest growth in population in the "sun belt" states such as Arizona, California, and Florida. Why did this happen? Geographers seek answers to questions of this kind by collecting and interpreting data. Perhaps by interviewing samples of people who moved to these locations, geographers found that the high cost of energy in colder regions was a major reason for growth. Other reasons for population growth besides immigration include better medical care and industrialization. Can you think of others?

POPULATION DISTRIBUTION.   Besides finding out about general population figures, geographers want to know where greater or lesser numbers of people live. We know that the United States has nearly 230 million people. Some regions have large cities with great concentrations of people while other regions are rural and have small populations. The geographer is interested in why that is so. For example, why does a small state like Massachusetts have nearly six million people and a large state like Nevada have fewer than a million? The uneven distributions interest geographers and help them understand how the land is being used.

Geographers use a variety of tools to study the features of the earth: maps, charts, graphs, tables, reference books, and photographs. All of these tools help geographers solve problems. For children to understand geography, they must understand how to use the tools of a geographer. Suggestions for teaching children how to use these tools appear throughout this text, but the main discussion is in Chapter 6. For now, remember that the geographer's method of study (inquiry) is essentially the same as the historian's, except that geographers collect and analyze data for a different purpose.

Political Science

Political scientists study people's attempts to establish and maintain order in both complex and simple societies by investigating relationships between authoritative power and those subjected to it. They do this by examining laws, the reasons laws are made, and the ways laws are enforced. Political scientists also study the people who run the government—how they get power, what their duties are, and how they carry out those duties. In short, political scientists analyze the relationships among people and the institutions that comprise a political system.

Political scientists use a method of inquiry similar to the other social scientists and use direct observation, civic documents, government publications, documented research, statistics, laws, and similar sources to answer questions such as, "How are laws made in different societies? How do members of different societies select their leaders?"

Development of political science concepts should begin in the primary grades. Children can cooperate in making classroom rules and regulations for class activities such as field trips or assembly programs. The involvement helps children attain higher levels of understanding about rules and behavior. For example, the early primary child's understanding of rules is that all rules reflect the infinite power of adults or authority figures. When children are about eight years old, they begin to see rules as based on group agreement and cooperative action. Through learning activities that develop the concept of rules, the child begins to understand basic ideas of rule making and develops a readiness to conceptualize deeper meanings that will be dealt with in later grades—more sophisticated ideas such as the Constitution, the government, other types of government, guaranteed freedoms, property rights, trial by jury, and the election process.

Economics

Most college-age youth find it easy to identify with the area of inquiry called economics, for this field deals with most people's desire to satisfy unlimited wants with limited resources. Referred to as the *scarcity concept*, it is from this idea that a family of economics learnings emerges. Because of scarcity, humans have attempted to develop methods to produce more in less time with less material, by which *specialization of labor* was discovered. From specialization has emerged the idea of *interdependence,* a reliance of people upon one another that necessitates monetary, transportation, and communication systems. From interactions of these factors, a *market system* developed through which buyers and sellers produce and exchange goods or services. Finally, governments are responsible for controlling segments of the market system to assure the welfare of all its citizens. Information about the economy helps one assess pressing issues of the day. This area includes the study of taxation, consumer economics, economic growth and development, and policies toward business.

Fundamental questions at each grade level include: "What are people's needs and wants? How do people meet their needs and wants in terms of goods and services? How are goods and services brought to the people?" Table 2–1 shows how some major economics concepts can be efficiently incorporated into the elementary social studies program. Of course, the scientific inquiry technique should be used as children explore related activities. Those activities will be explained in greater detail in Chapter 5.

Sociology

The sociologist studies humans by examining their interactions with one another in groups or organizations such as the family, government, church, or school. Sociologists analyze the values and norms these groups hold in common to discover how they become organized (or disorganized) or why they behave as they do. They study how groups form, how they operate, and how they change.

Sociologists organize their study of groups around many questions, such as "What kinds of groups do people in any given society form? What are the expectations of each group member? What problems do the group members face? How does the group control its members?"

To answer these questions, sociologists may visit a particular group, observe what the people in that group do, interview group members, or even live with a group for a short time to more completely understand its nature. This firsthand information is enough to get sociologists started, but they must check the validity of their information. By studying written material, television, films, radio programs, and a variety of other resources, they determine whether their original impressions contained inaccurate generalizations or unwarranted stereotypes. Sociologists share their findings with others through various means, of which one of the most popular is the *case study*. Case studies are reports of individuals or groups describing day-to-day conditions of their lives during a certain period. They frequently appear in elementary school social studies textbooks to provide children with real-life episodes that furnish clues to others' behavior.

The content of social studies programs, especially in the primary grades, is selected largely from the field of sociology as children are encouraged to investigate areas of group activity—a social characteristic especially meaningful in their own lives. Units usually center on *socialization*, the activities through which children are led to accept the folkways and mores of our society. By examining and accepting natural and artificial differences among individuals, children learn to predict human behavior in families, neighborhoods, cities, and the world.

Study of the family during the primary grades is usually followed by a study of neighborhood groups, community groups, special interest groups (such as a group

TABLE 2–1
Economics Concepts and Examples

Concept	Example
Production (study of goods and services provided by others)	*Bakery* (Grade 2) 1. Bakers use goods furnished by other workers. 2. The bakery is a source for many goods. 3. Work in a bakery is divided into specialized tasks for more efficient production. 4. Not all bakeries produce goods of the same variety or of equal quality.
Distribution (study of how goods and services are made available to consumers, i.e., selling, advertising, and shipping)	*Automobile Industry* (Grade 5) 1. Automobile dealers get the cars they sell from an automobile factory. 2. Many different workers help get the automobiles from the factory to the dealer and ready for the buyer. 3. Automobile dealers use attractive advertisements to encourage people to buy their goods. 4. Some automobile dealers are able to sell cars at a lower price than others.
Exchange (study of money and other mediums of exchange that enhance exchange of goods or services between producer and consumer)	*Bank* (Grade 4) 1. Banks are safe places in which to save money. 2. Banks lend to people who may not have enough money to buy what they want. 3. Banks provide checks for people who wish to pay without handling real money. 4. Banks pay people for the use of their money.
Consumption (study of needs and wants of the buyer and of the agencies responsible for protecting the buyer)	*Consumerism* (Grades 2–5) 1. Each person decides what to buy after evaluating what he needs most. 2. We buy some items because they satisfy basic needs and others because they bring us enjoyment. 3. Shoppers should examine the goods sold by several stores so they can select those that give them the most for their money. 4. The government protects the buyer from false claims and promises.

of friends), and school groups. Progressing through the grades, children increase their study of groups in cultures other than their own. Be sure to focus on concepts and generalizations rather than on some quaint characteristic a group might have for meeting its needs. For example, children should learn to collect data such as "young children from the Ibo village in Nigeria do not go to school as we do" not for the purpose of concluding that it is odd if children do not go to school as we do, but for the purpose of generalizing that "we usually think of education taking place in school, but children from other lands may learn by helping adults and practicing tasks they will perform when they get older." Children should experience and value the contributions of other cultures as they study unique group-centered concepts such as language, festivals, customs, education, and recreation.

Anthropology

Anthropologists study peoples to find out what they were like from earliest existence and what changed their lives throughout the years. They learn how people have existed—in their civilization's approach to language, literature, folklore, music, religion, art, law, and social institutions. When we study a society's contributions to existence, we refer to that society's *culture*—things its people do that are similar or dissimilar to the ways other people behave. Because of this great scope of study, anthropology has often been described as a universal social science—one that comprehensively studies people by looking at all aspects of their civilization.

Anthropologists examine a culture by visiting the lands of the people, living with the people, and recording what they do. This investigation is a *field study*, one of the most effective means of uncovering information about people. Of course, anthropologists support their findings by searching for additional information about a culture: conducting library research to discover what others have observed; examining artifacts (such as stone tools); or studying films, slides, or tapes of others' field studies. Also of great interest are a people's legends and stories. These stories often help anthropologists get a better idea of a culture they are studying, but may also lead the anthropologist astray. For example, Navajo mythology implies that they have always lived in the Southwest, but years of accumulating other anthropological evidence suggests that they arrived there from the north about seven hundred years ago. Children are fascinated by the legends and myths of other cultures, however, so they should be included as a source of information whenever possible. Sometimes these stories influence a person's whole life, as in the case of Heinrich Schliemann. When Schliemann was young, he enjoyed listening to myths about Greece and Rome and was particularly fascinated with the Trojan War and how the gods and goddesses took sides with the Greeks and Trojans. When Schliemann was growing up, most people believed the story of Troy's burning was just a myth. But Schliemann was not convinced. He had an opportunity to find out later in his life when he visited Asia Minor to investigate stories of buried cities in the area. After much looking, he finally found a huge mound of earth close to the Aegean Sea—an area where the ancient city of Troy was believed to have existed. Schliemann dug into the earth and discovered that the site had been the location of many cities, each built upon the other as the previous city had been completely destroyed—nine separate cities altogether. Archaeologists were summoned to use their special equipment and methods to search the area. They now think the Troy made famous in stories was the city found in the seventh layer of Schliemann's mound.

Of course, not every child will become a Heinrich Schliemann, but children's curiosity and willingness to pursue areas of interest should be capitalized on when studying people. Allow the children to examine artifacts, for example, and guess how they were used. Have them support their guesses by visiting museums, reading books, searching through pictures, asking resource persons, or talking to anthropologists. The exciting contribution anthropology brings to the elementary school program is an understanding of and respect for cultures that are non-Western. Children are able to discover that all civilizations have things in common and that all peoples have used their abilities to think and create to shape their environments and build their cultures.

Combining the Disciplines

Figure 2–5 summarizes the content characteristics of each of the social sciences as they might be applied to a study of Africa. Although some school programs approach instruction by maintaining the separate identities of each of the social sciences, most advocate an *interdisciplinary approach,* which combines two or more of the social sciences in one program. With this approach, children develop a more realistic picture of all the forces that influence human behavior.

Hymes considers *subject matter labels* critical for administrative and organizational purposes, but advises against focusing on them too narrowly.[6] Knowing content and how to organize knowledge helps you focus on what you teach, but no *real* educational opportunity can be limited to one subject matter label—learning comes in big packages.

DEVELOPING COMPETENCE

The extent to which you develop your personal qualities, your flexibility, and your content knowledge determines whether you will be considered a *competent teacher.* School districts are concerned about identifying competent teachers, as are teacher training institutions like yours and mine; therefore, many professional teacher training programs are characterized as *competency-based* programs. These programs specify observable teaching behaviors for the purpose of evaluating whether an individual reflects the appropriate knowledge, skills, attitudes, and behaviors necessary for successful teaching. The *generic* or general competencies necessary for a candidate to receive a teaching certification in the Commonwealth of Pennsylvania are listed here; compare them to those identified by your state, college, university, or local school district:

Each certification candidate shall demonstrate the ability to:
1. apply theory and research concerning the development, behavior and learning of children including those with exceptional characteristics and/or special needs;

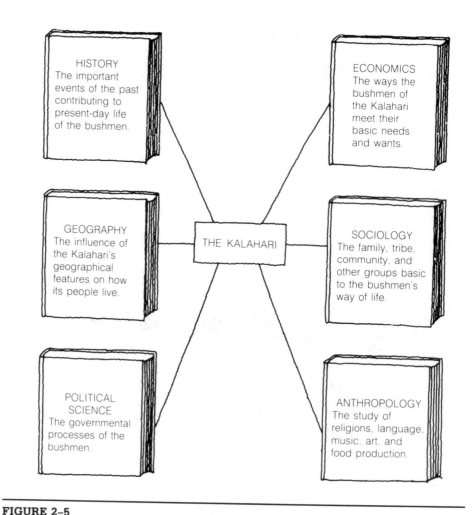

FIGURE 2-5

An Interdisciplinary Approach to a Study of Africa

2. prepare, select and use materials and media; modify commercial materials; and produce original materials;

3. use appropriate methods to carry out his/her role;

4. prepare, select and use evaluation procedures;

5. apply knowledge, techniques and skills of describing and analyzing professional, institutional and political situations in order to make educational decisions;

6. assess and improve reading, writing and speaking skills and/or make appropriate referrals;

7. promote better understandings and interrelationships among individuals and groups, of different races, sexes, religious beliefs, national origins and socio-economic backgrounds;

8. make the students aware of the world of work, its opportunities, and assist students in making the transition from the school to the community.[7]

Competency-based instruction specifies the behaviors, skills, attitudes, and knowledge demonstrated by effective teachers. These are some of the specific competencies expected of its student teachers by the University of Houston's Competency Based Teacher Education program in the area of the social studies:

- Justifies objectives and plans in terms of recognized curriculum guidelines and the characteristics of a particular teaching situation.
- Selects and uses a variety of films, books, current publications, documents, etc., to support learning objectives.
- Identifies and selects materials and resources compatible with objectives for a given pupil population.
- Organizes knowledge acquisition strategies around concepts and generalizations.
- Plans for valuing strategies that allow students to form and/or clarify their own values.
- Designs strategies to teach the use of scientific modes of inquiry and techniques of social scientists as tools for solving problems, making decisions, or applying and processing knowledge.
- Develops strategies to encourage pupil participation in social action projects.
- Identifies positive and negative attributes in teaching toward concept attainment.
- Uses dilemmas and questioning strategies to identify and clarify values.
- Uses questioning techniques consistent with a values clarification model.
- Helps students recognize the role of values in human behavior.
- Involves pupils in both independent and group inquiry.
- Involves pupils in situations which require the application of critical thinking skills to identify problem solutions and/or make decisions.
- Selects and implements activities to develop skills in gathering, processing, and analyzing data.
- Assists pupils in planning and implementing a social action project based on identified social studies goals and objectives.
- Identifies and implements activities for social participation through simulation, gaming, and role-playing.[8]

Students have a range of learning experiences, including field experiences, in which to develop these competencies. All through their professional program, prospective teachers are encouraged to develop individual teaching styles while being helped to constantly analyze and assess their progress toward meeting program standards. The University of Houston's list of competencies is representative of the desired competencies of elementary school social studies teachers today. Do you feel you are acquiring the knowledge and skills necessary to orchestrate a healthy and positive teaching-learning situation in the social studies?

ETHICS

Specialized competencies contribute to your becoming a professional, but you must also have an appropriate attitude of responsibility. Professional groups often call attitudes of responsibility "private systems of law," and one characteristic of a profession is that its members comply by that system of law, commonly called a *code of ethics.* In 1981, the National Council for the Social Studies published its proposed code of ethics for teachers of the social studies. The degree to which you adhere to these ethical principles will influence the quality of instruction you will provide to your students:

> *Principle 1:* It is the ethical responsibility of social studies professionals to set forth, maintain, model, and safeguard standards of instructional competence suited to the achievement of the broad goals of the social studies.
>
> *Principle 2:* It is the ethical responsibility of social studies professionals to provide to every student, in so far as possible, the knowledge, skills, and attitudes necessary to function as an effective citizen.
>
> *Principle 3:* It is the ethical responsibility of social studies professionals to foster the understanding and exercise of the rights guaranteed to all citizens under the Constitution of the United States and of the responsibilities implicit in those rights.
>
> *Principle 4:* It is the ethical responsibility of social studies professionals to cultivate and maintain an instructional environment in which the free contest of ideas is prized.
>
> *Principle 5:* It is the ethical responsibility of social studies professionals to adhere to the highest standards of scholarship in the development, production, distribution, or use of social studies materials.
>
> *Principle 6:* It is the ethical responsibility of social studies professionals to concern themselves with the conditions of the school and community with which they are associated.[9]

You may wonder how these ethical principles differ from competency statements. The distinction is fairly sophisticated at this stage of your training, but an illustration of each will help you see the difference. The competency statement describes a behavior we intend to exhibit:

> The teacher will choose strategies appropriate for the developmental level of the children.

The principle describes an attitude and value we should hold:

> The teacher will respect each child as a human being.

BEGINNING AS A TEACHER

Now suppose you have met the minimum qualifications necessary for attaining a position in elementary education. You begin your search for a job by checking the Career Development Center at your college, by reading the want ads of newspapers in communities in which you wish to live, or by making personal contacts with school administrators. Several places ask you to fill out an application; some may invite you for an interview. Interviews are usually carefully planned to be comfortable discussions during which the organization gets to know you and you get to know the organization. The interviewer will ask questions to elicit all the personal and professional information the organization needs to make its decision. Generally, you will be given an explanation of the position and its requirements, along with salary expectations. Salaries vary widely in the field. Starting public school teachers often receive in excess of $15,000 for a nine- or ten-month school year, with a full range of payroll benefits. Although salary is often a major factor in deciding to accept a professional position, it is wise to give careful consideration to other factors, too. Get to know the facilities, the administrators to whom you will be responsible, the number of children you will have in your care, the staff with whom you will work, and anything else that can influence your job satisfaction.

Imagine, now, that you have been offered and have accepted a teaching position. You now face the first big question of your professional career: "What do I do now?" You are not alone; this is the main concern of most new teachers. Lilian Katz described this concern for survival as a characteristic reaction of teachers in Stage 1 of her four developmental stages of teachers.

> **You are preoccupied with survival. You ask yourself questions such as "Can I get through the day in one piece? Without losing a child? Can I make it until the end of the week? Until the next vacation? Can I really do this kind of work day after day? Will I be accepted by my colleagues? (first year)"**[10]

During this period you will need support, understanding, encouragement, reassurance, comfort, and guidance. You need instruction in specific ways of handling complex behavior in children, especially since classroom management problems can cause intense feelings of inadequacy at this stage.

Katz's point is that the need to further your education and for exposure to new ideas changes as you gain experience. Administrators usually recognize this with a plan for staff development. Staff development programs generally address areas that need special attention, such as:

Orientation of new staff members to the school facilities

Planned field trips, workshops, or speakers to gain new ideas

Staff meetings for sharing concerns or ideas

Financial assistance to enable staff to take further course work or receive other kinds of formal training

Membership in major professional groups will also help you keep up to date in the field. The primary professional organization for elementary and secondary school social studies teachers is the National Council for the Social Studies. For information, write to: National Council for the Social Studies, 3501 Newark Street, N.W., Washington, DC 20016.

SUMMARY

Effective social studies teaching relies upon a sophisticated balance of personal and professional characteristics. Despite conflicting opinions as to what personal characteristics make a good teacher, most writers advance three criteria: (1) good teachers are fine people, who respect the needs of the children with whom they work (Maslow) as well as their unique talents (Taylor); (2) good teachers are flexible, and are willing to change to meet the demands of a particular learning situation; and (3) good teachers know what they are teaching and are well-informed in the subject areas of history, geography, political science, economics, sociology, and anthropology.

Professional characteristics of good teachers are usually described in the two areas of competencies and ethics. College or university teacher certification programs identify specific competencies (observable teaching behaviors) and direct learning experiences toward the development of accepted teaching practices. Ethical principles, on the other hand, are a "private system of law" that describe an individual's role in the professional field. The awarding of a teaching certificate demonstrates that an individual has attained the specific competencies and demonstrated the ethical principles expected of professional educators. But the initial certification does not imply that an individual is a "completed product"; most beginning teachers return to colleges or universities for additional training to keep up with new developments and to enhance professional skills. In addition to postgraduate programs, teachers often keep up-to-date with educational trends by seeking membership in professional groups such as the National Council for the Social Studies.

ENDNOTES

1. Mary Harbaugh, "Who Will Teach the Class of 2000?" *Instructor*, 95, no. 2 (September 1985): 31–35.
2. Abraham H. Maslow, "A Theory of Human Motivation," *Psychology Review*, 50 (1943): 370–76.
3. Calvin W. Taylor, "Be Talent Developers. . .As Well As Knowledge Dispensers," *Today's Education*, 57, no. 9 (December 1968): 67–69.
4. Frank Reissman, "Teachers of the Poor: A Five-Point Plan," *Journal of Teacher Education*, 18, no. 3 (Fall 1967): 326–336.
5. Albert Cullum, *Push Back the Desks* (New York: Citation Press, 1967), p. 19.
6. James Hymes, *Teaching the Child Under Six*, 3rd ed. (Columbus OH: Merrill, 1981), pp. 80–81.

7. "Program Approval Standards: Undergraduate and Graduate Programs" (Part II) *Policies, Procedures and Standards for Certification of Professional School Personnel* (Harrisburg, PA: Pennsylvania Department of Education, 1977).

8. Carl E. Schomburg, "Integrating the Social Studies Component in a CBTE Model," in *Competency Based Teacher Education: Professionalizing Social Studies Teaching* ed. Dell Felder (Washington, DC: National Council for the Social Studies, 1978), pp. 67–68.

9. "A Code of Ethics for the Social Studies Profession," *Social Education*, 45, no. 6 (October 1981): 451–453.

10. Lilian G. Katz, "Developmental Stages of Preschool Teachers," *Elementary School Journal*, 73, no. 1 (October 1972): 50–54.

3

Formulating Direct Instructional Practices

KEY CONCEPTS

- ☐ Teaching children to form concepts through deliberate, sequential, directed learning experiences
- ☐ Planning effective lessons that use concepts as organizational frameworks for teaching
- ☐ Formulating appropriate questions and teaching strategies to make direct instruction interesting, motivating, and meaningful
- ☐ Understanding the most appropriate uses of direct instructional strategies

> Every teacher wishes to be an excellent one. But each falls somewhat
> short of his aspirations. . . . There are varied reasons for this gap between
> a teacher's desired excellence and actual performance. In some cases the
> gap is caused by an inability to understand how students think. In others
> it is a result of a poor knowledge of subject matter or of an inability to
> maintain order in class. But often poor teaching is due to a lack of skill in
> selecting and using teaching methods![1]

Effective teaching is the central process of education and the major function through which societies foster their educational objectives. The complex processes of teaching, however, are not yet universally defined, and there is considerable disagreement about just which teaching practices cause the greatest changes in student learning. N. L. Gage says "changes [in student learning] are brought about not by revolutions in teaching practices or school organization, but by relatively straightforward attempts to educate more teachers to do what more effective teachers have already been observed doing."[2] Teachers, not the material or method, produce the most positive effects of instruction. The most promising or attractive materials and methods are only ordinary until a creative, eager teacher brings them to life, and the most mundane materials become interesting in the hands of skilled teachers.

Because of teachers' critical importance in fostering productive learning, I will not try to convince you that either an inquiry or a textbook approach is superior to all other approaches to teaching social studies. Inquiry teaching and textbook usage are important, but so are other techniques. (I would rather have children learn social studies from a great lecturer than from a poor inquiry teacher.) I will not name any single method as the solution for all that is wrong with the social studies; instead, I will describe what is available to teachers as acceptable options for instruction. The hope is that, once choices are made for the particular children, teachers will have the skills to develop a social studies program of value.

The first instructional option is *directed teaching*. Directed teaching occurs when the teacher specifies a particular concept as a learning outcome and patterns the learning experience to assure the desired conceptual attainment. Such learning experiences may be language-based, as in a textbook reading assignment, or activity-based, as in a field trip, but the goal is to organize instruction so as to lead children toward a particular concept, usually moving from relatively simple to more complex mental operations.

Unfortunately, what we know about the actual process of concept formation is meager:

> Psychologists have been attempting to get a hold on the thinking process for
> decades. . . .Yet, for all their efforts, we still have but a limited understanding
> of only some of the more superficial behaviors related to thinking. Inasmuch
> as this is true, we are naive to expect educational research to provide us with
> answers to teach a specific kind of thinking behavior."[3]

In other words, we cannot conclusively define or describe what goes on in the mind when someone tries to make sense of learning experience. Considering this severe limitation, we must approach our teaching responsibilities by working with what is now acceptable.

CURRENT THEORY

Contemporary thinking suggests that to learn effectively, one must be led through a process of "filling in" existing schematic or cognitive structures with new information. The process of relating information to existing conceptual schema is now thought to be the basis for understanding, for making sense of what is happening. Suchman explains:

> Conceptual growth is largely a matter of building new models from old. It is quite possible for a teacher to manipulate this process and lead students to form new concepts. The teacher can augment. . .by bringing real objects and events to the student's attention. In this way the teacher enriches the student's background of experience to enable him to build even stronger concepts. . . .The teacher can guide and facilitate, but the act of concept formation itself is in the final analysis the act of the learner.
> The teacher deliberately plans the sequence of events so that the learner emerges with a concept he didn't have before—a concept built of new pieces that the teacher helps to create. . .and old pieces that are retrieved from the student's storage. . . .When the student builds his own conceptual structures. . ., one thing is certain: Whatever concepts the student has at any given time are wholly meaningful to him, because they grew from his own thinking.[4]

The deliberate, sequential nature of instruction associated with concept formation also finds support from Frank Smith, a noted psycholinguist who asserts that concept formation is a process in which new experiences are associated with what the child already knows or believes. Smith defines learning as "making sense of the world"; he says that we all comprehend our world by "relating the unfamiliar to the already known."[5] Ausubel highlighted this critical process: "If I had to reduce all of educational psychology to just one principle, I would say this: The most important single factor influencing learning is what the learner already knows."[6] What this means is that, if you are considering "dairy farming" as a segment of instruction within the topic of Our Nation's Agriculture, for example, you must first determine the degree to which your children understand the concepts of "dairy" and "farms" before you begin to choose associated learning experiences. Some children, especially those in urban areas, may never have had direct experiences with a dairy farm. They may associate the milk they buy in stores with cows and pastures, but they could never have actually seen a real cow, heard it moo, smelled a pasture or barn, watched a cow being milked, or patted its big, wet nose. Because you judge these children's firsthand knowledge of cows or dairy farms as relatively embryonic, it would be profitable to arrange a field trip to a dairy farm as an initial learning experience. If you cannot arrange that experience, the children need at least a quality film or combination of other multisensory experiences before they will be motivated to examine the topic of dairy farming more extensively and more abstractly.

On the other hand, if you find the children's knowledge of the topic is much greater, it would be boring for them to have such basic introductory experiences. Rural children who live on or near dairy farms or have easy access to them would not need intensive, direct experiences. Instead, they would probably be able to begin with systematic investigations of more complex understandings, such as economic issues facing dairy farmers or the future of dairy farms in our increasingly technological society.

To help children process incoming information, then, we must first be sure that they have one extremely critical mental component—a previous exposure to a topic that serves as an internal "filing system" to help sort and classify new objects, events, or ideas into general categories of meaning called *concepts*. These categories help learners make sense of the vast amount of information they will accumulate throughout their social studies learning experiences. Smith contends that if learners do not have this conceptual filing system for incoming information, they may opt for one of these methods of coping with the learning situation:

1. *Rejecting the information*—When the incoming subject matter content does not register and we cannot connect it to what we already know, we tend to discard or ignore it.

2. *Miscategorizing the information*—If we choose not to throw out the unperceived information, we may make some attempt to comprehend it. However, the tendency for children is to misfile it. They may place it into a wrong category or simply allow it to float "unattached," thinking that it must belong there someplace.[7]

In our view of learning, comprehension is defined as the establishment of a conceptual filing system into which more and more information can be meaningfully categorized. Teaching for comprehension is the process of (1) providing *advance conceptual clues* by which we encourage learners to explore their system of related concepts prior to any learning experience; and (2) guiding the children's thinking so they can effectively categorize new information into existing conceptual structures.

THE STRATEGY

Directed lessons for guiding the comprehension of any social studies learning experience involve four steps:

1. Introduction
2. Learning experience

3. Comprehension development
4. Reinforcement and extension

We will call this four-step plan a *Directed Learning Episode,* or *DLE.* In the following sections of this chapter you will learn about selected practices for teaching toward concept development through the use of *reading materials* in the social studies. I have based my suggestions on reading materials because they are the most common instructional tools in the social studies classroom. The *DLE* is not meant for exclusive use with social studies textbook materials; the basic format can be adapted simply by substituting slide presentations, guest speakers, or any other direct source of information into the Learning Experiences section described later.

The Introductory Stage

For children to experience a high degree of success in understanding the material to which they will be exposed, three critical teaching activities must happen during the introductory phase of a DLE:

1. Associating the children's previous knowledge to the new material
2. Introducing new words
3. Setting a purpose for the activity

Associating Previous Knowledge

One fourth-grade social studies reading selection about a Native American Indian village, in which the major concept is "interdependence"—people's reliance on one another to survive—begins: "A long time ago, during the time of Thunder Moon, small children helped the people of the village meet their needs for food by collecting wild berries, nuts, and seeds."

The teacher's guide makes provisions for two possible problems with this selection. The first has to do with the reference to "Thunder Moon," and the second is the probability that not many fourth-graders would understand that small children's contributions would be so crucial to a village's survival. The teacher is encouraged to tell the children that the old American Indian calendar was organized by "moons" rather than "months" and that the children's responsibilities in the Native American culture was different from those in the children's own lives.

Creative teachers might find ways to do a bit more with these ideas; they might find out what the present month is in the old Native American calendar and how the Indians kept a record of days. The children might then write that day's symbol and even use it in different contexts during their school day, writing it on their assignments or on the classroom calendar. Innovative teachers might display pictures from various cultures to show how different the world was in the past and how children contributed to the survival of other social groups, too. The important point, however, is that teachers preview the selection to determine what unfamiliar areas

*Many teachers believe that directed learning
experiences are the most efficient and effective means
for children to develop social studies concepts and
generalizations.*

might impede comprehension and provide help in those areas prior to the learning experience itself. This is old advice, but recent research adds support for this crucial teaching practice. Carver found that when children fail to adequately comprehend written material, it is primarily because they do not possess the necessary experiential background to relate to the new information.[8] There are a number of motivational techniques to help children bridge the gap between previous encounters and new experiences.

Motivational Techniques

PAST EXPERIENCES/NEW MATERIAL.   Sometimes a brief question or comment will bridge the gap between what the children have already experienced and new reading material. For example, you may say, ''Yesterday, you'll remember, we learned where Kenya was located on our globe. We found that Kenya was located

Questions Comments

on a continent. Who can remember the continent's name? Africa is right. See if you can locate Africa on the globe." Write the word *coffee* on the board. Show some coffee ads from newspapers and invite the children to smell a freshly opened can of coffee. Ask them, "How many of your parents drink *coffee?*" Remind them that coffee is grown in Kenya and that today they will be reading about the Komu family who helps raise coffee in Africa.

EMPATHY. A second motivational technique is to encourage the children to empathize with groups or individuals whose conditions are similar or dissimilar to their own. For example, the reading selection for a lesson on Kenya could be introduced this way: "Yesterday you read that the mother does much of the tending of the coffee for the Komu family and the children go to school. But did you ever think about why the children go to school only during the dry season? Because there is no schoolhouse. Classes are held outdoors under a big tree." Then encourage the children to read and compare the kind of school the Komu children attended to their own.

POSE QUESTIONS. A third motivational technique is to pose a puzzling question or problem. You know that children are full of questions as they continually attempt to discover the hows, whats, and whys of life. They are extremely curious, a characteristic that should be a highly motivational tool for classroom teachers. You could introduce a reading assignment by motivating children this way: Arrange on a work table a number of tools used by early American farmers. Ask questions about the types of tools the children see: "What are these tools? Are these hand tools or machines? These are tools used by early American farmers. What kind of tools are they?" The children can then be directed to read about early American farm tools and then use the information to explain how the tools on the work table were used.

In these three examples, then, we have examined popular introductory approaches. The aim of such techniques is to stimulate children to develop intrinsic motivation for their own learning, so they will comprehend material better and remember it longer. This initial part of the DLE is extremely important because it establishes a readiness framework for the remainder of the strategy. It deals with the motivational aspect of learning by addressing the educational tenet, "You cannot teach children something unless they want to learn it." We all hope that children will become self-motivated and seek to learn because *they* want to. Those situations occur when a child asks you to teach him to throw a ball or help him locate reading material about constructing a tree house—the motivation is already there in the form of strong personal needs. Motivation to pursue reading assignments in social studies textbooks does not surface as freely. You must do something to stimulate children to *want* to read the material you and your school district consider important.

These are not rigid recommendations to follow to the letter before each learning activity. You must adapt your techniques to the type of material you will present. A relatively simple selection may require only a short discussion; a more difficult selection may require much more—real objects, pictures, chalkboard lists, or other types of background building. Each learning experience requires a different kind of advance preparation, depending entirely upon the difficulty of the selection and your knowledge of the learners' backgrounds. In preparing to guide your children through any learning experience, analyze the content, evaluate the children's backgrounds, then choose the appropriate strategy.

Introducing New Words

Understanding social studies concepts also depends upon knowledge of the vocabulary in the reading selection, so you must give special attention to new words before the children read the material. Early primary-grade materials usually use words already familiar to the children's listening/speaking vocabularies, but in subsequent grades, "new words" such as *junta, boycott, shaman, cassava,* or *Nneki Mgobo* may gradually enter the reading materials. The entry of new words is carefully controlled in basal readers, but social studies textbooks often confront children with a larger proportion of unknown new words. The social studies vocabulary is often more difficult and presents a major deterrent to fluent reading: new terms appear at a faster pace and with fewer repetitions; many complex concepts are introduced with little explanation (one geography book, for example, actually contains over two hundred new terms in one section); more facts are presented; references to previously developed ideas often make it impossible to use a textbook other than from beginning to end; and children may find the expository writing style less interesting than the narrative style and dialogue of their reading books. Even though the more recent elementary social studies reading materials have been carefully graded and the content presentation made more interesting, their specialized vocabularies remain a serious problem for many youngsters. Because the specific vocabularies are prerequisite for understanding broader social studies concepts, you must be sure to help children understand their meanings. To do so, however, you must first be aware of the types of word difficulties especially common to social studies reading materials.

SPECIALIZED VOCABULARIES.   Children often encounter words in the social studies that they will rarely, if ever, find in other school subject areas. Nonetheless, it is often necessary that they know these words, and the teacher should carefully explain and illustrate them before the children read. Examples of specialized social studies vocabulary are *tundra, latitude, consumer, legislature,* and *archaeologist.*

MULTIPLE MEANINGS.   Social studies materials frequently contain words that have different meanings from the single meaning the child knows. Consider the word *measure.* In music class, the teacher may refer to *measure* as the division of a musical staff into equal beats of time. In arithmetic class, *measure* becomes the process of determining an object's dimensions. On the playground, *measure* may mean the act of judging one's ability against another's. Now, when used in a social studies textbook, *measure* refers to a specific law or statute. Other possibly confusing words include *chief, note, mouth, fork, bill, foot, draft, cradle, range, belt,* and even words such as *steppes* (a *homonym*).

SIMILES AND METAPHORS.   Similes and metaphors are common in young children's reading materials. They are figures of speech in which one thing is likened to another; for example, "The explorers to the strange new land must have had hearts *as big as whales."* I asked some third-grade children what this sentence meant. Several thought it meant the explorers were giants who had extremely large body parts. They had difficulty understanding that the author wanted to depict the explorers as brave men through the use of an exaggerated comparison. The frequency of such comparisons increases as children read books at more mature levels. Their interpretations are usually proof of the need to provide special attention to sentences of this type. Other examples include "quiet as a mouse," "fast as a deer," "cool as a cucumber," and "quick as a cat."

FIGURATIVE LANGUAGE. Figurative terms contain colorful words that make a description more vivid and imaginative and result in an image completely different from the intended literal description. They may present a potential problem to readers who have a tendency to think only in concrete or literal terms. Examples of figurative terms are *iron curtain, hawk, dove, carpetbag,* and *party platform.*

Young children bring meaning to new experiences only in terms of their previous experiences, so you must anticipate the words that might confuse the children and help them understand intended meanings of words as they appear in the material under study.

Methods of Presentation

Teacher's guides for social studies textbooks usually list words whose meanings may need clarification. Teachers are urged to write these words on a chalkboard or word chart and use one of several techniques to help children understand the words before they read.

DIRECT EXPERIENCES. Provide real experiences that will establish a concrete background for understanding new words. Think how much more meaning children would have of the word *serape* if a real one were on exhibit alongside its word symbol. My college students are often skeptical at this suggestion and ask me how they would be able to obtain such items for their own classrooms. My response is simply, "Send a note home prior to studying a topic and explain to the parents that you are in need of certain items related to that topic and *get ready."* Through my own elementary school teaching experiences, I've always ended up with more than I could handle by using that technique. Dolch illustrates the value of direct experience:

> The average adult tries again and again to tell children with words what things are. . . . The child asks, "What is a snake?" The adult says, "An animal that crawls along the ground." The child imagines such an animal and asks, "But his legs will be in the way." The adult says, "Oh, he hasn't any legs." So the child takes off the legs and sees a legless body lying there. "But how does he crawl around without legs?" "He wiggles," says the adult. The child tries to make the legless body wiggle. "How does that get him to go forward?" The adult loses his temper. The peculiar way in which part of the snake pushes the other part cannot be described. It has to be seen. Let us go to the zoo.[9]

AUDIOVISUALS. Realistically, you will often not be able to show children the things they will read about. When you need to, *share* the pictures in textbooks, other photographs, slides, or transparencies to illustrate key words. Much less time is needed to establish word meaning with a photograph and accompanying word label than with a verbal description.

DIRECT EXPLANATION. Sometimes, when dealing with words of multiple meanings or figurative terms, you can best communicate a meaning with direct explanation. When a word like *change* is introduced, for example, you should use it in various contexts. To illustrate, you may say, "Our new word for today is *change*. Who can tell me what *change* means when I say, 'The grocer gave me *change* for my quarter?' I'm going to use the word again, but this time it will mean something different. Listen to what I say and then tell me what *change* means. Here we go. 'The leaves *change* color in the Fall.' What does the word *change* mean now?" Be careful in verbal explanations of new words, though, especially to primary-grade children; there are shortcomings to this technique:

> One difficulty with this procedure is the danger of relying on superficial verbalizations. Meanings that are clear to the teacher may be quite hazy to the child. Many of the classical boners are due to superficial and inadequate grasp of word meanings. It is not sufficient to tell a child that *frantic* means *wild,* or that *athletic* means *strong;* he may try to pick *frantic flowers* or pour *athletic vinegar* into a salad dressing.[10]

QUESTIONS. Use appropriate questions to stimulate word recognition skills. Fitzpatrick suggests four types:

Definition Question For example, "What does *school* mean in the sentence: He met a *school* of fish as he dove deeper into the water?"

Semantic Question For example, "List some other meanings for the word *school.*"

Synonym Question For example, "Look at the underlined word in the sentence: President Roosevelt began a program of *relief.* What other words can you substitute for *relief* without changing the meaning of the sentence?"

Antonym Question For example, "What words could you use for *relief* to make it have an opposite meaning?"[11]

CONTEXT CLUES. Perhaps the most widely recommended technique for helping children recognize new words is through the use of context clues—utilizing cues from the way a word is used in a sentence to derive its meaning. Often, social studies textbooks use this technique when presenting new words so teachers are not forced to spend a great deal of time explaining new words before a selection is read. A brief explanation of the word may be given in parentheses or in a footnote; for example, "The *padre* ordered the sacrifice of a young lamb. (A *padre* is a priest in Mexico.)" A synonym, clause, or phrase that explains the meaning of the word can be inserted in the sentence: "The cattle were branded by the *vaquero,* a Mexican cowboy." A new word is emphasized by italics, quotation marks, or boldface type: "Puerto Rico is a 'possession' of the United States." A direct explanation of the word can be presented in a full sentence: "The Post Exchange is one of the busiest spots on an Army base. The Post Exchange is a nonprofit store which sells small articles for personal use and is sometimes abbreviated PX." You should call the children's attention to these techniques as they progress through the reading assignment.

Often, however, new terms are presented in the reading material without such helpful explanations. Children usually have little trouble picking out those words and discovering their meanings if they have previously met the words, even if the meetings were only listening experiences. Consider, for example, how children would use context clues to decipher the unknown word in these sentences:

> The Hawaiian Islands were formed when great [unknown word] under the sea erupted.
>
> The rocks and ashes from the [unknown word] cooled and formed small patches of land in the Pacific Ocean.

If you sense that children will have difficulty with some words in their reading, prepare situations in which they can experience words in context before they meet them in textbook print, so they will recognize them. If, however, you simply list new words on the chalkboard or define them in isolation, you risk the development of inappropriate or inaccurate definitions. Consider the teacher who listed on the chalkboard five new words, one of which was *skim*. She asked the children to look up a meaning of each word and write them in their special social studies vocabulary notebooks. One child looked up *skim* and wrote the following definition in her notebook: "*skim*—to remove cream from milk." Imagine her confusion when she encountered this sentence in her reading: "*Skim* over the documents so we can be sure they are ones we need." Of the four or five definitions in the child's dictionary, she selected the wrong one. The word would have been more understandable if the teacher had used it in a similar context before the child encountered it in the reading assignment.

Setting Purposes

The introductory phase of the *DLE* usually culminates in a purpose setting statement, a "launching pad" from which children propel themselves into the reading material. It stimulates awareness of the reading material and identifies the reason the assignment has been given. Rather than saying, "Read pages 198–201 for class today," the teacher can lead the children with this statement: "We are going to be reading about groups that came to America searching for freedoms that were very important to them. As you read pages 198–201, think about the reasons these groups of people had for leaving their homelands." This kind of statement gives the children direction and prepares them to look for information to use in a follow-up discussion.

Purpose setting statements let children know *why*. They should be made immediately before the children actually begin the reading task. "Read to find out. . ." cues the children that a purposeful endeavor is at hand. Ask primary-grade children to read a selection "to find out why bells ring every half-hour on a ship." Ask an intermediate-grade child to read to prepare informative arguments for a class debate or to follow the directions to construct a table model of an oil derrick. These announced reading purposes prepare the student for the time when he can establish individual purposes independently. The goal is the reader who sets his own purpose by asking himself, "I wonder why banana farmers cut the stalks while the fruit is still green?" and then reads to find out. He also sets his own purpose when he checks a new chapter's headings, such as "Growing Lettuce," and turns it into a question: "What is the best way to grow lettuce?"

In the early primary-grade classroom, initial purpose setting statements are usually concrete, based on a single piece of information that is plainly stated in the text. The purpose setting statements are simple because reading assignments are usually broken into small segments, and young children are just learning how to get basic meaning out of the printed word. In subsequent grades, however, purpose setting statements that focus on one or two discrete items of information are considered inappropriate. Frase has established that by narrowly focusing the learner's attention on specific bits of information, we may enhance memory of that portion of the selection, but cause failure to establish the overall concept.[12] Of these two examples, which would be most appropriate in a fourth-grade classroom?

> **"Read to find out what is the most common occupation in China."**
> **"Read to find out how the Swiss provide for their needs and wants in spite of limited natural resources."**

Notice that the second statement goes beyond asking the children to read for specific information, but establishes a framework onto which children can organize the information they will read. Now the reader is able not only to recognize important elements of the reading selection, but also relate those elements to a higher order design.

There are many different purposes for which children are asked to read a social studies assignment, and, to be able to initiate good follow-up discussions, it is important for teachers to understand exactly the types of thinking these different purposes help promote.

BLOOM'S TAXONOMY.   Familiarity with Bloom's taxonomy of cognitive objectives will help you choose appropriate purpose setting statements. Bloom identified six levels of intellectual behavior that the schools should promote.[13]

Level 1: Knowledge   The student is asked simply to recall specific information from the reading assignment: "Read to find out when Christopher Columbus sailed for the New World."

Level 2: Comprehension   The student is asked to "personalize" content by "putting it into her own words," in any other parallel form of communication (for example, to draw a picture based on the reading assignment), or to discover relationships among the concepts: "Read to find out how Hopi hogans are constructed. Be prepared to use the materials at the work center to make your own model of a hogan based upon what you've read."

apply it

Level 3: Application The student is asked to *use* the content to solve a unique problem, stimulating transfer of learning: "Read about the process of amending the Constitution of the United States. Then, come up with a plan whereby our classroom constitution can be changed if a need arises in the future."

identify parts

Level 4: Analysis Students are asked to identify and comprehend the parts of a process or pattern of communication. They must apply rules of logic and sound reasoning to test the validity of an argument: "Some people in the selection say 'America—love it or leave it.' Read the next page and tell whether such reasoning is sound or unsound."

supply solutions

Level 5: Synthesis Students are asked to combine ideas and supply original, creative solutions to problems: "Read the selection on state symbols, then think of a possible new symbol for our state."

judge

Level 6: Evaluation Students are asked to judge the value of ideas, procedures, or methods: "Read pages 191–194 and tell whether or not you agree with the author's view that factory owners of the late 1800s were abusive to their workers."

Bloom's taxonomy, shown in Figure 3–1, offers a concise, practical reference for creating instructional purposes that go beyond mere recall of facts. Become familiar with the thinking processes associated with each level and learn to select from among them as you give children direction for any learning experience.

Bloom's taxonomy is *hierarchical*; that is, children need to *know* something before they can be expected to *comprehend* it. Comprehension means to combine,

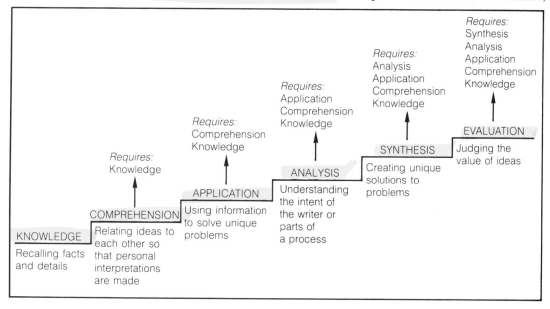

FIGURE 3–1
Bloom's Levels of Cognitive Behavior

through a complex thinking process, facts and other informational data to form concepts. Children must *know* something and *comprehend* it before they can be expected to *apply* their understandings to solve unique problems. Likewise, each subsequent thought process continues to combine with the lower processes so that all levels are in operation when we ask children to become involved in *evaluating* something. If we accept the notion that thinking skills are hierarchical, we must agree that the further up we move toward *evaluation*, the more highly sophisticated and complex an individual's thinking has become. Teachers who believe that children should be deliberately led through classroom activities that help them achieve lower-level skills before they can achieve the higher-level ones are employing the directed learning philosophy. They select the precise information and concepts they believe the children should acquire and design their instructional plans to ensure content acquisition before dealing with higher thinking skills. The Taba approach and several other social studies instructional practices operate from the premise that children should be carefully and efficiently directed from the bottom of the hierarchy upward toward development of higher-order skills. Although some teachers stop at the *comprehension* level, most teachers want their students to think more deeply about what they are learning. Concepts are important, but if all instruction stopped at that point, students would rarely have the opportunity to employ divergent thought to solve problems.

Suppose a teacher is responsible for teaching the concept of law, as shown in Figure 3–2. Based on the material, the teacher decides that higher-order thought processes will be difficult to reach unless the children are first able to comprehend the material. Therefore, culminating a short introductory discussion, she asks the children to "Read Lesson 1 to find out why people need laws." This teacher must then follow up the reading with a sequence of experiences to help the children comprehend the material. She realizes that *comprehension* involves special thought processes that need careful development—she knows that comprehension does not occur automatically, but depends on special thinking skills that are fostered through competent instruction. The *purpose* for the activity, then, determines what happens in the DLE immediately after the children have been exposed to information. Now let us suppose that, after comprehension has been established, the teacher wishes to personalize the information to a greater degree following the discussion. She may then choose to extend the lesson by establishing small groups and asking each to think about this problem: "Based on what you know about laws, design a set of rules to regulate the conduct of our class members." Or she may prefer to have the groups apply creative thinking to problem solving, and say: "Here is a study sheet showing a fast growing neighborhood in a large city. What do you think would happen if no laws existed there?" She might then ask each group to write three laws they think the neighborhood would need to adopt. In each case, the teacher has demonstrated her awareness that children *must* go beyond comprehension, through special thought processes that encourage deeper immersion in the material. Only through mastery of those processes can children acquire higher-order thinking skills.

This description highlights one flaw in the application of elaborate taxonomies such as Bloom's. Comprehension, or the formation of concepts, must be thought of as a process all its own. It describes the process of organizing incoming data *only* and does not involve any of the higher-level thought processes such as application (which also requires special thought processes of *its* own). Many educators, however, commonly categorize under "comprehension" processes that go far beyond

Lesson 1   Society Needs Law

Could you imagine living in a society without laws? Picture what it would be like. What would happen to power and how it is used? Because we value justice and the control of power, we follow laws and expect others to do the same.

In earliest times, laws were really only customs. There were no elected officials who wrote laws or police who enforced them. Sometimes the most important customs were written down so everyone would know what was expected. When one tribe overran another, the customs of one group would be mixed with those of the other.

As tribes were conquered or joined together under a strong leader, kingdoms appeared. As kings became more powerful, they spread their customs over larger areas. The kings had power to make the laws, enforce them, and punish those who disobeyed.

In the country of England, a custom developed which improved the way laws were applied to the people. The English king began to appoint judges whose job it was to settle disputes. They recorded their decisions in books. The judges were to be fair and to read the decisions of other judges so that the laws could be applied justly and equally throughout the country. The books of "common law" helped people understand where they fit under the laws.

In 1215, King John of England was forced to sign a paper called the Magna Carta. In it, he promised not to raise taxes without the consent of the nobles and the church. He also agreed to let juries and judges decide if someone was guilty of breaking a law. Even he, the king, had to respect the laws. The belief in rule by law and the ideas found in the English "common law" were brought to America with the first English colonists.

As the colonies grew, arguments with England happened more often and were very bitter. The colonists went to war with England over these arguments. On July 4, 1776, a meeting of representatives from the 13 English colonies took further action. They signed a

298

FIGURE 3–2

Sample Textbook Selection Dealing with the Concept of Law (From SCOTT, FORESMAN SOCIAL STUDIES, Book 7, William Stepien. Copyright © 1982, 1979 Scott, Foresman and Company. Reprinted by permission.)

the ability to organize information, such as the processes of critical evaluation and creative problem solving. I argue that only the first two levels of Bloom's taxonomy pertain to information processing and that dimensions of the upper levels require comprehension as a *necessary base* for the subsequent, special thinking abilities. Unfortunately, this argument brings us full circle to an earlier point: we know very little for certain about children's thinking. Still, you must keep comprehension in mind as a guide for choosing appropriate teaching strategies.

When teachers choose a *purpose* for the lesson, they establish a direction of instruction toward which all subsequent activities are planned. Bloom's taxonomy is a useful guide for establishing purposes and for selecting instructional activities. It is important to remember, though, that all levels above the *knowledge* level involve a *process* of thinking, so when your purpose centers on any particular level, you must elicit associated thinking processes. We will consider only comprehension processes in this chapter. Chapter 5 will treat the sophisticated processes of solving problems (*application, analysis,* and *synthesis*), and Chapter 6 will deal with *evaluation*. As a flexible teacher, you must examine the material to which your children will be exposed and decide the major purpose for presenting it. If the purpose is comprehension, you must choose an associated strategy; if the purpose is something else, you must use a strategy associated with that level. You can make these decisions by establishing some "if . . . then" relationships; for example:

If I want to insure meaningful understanding of the content, *then* a comprehension process must be used.

If I want the children to solve unique problems with the understandings they developed, *then* an application process must be used.

If I want the children to design creative, original solutions to unique problems, *then* a synthesis process must be used.

If I want the children to share their personal feelings on a topic, *then* an evaluation process must be used.

In other words, if you decide the material is such that any or all of the thought characteristics should be treated after a learning activity, then you must be prepared to lead the children through the associated processes. What special thought characteristic, for example, would you be likely to stress after requesting that children read the sample text selection in Figure 3–3? Do you agree that *evaluation*, or the expression of personal feelings, is most apparent? To help the children evaluate, we must do more than simply ask "How do you feel about . . . ?" We must lead the children through the *process* of establishing a personal opinion. (You will find suggestions in Chapter 6.) Likewise, if comprehension is important, we must do something more than ask a series of unplanned questions.

Because the introduction is such an important component of the DLE, there is sometimes confusion over how much time to spend on that section. Suppose you are introducing a friend to someone she has never met before. You might say, "Beth, I would like you to meet Larry, who loves skiing as much as you do." A brief *introduction* (if it is a good one) establishes a common bond between the two individ-

PEOPLE WATCHERS

Some scientists do not wear long, white laboratory coats. And only rarely do they squint into microscopes. These scientists are called **social scientists.** They study people.

There are many different kinds of social scientists. But all of them search for similar clues. They want to find out how people act and why they do certain things.

Some scientists study the people of different cultures to learn their ways of doing things. These scientists are **anthropologists** (an' thrə päl' ə jəsts)

Anthropologists often live with the people of the culture they are studying. They try to watch, listen to, and feel the world of these people. But an anthropologist must be a good reporter when describing other cultures. Facts, not opinions, must be reported. Do you think it would be difficult for an anthropologist who believed in one god to write about a people who believed in many gods? Why or why not? Do you think that the report might be mixed with opinion?

FIGURE 3–3

Sample Text Describing Social Scientists (Bowmar/Noble Social Studies: People and Culture. Copyright © 1980 Bowmar/Noble Publishers, Inc. Reprinted by permission.)

uals by emphasizing past experiences, motivates them to explore that interest more deeply, and may encourage them to talk about skiing and other subjects. A poor introduction—"Beth, I'd like you to meet Larry"—leaves both individuals unsure of where to go from there. Likewise, a good introduction to a DLE briefly introduces the reading material to your children by relating the new topic to previous experiences, helping them clarify new terms, and motivating them to pursue the subject matter that makes up the main body of the lesson. If motivated enough, your two friends may spend this first meeting talking and getting to know each other, asking questions of each other, and expecting direct answers in return. *Reading* a textbook assignment is similar; the children will have questions in their minds (purposes established by the teacher) and read attentively to find answers to those questions. If your two friends decide to learn more about each other or to further explore common interests, they may agree to see each other again. Likewise, *follow-up* and *extension* activities give children a chance to reinforce what they have been exposed to in their reading or to further explore an interest.

Remember this explanation whenever you plan to teach a textbook reading assignment, because a problem that constantly surfaces when I ask my students to prepare their first DLE is the extraordinary amount of time they devote to the introduction. Simply because there are new words to introduce and a background to establish, they want to apply all they know about direct experiences and take field trips, show films, or invite resource people for that introduction. They are not keeping the parts of the DLE in perspective when they do that. The purpose of the *entire* learning experience is to establish meaningful comprehension of new ideas. A long, drawn out introduction only belabors the task, often creating anxiety in the children and a frustrated desire to "get on with it." Keep the introduction short and to the point—the remainder of the DLE has a purpose, too. Suppose you decide that a field trip *would be* appropriate for a topic—at which point would it fit best in the DLE?

THE LEARNING EXPERIENCE

Selecting sources of information for your social studies program and using the sources effectively are professional behaviors associated with any theory of learning. There are dozens of types of sources from which to choose. In learning about community workers, for example, there may be no substitute for visiting a firehouse to see the fire engines, to hear the chatter of the two-way radio, to try on the firehat, or to listen to firefighters explain their duties. At other times, objects such as kimonos, kinaras, or tabis might be brought to the classroom to enlighten children about other cultures. Bricklayers, craftsmen, artists, or musicians can visit the classroom to share expert skills or information. Movies and tape recordings offer valuable learning experiences. Children's literature offers information, emotion, and creative possibilities. All these sources of information appear in abundance in good social studies programs, but it has been estimated that up to 90 percent of all elementary school social studies content is communicated through a combination of social studies textbooks. For that reason, we will continue to examine our format for that strategy, with the expectation that you will be able to substitute a film, recording, or other learning experience as a major learning activity in the teaching sequence.

Reading the Selection

After an introduction to their reading selection, children begin to initiate the main component of the entire procedure—the actual reading. The children have a purpose for the reading and are now reading to fulfill it. During this *silent* reading time, you should circulate among the children to determine whether they are having trouble understanding. In most instances, you should provide immediate help for the children, but if a problem seems to persist, you may want to plan reinforcement activities to remedy the situation.

READING RATE.   The major reading skill to emphasize during silent reading is establishing an appropriate *reading rate*. Reading rate must be adjusted to the various purposes for reading. For example, when it is clear that an author is sharing a personal experience, you can tell the children they can relax and read quickly because the purpose of the assignment is to enjoy the author's account. A sample of this type of selection is this account of a Chinese-American, telling of his parents' arrival in the United States.

> My parents came here from Canton, a city in southern China. They came with many other Chinese during the gold rush in the 1800s. It was very difficult for them—they couldn't buy a house, they couldn't rent an apartment, they couldn't get a job because they were Chinese. Today, doors are opening for our people, more so than ever before.[14]

When a reading selection begins with a question, the children can read a bit more quickly because they are clued into the fact that they are reading to locate specific information. They merely read through the text until they find the answer.

> What materials could Australian Aborigines use many years ago to build shelters? Most of the time they built temporary shelters called *lean-tos.* They used sticks to build a wooden frame for the shelter and then covered the frame with leafy branches and grasses. But, most Aborigines did not build any kind of shelter. They stayed warm on cold nights by building fires. Several Aborigines crowded around the fire and rubbed warm ashes on their bodies when the fire died.

Finally, slow, careful reading is necessary when the material contains many factual details or complicated instructions.

> The Congress is comprised of all the members of the Senate and the House of Representatives. Congress passes laws for all the people of the United States to follow. In 1973, Congress passed a law empowering the President to make new coins for our nation's bicentennial year of 1976. The new coins were to be ready by July 4, 1975, a full year before the bicentennial. The silver dollar, half dollar, and quarter each had special designs and the dates 1776–1976 on one side.

Because we expect children to read for a variety of reasons and to eventually adjust their rates to satisfy those reasons (income tax forms, newspapers, magazines), encourage them to be flexible in their rates for successful reading of social studies materials.

Aiding Comprehension

What is commonly done in our schools to help children comprehend their educational materials? Dolores Durkin sought to answer that question by observing classroom instruction in a number of fourth-grade classrooms. To start, she needed a definition of *comprehension instruction* so she could recognize it when she saw it. Unable to find a definition in the professional literature, she set out to formulate her own. One possibility was to define comprehension instruction as "everything that helps children to read"—word recognition, phonics, and so on. In other words, teaching comprehension would be analogous to teaching reading. A second possibility was to exclude all instruction associated with single isolated words and include only attempts "(a) to teach children the meaning of a unit that is larger than a word, or (b) to teach them how to work out the meanings of such units." Using this definition, Durkin observed comprehension instruction during only twenty-eight minutes of a total of 4,469 minutes of observation—less than *one percent* of the time! Durkin commented, "Practically no comprehension instruction was seen. Comprehension assessment, carried on for the most part through interrogation, was common. Whether children's answers were right or wrong was the big concern."[15]

Durkin thus showed us that teachers appear to be more interested in *testing* comprehension than *teaching* it. We can teach comprehension directly through good questioning techniques, but only if we design a systematic, sequential pattern of questions to help children unlock meaning. Dewey described the "art of questioning" this way:

1. Questions should not elicit fact upon fact, but should be asked in such a way as to delve deeply into the subject, i.e., to develop an overall concept of the selection.
2. Questions should emphasize personal interpretations rather than literal and direct responses.
3. Questions should not be asked randomly so that each is an end in itself, but should be planned so that one leads into the next throughout a continuous discussion.
4. Teachers should periodically review important points so that old, previously discussed material can be placed into perspective with that which is presently being studied.
5. The end of the question asking sequence should leave the children with a sense of accomplishment and build a desire for that which is yet to come.[16]

Taba pointed out the difficulties of teaching methodologies that do not adhere to Dewey's suggestions:

> A closed question such as, "When did Columbus sail?" permits only one child to respond. If the first student knows the answer that's the end of it. The teacher must then ask a second question to elicit another fact. A series of closed questions inevitably develops a teacher-student, teacher-student sequence. It also prevents the child who has a particular piece of information to offer from entering the discussion if the teacher does not ask "the right question."...A teacher whose opening question lacks focus may himself be unsure of the focus or the purpose of the discussion and his students will suffer accordingly.[17]

Unfortunately, closed questions permeate many classroom comprehension discussions. Some teachers repeatedly begin their approach with "Let's answer a few questions to see if everyone understands what we've just read." To which Manning says, "If the students know the answer to the question. . .why ask? And. . .if the students do not know the answer to the question. . .why ask?"[18] Manning advises replacing such questioning sequences with more appropriate direct teacher instructional processes.

Realistically, teachers can ask many different kinds of questions, and good social studies teachers *must* use a variety of the "right" kinds of questions. The kinds of questions you choose, however, are primarily determined by the established *purpose* for reading. When trying to determine whether children have grasped the main idea of a selection, a teacher might begin discussion with "Tell in your own words how the mountains affect the lives of the people in Peru." A crucial component of effective questioning is to tie the stated purpose for reading to the initial question. A teacher might state the purpose for reading this way: "Please read pages 195–196 to find out the three branches of the federal government." Then after the children have finished reading, she can ask, "What are the three branches of the federal government?"

The logic of the connection between *purpose* and *initial question* is apparent, but we sometimes neglect to make that connection. Be sure to keep in mind the necessity for this connection and ask yourself, as you develop your discussion sequence, "Why did I assign that reading?" Then, the process of framing your questions will become much easier.

The description of Bloom's hierarchical taxonomy was to help you understand the different levels of thinking associated with purpose-setting statements. Many educators also pattern their comprehension questions on the various levels of the taxonomy.

Advocates of the position that comprehension involves a series of hierarchical thinking abilities suggest that comprehension questions can be generated either as an *inductive process* or as a *deductive process*. In Figure 3–4, the left-hand arrow indicates an *inductive approach* because the questioning sequence begins with an initial discussion of facts and details and progresses through higher levels toward critical thinking. The teacher might begin a sequence with a question such as: "As you think of Captain John Smith, what were some of the things he did?" The teacher would list the responses on the board and pursue a discussion of Smith's actions

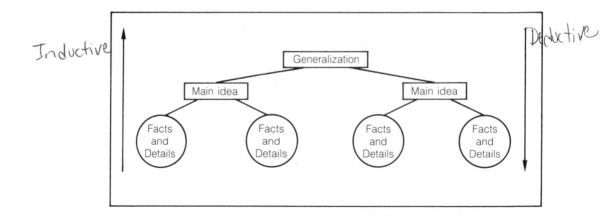

Inductive   *Deductive*

FIGURE 3–4

Interrelationship of Levels of Comprehension

along with his motivation for taking those actions. After establishing a base of understanding, the teacher would eventually culminate her discussion with a high-level thought question: "Now, what kind of a person would you say Captain John Smith was?"

The right-hand arrow in Figure 3–4, a *deductive approach*, starts out with the higher-order question (Bloom's evaluation level, for example) but does not stop there. Once the question is asked, and the children's feelings are shared, the children are always asked to support their judgment. For example, the teacher's first question might be: "From all you've read about Captain John Smith, what kind of a person do you think he was?" In other words, the children are asked to make critical evaluations in the opening question. The teacher then steadily asks the children to support their feelings with the question, "What did he do to make you feel that way?" As the children offer support for their feelings, the facts, details, and main ideas from their reading become useful bases for their arguments.

In both these questioning sequences, teachers generate the same kind of thinking, but have approached the sequence from different directions. Both directions take the children through the reading selection by creating a unified concept of the material. The direction you choose for a questioning sequence is primarily determined by the purpose you establish for the reading. If you tell the children to "read pages 49–50 to find out what kind of person Captain John Smith was," your first question should be "What kind of a person do you think he was?" Imagine the difficulty children would have if you stated the same purpose but asked as your first question, "What were some things John Smith did?" The rule is: always relate your first question to the established purpose and go from there. Planning a sequence of discussion questions is a complex skill, especially for someone who is trying it for the first time, so some teachers feel more comfortable following a guide during their initial efforts.

The Taba Approach

The Taba approach is a popular technique for organizing questioning sequences in the social studies classroom. According to Hilda Taba and her associates, concept formation begins with recognition of the special qualities of things and examination of characteristics or properties that separate one thing from another. From this knowledge base, the teacher helps children organize their thinking with a specified series of questions. To illustrate, let us suppose that a primary-grade teacher has just returned with her class from a field trip to the supermarket. She might help the children organize their thinking with a pattern of questions like these:

Teacher	*Children*
"What did you find at the supermarket?"	List items they saw at the store (*factual data*)
"Do any of these items seem to belong together?"	Use colored chalk to group items (e.g., fresh vegetables, canned goods, meats, machinery, etc.)
"Why did you group these items together?"	Verbalize common characteristics of items in each group
"What would you call each of these groups?"	Decide on a label that encompasses all items in a group
"Could some items belong in more than one group?"	Discover different relationships
"Can you find a different way to group the items?"	Discover additional relationships (*concept development*)

As children progress through this activity, their concept of *supermarket* becomes somewhat more sophisticated because their teacher (1) provides a concrete experience to relate to the reading material, and (2) sequences questions to help organize the experience. The understanding of *supermarket* will continue to grow and change as continued experiences become integrated into each child's life and into adulthood. Because it encourages children to think at levels beyond basic concept development, the Taba program extends the conceptual base through a process of developing *generalizations*.

Developing Generalizations

Concepts are most often represented by a word or phrase, such as *neighborhood, minority group,* or *inflation,* to help one organize or categorize information. Like concepts, generalizations are the products of grouping items that have similar characteristics, but generalizations indicate higher levels of thinking in that they state relationship among two or more concepts. "Modern transportation and communication systems help to make possible easier lives for people in metropolitan areas," is a broad statement that contains two or more concepts and establishes

Skill in designing and asking good questions enhances the learning process and creates interest and enthusiasm.

a relationship among them. Can you name the concepts included in the generalization?

The generalizing process is among the most important goals of elementary school social studies instruction. You should capitalize on every opportunity to have students generalize about their social studies experiences, because generalizing demonstrates a sophisticated ability to gain deeper meaning from data. Children should have the freedom to express personal interpretations of shared experiences in a nonthreatening atmosphere, where no one is criticized for offering a "wrong" or "silly" statement. You must encourage them to offer interpretations and to support them by reexamining data from their experience so they will see how their ideas can change as they study the data more carefully. This example illustrates how one teacher conducted a discussion to help children recall important information, again following a trip to the supermarket, and to generalize beyond the data (the question sequence is an adaptation of the Taba approach):

Teacher	*Children*
Developing Concepts	
"What did you see at the supermarket?"	List items they saw at the store.

"Which of these things can be put together? Why?"

Group items into categories.

"What shall we call each of the groups?"

Generate labels as the teacher lists items beneath each label.

Developing Generalizations

"What foods or supplies come from the neighborhood where the store is located?"

Generate list of items.

"What foods or supplies come from outside the neighborhood?"

Generate list of items.

"How do the stores get the things they sell?"

Children hypothesize (guess) solutions to the question as the teacher lists them on the chalkboard.

(At this point the teacher allows the children an opportunity to search for data to support or reject their hypotheses [library books, guest speakers, etc.].)

"Which reasons were correct? Which reasons need to be changed? Why? Should we add some reasons?"

Children use their data to support or reject their hypotheses.

"What can you say about the super-market and the ways it gets its food and supplies?"

Offer statements of relationship between workers and the services they provide; for example, "People in supermarkets need other people to furnish foods and supplies."

This example shows how a social studies program can promote development of higher-level thinking skills. Knowledge and details are the foundations to support these higher-level processes, not data for the children to commit to memory. A sample progression might look something like this:

Fact: Columbus discovered America in 1492 (and other facts)

Concept: Exploration

Generalization: European rulers sought to extend their influence by exploring new continents.

The Taba approach provides a solid framework of sequentially ordered questions for promoting the mental operations necessary for development of concepts and generalizations, as outlined in Table 3–1.

TABLE 3-1
Taba's Pattern of Comprehension Questions

Child's Responsibility	Teacher's Question	Teacher's Responsibility
1. Enumerate items	1. "What do you see here?"	1. List items on chalkboard, chart, etc.
2. Find similarities among items to serve as basis for grouping	2. "Do any of these items belong together? Why?"	2. Underline in colored chalk, mark with symbols
3. Label the groups	3. "What would you call a group of these items?"	3. Record names
4. Regroup and relabel	4. "Could we put some of these items into more than one group?"	4. Record responses
5. Summarize information into one sentence	5. "Can someone say in one sentence something about all these groups?"	5. Encourage several responses

The Taba program developers stress the importance of consistently following the questioning sequence shown in Table 3–1. They feel that unless teachers adhere to the basic form, there is little chance that what is done in social studies will improve children's thinking skills. The belief is that if children repeatedly go through the process of answering questions from a predetermined sequence, they will internalize the procedure and begin to create patterns on their own. Through such a process, we *teach* comprehension skills.

A PERSONAL PATTERN OF QUESTIONING.   Although many teachers enjoy the freedom of choosing a questioning sequence that matches their teaching style and individual student needs, other teachers, when they are given specific guidance, appear to be more comfortable leading group discussions. Morgan and Schreiber believe that teachers should be so skilled that they are able to engage young children in meaningful discussions by selecting *their own* classification schemes for questions. They comment:

> Any discrete categorization of questions is inherently artificial. It seems more reasonable to conceive of classroom questions as being on a continuum. One extreme of the continuum may be characterized by lower levels of mental activity such as pure recall. . .and questions which are likely to have one "correct" answer. The social studies classroom in which questions of this type predominate will tend to be teacher dominated, with minimal student involvement. . . .Conversely, questions at the other extreme of the continuum involve more complex, higher mental activity. . . .Student participation in class discussions would consume a greater proportion of class time.[19]

Figure 3–5 is an example of Morgan and Schreiber's advice. At which point of the continuum would you place each of these questions?

FIGURE 3–5

Continuum of Personal Discussion Questions

1. Who was the first president of the United States?
2. How would the world be different today if the Axis powers had defeated the Allies in World War II?
3. Do you think the Russian people are really as unhappy as the writer described?
4. Describe the operation of Henry Ford's first assembly line.

Whether or not we agree on our exact placements is immaterial; what *is* important is that you are able to sense what comprises a "lower-level" and a "higher-order" question. We both should have identified questions 1 and 4 as lower-level questions, though, because they deal with specific information. Questions 2 and 3 should have been classified as higher-order questions because they require of the student more reflection, originality, and expression of personal feelings.

We can construct many questioning patterns, but the main consideration that should guide your thinking is knowing where you want to go with it. For example, one teacher who wished to draw on material the children had just finished reading to lead them toward developing a generalization used this approach:

Teacher: Can someone tell me the name of a popular food eaten by children in Mexico?

Child 1: Tacos.

Teacher: That's correct. And what are tacos made from?

Child 2: They're flat cornmeal cakes filled with chopped meat, cheese, and vegetables.

Teacher: Has anyone here eaten a taco?

Several children relate positive experiences; plans are made to make tacos in class as a special project.

Teacher: Tacos are a special food eaten by children of Mexico. Are there any special foods that children in the United States enjoy?

Children: Hamburgers! Hot dogs! Pizza.

Teacher: My goodness. Does that mean you eat those foods every day?

Child 3: No. We just like them as favorites.

Teacher: Just as the Mexican children like tacos?

Children: Yes. I don't think they eat tacos every day either.

Teacher: What can you tell me about special foods?

> Child 4: We all need food to eat, but people in different countries choose to eat special foods they themselves like to eat.
>
> Teacher: Very good. You did a lot of good thinking today.

Notice that the teacher led the children through a discussion of the data toward an appropriate generalization. Your guidance is important in this area for you must guard against formation of generalizations that are too broad ("All Japanese wear kimonos") and against forming generalizations without sufficient evidence.

SUSTAINING CLASSROOM DISCUSSIONS

Whether you choose a less structured, hierarchical approach such as Bloom's or a patterned approach such as Taba's, the key is to organize classroom discussions so that they have a goal beyond the regurgitation of factual data. To achieve your goal, you will sometimes need to ask questions or offer comments other than those that form the major part of your strategy. *Probing* is a popular technique of sustaining classroom discussions. This process, mastered centuries ago by Socrates (and referred to as the Socratic method), remains a valuable teaching tool today. By probing, Socrates was able to prod students (offer them hints) if they were unclear in an answer or unable to answer a question at all. To understand the technique, you must realize that it is comprised of two subprocesses: *prompting* and *clarifying*.

Prompting

Prompting utilizes short hints or clues whenever a child gives an incorrect response to a question, usually of the lower-level type. Several prompts or leading questions help the child organize her thinking patterns relative to the original question.

> Teacher: How does the process of gerrymandering work?
>
> Student: I'm not sure. I don't know.
>
> Teacher: How does an individual state establish voting districts?
>
> Student: The state is divided into sections, which have about the same number of people in each section.
>
> Teacher: That's right. Now can you tell me who is responsible for establishing those districts?
>
> Student: Oh, I see. The party controlling the state government at the time can use their power to set up districts unequally so that its voting strength will be as strong as possible, and the opposing party's strength will be as weak as possible.

Children are not told that their initial response is wrong; instead, they are led, reinforced, and encouraged. Since the teacher does not imply that a student's initial response is incorrect, prompting also helps to enhance the student's self-confidence.

Clarifying

Clarification calls for enlargement or restatement of a student's original answer. The teacher uses clarification when an answer is correct but does not come up to expectations for accuracy and completeness, or when children are asked to defend a position when there may be differences of opinion. Thus, clarification can usually be applied to questions at the higher levels of thinking.

> Teacher: Would both Democrats and Republicans gerrymander in our state if they had the chance to do so?
>
> Student: Yes, I think so.
>
> Teacher: Can you explain your reasons for feeling as you do?
>
> Student: I think it's hard for people to be fair when so much is at stake.

The probing technique helps children express ideas individually and intuitively. It enables learners to operate on all levels of thinking while they develop solutions to problems. The success of your questioning technique, however, depends on your ability to adapt questions to the individual without expecting the same quality of response from all students.

To influence class discussion interaction, the teacher also needs to be familiar with forms of verbal and nonverbal language that communicate her attitude toward what the children are contributing.

WORDS OF PRAISE.   Offer words of praise for children's sincere efforts. A spontaneous, honest reaction such as "Yes, I understand," "Go on, you certainly are on the right track," "All right!" "Um-hm, that's something to think about," or "I'm listening," lets the children know you are paying attention to what they are saying and encourages them to continue.

EYE CONTACT.   Another technique of letting the children know that communication lines are open is to *maintain direct eye contact with the child who is speaking.* All too often we tend to glance down at the teacher's guide or lesson plan or think ahead to the next question with faraway looks in our eyes. You must let the child know you are interested in what he is saying and that you are trying to understand.

BODY LANGUAGE.   Use body language to offer support as children contribute to class discussion. A smile, nod of approval, or pat on the back indicates your satisfaction with a child's efforts and lets him know you appreciate his active participation.

Any of these approval techniques, alone or in combination with one another, initiates a positive interaction pattern between teacher and students. Avoiding eye contact, apparent disinterest, frowning, sarcastic comments, impatience, or ignoring children does the opposite. It establishes roadblocks that terminate the children's talk and says, in effect, "I want you to stop talking." Instead of such roadblocks, consider using verbal and nonverbal signals that reinforce discussion. These are examples of verbal reinforcement:

Words:	great, fascinating, positively fabulous, splendid, right, correct, unmistakable, exciting, powerful, wow
Sentences:	That's clever.
	That shows a great deal of good thought.
	I like the way you explained it.
	You make being a teacher very rewarding.
	You really thought that one out well, didn't you?
	You catch on very quickly!
	I like that—I really didn't know it could be done that way.
	You did some great thinking today!

These are examples of nonverbal reinforcement:

Facial:	smiling, winking, nodding, raising eyebrows, widening eyes
Bodily:	shaking head, thumbs up, signaling O.K., clapping hands, sitting on desk near students, touching, hugging

Visual Organizing Strategies

WEBBING.   Although oral discussion strategies are critical teaching tools, *visual organizing strategies* often help children focus on major ideas and understand relationships among details. One device for facilitating comprehension of social studies content is the *semantic web*, a technique introduced by Freedman and Reynolds.[20] A semantic web has four basic elements: core questions, web strands, strand supports, and strand ties.

The *core question* serves as the focus of the web. All the information generated in a discussion should relate to the core question, so the core question should create the possibility of several answers. An example of a core question is: "What words would you use to describe William Penn?" The core question is placed in the center of a growing matrix (Figure 3–6).

All subsequent information relates to this core question. The immediate responses to the core question are *web strands* and are placed systemmatically around the core question, as shown in Figure 3–7.

The facts or inferences the students use to support each web strand are *strand*

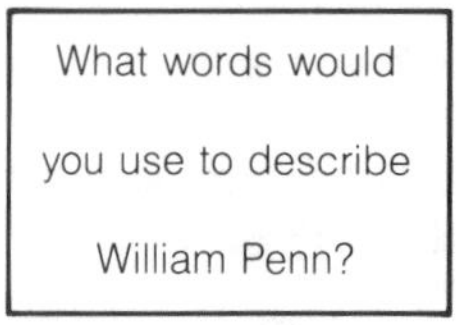

What words would

you use to describe

William Penn?

FIGURE 3–6

The Core Question of a Semantic Web

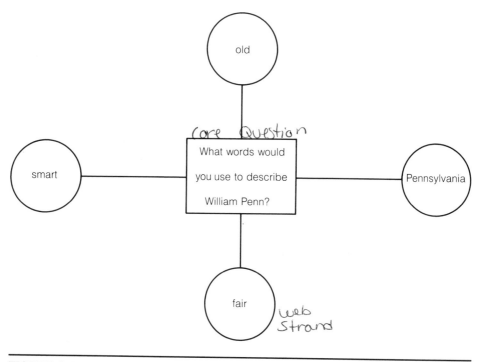

FIGURE 3–7

The Core Question and Web Strands of a Semantic Web

supports. The strand supports extend from each web strand, as shown in Figure 3–8. The possible relationships among the strands are called *strand ties.* "Smart" and "fair," for example, may be related in that they describe William Penn's personality characteristics. Likewise, each of the other characteristics are related to some degree. The teacher's responsibility is to probe and prompt the children until they discover some of those relationships.

Semantic webs can be constructed for many purposes. Here are some possibilities based upon Bloom's taxonomy:

- Comprehension
  "What are some major events from the history of Pennsylvania?"
- Application
  "How can we find out which of these events children in our school would most like to personally witness if they could go back in time and watch our state's great leaders in action?"
- Analysis
  "What did George Washington mean when, just days before he crossed the snowy and icy Delaware River in 1776, he said, "I think the game will be pretty well up.""

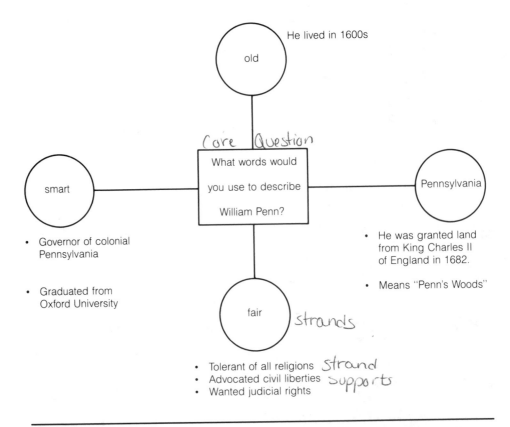

FIGURE 3–8

A Semantic Web with Core Question, Web Strands, and Strand Supports

■ Synthesis
"How would the history of Pennsylvania have been changed if it were settled by the Chinese rather than the British?"

■ Evaluation
"What event would you choose to watch if you could personally witness any event from Pennsylvania history?"

Because semantic webs can be used for such a variety of questions, it is quite a versatile technique. Teachers can also adapt the basic webbing technique in a number of ways. Rather than simply draw webs on the chalkboard or chart, you may wish to introduce your children to a stuffed toy spider called "Spike." Tell the children that Spike is a special spider because he always asks good questions and that he loves to stay in your classroom because the children are so helpful in answering his questions. Place Spike in the center of a circle of children next to a question printed on a sheet of construction paper (core question). Attach a long string of yarn to Spike, which you will use to construct Spike's "web." Request responses to Spike's question and, making sure each response is different, ask the children to print their answers on sheets of construction paper and display it for all to see (web strands). Then, pass Spike and the yarn to each child in turn and ask each youngster to explain the relationship between his answer and the question (web strands). Finally, encourage the children to offer ideas as to why each of their answers is connected by Spike's web.

INFORMATION RETRIEVAL CHARTS. The purpose of a retrieval chart is to help students categorize information into conceptual blocks. Retrieval charts typically consist of two interrelated elements: (1) the concept labels and (2) the information to be categorized. Table 3–2 shows these two retrieval chart components. After you have guided the children through a purposeful learning experience, display a chart and ask a main idea question, such as "What did you find out about different neighborhoods?" As the children suggest information, ask them to identify the category into which their comments can best be organized.

When the children finish organizing the mass of information, the teacher should use the retrieval chart to help them make generalizations. For example, you might ask, "What can you say about different neighborhoods and the things people do in them?"

Some teachers object to retrieval charts because they feel it offers too much "spoon feeding" of information. It's true that it isn't a good idea to lock students into any single system of information retrieval, but if retrieval charts are used wisely in combination with other devices, they can remain valuable teaching tools.

GUIDE-O-RAMAS. The guide-o-rama helps students process the major concepts of a reading selection. The guide-o-rama's six-step procedure provides a reading road map that emphasizes both comprehension and flexibility of reading rate. Wood and Mateja explain the process: *First*, determine the overall purpose of your

TABLE 3–2
Pattern of a Typical Retrieval Chart

	Buildings	Traffic	Land
City	Tall office buildings Large apartments Many stores	Many cars Buses Automobiles Taxis	Few trees Little grass Much cement and roads
Suburbs	Houses for one family Shopping malls Shopping centers	Shopping areas have many cars Short streets have few cars	Many trees Grass Shrubs
Country	Houses for one family Barns	No busy streets Cars and trucks	Farmland grows crops Trees Grass

reading assignment. In Figure 3–9, the teacher wants children to understand the events leading up to the Revolutionary War. *Second*, choose the essential sections that directly relate to the purpose. *Third*, develop questions or content statements to help children comprehend the selection. *Fourth*, design a novel, interest-capturing guide format to stimulate interest. *Fifth*, present the guide to the children, usually as a duplicated sheet or chart. Explain its purpose and "walk" the children through the guide to familiarize them with the procedures. Allowing the children to work in pairs or small groups helps promote positive learning. *Sixth*, have the students share their guide-o-ramas and talk about their responses.[21]

The guide-o-ramas, as with other forms of information processing we have discussed, are direct teaching strategies for aiding comprehension. These content-based strategies help students take a greater step toward learning social studies materials.

Children's Own Questions

A final major responsibility in questioning is to plan sessions during which children discuss questions that are important to them. You can do this orally, set aside places where children can write questions whenever they wish, make tape recorders available, or simply encourage children to talk about things informally. In learning to listen to the questions children ask, you often find rich material for class exploration. Listen to these questions asked by elementary school youngsters and imagine the possibilities for discussion:

"Why are there so many fights and arguments on the playground?"

"Can a rocket ship get lost in the clouds?"

"Why is there no smoke from the fire on the sun?"

"Are elephants really afraid of mice?"

"Where does the garbage go after the garbage collectors throw it on the truck?"

You can understand how teachers who feel pressures to get through the daily routine often neglect questions like these. Take time to listen to your children, though, because they need to be heard and to learn. Their understanding of their world is incomplete and their questions about the "unanswerable" often provide "precious moments" of innocence that we all enjoy remembering:

"Do the clouds have bones?"

"The vet said our cat has to go on a diet. He eats mice when he goes out. How many calories are in a mouse?"

"My father said that when someone is born, someone dies. I was born at 1:20 on June 28, 1975. How can I find out who died when I was born?"

Everyone agrees that good teachers should know how to ask good questions. Through good questioning techniques, we not only encourage effective thinking but we also help build positive relationships. Simply asking good questions is not enough,

The English Colonies

(interview with a colonist) Purpose: Imagine that you were a colonist when Great Britain had control over America. Describe how you felt at each of the events on pages 159–164.

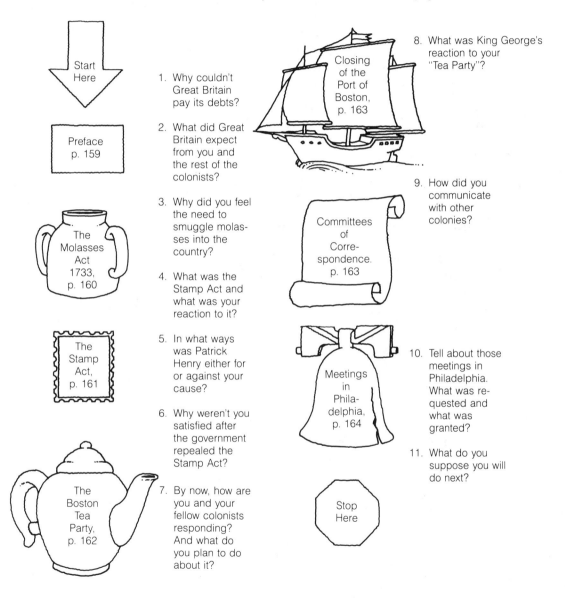

Start Here

Preface p. 159

1. Why couldn't Great Britain pay its debts?

2. What did Great Britain expect from you and the rest of the colonists?

The Molasses Act 1733, p. 160

3. Why did you feel the need to smuggle molasses into the country?

The Stamp Act, p. 161

4. What was the Stamp Act and what was your reaction to it?

5. In what ways was Patrick Henry either for or against your cause?

6. Why weren't you satisfied after the government repealed the Stamp Act?

The Boston Tea Party, p. 162

7. By now, how are you and your fellow colonists responding? And what do you plan to do about it?

Closing of the Port of Boston, p. 163

8. What was King George's reaction to your "Tea Party"?

9. How did you communicate with other colonies?

Committees of Correspondence. p. 163

Meetings in Philadelphia, p. 164

10. Tell about those meetings in Philadelphia. What was requested and what was granted?

11. What do you suppose you will do next?

Stop Here

FIGURE 3–9

A Guide-O-Rama for Fifth Grade American History (From Dick Cunningham and Scott L. Shablak, "Selective Reading Guide-O-Rama: The Content Teacher's Best Friend," Journal of Reading 18 [February 1975]: 380–382.)

however—we need teachers who can listen and encourage children to ask questions of their own. By doing so, we create an environment in which children express their ideas and feelings freely and where they know they can be heard.

Although we have talked about questioning and discussion techniques under the topic of using the social studies textbook, you must understand that the principles apply to questioning and discussing *any* learning experiences, including field trips, films, listening to speakers, and so on. These interaction techniques are valuable tools in the repertoire of any teacher, but especially that of the social studies teacher.

FOLLOW-UP AND EXTENSION ACTIVITIES

Follow-up and extension activities are the culmination of the entire DLE procedure. They provide additional practice on certain skills through workbook or other seatwork assignments or through special projects or independent activities that encourage children to apply or extend concepts to a variety of situations. This list of the activities represents only a sampling of the hundreds of possibilities:

Have children illustrate major learning by drawing a picture, dramatizing, making a model, and so on.

Have special projects such as games or cooking going on around the classroom.

Make large table models of places from plasticene, clay, cardboard, or wood.

Have children pretend they are among the first Jamestown colonists, for example. Ask them to write a letter to a friend in England telling about life in the first year of the settlement.

Make a "fashion magazine" or "catalog" as it might have been published at another time in history.

Bring in foods described in the textbook and encourage the children to taste them.

Paint a mural to show the major characteristics of a culture.

Construct time lines to illustrate the sequence of important events.

Develop charts and graphs to summarize important data.

Go on a field trip or invite a resource person to speak in the classroom.

Show a film to reinforce main ideas from the text.

By reading professional journals and organizing an idea file, you will begin to accumulate ideas for experiences that will bring more meaning to reading assignments. Remember, though, that these activities *must* be part of the total learning experience, not "extra busy work" or "icing on the cake" that gets done only because we have a few minutes to kill.

One technique for this phase of the DLE when a reading assignment is the major learning experience is directed *silent* or *oral rereading*. If, however, the comprehension section part of the DLE was successful, you would need to spend little time on rereading the material—orally or silently. But if you find in your questioning sequence after the initial reading that children have had significant comprehension problems, then you might want to have them reread certain parts to clarify key points. Therefore, the first purpose for silent or oral rereading is to *clarify ideas*. To help children in this area, keep these activities in mind.

Read captions under pictures or illustrations before discussing their content

Reread orally or silently from short selections that have already been read silently for the purpose of clarifying meaning

Reread orally to defend a position or prove a point

Reread orally to explain complicated directions for completing a project

The second major purpose for oral rereading is *personal interpretation*. In this realm, the oral reading experience becomes an opportunity for children to share something interesting with others. You should rarely expect children to read orally before they have been given an opportunity to read the selection silently for meaning. Recall how many times you may have been asked to read orally in school before you had an opportunity to "practice" first. When you finished your part, did you ever fear the teacher would ask you a question on what you were reading and that you would not be able to answer because you "didn't listen"? You may have also proven the importance of prior silent reading when you "peeked" ahead in the book while another child was reading aloud so that you wouldn't make a mistake when it was your turn.

Young children enjoy reading aloud, but they need certain skills for the oral reading activity to be worthwhile. The good oral reader should be able to pronounce words clearly and use a voice to suit the mood of the selection. Encourage children by leading them something like this:

"Read the line that tells you what Maria wanted."

"What two words tell you that Maria wanted the sheep badly?"

"Read the sentence that Maria said, exactly as you think she said it."

Other opportunities for purposeful oral reading are to:

Put on a short skit for another group of children

Give a puppet play in which the dialogue is read

Ask children to bring their library books to the reading circle and let them tell something about their books and read an interesting portion in the library book that supports or rejects an idea from the textbook

Have the children use flannel board cut-outs to tell part of the story or to depict the action while they read selected portions aloud to the group

Let one child silently act out part of a story while the other children look for the place where the action occurs in the story; whoever finds the correct portion may read it aloud to the others

Ask the children to read only the dialogue in a story, with each child reading a particular part; let one child act as narrator to read necessary descriptions of the setting, etc.

A superior reading lesson from the social studies textbook keeps comprehension in the foreground and oral or silent rereading as a "back-up" to help children clarify important points or to bring personal interpretation into the reading material.

Besides reinforcing concepts developed during the actual learning activity, follow-up experiences can enrich children's thinking through activities at higher levels of Bloom's taxonomy. D. B. Holzwarth's class in Upper Darby, Pennsylvania, studied Pennsylvania as a unit in its social studies program. After classifying and summarizing information from a number of learning resources, Mrs. Holzwarth's class became particularly interested in Pennsylvania's symbols—its nickname as the "Keystone State," mountain laurel as the state flower, and so on. Capitalizing on this interest, Mrs. Holzwarth challenged her class to choose a state symbol that did not already exist. After much independent research, groups offered suggestions such as a ladybug, praying mantis, or firefly. Justifying each choice became a particularly engaging process—friendly arguments raged back and forth as the benefits of each choice were presented. Finally the class voted, and perhaps swayed by its widespread summertime presence and Latin name *Photuris Pennsylvanica*, decided that the *firefly* would be most appropriate. Surprisingly, this classroom project received publicity in the local newspaper, where the district's state congressman read about it. He visited the classroom, congratulated the children, and introduced their idea in the next session of the legislature. The firefly is now the official state insect of Pennsylvania. What an ideal way to experience the process of active decision making and to learn about the function of state government!

A SAMPLE DLE

The following scenario describes the complete process of carrying out a DLE in a fourth-grade classroom. It pulls together all the sections of a DLE and illustrates a sound textbook-based social studies lesson.

Mr. Kurlak: (Brings children's attention to a photograph on the opening page of the reading assignment. The photograph shows archaeologists examining a dig.) What do the television character James Rockford and the people in this picture have in common?

Bernard: Rockford is a detective who looks for clues to solve crimes. These people look like they're trying to find something, too.

Mr. Kurlak: That's good thinking, Bernard. They both try to solve mysteries. These people are not called detectives, though. Does anyone know what they are called?

(None of the children answer.)

Mr. Kurlak: People who study clues to solve mysteries of the past are called *archaeologists*. (He writes the word on the board.) They are like detectives who learn about communities of long ago. As we read this assignment, be good detectives, or archaeologists, and look for the ways people lived in the past. But, before we read, I'd like to ask a question: How many of you have ever been to a place where you were all alone, surrounded only by forest and wildlife?

Inez: We went on a camping trip to the mountains. My brother and I went for a walk in the woods and we got lost. It was scary. (Other children offer similar experiences.)

Mr. Kurlak: It sounds like many of you have been in far out places in the country. If you have, you can begin to get an idea of what the world was like before people started settling in communities—especially you, Inez. I'd like you to read pages 118–21 to find out some ways people provided for food and shelter before there were cities and to compare their life with life in cities.

(The children all read for the stated purpose.)

Mr. Kurlak: Where did the early people get food, shelter, and clothes?

Charles: They moved around quite a bit to find animals to kill and to get wild berries and vegetables.

Kathy: When the food gave out in one place, they moved on to another spot.

Mr. Kurlak: Very good. The people led what is called a gathering life. How would you feel to be constantly looking for food like that?

William: I wouldn't like it. I'd be afraid of the animals or what would happen if there was a drought that killed all the plants.

Mr. Kurlak: That's exactly how the early people felt, William. Suppose you were living back then, what kinds of things would you suggest to the other people to make your lives easier?

Sonja: I'd tell them to join together. That way people could grow their own crops.

Rebecca: And raise their own animals.

John: Yeah. And then they wouldn't have to wander all around to get their food.

Mr. Kurlak: Let's go back to our reading and find the place where one of the early people described his fear of being killed by an animal. Would someone read the part to show how that person felt at the time?

(Anita reads the part aloud with expression.)

Mr. Kurlak: Thank you, Anita. The passage shows us that people had many enemies long ago. I'd like to have you think about the ways cities changed those problems. There is a chart on the board with two categories: "life before cities" and "life in cities." I'd like you to tell me how people got food before there were cities and then after there were cities. Then we'll continue down the chart. Ready?

	Before Cities	*In Cities*
Food		
Jobs		
Homes		
Transportation		

(The children complete the chart.)

Mr. Kurlak: To finish our lesson today, I would like to ask you to group yourselves by fives. Pretend that you are planning an ideal city of the future where all of our present problems would be solved. What are some of our present problems?

Children: Water . . . housing . . . pollution . . . too crowded . . .

Mr. Kurlak: Your special project is to spend time discussing ways to solve these problems for our ideal city. Choose the problem you would like to talk about and think of all the ways it could be solved.

SUMMARY

Learning can be accomplished in several ways. On one extreme we find teachers and children who are most comfortable in an environment that accommodates individual learning styles, small-group activities, and a great deal of self-direction and independence. At the other extreme are those teachers and children who require more structure to do their best work. They respond best to formalized lessons presented to the large group, preferably with a textbook as the core of the program.

There is room for both variations in a social studies program; the main idea to keep in mind is that whatever approach you choose, make sure it matches your personality, philosophy, and area of competence.

In presenting formalized lessons to the entire group from a textbook, teachers often follow the Directed Learning Episode format. Regardless of how creative you become within the context of directed teaching, there are approximately four steps you will take to assure adequate comprehension:

1. Introduce the lesson
   * Clarify word meanings
   * Relate past experiences to new material
   * Motivate the children to read
   * Establish clear purposes for reading
2. Read the selection silently
   * Observe the children to detect problems
   * Encourage variable reading rates
3. Teach comprehension skills
   * Use a questioning guide, such as Taba
   * Compose your own questions
   * Utilize visual organizing strategies
       webbing
       information retrieval charts
       guide-o-ramas
   * Respect children's own questions
4. Follow-up and extension activities
   * Special projects to extend learnings
   * Reinforcement activities to strengthen concepts

Some of you may look at all that is involved in developing a DLE instead of just teaching page-for-page from a textbook teacher's manual and say, "Why bother? After all, the manual was written by experts in the field who really know the social studies." To an extent, you are correct. Manuals can be very helpful, especially for student or beginning teachers. As guides, though, they must be viewed as suggestions, not as prescriptions. Do the experts in the field know your fifth-graders as well as you do? You will probably want to start your career by using the teacher's guide closely, but as you gain experience, adapt it to the changing needs of the different groups of children you will teach each year. The DLE allows you to constantly change your teaching ideas within a framework of sound planning.

ENDNOTES

1. R. Murray Thomas and Sherwin G. Swartout, *Integral Learning Materials* (New York: Longmans, Green, 1960), p. 1.

2. N. L. Gage, "Teaching Effectiveness: Give Us the Tools and We Will Do the Job," *Education Forum* (Boston: Houghton-Mifflin, Fall 1985), p. 2.

3. Roger Farr and Sam Weintraub, "Editorial: An Argument for Research," *Reading Research Quarterly* 9, no. 2 (1973–1974): pp. 131–132.

4. Hilda Taba, *Teacher's Handbook for Elementary Social Studies*, (Palo Alto, CA: Addison-Wesley, 1967).

5. Frank Smith, *Comprehension and Learning: A Conceptual Framework for Teachers* (New York: Holt, Rinehart and Winston, 1975), p. 92.

6. David P. Ausubel, "In Defense of Verbal Learning," *Educational Theory II*, no. 4 (January 1961), p. 16.

7. Frank Smith, *Understanding Reading: A Psycholinguistic Analysis of Reading and Learning to Read* (New York: Holt, Rinehart and Winston, 1982).

8. R. P. Carver, *Reading Comprehension and Reading Theory* (Springfield, IL: Charles C. Thomas, 1981).

9. Edward W. Dolch, *Psychology and Teaching of Reading* (Champaign, IL: Garrard Press, 1951), p. 309.

10. Albert J. Harris, *How to Increase Reading Ability* (New York: Longmans, Green, 1961), p. 409.

11. Mildred Fitzpatrick, in Miles V. Zintz, *The Reading Process* (Dubuque, IA: William C. Brown, 1970), p. 186.

12. L. T. Frase, "Purpose in Reading," in *Cognition, Curriculum, and Comprehension*, ed. J. T. Guthrie (Newark, DE: International Reading Association, 1977), pp. 42–64.

13. Benjamin S. Bloom, *Taxonomy of Educational Objectives: Handbook 1, Cognitive Domain* (New York: David McKay, 1956).

14. Richard K. Jantz, *Scott, Foresman Social Studies Book Three* (Glenview, IL: Scott, Foresman, 1979), p. 210.

15. Dolores Durkin, "What Classroom Observations Reveal About Reading Comprehension Instruction," *Reading Research Quarterly 24*, no. 4 (1978–79): 481–533.

16. John Dewey, *How We Think* (Boston: D. C. Heath, 1933).

17. Hilda Taba et al., *A Teacher's Handbook to Elementary Social Studies: An Inductive Approach* (Reading, MA: Addison-Wesley, 1971), p. 105.

18. John C. Manning, "What's Needed Now in Reading Instruction: The Teacher as Scholar and Romanticist," *The Reading Teacher*, 39, no. 2 (November 1985): p. 136.

19. Jack C. Morgan and Joan E. Schreiber, "How to Ask Questions," *How To Do It Series*, no. 24 (Washington, DC: National Council for the Social Studies, 1969), p. 2.

20. Glenn Freedman and Elizabeth G. Reynolds, "Enriching Basal Reader Lessons with Semantic Webbing," *The Reading Teacher*, 33, no. 6 (March 1980): 677–684.

21. Karen D. Wood and John A. Mateja, "Adapting Secondary Level Strategies for Use in Elementary Classrooms," *The Reading Teacher*, 36, no. 6 (February 1983), 492–496.

Working Effectively in Groups

KEY CONCEPTS

- ☐ *Understanding the importance of practicing democratic social behavior in the classroom as a prerequisite to group work in the social studies*

- ☐ *Identifying appropriate procedures and routines for starting group work in the social studies*

- ☐ *Using a wide range of flexible grouping programs in the social studies curriculum*

- ☐ *Perceiving how group projects contribute to the overall democratic principle of learning to work and share with others*

Much of school life seems to be built upon. . .isolation. For example, what are teachers teaching children when they call for recitations with the preface, "Now, Johnny, I want to hear what *you* have to say. Don't anybody else help him!" Homework is given out with the admonition: "Make sure it's your *own* work.". . .I realize that a purpose of this isolation is to enable the teacher to evaluate and rank her pupils. But every day? And at such a cost?[1]

Whole-class instruction is appropriate in the social studies—teachers routinely use instructional techniques such as textbook assignments, media presentations, guest speakers, or lectures with the entire group. Whole-class instruction is an efficient, effective form of teaching. Children can learn some important group work sensitivities in a whole-class setting. For example, when children watch a film or read a text assignment and discuss what they have found, they share ideas with one another by taking turns, listening attentively while others talk, and showing consideration for others. These skills are important to learn and help establish readiness for subsequent small-group responsibilities. Unfortunately, in many schools, whole-class instruction is the only pattern of social studies learning our children are exposed to, because some teachers perceive that classroom management problems are easier to control if children are taught in a formalized large group where they are physically separated from one another. If you choose whole-class instruction, do so because it is the best means to achieve a specific instructional goal, not because it is a convenient way to control the children.

We discussed specific uses of whole-class instruction in Chapter 3 as they relate to a DLE. In this chapter we will examine how teachers choose follow-up and independent activities that give children opportunities to plan together, to work toward common goals, and to interact with one another. These responsibilities foster many important instructional goals, not the least of which is to teach and practice democratic social behavior.

The classroom environment provides many direct opportunities for promoting democratic behavior. In attempting to democratize the classroom, teachers move children from childhood's natural passive dependence on authority toward personal responsibility and interdependence. Democratic classroom practices comprise only one of several effective ways to teach elementary school social studies, but the social studies program, with its many opportunities for group work, provides the most appropriate environment for teaching skills of democratic functioning. The two major stages through which groups move when a teacher plans to maximize democratic functioning are whole-group orientation and establishing responsibilities for group work.

Whole-Group Orientation. This stage involves changing a collection of individuals into a large classroom group. When children enter the classroom on the first day of school, they are full of many questions: What is going to happen here?

Who are these people? What are they like? How do I fit in? The whole-group orientation stage is comprised of a series of activities to help children understand what their new classroom system and environment will be like.

Establishing Responsibilities for Group Work. After a few weeks of orientation activities, children begin to develop basic concepts of democratic living. From there, you can diversify by helping children understand how members should act in small groups formed specifically for special instructional purposes.

Groups are important to all of us; as humans we are social beings who have a basic desire to belong to groups. It is not human nature to want to be alone. Babies are born into their first social group (the family); their personal attachments begin there and progressively increase as they explore and expand their relationships with others. Like the family, interaction with various groups influences personal identity, so the quality of one's life depends greatly upon personal group skills and knowledge of group processes. What is a group? Johnson and Johnson define a group as a "collection of persons who are in cooperative, face-to-face interaction, each aware of his or her own membership in the group, each aware of the others who belong in the group, and each getting some satisfaction from participating in the group's activities."[2] This chapter focuses on this concept of "group," a collection of children who join together in productive working units.

Productive groups just don't happen; they must be carefully orchestrated. Good groups require a skillful, patient teacher who understands that a variety of developmental hurdles must be conquered before a collection of individuals evolves into the entity we refer to as a "group." Although the use of small-group instruction involves some risks to classroom management, appropriate precautions and a sound transition from whole-class instruction ensure smooth movement into the flexible use of various instructional groups.

WHOLE-GROUP ORIENTATION

A major factor in establishing and maintaining effective groups in the social studies classroom is the children's and teacher's ability to get along pleasantly together. For both, this involves

- Developing a positive sense of self
- Understanding others
- Relating to each other positively
- Becoming comfortable and accepted in the classroom

Before children can begin to understand their roles in a new social group (the classroom), they must first acquire a positive sense of their own identities. They must feel good about themselves; only as children accept themselves as separate, unique, and worthwhile individuals can we expect them to enter into successful relationships with others. In the early grades, then, teachers must offer experiences that help children grow in self-confidence; those experiences begin on the very first day of school as teachers plan and organize the classroom environment for the children.

COMING TO SCHOOL

The first thing a child looks for in the classroom is *you*. Be at the door to welcome each child. Offer a cheerful hello and add something special as each child comes in: "I like your yellow shirt" or "You sure look ready for school today!" It is important for the child to be greeted by a warm and supportive teacher, for the initial impressions children have about their new classroom environment will be the lasting ones. Children will make further judgments about school as they walk into the classroom, so make it an inviting place by arranging bulletin boards, displays, and furniture in ways that show children the classroom is everyone's, not exclusively the teacher's. Is there a personal name tag on each child's desk? Are the seats arranged so the children can see each other, or are they all directed toward the teacher? Have you used dividers, screens, or bulletin boards to make the space inviting?

As the children enter the room, capitalize on their *names* to expand the development of self-concept and to create an understanding of the new social group. An excellent way to organize this part of your program is to choose a theme for introducing the children to each other. Before the first morning in a primary-grade classroom, you might, for example, decorate your room with pictures of popular, likable bears—teddy bears, Winnie-the-Pooh, Paddington, and Corduroy. Prepare simple bear-shaped name tags and arrange the tags, each not yet bearing a child's name, on a colorful bulletin board captioned, "A Beary Special Group." Introduce the children to a special bear puppet, "Bear the Magnificent. . .Beary for short." Have Beary greet the boys and girls with a nonthreatening roar and "Good morning boys and girls. I am so happy to see you today and you all look so nice. I was lonely without you. We'll have fun each day playing, talking, and learning." Then, making Beary appear startled, call his attention to the bulletin board on which all the blank name tags are displayed. "Good gracious," roars Beary. "I've never seen so many bears in my whole life! A wall full of bears that all look the same! Quickly, bears, tell me your names." Then, making Beary appear to be talking to one of the tags, say, "Please tell me your name." The bear tag should respond, "Teddy." Then repeat the request ("Please tell me your name") and the response ("Teddy") for five more bears, with Beary appearing more frustrated each time: "Hold it—this just won't do," says Beary. "Are you trying to play games with me?" The little tags reply, "No, we're telling the truth!" The teacher can then turn to the children and say, "We have an awful problem. We must have new names so we can tell who is who. I know! We can use each of *your* names. How does that sound, Beary?" Beary eagerly agrees, but then becomes puzzled: "But I don't know their names yet." The teacher then asks the children to introduce themselves individually to Beary as she writes each name on the tags. (Remember to use upper- and lowercase letters.) Then pin each tag on the child's shirt and say, "Now this is better. All of the bears have new names." Then, Beary can repeat his request ("Please tell me your name") to each child and the child can respond. Happily, Beary responds, "Now the school year can begin!"

After this introduction activity, you may want to play a short action game with the children, keeping the bear theme central. Tell the children that bears are lots of fun and that school will be fun this year, too. Ask Beary if he is happy to be in this classroom and have him respond cheerfully, then encourage the children to join you in the action song, "If You're Happy and You Know It" using these phrases: ". . .say roar, roar. . .clap your paws. . .do them both. . .!" You can expand on this aspect of individual understanding on subsequent days with these suggestions:

Sing the children's song "Thumbkin" and perform the actions with the youngsters. Repeat the song several times, inserting children's names:

Where is (*child's name*)?
Where is (*child's name*)?
There she is. (Child stands up)
There she is.
How are you today (*child's name*)?
Very well, I thank you. (Child bows)
Run away. (Child sits down)
Run away.

Construct a "talking book." Take a photograph of each child and mount them on separate pages. Begin a tape recorded narrative such as, "This is a picture of Caroline Montego." Invite the child to continue with information such as color of hair and eyes, age, home address, hobby, interests, and so on. Children will enjoy frequent replays of this book as they get to know one another.

Reserve a small area in the classroom for a "Me Display." Each week, let a different child take a turn making a bulletin board or other display about himself. Ask him to bring in pictures, toys, hobbies, or other things from home to show interests, skills, or other characteristics that help his classmates become aware of him as a unique individual.

Play the "Police Officer and Lost Child" game. Select one child to be a police officer and another child to be the parent of a lost child. The parent requests, "Police officer, please help me find my lost child." The police officer asks, "What does your child look like?" The "parent" then describes one of the children in class. When they identify which child the parent is describing, the parent becomes the police officer and the child becomes the parent.

From these and other introductory activities, you get to know the children and they get to know one another. As they gain initial confidence, children are eager to participate in other activities that help them understand their place in the group.

Birthdays

Part of the fun of going to school is the special recognition children get on their birthdays. Enhance that joy with a special bulletin board displayed on the first day of school. This display is valuable not only for the recognition it brings to children, but also for introducing them to the concept of days, months, and year. Cut construction paper to form the engine and cars of a train, making a car for each month.

FIGURE 4-1

Sample Birthday Chart for Primary-Grade Classrooms.

Print the names of the month above each car, insert a photo of each child in the windows, and print the birthdates below the pictures, as shown in Figure 4–1.

A highlight of the school year is the celebration of special days, but no party or occasion seems to bring as much excitement as the planning and execution of a birthday party. Most kindergarten or primary grade teachers set aside a special time during the day when the birthday child is allowed to share her special day with the others. Here are some suggestions for these special days:

Paint a chair with bright paint and decorate it; this "birthday chair" is for use by a child only on his birthday.

Make a crown from construction paper, decorate it, and label it with the child's name, date, and age. The child can wear it during the birthday party and take it home as a souvenir.

As a group, sing "Happy Birthday" and/or "For He's a Jolly Good Fellow" to the birthday child.

Classroom Helpers

Individual contributions to group welfare can be effectively demonstrated by assigning helpers for specific classroom duties. You can decide who the helpers should be on a daily or weekly basis, but make it a consistent part of the schedule. There are several ways to organize this facet of your program; the following suggestions may prove helpful for kindergarten and first-graders. All of them promote a sense of identity and of belonging to a group (see Figure 4–2).

Begin the year using concrete materials to indicate individual responsibilities. For example, you can place a child's photograph and a sponge next to each other on the "Our Helpers" bulletin board to indicate who is responsible for cleaning the

FIGURE 4–2

Classroom Helpers Bulletin Boards

table after snack. A straw and a photograph indicate the straw arranger, a photograph and napkin the napkin passer, and so on.

As the children begin to recognize their names, print them on "smile faces" and associate the smile faces with the labeled concrete object. A "Happy Helpers" bulletin board is an attractive way to organize the materials.

As a final stage in this developmental process, organize a special "Helping Hands" bulletin board, on which one hand is labeled with the classroom responsibility and the other with the name of the child assigned to it. To avoid disagreements as to whose turn it is to do what job, print the completed job on the back of the hand with a child's name.

Children enjoy assuming responsibility in the classroom and enthusiastically meet their tasks each day, especially if they are motivated by colorful charts or bulletin boards.

Attendance Charts

Charts that show who is present or absent each day help young children recognize that separate individuals comprise their group and help them learn to recognize each other's names.

Mount the children's photographs or small self-portraits on red construction-paper apples labeled with their names. Make a large apple tree from green and brown construction paper. As they arrive at school each day, the children find their apples and place them on the apple tree. During large-group time, the children can look at the chart to see who is absent.

Mount library book pockets on a bulletin board, each pocket illustrated with the child's photograph or self-portrait. Print each child's name on a card large enough so that the child's name can be read when the card is placed into the pocket. As the children come to school each day, they place their name cards into their corresponding library pocket.

To promote future graphing skills, make a series of cardboard dolls representing the boys and girls in the classroom. Label each doll with the children's names. As they enter the classroom, the children place their dolls in the "Here Today" row; when everyone has arrived, you take the absent children's dolls and place them in the "Absent Today" row. During group time, help the children count the number present, the number absent, the number of boys present, girls present, boys absent, or girls absent (see Figure 4–3).

Activities like these show young children they are valued and loved. The security that comes from a warm, accepting teacher gives young children the confidence to form relationships with others. Democratic classrooms must be firmly based upon a child's development of a positive sense of self. Without this clear perception, children will not see themselves as worthy persons capable of making personal deci-

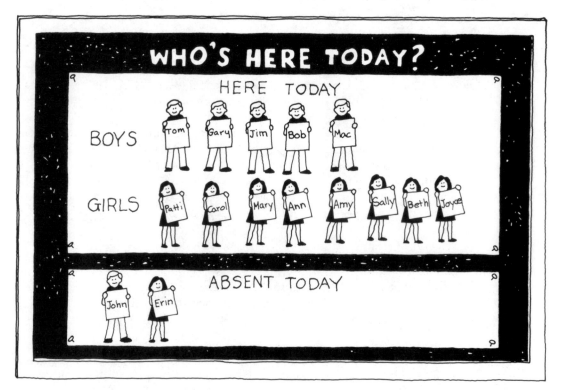

FIGURE 4–3
Attendance Chart

sions. Some teachers extend this informal personal and social aspect of their program by choosing from special programs for promoting self-confidence and social awareness. These programs are based on the premise that children must have opportunities to express personal feelings and participate in activities with others in an environment of acceptance. Two of the most popular programs are Magic Circle and DUSO.

THE MAGIC CIRCLE.   Uvaldo Palomares created a program for enhancing a child's ability to develop high self-esteem. This widely used *Magic Circle* program consists of fifteen- to twenty-minute sessions with groups of five or six or more children that encourage interaction and acceptance. The Magic Circle involves cuing, encouraging active listening, varying procedures, and feedback.

Cues. Sitting in a circle with seven or eight children, the teacher gives a cue and waits for a child to respond. Discussion cues are grouped into three categories:

1. *Awareness* cues are the teacher's requests for a child to describe "Something that made me feel bad" or "What I like about my pet."
2. *Mastery* cues call for the child to describe "Some things at school that I can do for myself" or "Something I was afraid to do but I did anyway" or "Some things I can't do for myself."

In a Magic Circle, teachers offer children a cue and encourage them to share their feelings about it.

3. *Social interaction* cues ask the children to talk about "A time we did something for each other" or "How I made someone feel good" or "Somebody did something that I didn't like."

Teacher encourages active listening. After a child talks about the subject of a cue, the teacher encourages active listening with questions such as "How did that make you feel?" or by paraphrasing a child's statement, such as, "When you were telling us about the lake, you mentioned how much you like to swim. You said it as if it made you very proud." As each child talks, the teacher looks at him calmly and nods, smiles, or uses other gestures to indicate interest. When each child finishes contributing, the teacher thanks him for his idea.

Teacher begins to vary the procedure. The teacher can vary the procedure by reviewing what each child has said when conversation slows, perhaps by saying, "Let's see where we've come. . ." and then asking if anyone in the group can review what was said. She can focus on similarities and differences by saying, "Jim said something that sounds like what Amy was saying. Who can tell us what it was?" She can also encourage shy children with an invitation such as "Jane, would you like a turn today?" But the teacher should not force children to speak.

Teacher leads a roundup. At this point, all the contributions are summarized and the feelings associated with each event are identified. The teacher may say, "Let's go back and tell what each person did" or "Who can feed back just the feeling?"

A teacher who is sensitive to the Magic Circle technique would plan sharing and discussion sessions like this one described by Mary Olsen:

Teacher:	Some words people use make us feel bad or make us feel happy. Different words make different people feel bad. I don't feel happy when someone calls me stupid. Did someone ever use words that made you feel bad or unhappy?
Billy:	My sister calls me "stinky."
Teacher:	How does that make you feel? (No response.)
Teacher:	Do you like to be called "stinky"?
Child:	No. It makes me feel bad.
Teacher:	Would someone else like to share a word?
Susan:	It makes me feel bad when someone says, "Shut up."
Teacher:	I know what you mean, it makes me feel angry when someone says "shut up" to me.
John:	Big boys say, "Get out of here."
Teacher:	How does that make you feel?
John:	I don't like it.
Susan:	My sister calls me "stupid."

Chris:	"You can't play." I don't like it when they say that.
Teacher:	I can tell by your voice that you feel hurt when someone won't let you play. Alice, you look like you have something to say.
Alice:	My brother calls me "puny." I don't like it.
Teacher:	It isn't a nice feeling inside when a brother calls you "puny." Did anyone ever say some words that made you feel happy? (Two children start to smile but don't respond verbally to the questions.)
Teacher:	I can tell that you're thinking of something that makes you happy because you're smiling.
Chris:	You get to ride a trike.
Teacher:	How would that make you feel?
Chris:	I'd say, "Goodie," and I'd tell everyone.
Susan:	(blurts out) I like you!
Teacher:	How does that make you feel when someone says, "I like you"?
Susan:	It makes me feel good.
Teacher:	It makes me feel happy when my son says to me, "Mom, that pie was delicious." John, what did someone say to make you feel good?
John:	Someone said, "You're nice."
Teacher:	How did that make you feel?
John:	I liked it.
Susan:	I like it when it's my birthday.
Teacher:	What do you like about your birthday?
Susan:	The presents make me happy.
Teacher:	(smiles and nods) I like presents, too. Words can make people feel happy or sad. Different words can make people feel happy or sad. I'm going to say something that might make you happy. I think you did a very nice job of sharing how you feel.[3]

In this example the teacher encourages the children to talk openly about their experiences and emotions. The Magic Circle guidelines were not rigidly or mechanically followed, but the teacher's active and friendly leadership helped the children to recognize and accept each other's feelings. The Magic Circle program, under the leadership of Palomares, has lesson plans and teacher's guides to help improve children's self-confidence and awareness. Complete teacher's guides and session formats can be obtained from: Human Development Training Institute, Inc., 7574 University Avenue, La Mesa, CA 92041.

THE DUSO KIT. Another source for self-awareness goals is the Developing Understanding of Self and Others (DUSO) Kit, a program of activities to help children understand social-emotional behavior. The materials, contained in a large metal carrying case, include:

1. Teacher's Manual—contains a wealth of activities and special guidelines for their use.

2. Storybooks—contain theme-centered stories designed to catch the children's imagination. Each 10″ × 12″ storybook contains forty-one stories and 200 full-color illustrations.

3. Records or cassettes—songs and stories are done in this form to heighten the children's interest. They contain the "Hey, Duso" and "So Long, Duso" songs that mark the beginning and ending of each story.

4. Posters—More than thirty posters are included with the kit. Each poster summarizes in pictorial form a major point from each story.

5. Puppets—Two puppets make up the central characters in the program, Duso and Flopsie. Duso is an understanding dolphin who helps lead children to a better understanding of behavior; Flopsie is an inquisitive flounder who provides a model for change. Other puppets are used in various ways.

6. Miscellaneous—Role playing situations and puppet plays help children dramatize real-life situations.

The program follows this cycle: A stimulating story presents a problem situation. The story is followed up by positive discussions. A role playing or puppet activity involves children in dramatizing a similar situation. The manual suggests several supplementary individual or group activities. For more information about the DUSO program, write to American Guidance Service, Inc., Publishers' Building, Circle Pines, MN 55014.

In choosing a program for your social studies curriculum, you must have a clear idea of just what you're after. In making your choice, I suggest you consider: What kind of individual do you want to help develop? What sorts of goals do you want for your personalization program? What kinds of learning activities will be available? What skills do you need to help your children develop? At what age should your program begin?

The First Day for Older Children

Older children require acceptance too, of course, but should be offered activities more suitable for their developmental needs, so you may need to vary their experiences. Here are suggestions for introductions on the first day of school.

Design posters with the twelve signs of the zodiac. Include the dates, characteristics, and a symbol for each. Hang the posters around the room. Give each child two large sheets of tagboard and two pieces of string. Punch holes in the tagboard and tie them together with string so they will hang over the children's shoulders like a sandwich board. Ask the children to divide each piece into three equal sections and number sections 1–3 on the front and 4–6 on the back. They then complete their sandwich boards by illustrating information for each segment:

What is your favorite school subject?

What do you enjoy most outside of school?

What is one personal characteristic of yours that you are most proud of?

What do you admire most in other people?

What is one thing you do very well?

What do you like to do with others?

When the boards are finished, the children gather near the posters bearing their astrological signs. While they are there, ask them to compare their boards with others. Are they somewhat alike? Which of their characteristics are like and unlike those on the posters? What did you learn about the others in your group?

You can have the children make a "This is Me" T-shirt collage. Pass out pieces of drawing paper cut into the shape of T-shirts. Ask the children to cut out from magazines pictures that show their interests, experiences, or favorite things and paste these clippings on the T-shirt shapes. Label each T-shirt with the child's name and attach it to an illustrated clothesline on a bulletin board captioned "We Hang Out in Mr. Robinson's Room."

The children will enjoy creating a classroom directory. Take individual photographs of all the members of your class. Mount the photographs in a booklet and label each. Ask the children to fill in data about themselves—family characteristics, address, phone number, hobbies, interests, abilities, favorites, and so on.

You can prepare a chart like the one in Figure 4–4 with the children's names listed down one side and categories of information across the top (hobbies, pets, etc.). Divide the class into groups and fill in the chart together. Take time to share responses and use the information for activities such as graphing or creative writing.

Children in the middle- and upper-elementary school grades enjoy the recognition associated with helpers' charts, birthdays, and other routines described for the early years, but you must adapt the classroom displays and patterns of interaction during the associated activity for the older child. One teacher led her children through the development of a classroom constitution as an experience in understanding the sophisticated relationship between individual and group responsibility.

Grade Six Constitution

We the students of Grade 6, Room 14, in order to form a more perfect class, do establish this *Constitution of the Sixth Grade.*

ARTICLE I. OFFICIALS
1. There will be two branches of our government: the *executive branch* and the *legislative branch.*
2. The executive branch is made up of the president, vice-president, secretary, and treasurer.
3. The legislative branch is made up of all the rest of the members of the class.

	COLOR OF EYES	COLOR OF HAIR	FAVORITE SONG	HOBBY	PET
MIKE					
JUDY					
STANLEY					
ROSE					
JEFF					
BRIAN					
MELISSA					
ELIZABETH					

FIGURE 4–4

Classroom Chart of Individual Class Members

4. Two candidates each for the offices of President, Vice-President, Secretary, and Treasurer shall be nominated the Friday before the third Monday of each month.
5. Election of officers shall take place the third Monday of every month by secret ballot.
6. A student may hold a term of office only once.

ARTICLE II. QUALIFICATIONS OF OFFICERS

1. Everyone automatically becomes a member of the legislative branch when he enters Room 14 as a student.
2. Students must have these qualifications to be an officer:
   a. must be a member of Room 14 for at least two weeks.
   b. must be honest and trustworthy.

ARTICLE III. DUTIES OF EXECUTIVE BRANCH

1. *President*
   a. The President shall run all class meetings.
   b. The President shall take charge of the class in the teacher's absence.
   c. The President shall help the substitute (show him or her where things are).
   d. The President shall appoint class helpers.
2. *Vice-President*
   a. The Vice-President shall help the President when necessary.
   b. In the absence of the President, the Vice-President shall take over.

3. *Secretary*
   a. The Secretary shall take notes at all class meetings.
   b. The Secretary shall take care of all class mail (letters, thank-you notes, etc.)
4. *Treasurer*
   a. The Treasurer shall take care of all class funds.

ARTICLE IV. DUTIES OF LEGISLATIVE BRANCH
1. To approve, by majority vote, class helper assignments.
2. To approve, by majority vote, any decision for which the class is responsible, including birthday celebrations, holiday parties, and so on.
3. To volunteer for class helper assignments:
   a. clean chalkboard
   b. feed fish
   c. water plants
   d. pass out papers
   e. take lunch count
   f. class librarian
   g. greet room visitors
   h. keep art materials orderly
   i. check attendance
   j. run errands
4. To approve, by two-thirds vote, any amendment to this constitution.

ARTICLE V. PRESIDENTIAL VACANCY
The Vice-President shall take over if the President's office is vacant, followed by the Secretary, and then the Treasurer.

ARTICLE VI. CLASS MEETINGS
Meetings shall be held each Friday from 2:30–3:00 p.m.

ARTICLE VII. AMENDMENTS
1. An amendment may be proposed by any member of the class.
2. An amendment must be approved by two-thirds vote of the legislative branch.

Amendments

AMENDMENT I.
An elected official shall temporarily give up any classroom helper jobs held during his or her term of office. (Approved: February 10)

Play, conversation, work, and other cooperative ventures within the normal daily routine help children develop group work skills and sensitivities from kindergarten throughout the elementary school years. Specific group work skills for the social studies program are more complex, however, and entail special skills other than those practiced during introductory situations. To describe specific group work skills for the social studies, then, let us assume that the children have never worked together formally in a subject-related situation, so we must first help them understand the nature and purpose of formal group work.

ESTABLISHING RESPONSIBILITIES FOR GROUP WORK

We must approach group work with children with patience and understanding, especially if they have never experienced activities of a cooperative nature. With proper encouragement and support, youngsters can be effectively led toward discovering the skills and developing the interest necessary for cooperating with others in a group setting. Ideally, they will master the skills of group behavior in practical ways by actually involving them in exemplary situations. To get an idea of good group membership, the children need to conceptualize how individual behaviors contribute to its effectiveness. Children must realize the importance of eliminating barriers to the accomplishment of group objectives and of solving problems with the highest quality of interaction among the members. Groups must be aware of certain responsibilities before they can expect to function effectively:

1. Groups must establish and understand their goals.
2. Members must not feel threatened while sharing their ideas and feelings with the group.
3. All members should share ideas and feelings accurately and clearly.
4. Leadership and participation should be equally shared.
5. Group responsibilities vary according to the group's purposes.
6. Conflicting solutions are to be encouraged because they promote creativity and decision making, but excessive competition and pressure should be avoided.
7. Group cohesion is important. Work toward a high level of acceptance and trust among group members.

Begin to demonstrate the dynamics of group interaction by putting children into situations that illustrate the value of cooperative responsibility. I use the following sequential game strategy to accomplish this goal; it is valuable at all grade levels in the elementary school prior to beginning any formal group work.

PUZZLE SQUARES.   Puzzle Squares, a simple nonverbal game, creates an environment for understanding the limitations of achieving a group goal when all communication is prohibited. As the children attempt to reach their goal without communication, you will observe reactions of anxiety, frustration, fear, aggression, hostility, and indifference. After the activity, you should discuss these feelings and their causes at length.

Materials

1. Cut out five heavy tagboard squares, each about five inches. It is advisable to begin with five because the recommended group size for elementary grades is four to seven members per group.
2. Cut each square into three segments following the patterns in Figure 4–5.
3. Scramble the fifteen pieces and put them into a large manila envelope.
4. Repeat the procedure for each set of five children in your classroom.

Goal

Each child in a group must use the puzzle pieces to complete a five-inch square consisting of only three pieces.

FIGURE 4–5

Patterns for Puzzle Squares

Procedure

1. Place children into groups of five and have them select a group leader.

2. Give each group leader an envelope containing fifteen puzzle pieces.

3. On signal, the group leader opens the envelope and randomly passes three puzzle pieces to each group member.

4. Students are directed to examine each of the puzzle pieces and try to make a square from them. Signal the students to begin. Allow approximately thirty to forty minutes of working time. If the students discover their segments will not form a perfect square, they may exchange pieces with other members of their group, but only under these rules:

   No talking. The game must be played in complete silence.

   No eye signals, hand signals, or gestures. Communication of any kind is discouraged.

   No taking of another puzzle piece from another player, unless he or she first offers it to you.

5. When the time is up and several puzzles have been completed, discuss questions of this type:

   How did you feel when you first started working with the group?

   Did you find it difficult to cooperate with others as you kept working?

   What were some of the problems that resulted from not being able to communicate?

   What feelings did you have toward the other members of your group? What made you feel that way?

   How would it help to be able to communicate with the others in your group?

   What are some ways you would have used to communicate with them?

   What would happen to our city, state, country, or world if people followed the same rules for communication that you had for your game?

You would be wise at this point to ask the children to think about and suggest any "rules" they feel would make their group projects effective experiences. Then, move to the second phase.

   THE DIRECTION GAME. After realizing the limitations of completing a task with no communication, children must be made aware that the communication process may present other special problems, especially when one person does most of the talking. Misunderstandings and conflicts may arise if one person dominates a conversation. A simple activity establishes this principle.

Materials

1. Use one piece of heavy 8½ × 11-inch paper for each group of four to six students.
2. On each piece, draw the design shown in Figure 4–6.
3. Give each child a blank piece of 8½ × 11-inch paper and a crayon or pencil.

Goal

Each child in a group must listen to directions and accurately copy the design.

Procedure

1. Form groups of four to six children each.
2. Direct each group to choose a leader. The leader's responsibility is to orally present directions for completing the design.
3. Give a blank paper and crayon or pencil to each of the other members of the group. Students should shield their papers from each other.
4. Direct the children to listen carefully to the leader's directions as they attempt to draw the design from the description. They must follow these rules.
   Only the leader may talk.
   Directions must relate to the figure only, and at no time should the leader tell the other children whether they are right or wrong.
   Only verbal communication is allowed. No hand signals or other specific guidance may be given.
   Members of the group may not ask questions.
5. Allow about fifteen to twenty minutes for completing this task.

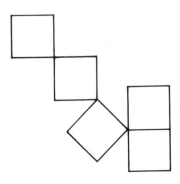

FIGURE 4–6
Design for the Direction Game

6. Ask questions patterned after those suggested for Puzzle Squares.

7. Present a second design to the class. Give the same directions, but this time, allow pupil dialogue.

8. Compare the accuracy of the first attempt to the second attempt, and ask the children to discuss why the second set was more precise.

This is a good time to extend the "rules" the children began to develop after they first discussed Puzzle Squares. Students will show greater insight into the mechanics of effective communication and cooperation after these direct experiences. If you really want to develop the concept of good communication and cooperation in groups, involve your students.

THE GOSSIP GAME. This game is designed to show that even when two-way communication is permitted, the level of an individual's involvement and interest affects the quality of communication within a group.

Materials

1. A short story containing many details that can be composed by a small group.

2. Tape recorder.

Goal

The children can see how stories change as they are heard and retold to other people.

Procedure

1. Select three or four students to leave the room for ten to fifteen minutes on a "special errand."

2. Have a group or the entire class secretly construct a short story full of many details and incidents. Copy it on paper for later reference.

3. Call one of the students back and have the story read to him. Tape record the reading.

4. After the student hears the story, the second student who left on the "special errand" is called back to the room and listens as the first student tells her the story as he heard it. Record this version also. The progression is repeated until all the pupils who have left the room are back and have recorded their versions of the changing story.

5. Play back all four taped versions of the story. The class listens to hear how each version varies from the way the story was written.

6. Discuss with the class why the original story changed as each individual told his or her version.

Now is an excellent time to encourage the children to suggest ways that classroom communication could be made more effective. Suggestions can be compiled and illustrated in a chart or bulletin board to refer to whenever difficulties in classroom communication arise, as in Figure 4–7.

For teachers interested in grouping children for specific social studies communication purposes, a variation of the Gossip Game technique may be appropriate. The same game procedure is followed, but instead of individually sending three or four students out of the classroom, send three *groups,* each group of the same number. After a story is constructed, bring each group back and have the students listen to the story. Then have each group decide how to retell the story. This can be an excellent transitional activity; the children can discuss the similarities of their "rules" for good discussion and the characteristics of good group work.

Now that the children have seen the characteristics of good group work, the teacher can initiate grouping techniques in the classroom. Chances for successful group work are enhanced when the children have been prepared for it.

When we initially guide children into group work specifically designed for the social studies, we must be sure to offer projects that do not involve complex responsibilities. Making an illustration, map, information retrieval chart, graph, model, or chart that organizes or represents material they have already studied helps the children build cohesiveness and moves them toward increasingly sophisticated group work skills. Such activities are often planned to follow guided, whole-class instruction. As the children establish suitable group behaviors, you can gradually offer them

OUR RULES FOR GOOD GROUP WORK

1. Talk clearly so others will understand.
2. Listen carefully when others speak.
3. Follow our leader's directions carefully.
4. Sometimes we may write what we want to say instead of talking to one another.
5. Cooperate with others to get the job done.
6. Take care of our work materials and supplies.
7. Respect the contributions of others.
8. Support ideas with good evidence.

FIGURE 4–7
Sample Group-Work Guidelines

more complex responsibilities: creating dramatic skits, organizing an antilittering campaign, designing a classroom flag, tackling an intense issue, or illustrating an aspect of life in the twenty-first century. These possibilities call for expression of different information or contrasting points of view about an idea, theme, or topic; therefore, greater cohesion and skilled work habits are necessary. Group work thus offers children the opportunity to process information or explore ideas in ways that otherwise would not be possible. And if we want to offer children opportunities to use thinking abilities higher than Bloom's comprehension level, we must engage them in appropriate processes, most of which involve group or individualized responsibilities.

Group work skills develop over an extended period of time through much practice. Working with others for special purposes is a developmental process that needs carefully sequenced experiences throughout the elementary school grades. Table 4–1 presents a suggested developmental plan. Beginning in the early grades, then, you will want to plan gradual transition from whole-class projects to coordinated small-group activities established for special purposes. Inherent in such a scheme is a gradual transformation of classroom space arrangements and work habits to encourage greater individual emphasis in the social studies program. Movable tables, desks, and chairs offer much flexibility. Figure 4–8 shows classroom arrangements for accommodating group projects. There are many variations of these examples, but the point is that the physical arrangement of the classroom should be such that children can easily discuss, share materials, and carry through projects in comfortable, stimulating work areas.

TABLE 4–1
Developmental Plan for Establishing Group Work Skills

EARLY GRADES		LATER GRADES
PHASE ONE	PHASE TWO	PHASE THREE
Short, one-day arrangement 5–6 children meet together to address a situation planned by teacher Sharing of group findings is informal, no established leadership	Two- or three-day arrangements, becoming somewhat more formal Chairperson is selected, organizes group and apportions tasks among members Various resources used to gather information, usually on a single topic Members report findings individually on the topic	Longer arrangements, up to two weeks Groups varied and flexible Chairperson selected to coordinate group's efforts Findings, from a variety of sources, are shared; one report planned as sharing project Planning throughout is done primarily by children; emphasis on self-activity

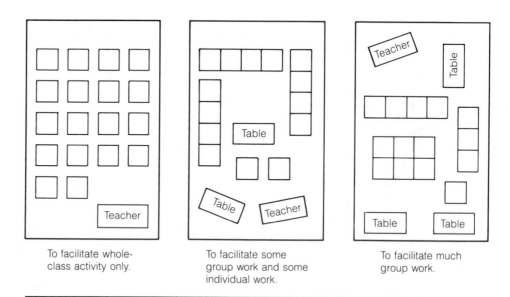

To facilitate whole-class activity only.

To facilitate some group work and some individual work.

To facilitate much group work.

FIGURE 4–8

Classroom Arrangements Designed to Accommodate Group Projects

Determining Group Membership

How group membership is determined depends upon the *needs of your children*. Good teachers constantly evaluate children throughout their learning experiences; they observe progress to determine whether changes should be made in the instructional program. These perceived needs are then translated into alternative instructional strategies. The *purpose* of grouping in one social studies program might be to provide children with opportunities to research and explore an area of interest the teacher has seen developing after the children watched a film on the caste system of India. Another program might group its children because of an observed need to summarize and deepen the children's understandings of the industrial countries of Western Europe. Social studies groups are thus determined on the basis of two interrelated factors: (1) observed needs and interests of the children in the classroom, and (2) the specified purposes for choosing the group work approach.

Burron and Claybaugh illustrated the relationship between these two grouping considerations by describing a large group of cattle and placing the reader in a situation where a rancher has asked him, as a beginning ranch hand, to divide the herd, on paper, into as many subgroups as possible according to what he considered the most logical order. (An example of a subgroup formed from the large group below might be "dairy cattle.") The reader's possible permanent employment is determined by how well he does the job. Try the problem:

On a certain ranch in eastern Colorado there is a large herd of cattle. Some of the cattle are males and some are females, some cattle can be found which do not give milk. A part of the herd is comprised of calves. The cattle in the herd are either black or brown. All of the cattle with horns are brown, but not all of the brown cattle have horns. A part of the herd is made up of dairy cattle; the other part of the herd is made up of beef cattle. The cattle in the herd are from Texas, Wyoming, and Colorado. Some of the cattle are fed hay, and some of the cattle are on green grass. Not all of the cattle from Colorado have eaten green grass.[4]

Purpose of Grouping

Regardless of the *characteristics* you selected for grouping the cattle, you cannot be sure you grouped them logically because you do not know the *purpose*, an important principle in grouping, that the rancher had in mind. Suppose, however, the rancher's major purpose was to separate the dairy cattle from the beef cattle. You would not have formed the final groups on the basis of sex, would you? Likewise, if you wish to supplement a textbook reading assignment by encouraging children to pursue special interests developed through the initial textbook exposure, you would group children according to common interests and not on the basis of some other characteristic, such as reading level. You *must* relate the subgroup membership to your primary purpose for establishing subgroups.

HOMOGENEOUS AND HETEROGENEOUS GROUPS. Any group in which members are selected on the basis of a common characteristic (such as interest) is a *homogeneous* group. In a group of hay fed cattle, for example, food is a common characteristic shared by all the group members, even though the group would include members with like characteristics (there may be many males and many females) and different characteristics (there may be some dairy cattle and some beef cattle). Likewise, even if you form subgroups according to *one* characteristic, each subgroup will still reflect other likenesses or differences. When there is no attempt to establish group membership on the basis of some common characteristic, we call it a *heterogeneous* group. So we can deduce that most groups are homogeneous only in reference to one common characteristic, and, for all other characteristics, the group is probably heterogeneous.

Since so many characteristics can be used to group youngsters for different social studies purposes, you should establish a variety of purposes for your teaching. As your purposes for teaching and needs of the children continually change, your groups should also change. In other words, effective grouping involves *flexibility*.

Interest Groups

Once the children have been adequately introduced to the topic, you may wish to form subgroups on the basis of common interests in a particular topic. Common interest binds the members together and creates a high level of motivation and self-direction. Generally, children who have similar interests in a subject come together and supplement the ideas found in their textbook by preparing a group project. One teacher, after using the DLE format to lead his class through textbook readings on various communities, decided that specialized group work would help establish the generalization that people work together to get things done. The following illustration describes how that teacher, Mr. Long, organized interest groups following textbook reading with his second graders.

First, the children read about different kinds of communities (urban, suburban, rural) and about the ways that people work together in communities to get things done. Mr. Long sensed a great deal of remaining interest in the topic and knew the children enjoyed working together on special projects dealing with social studies topics. So he planned a whole-class discussion about what projects the children might be interested in doing.

Melvin: We could build a model of our community showing where all the houses and buildings are.

Aneatra: I'd like to do a big painting to show how a large town gets its bread.

Robert: I've been collecting picures of people doing different jobs in the community. Could we make a bulletin board showing all the special community workers?

As the children contributed their ideas, Mr. Long wrote them on the chalkboard, guiding the whole group as they became involved in the process of *planning together*. Intermittently, Mr. Long reinforced ideas with supportive phrases such as, "I think that's a great idea" or "You're really cooking today." In this way, he not only received a great number of ideas, but he also encouraged the others to listen to the ideas as they were offered.

Mr. Long: We have some wonderful ideas here. I'm proud of the exciting projects you suggested. Now take a few minutes to think about the project you would most like to work on.

After allowing the children a short time to plan, Mr. Long listed children's names beneath each project title he had written on the board.

Mr. Long: How many of you would like to work on the model of our community? (and so on).

After all the interest groups were formed, they examined the room to decide where they would need to work. One group chose the large worktable for their community model; the group collecting pictures of communities pushed together a group of desks to form their work area near the large bulletin board; and the group planning the large painting decided to tape a large sheet of butcher paper to a blank wall along the back of the room. The next day, the groups planned their work and selected materials to begin their projects. They collected boxes, colored paper, scissors, paste, thumbtacks, old magazines, etc.

Mr. Long: Now that each group has organized itself and is ready to begin work, I'd like to have you think about using the next two social studies class periods to finish your projects. I'll walk around from group to group to help if you have any problems.

Mr. Long visited each group for a short period during this planning day to be satisfied that each boy or girl had a fair amount of work to do. He was pleased to see how the community model group divided itself even further into downtown, park, and residential subgroups. The work progressed satisfactorily as the children shared their ideas and tried to make each project successful. On the second day, however, an important problem surfaced within the community model group: the children from the residential area subgroup made their streets from white construction paper while the downtown subgroup chose black. When both parts were put together on the second day, the difference was apparent. The teacher asked both subgroups to talk to find out what could be done to solve their problem. Finally, after a short deliberation, the residential subgroup decided that "dark is more like what streets really are."

As with the community model group, the workers on the bulletin board group worked cooperatively to complete their project. They searched through magazines in the classroom and at home to find pictures that best illustrated the types of communities they read about in their textbooks. They cut out the pictures, mounted them with paste on colorful construction paper, and tacked them to the bulletin board. They worked well together combining their efforts and ideas.

Each of the other interest groups also worked together to complete their special projects. When they were completed, Mr. Long brought together the entire class and invited each interest group to share its results.

Mr. Long successfully used interest grouping for purposes directly related to textbook reading: (1) he helped reinforce the information presented by involving children in the projects, (2) he deepened the idea that things are done better when everyone works together and helps one another, whether in a community or a classroom, and (3) he provided a "hands-on" experience through which children are able to learn more readily and able to channel their creativity.

You should form *interest groups* according to these general criteria:

- Discuss the topic of study with the children to see what interests have developed (plan together).

- Invite the children to associate themselves with the group in which they have the most interest.

- Allow the groups to participate in a planning session where they can decide where they will work on their projects and what materials they will need.

- Give the groups enough time to complete their projects.

- Serve as a *facilitator* during the project work periods: be available to talk with children about special problems, offer suggestions, give verbal support, and so on.

- Bring together the entire class for each group to share the results of their efforts.

Research Groups

Grouping children for research on special topics is similar to interest grouping. Under research grouping, though, children are brought together to collect and organize information beyond their textbooks for the purpose of sharing it with others in oral or written reports, art or construction activity, creative skits, and so on. Research groups can also be formed when children become especially interested in studying a specific topic. Somewhat related to *inquiry* (Chapter 5), special research groups delve into supplementary materials to deepen their understanding of the general textbook information or to compare sources of information to judge whether the textbook was accurate in its interpretations.

Here is an example of one teacher's approach to grouping children for research purposes.

Ms. Javier led her fifth-grade children through several lessons from their textbook focusing on change within urban society. Yesterday, in this suburban schoolroom, the class read about and discussed how modern technology brought about new forms of city transportation—especially the role of automobiles in the rise of suburbs. To review yesterday's lesson, Ms. Javier asked this question:

Ms. Javier: How did new transportation technology affect life in the cities?

Beth: It gave people a chance to spread out and move to the suburbs.

Ms. Javier: That's good, Beth. The automobile, especially, meant that people could move to the suburbs if they wanted to. But we're facing a problem in our country today that makes it harder for people to live in the suburbs and causes many families to move back to the cities. Can anyone tell me what it is?

Russell: The high cost of gasoline. I hear my parents talking about it all the time.

Ms. Javier: Yes, Russell, you're correct. Let's keep in mind that gasoline is expensive but that some families would rather live in the suburbs than move back to the city. What could they do?

(Children give no response, but are obviously interested.)

Ms. Javier: Let's look at the map and find our community, Oakdale. Suppose you want to go from Oakdale to Stuart's Department Store in downtown Metropolia. Who will come to the map and find Oakdale. . .that's it, Juanita, keep your finger on the place. And now, we need someone to locate Stuart's in center city Metropolia. Very good, Robin. Now, Juanita, mark Oakdale with your red crayon and Robin, mark center city Metropolia with your green crayon. We must find out about traveling from Oakdale to Metropolia.

At this point, Ms. Javier established three research groups. Research Group 1's role was to study the large map to determine whether any public transportation was available for their trip. If so, the children were to name the various forms (train, bus, etc.), describe the routes, compare travel times of each with the automobile, examine the differences in cost, and decide which route they would take, evaluating advantages and disadvantages of each. Ms. Javier helped the children by providing brochures, timetables, and the like. Research Group 2's role was to design a survey questionnaire to use while interviewing citizens of Oakdale to determine what places in the city are traveled to most regularly and how the people get to those places. These are sample questions:

Oakdale Elementary School
Transportation Survey

1. Where do you go?   2. How do you get there?
   ☐ Park   ☐ Bus
   ☐ Movies   ☐ Car
   ☐ Shopping   ☐ Walking

The children were to tally their results to identify the means of transportation used *most often*. Research Group 3's role was to predict and hypothesize about future transportation innovations. The group was challenged to consider the current energy situation and to create new ways to travel from their suburban community, keeping in mind that all gasoline-powered vehicles would be banned for public transportation.

Each group was given three class periods to collect its data and plan a method of sharing them with their classmates. This type of sharing brought together all aspects of the problem examined by the children.

Research groups used with textbook study should be formed along these guidelines:

- Establish a firm foundation of information from the textbook.
- Create a puzzling dilemma related to the topic so the children will be motivated to explore ideas beyond the textbook.
- Group children to explore various phases of the dilemma.
- Supply research materials or encourage the children to uncover their own data through interviews and survey techniques.
- Allow the children ample time to complete their separate areas of research.
- Be available for each group during the research time. Talk with children, offer encouragement, stimulate thinking, and so on.
- Ask each group to share the results of its work with the rest of the class.

Ability Groups

Grouping children according to mastery of skills or understandings is a popular practice, especially for subjects such as reading or arithmetic. In social studies, ability groups are formed by dividing children into groups of somewhat equal ability in performing certain skills such as reading maps. Children who have been diagnosed as "better map readers" are placed in one group, and the others in one or more additional groups. The organization we often find in ability grouping is this:

1. Children who are ready for grade-level work.
2. Children whose ability exceeds grade-level work.
3. Children whose ability is much below grade-level expectations.

Because these children require different instruction as well as different materials, teachers often divide their classes into three groups whenever appropriate instructional goals dictate. This group plan gives the teacher a valuable framework upon which to develop meaningful, individualized instruction. Used properly, ability groups narrow the range of differences teachers face during any instructional period and help to focus on the needs of specific children.

Despite these advantages of ability grouping, there are serious objections to the way grouping methods are used. For example, once three ability groups are established at the beginning of the school year, there is rarely any change in composition of groups throughout the year. The "slow child" is quick to discover his place in class, as is the "superior child." Year-long membership in relative groups often stigmatizes the "slower" child and frequently develops a snobbishness in the "faster" child. Teachers often attempt to minimize such stereotypes by labeling ability groups with names like "Hummingbirds," "Bluebirds," and "Canaries," or "Steelers," "Cowboys," and "Rams," or "A," "B," and "C," or as one unempathetic teacher, "Roses," "Tulips," and "Weeds." Despite such attempts, children *always* find out what their classification is, causing the major objection to ability grouping. Another serious objection is the tendency of teachers to use the *same* books to cover the *same* material with the children, but at a quicker pace (with enrichment activities to take up the extra time) for the "faster" child and a slower pace for the "slow" learner.

When grouping on the basis of ability, the key idea to remember in preventing these shortcomings is *flexibility*. As we recall from Taylor's talent totem pole, children have different academically oriented characteristics and are above average in at least one. Therefore, if we are flexible in our reasons for grouping, we will find that a child may be in a low group for reading textbook assignments, but in a high group when designing a construction project, or vice versa. This point brings to mind a former sixth-grade student of mine named Robert, classified by all his previous teachers as "slow" and "disinterested." Predisposing Robert to a life as a dropout was incomprehensible to me, so I sought every avenue to get him interested in schoolwork and in school. How to do that with a fourteen-year-old sixth grader reading on a primer level? As it turned out, by involving Robert in projects where he experienced success rather than repeated failure, he soon began to become more spirited and involved in his work. Even though he had trouble with the "easiest" first-grade basal readers, Robert could read directions for construction activities and make things expertly—an outstanding craftsman. Assuming leadership in these kinds of social studies group projects brought great pride and joy to Robert while helping him win the respect and admiration of his classmates. Years after losing contact with Robert, after he left my classroom and I had left the school district, I returned to visit and saw this ad in a local newspaper: "Robert _____'s Construction Company." Asking around, I found that Robert now owned one of the most successful businesses in the area.

Of course, not all your "slow learners" will become as successful as Robert (and neither did mine), but should they not at least be given a chance to exploit their strengths rather than simply cope with their special needs? So, whenever you group for special needs in the social studies, keep the groups *flexible* and disband the group once the needs have been addressed.

Here is one teacher's approach to ability grouping:

Mrs. Grego consistently observed her fourth-grade children to evaluate their map reading abilities and to discover, at their earliest stages, any problems in this skill. She tabulated her information on a large class summary sheet and, on the basis of her information, developed special instructional groups.

Her summary sheet shows that Mrs. Grego could put Margaret and John (among others) into a group in which material for promoting skills in *reading cardinal directions* (north, south, east, and west) would be used. John, Theresa, Margaret, and Everett would be among those grouped for the purpose of reinforcing understandings of *map scale*, while David and Sara have indicated appropriate mastery of all necessary map reading skills and are ready for new, challenging encounters with enrichment activities. To facilitate success with appropriate materials, Mrs. Grego planned this activity for Group 1: Before being exposed to this direction reading activity, the entire class worked on points of direction in relation to the earth. In a series of outside lessons, the children's attention was called to the different positions of the sun at different times of the day until they understood the concept of east and west. North and south were established with a compass. Children played directional games such as "Simon says . . . girls take two steps south . . . boys turn to the east . . ." and so on. After these activities and some additional simple map work, Margaret and John still had difficulty reading directions on maps. To give them extra practice, Mrs. Grego prepared a "secret code map" which the two children were to follow until they found their special treat (Figure 4–9).

At the bicycle rack, John and Margaret found a note that read, "Go *east* to the sandbox. Read your next direction on the note in the pail." As the children went from location to location they were required to chart their course on the map Mrs. Grego provided. The last direction read, "You are here. The big

Longlake Elementary School
Class Summary Sheet

Student Name*	Recognizing Map Symbols	Locating Places	Reading Cardinal Directions	Understanding Map Scale	Reading Special Purpose Maps	Special Notes
Sara	✔	✔	✔	✔	✔	Plan enrichment project
Elnora	✔	✔	✔	✔	✔	
John	✔	✔				
Theresa	✔	✔	✔			
David	✔	✔	✔	✔	✔	Plan enrichment project
Margaret	✔	✔				
Everett	✔	✔	✔			

*Check indicates no need for special attention.

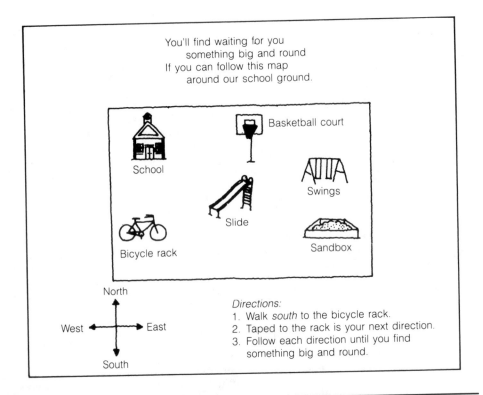

You'll find waiting for you
something big and round
If you can follow this map
around our school ground.

Basketball court

School

Swings

Slide

Bicycle rack

Sandbox

North

West ←→ East

South

Directions:
1. Walk *south* to the bicycle rack.
2. Taped to the rack is your next direction.
3. Follow each direction until you find
   something big and round.

FIGURE 4–9

Map Reading Activity

round surprise is a basketball hidden behind the basket support. You may each shoot baskets for three minutes." Mrs. Grego checked their "secret code maps" to see if the directions were correctly plotted.

Keeping direct involvement in mind for the other children, Mrs. Grego provided each of the other groups with activities designed to reinforce or extend important social studies map reading skills. Other skills areas within the social studies should be reinforced and extended similarly: specialized reading skills such as word recognition or comprehension, reading charts and graphs, or independent study skills.

When teachers use *ability groups* with textbooks, they should follow this basic format:

- Diagnose the special needs of your children.
- Group children on the basis of their needs.
- Disband the group once the needs are addressed.
- Establish a flexible grouping pattern.
- Be available for special help as each group works on its assignment.

Grouping children as a means to deal with individual differences can be a major contribution to the successful use of textbooks in the social studies program. Remember you must be flexible in your approach. A child may be in one group based on skills needs and in another organized for pursuing individual interests. A group experience must match its purpose, and the purpose is determined only after carefully observing the children.

Know your children well enough so that you can tell who are the most self-directed in their work. These should be the first to try a small-group project.

Start deliberately. Wait until you have established the appropriate rapport with and among the children.

Select a simple, well-defined task that the group can assuredly complete successfully.

Offer individual assignments for the rest of the class.

While the rest of the class is working, meet with the small group. Designate a leader and explain what learning resources the group members can use to complete their task.

Gradually introduce the small-group technique to one group at a time until the whole class is familiar with working that way. Acclimating the entire class to a pattern of small-group activity can take up to two months.

Since group work is to be as independent as possible, supervise only as needed. Be prepared to answer questions or redirect efforts, but resist the temptation to overdirect.

Evaluate group progress continually. As their work progresses, involve the children in class discussions about their abilities to follow group work standards. Keep a watchful eye on those who may not yet demonstrate an appropriate sense of responsibility. After you move these children into groups, it may be a mistake to remove them entirely for unacceptable behavior. You may want to cut back on the amount of time they spend in groups or even move the child to another group, but removing them eliminates the opportunity to learn the skills and behaviors they do not have.

Difficulties

Group work in the social studies can present a few difficulties at any grade level. Recognizing these problems will help you stop them before complicated situations arise.

INITIATING GROUPING. Children who have never participated in grouping activities do not understand the techniques. Therefore, you must promote understanding by introducing the children to the procedure they will follow.

CHILDREN'S READINESS FOR GROUP WORK. Remember that some children, especially in the early primary grades, will not have the maturity necessary for sharing responsibilities and getting along with the others. Functioning as a group member is a learning experience, so do not force someone into it until he has shown appropriate readiness. For the reluctant child, plan individual activities but constantly encourage group orientation.

DOMINATING THE GROUP.   Often, one or two children seem to take over the group. These youngsters are forceful in their wishes and feel secure in speaking their minds on every issue, expecting the others to follow their lead. You should not attempt to quench the spirit of these leaders even though their viewpoints do not conform to the majority. Instead, encourage all children to speak their minds and to arrive at a decision on the basis of one of these three methods:

Consensus   Perhaps the most appropriate technique for social studies groups, all members offer suggestions so that the group as a whole can agree on a common plan of action.

Compromise   This technique is a form of "give-and-take" where members of a group with sharply conflicting ideas each modify their positions so that agreement can be reached.

Voting   Perhaps the most popular decision-making process among children, this technique simply decides the direction of a group by moving toward the wishes of the majority of its members.

To illustrate how each of these techniques could be used to solve an impasse, consider the following:

A sixth-grade class, while building a model of a Navajo Indian village, argued over the shape of the Navajo houses, called *hogans*. Some said the shape of the hogan under construction was right; others argued that something was wrong. Naturally, the group decided to clear up the controversy by taking a *vote*. The vote ended up three to two in favor of the shape under construction, resulting in unhappy losers. The teacher joined the disagreement at this point and asked whether a satisfactory solution was arrived at through voting. "Nope," was the response, and further discussions ensued. The three children showed their teacher a picture of a crude brush and mud hut they had been using as their model. "But we saw other pictures of hogans showing much larger houses," argued the contenders. The teacher encouraged a library visit to relocate the picture, and the group agreed to wait until the skeptics could offer a *compromise*. Soon they returned, book in hand, ready to prove their point. Indeed, they found that the hogans under construction were from the primitive Navajo civilization, while the hogans—large, permanent structures of earth-covered logs—found by two children were from a more advanced Navajo civilization. After a short discussion, the group agreed that their model village should show both types of hogans, one labeled "primitive" and the other "advanced." So in a very short time, the children moved from *voting* to *compromise* to *consensus*.

You should encourage children to handle their own problems in group settings, but be near to furnish appropriate guidance. In this way, children not only learn about social studies content in their group work, but also get firsthand experience in the operation of a democratic system of decision making.

ACTIVITY-CENTERED INSTRUCTION

A fundamental purpose for grouping children in the social studies program is to provide opportunities for active, democratic, social exploration. Group skills are prerequisite to a comprehensive social studies program in which individual differences are accounted for and paths of thinking are open to all. Through development of effective group work skills, children move from a narrowly focused path toward acquiring concepts and competence (in which children do what they do because there is no other choice) toward a road of varied opportunities where the activity itself is a primary reward—where children do what they do because they *love* doing it.

Which type of motivation do we value for the citizen of the future? Obviously, the second; when children love what they are doing and choose to do it of their own accord, chances are they will try harder, learn more quickly, and meet responsibilities with greater initiative, imagination, and drive. Our future citizenry needs that spirit to be able to come up with new ideas and take a chance on using them.

An activity-centered curriculum is basic to developing citizens like these. Certainly, there are times when directed learning is necessary, but we must continually add new learning materials and novel learning approaches. Variety nurtures an openness to experience.

During the late 1960s and early 1970s, a drive to popularize activity-based, or informal education, for use in elementary school classrooms was led by Carl R. Rogers and John Holt. Rogers implored educators to redefine their major title as *facilitator* rather than *teacher*. He explained the differences in those two titles with his "mug and jug" theory:

> The teacher asks himself: "How can I make the mug hold still while I fill it from the jug with these facts which the curriculum planners and I regard as valuable?" The attitude of the facilitator has almost entirely to do with climate: "How can I create a psychological climate in which the child will feel free to be curious, will feel free to make mistakes, will feel free to learn from his environment, from fellow students, from me, from experience? How can I help him recapture the excitement of learning which was his in infancy?"[5]

Holt's perceptions of the learning environment were similar to Rogers's:

> We do not need to "motivate" children into learning by wheedling, bribing, or bullying. We do not need to keep picking away at their minds to make sure they are learning. What we need to do, and all we need to do, is bring as much of the world as we can into the school and the classroom; give children as much help and guidance as they need and ask for; listen respectfully when they feel like talking; and then get out of the way. We can trust them to do the rest.[6]

Characteristics

Informal education exemplifies a teacher's feeling that children learn most effectively when they have some say in how or what they will learn. Strategies emphasize learning as a *process*, not a *product*, that takes place in an environment reflecting these characteristics:

Respect for the children's right to pursue individual interests and activities

Provision for active exploration, manipulation, and physical action in the learning process

Encouragement of direct social contact with people whereby children acquire verbal knowledge from others

Realization that children learn efficiently when they proceed at their own pace and with their own learning style

Teacher attitude that learning should be exciting and enjoyable

Movement from teacher-directed learning to child-centered learning, with the teacher as a diagnostician, guide, arranger, and motivator

Teachers relinquish the role of authority figure and accept the role of facilitator. Teachers prepare the classroom environment with a rich variety of materials and allow children to choose activities freely with one another and to pursue any one activity for as long as they wish. A basic teaching strategy associated with informal learning is that of *problem solving* or *inquiry*, which we will examine fully in Chap-

TABLE 4-2
Comparison of Formal and Activity-Centered Classrooms

Teaching Considerations	Formal Instruction	Activity-Centered Instruction
Room arrangement	Assigned seating—usually desks in rows; movable furniture for other types of grouping	No assigned seating—variable patterns distributed throughout the room
Assignment of work	Large- or small-group instruction directed by the teacher; usually common assignments	Individualized or independent study with opportunities to choose what to do and when to do it
Classroom materials	Textbooks, workbooks, dittoes, worksheets; various supplementary activities	Books and materials of all kinds organized into thematic centers
Social interaction	Teacher controls discussions, usually the major form of interaction	Children are free to talk openly among themselves and with the teacher

ter 5. The inquiry approach encourages youngsters to ask questions and search for answers.

Besides problem-solving strategies, many action-oriented classrooms use a variety of learning centers. A learning center is any area in or out of the classroom in which children assume individual responsibility for their own learning. We will discuss social studies learning centers more comprehensively in Chapter 6, but for now, consider these points as you think about moving toward an activity-centered classroom.

1. If a teacher wants to emphasize individualized learning more than whole-group instruction—if she wants to change her role from instructor to facilitator—the arrangement of space must move away from the traditional room in which the teacher sits in front of the class and students sit in rows facing the teacher toward more flexible use of space in which children can learn individually in small groups and as a whole class.

2. If a teacher wants to emphasize self-initiated and self-directed learning rather than teacher-directed learning, books and materials must be readily accessible and plainly marked. The room must permit easy traffic flow and accommodate children who need quiet or solitude as well as those who work in groups.

3. If a teacher wants to promote active rather than passive learning, she needs an abundant supply of materials children can touch and manipulate.[7]

The major differences between formal instruction and informal instruction are shown in Table 4–2.

SUMMARY

Effective group work in the social studies does not happen by chance; it involves special skills that need to be learned through experience over a period of time. Teachers need patience and understanding to help children develop group work skills; it is not until third or fourth grade that some children are socially mature enough to handle it. For that reason, the early primary grades provide many "readiness" experiences: a social climate in which children develop a positive sense of self, learn to understand others, relate to each other, and become comfortable and accepted in the classroom. Effective classroom communication is easily fostered through programs such as the Magic Circle or DUSO and established classroom routines. Social learning activities (such as "Puzzle Squares," "The Direction Game," or "The Gossip Game") help children "try out" the roles of group members who work together to achieve a common goal. These direct learning aids help them construct their own guidelines for effective group membership. Eventually, the children learn to participate in special, flexible social studies groups such as whole-class groups, interest groups, research groups, or ability groups that promote interactions and democratic action. These behaviors are important for many reasons, but they especially contribute to successful use of special social studies instructional techniques involving action learning and independent inquiry or problem solving where children must work individually or in small groups.

Group situations are intermediate experiences for making the transition from formal to informal instruction. They reflect the teacher's sensitivity to individual differences by adjusting the instructional program to children's needs and interests. Group work as a supplement to large group instruction enhances the child's achievement potential.

ENDNOTES

1. Rachel M. Lauer, in Mary Greer and Bonnie Rubinstein, *Will the Real Teacher Please Stand Up?* (Pacific Palisades, CA: Goodyear, 1972), p. 144.

2. David W. Johnson and Frank P. Johnson, *Joining Together* (Englewood Cliffs, NJ: Prentice-Hall, 1975), p. 2.

3. Mary Olsen, "It Makes Me Feel Bad When You Call Me 'Stinky'," *Young Children* 26, no. 2 (December 1970): 120–21.

4. Arnold Burron and Amos L. Claybough, *Basic Concepts in Reading Instruction* (Columbus, OH: Charles E. Merrill, 1972), p. 81.

5. Carl R. Rogers, "Forget You Are A Teacher," in *Educational Psychology*, ed. Meredith D. Gall and Beatrice A. Ward (Boston: Little, Brown, 1974), p. 102.

6. John Holt, *How Children Learn* (New York: Pitman, 1967), pp. 185–89.

7. Charles E. Silberman, *The Open Classroom Reader* (New York: Vintage Books, 1973), p. xx.

5

Activity-Based Instruction: The Inquiry Process

KEY CONCEPTS

- ☐ Understanding the thinking skills associated with different types of inquiry

- ☐ Planning social studies learning experiences that involve children in the inquiry process

- ☐ Developing in children a spirit of curiosity and independent thought that initiates lifelong interest in searching for knowledge

- ☐ Respecting the many legitimate ways of learning and the many ways of thinking that an educated citizenry uses to address perplexing problems

> Teachers have always been somewhat ambivalent about what it is they do for a living. An excellent case in point concerns their conceptions of the human mind. For example, there is the type of teacher who believes he is in the lighting business. We may call him the Lamplighter. When he is asked what he is trying to do with his students, his reply is something like this: "I want to *illuminate* their minds, to allow some light to penetrate the darkness." Then there is the Gardener. He says, "I want to *cultivate* their minds, to fertilize them, so that the seeds I plant will flourish." . . .The Muscle Builder wants to strengthen flabby minds, and the Bucket Filler wants to fill them up.[1]

- determined by personality of teacher
- how the teacher was trained
- varies on each topic
"   "   "   child

How do *you* view the teaching process? Shall you scatter the seeds and apply the fertilizer? Or mold the child as a Sculptor would? Perhaps someone has advised you to become a Builder—to provide children with a firm foundation and steady framework. It is not my intention to poke fun at teaching with these metaphors, but think how often we stereotype teaching as something we do *to* children when we describe the learning process: a learned person (the teacher) dispensing answers (knowledge) to another person (the student). In reality, teaching is a multifaceted talent; one of the abilities it involves is to effectively, efficiently, and directly communicate information. But if *all* we do in the social studies classroom is to communicate information directly, we deny a basic educational principle: "Learning is something children must do for themselves." If children always sit and listen to someone tell them things, they eventually lose interest and motivation to learn how to learn by themselves.

SETTING THE SCENE FOR INQUIRY

At some point, you will need to move from standard methods (a Directed Learning Experience, for example) to new methods. Your observations will alert you that it is time to make changes—the children will seem restless, their projects and assignments less innovative. The need for change from directed learning toward inquiry comes sooner for children who have had *group experiences*, but two or three months into the school year will find children needing a change to more active learning, as shown in Figure 5–1.

One point to remember as you plan to make such a move is that children may outgrow the regular presentation of social studies content through the DLE, but *they do not outgrow their age.* They are still only two or three months older than they were at the start of school, so do not take anything away completely to start something new. If we accept the idea that children learn best through experiences, then we must involve them in transitional activities that will "feed in" more stimuli and help move them toward our ultimate goal of learning through inquiry. Introduce children slowly to any new pattern of instruction. Fisk and Lindgren warn that "the presence of any new element in a classroom is potentially distracting. . . .Introduc-

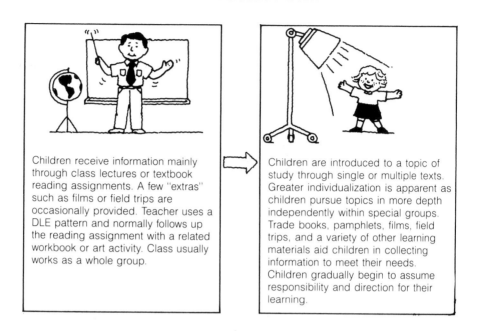

Children receive information mainly through class lectures or textbook reading assignments. A few "extras" such as films or field trips are occasionally provided. Teacher uses a DLE pattern and normally follows up the reading assignment with a related workbook or art activity. Class usually works as a whole group.

Children are introduced to a topic of study through single or multiple texts. Greater individualization is apparent as children pursue topics in more depth independently within special groups. Trade books, pamphlets, films, field trips, and a variety of other learning materials aid children in collecting information to meet their needs. Children gradually begin to assume responsibility and direction for their learning.

FIGURE 5–1

Movement from Directed Learning to Child-centered Instruction

ing a number of [new stimuli] all at once produces a situation in which the children's cognitive systems collapse under an 'overload of input,' as my computerized friends and colleagues would say."[2] Hurrying may result in a temporary collapse of classroom confidence, delays in progress, and reluctance to continue with the approach, so you will want to help children make an easy transition from directed learning to inquiry.

Spend time at the beginning of the school year with directed lessons. As a new teacher, these lessons help you "get your feet wet" and give you time to know your children.

When you notice the children's readiness to move on, begin to group for special purposes, as described in Chapter 4. One outcome of group-work projects is awareness of the process involved in completing learning-related tasks cooperatively. This outcome not only justifies group work in the social studies, but contributes to the children's motivation to work further with peers to solve unique problems. As the children are learning to work in groups, you will still utilize the DLE in some instances because you know it is not good to take everything away at once.

Because it is also not good to introduce everything new at once, make gradual additions to all-group and small-group activities. Exhibits, which Holman refers to as "mini-museums," stimulate children to ask questions. Whatever you call them, arrange daily exhibit areas in your classroom to surprise the children. Today's exhibit might be a ship's bell, origami, foreign coins, a butter churn, a cotton boll, shark's teeth, colonial tools, a tape recording of city sounds, or a sombrero. You can use the school resource center or ask parents for display items, but when they are placed in the "mini-museum," they are treated like exhibits in the best public, child-oriented museums—not with a "hands-off" policy, but one that invites touching and exploring. Good *pictures* also deepen interest in places or people the children are studying and stir them to ask more questions. Even kindergarten and first-grade children who cannot yet read words can read pictures. Exploit pictures as tools to encourage children to ask questions and to find new, more detailed information. Like a "mini-museum," the picture area can be decorated as a "Great Gallery." Finally, the *books* you make available for browsing as well as those you read to the children strengthen their real-life or school experiences and present new adventures that stimulate interests.

Children's natural curiosity must be allowed to surface in the classroom. By arranging opportunities for this to happen, you "inform" the children that you value and welcome their curiosity, which is a prerequisite to further inquiry. After arousing their curiosity, encourage children to tell what they already know about a topic

Displaying real things in the classroom stimulates children to express their natural curiosity.

on display—they will especially want to describe previous experiences. Then encourage them to express their ideas about the exhibit, picture, story, or whatever you have chosen by telling what they liked about the experience, asking questions, drawing a picture, putting a series of materials in correct sequential order, relating what they can remember about a story, or talking about the experience while the teacher records comments on an experience chart. All these activities stimulate a wish to discover new information and to describe what they find. The total process is a rudimentary form of inquiry, and a necessary initial step for further skill development.

Initially, it is up to the classroom teacher to bring in new materials to stimulate curiosity. One teacher, for example, brought in a stiff brush used by dog groomers and displayed it at her curiosity center. Almost instantly some of the more outgoing children began looking at it, touching it, and talking about what it might be. The teacher watched them and listened to their conversation, occasionally asking open-ended questions or making comments to encourage the children to talk and inquire more deeply about the item. One girl put the brush to her hair and tried to brush it. She was surprised to see just how stiff the bristles were. Naturally, the other children had to try, too.

Linda eventually identified the object. Her mother was a veterinarian and Linda often helped around the office. She was obviously thrilled to share her knowledge and experiences with her classmates. Interest in this one item led to several other social studies experiences: Linda's mother came to class to tell about her job; the children shared books about caring for animals; the teacher arranged a trip to the local SPCA; and the class explored recommended practices for animal care more deeply.

You can see from this example that it is a good idea to plan what you bring to your curiosity center rather than select items hit-or-miss. You want something to happen at the center—interests to grow and concepts to develop and strengthen as you extend the activity based on the children's comments and questions. The follow-up activities you arrange are limited only by your own imagination and resources.

Besides the curiosity center and related follow-up activities, what will help children practice the skills of inquiry? They must learn that scientists not only try to find out as much as they can about things that interest them, but must also keep records of their findings. Suppose you wish to interest your young scientists in a collection of seashells as a curiosity experience leading to further activities for studying the seashore as a geographic area. You might begin by inviting the children to explore the seashells and asking an open-ended question: ''What can you tell me about these seashells?'' The children will examine them closely to compare colors, shapes, textures, and sizes. You might ask them to make separate collections based on these and other criteria. The more ways you encourage them to separate the seashells, the more sophisticated their level of beginning inquiry will become. You will want to keep a record of the children's investigations: a simple graph can show how many items were classified into each group or an experience chart will summarize and record information. Children like to add to collections objects from home or things they find on the way to school. You may want to set up a special system of file cards like the one in Figure 5–2.

Depending on the children's ages, you may have to do the actual writing, but for the illustration, ask the child to trace the object and color it in. Recording information this way helps develop the more directed, purposeful observation and questioning techniques that are part of mature scientific inquiry.

These group- or individually-oriented "curiosity experiences" provide springboards for questions or comments that eventually serve as the key motivator for inquiry. During these experiences, stay attuned to the children's enthusiasm so you can seize upon their interests and move them into the inquiry technique itself. The beginning problem solvers will want to make significant learnings out of everything—a trip to the farm, a ride on a truck, a visit by a carpenter, cooking a pot of won-ton soup, or breaking a piñata. They seek new "happenings" and strive to unlock answers to all the questions these experiences stimulate. This is problem-solving or inquiry time, it is planning time, investigating time, organization-of-ideas time—when children use their energies, minds, and skills to seek answers to all that enthralls them. Figure 5–3 summarizes the transition process from directed learning to inquiry.

THE INQUIRY PROCESS

We often refer to programs that reflect the active, problem-solving nature of learning as inquiry approaches. Although there is no real consensus on a definition of

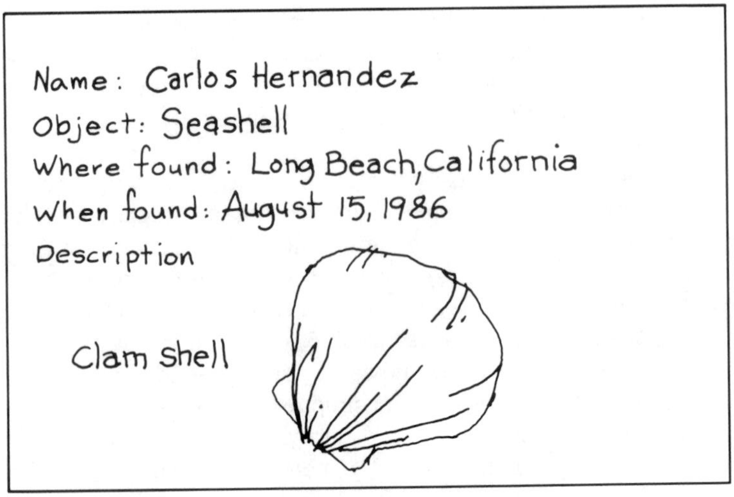

FIGURE 5–2
An Information File Card

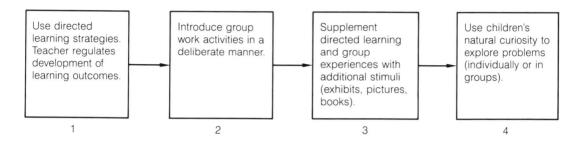

FIGURE 5–3

Transition from Directed Learning to Inquiry

inquiry, the teaching strategy has gained nearly unanimous approval among social studies educators. But when educators describe what they mean by inquiry, most of them offer an adaptation of John Dewey's model that was rejected, as you recall, as part of the "fads and frills" of the progressive education movement during the early part of the century. Essentially, Dewey's model contained four components: (1) awareness of the problem; (2) developing a hypothesis; (3) testing the hypothesis; and (4) developing conclusions.

Awareness of the Problem

Generate a meaningful problem for the children to solve. You usually need to arrange problems during the first few inquiry episodes, but with repeated experiences, children can define their own. The first problems need not be earth-shattering; developing the process of inquiry is an important learning outcome in itself. But the problem must hold a certain degree of mystery for the children to capture their interest. For the problem to be effective, we must also be aware of Bruner's advice that the problem "match" what the children already know. If the children are confronted with a problem with which they have little or no previous experience to associate, they often reject the problem because of its unfamiliarity. On the other hand, the problem should not be simply a unique opportunity for the children to "rehash" information they already know. Instead, the problem situation should be balanced between what children already know and that which is new to them. That balance seems to stimulate elementary school children's greatest need to explore and search for answers.

According to Dewey, this first step of the inquiry process is crucial; if children cannot accurately define a problem based on previous experiences or if they aren't sufficiently motivated to pursue it, the subsequent steps of the process are futile.

Developing a Hypothesis

Once children *know* what the problem is and *want* to pursue it, they must be led systematically and creatively to think about a solution. Assuming that we meet the criteria for selecting a problem, the teacher might ask: "What do you already know about these items? What have you already learned that we might be able to use now? How could this information help us come up with answers to our problems? What are some answers you can suggest based upon what we've just discussed?" The purpose of these questions is to help children associate information they already know and to encourage them to offer assumptions, or *hypotheses*, about the solution to their new problem. Formulating hypotheses involves a certain amount of risk to the child, so teachers must be especially careful to value individual contributions. Remember that these assumptions are, in most cases, nothing more than "predictions." Definitive solutions and opportunities to reject hypotheses arise when children become involved in carrying out their investigations and selecting the appropriate data that support or refute the hypotheses.

Testing Hypotheses

This step involves assigning group responsibilities and developing techniques of gathering information. Children must choose from a variety of sources to gather and organize information: books, magazines, resource people, original research, museums, pictures, films, filmstrips, and so on. The children check and recheck different sources of information as they organize their data in terms of relevance to the stated hypotheses. They must constantly ask themselves, "What do I know about the problem? Does what I know provide a good solution? What other information do I need?"

Developing Conclusions

In this phase, children are led to test hypotheses and formulate final conclusions. They classify and categorize their information to defend their hypotheses, then summarize their findings and share what they have found with their classmates. Popular sharing techniques include maps, charts, bulletin boards, drawings, oral reports, written reports, dramatic skits, replicas, and demonstrations.

Inquirers try to discover things in an orderly way; the procedures and skills they use are the *scientific method*. These are the steps of the scientific method:

1. Scientists observe and question something.
2. Scientists decide exactly what they want to find out. What is the problem?
3. Scientists recall what they already know about the problem.
4. Scientists develop hypotheses, or predictions, based upon their previous experience.
5. Scientists search for information to prove what they think is true. They compare and classify things that are alike.
6. Scientists organize their data, interpret it, and let others know the results.

Besides understanding the pattern of inquiry, we need to understand the range of mental abilities that come into play when we involve children in inquiry. In Chapter 3 we discussed Bloom's hierarchical thinking categories—knowledge, comprehension, application, analysis, synthesis, and evaluation. There is no evidence that we must lead children sequentially through all the steps before they can form meaningful opinions, but for the child to function at a higher level, all prerequisite skills must be accounted for.

CLOSED-ENDED INQUIRY

For the inquiry teacher, complex learning outcomes become associated with more advanced thinking abilities. Learning is something that logically involves a higher-level thinking skill; *using* information to solve a unique problem as exemplified by Bloom's *application* level. Suppose that a teacher has chosen to use a DLE format while reading a selection about the contributions of the assembly-line technique to American industry (see Figure 5–4). Her instructional goal may have been to deepen the children's concept of "division of labor" by examining the separate jobs necessary for production of certain goods in a factory. The resulting follow-up discussion would then consist of a series of questions in which the teacher might use the Taba approach, a personalized questioning strategy, a webbing technique, charting, or another information-processing activity for pulling knowledge together into meaningful thought categories (concepts). The teacher might then ask the children to draw a picture of the assembly-line process or encourage them to act it out as a follow-up activity. The basic goal of either of these activities is *comprehension* because the children must express *their understanding* of the concept of "division of labor" through the drawing or the skit, and the teacher evaluates the results of their efforts on this basis. Both activities, as appealing as they may be, do not require the children to do anything more with the content than represent it in some way.

Let us say the same teacher wanted to encourage higher-level thinking involving the same material. She is satisfied that the children have a good grasp of the "division of labor" concept, but wants to know if they can *apply* their understanding to new situations. In effect, can they solve new problems with the understandings they have just acquired? Just as teaching toward the comprehension level involves guiding the children through a unique process of concept development (the DLE and its components), the *application* level also involves a unique thinking process—a problem-solving or *inquiry process*. In short, to take full advantage of the thinking involved at the application level, we must *teach* the process of thought associated with that level. As we must *teach* comprehension rather than *test* it, we must also be reminded to *teach* application rather than test it. Since application-level thinking involves inquiry processes, Dewey's pattern of instruction is appropriate here. The "division of labor" teacher used this pattern by providing her children with construction paper dittoes, each of which depicted a section of a house to be constructed. Each child was to cut out each part of the house (roof, chimney, door, window), color it, and paste the sections together. After a specified time period, the number of completed houses was counted. The teacher then asked the children to speculate how they might improve their production. They analyzed the situation

From Woolen Mill to You

Mrs. Payne's class wanted to find out how wool from sheep is turned into cloth. Every child got a chance to turn a piece of raw wool into woven cloth.

Making woolen cloth in a mill is different in some ways from the way the children made theirs. First, woolen mills have big machines that do the carding, spinning, and weaving much faster than it can be done by hand. Second, different workers in a woolen mill work on different parts of the clothmaking job. One group of people works on the carding machines; another on the machines that spin the wool into yarn, and so on. This way the mill can produce goods much faster than if one person took one piece of wool through all the steps in clothmaking.

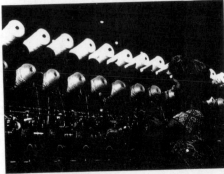

The people who work at the various jobs in a woolen mill are interdependent. And the mill itself is part of another interdependent **system.**

system, set of things or parts that make up a whole.

(Pictures from top to bottom) A carding machine at a South Carolina mill; spinning machines; weaving looms.

FIGURE 5–4

Sample Textbook Selection Dealing with Economics Concepts (From SCOTT, FORESMAN SOCIAL STUDIES, Book 3, Richard K. Jantz. Copyright © 1982, 1979 Scott, Foresman and Company. Reprinted by permission.)

based on their previous experiences, predicted a technique they thought would work, and found that assigning special workers to each of the cutting, coloring, and pasting jobs in assembly-line style would increase production twofold. The children applied concepts of the assembly line to a problem that required use of similar principles, but in a different context. What we look for in this category is whether children are able to transfer their learnings to new situations. To think successfully at this level, children must be able to predict and hypothesize, explain and support their predictions, and verify the predictions.

PREDICT AND HYPOTHESIZE. This thinking can best be done in response to a question such as, "What can be done to increase the number of houses produced?" Knowing the effects of division of labor on industry, children should be able to predict what might happen if the concept of mass production was applied to their construction project.

EXPLAIN AND SUPPORT PREDICTIONS. The children must be able to construct a chain of facts or processes that explain whether a prediction is valid. Questions such as, "What makes you think that would happen?" or "What would be needed for that to happen?" lead children to decide whether their explanations are sufficient. In the case of mass production, the children should know the processes involved and the conditions under which mass production is most beneficial to determine whether it would solve their immediate problem.

VERIFY THE PREDICTION. Children must verify that their proposed solution is the only possible, or best possible, answer. Questions such as, "Can someone offer a different solution to our problem?" or "What do you think will happen as a consequence of our choice?" lead the children to develop additional chains and offer divergent views to problem solution.

Application is the act of solving a problem that requires use of generalizations, facts, and other appropriate types of thinking. In the example of the house construction activity, the teacher decided it was best to put the children into a problem situation *after* she had led them through comprehension activities. This technique is *inductive* teaching. An inductive strategy arranges the sequence of learning so that it proceeds from the specific to the general, or from lower-level thought to higher. Other teachers who feel the thought processes of the application level are important may prefer to organize their instructional sequence in a *deductive* strategy, arranging experiences so that the children's thought processes evolve from the general to the specific, or from higher-level thought to lower. For example, the teacher might have presented the paper-house problem to the children *before* they saw the assembly line film, then asked them to make predictions based on their previous experiences. The children would then need to discover and analyze supporting evidence gathered from the film and other information sources to develop a solution to their unique problem. The goal of both methods is to encourage children to solve a problem through the inquiry process, but the content is handled differently. The teacher who uses the inductive method presents information directly to be sure the appropriate concepts are developed. This is the way directed lessons or textbook-based social studies programs extend inquiry experiences. The teacher who uses the deductive approach offers information sources and encourages children to discover their own supporting evidence.

Regardless of whether we choose an inductive or a deductive direction, whenever we challenge children to solve unique problems with specific, supportive evidence, we refer to *closed-ended inquiry*. It is closed-ended because the solution must be based upon application and analysis of concrete evidence, whether that evidence is organized by the teacher or acquired by the children themselves. Basically, then, teachers may choose to offer closed-ended inquiry episodes in either of two ways:

Inductive closed-ended inquiry
Teacher presents information and guides comprehension
Teacher presents unique problem or issue
Children analyze the information presented to them to determine how it can be applied to the problem
Children develop solutions and test them based upon their ability to apply the information

Deductive closed-ended inquiry
Teacher presents children with unique problem and encourages them to predict a solution based upon previous experiences
Children acquire information through various sources
Children choose and analyze information they need to solve the problem
Children propose and test solutions based upon the evidence they discover

OPEN-ENDED INQUIRY

A second type of inquiry is closely associated with Bloom's *synthesis* level. In *open-ended inquiry*, children are encouraged to develop their own ideas or solutions to problems. Before this stage, we primarily encourage *convergent thought*, in which solutions to problems are restricted to the content involved. On the synthesis level, however, we must recognize *divergent thought*. From our assembly line example, recall that it required children to solve a unique problem through the application of specific information. One could judge whether the children were functioning at the application level if they solved the problem by applying information about an assembly line as it is used in an automobile factory to their problem of constructing a greater number of houses. Some may consider that process creative, but it is not creative as defined by Bloom's taxonomy because the solution was not original. If the children had devised their *own* plan to produce more houses, we could consider their thinking to be creative. The line between the two categories is thin, but should nevertheless be addressed: in *application*, we judge "correctness" by whether previously learned information is used to solve a problem; in *synthesis*, we do not have a predetermined solution in mind. Because the outcome of open-ended and closed-ended inquiry is different, each involves slightly different guidance strategies.

GUIDING CLOSED-ENDED INQUIRY

As explained earlier, the way a problem is presented determines whether a closed-ended inquiry episode is inductive or deductive. The instruction sequence and teacher's and learners' roles vary with each alternative. Most teachers appear to prefer inductive closed-ended inquiry because it is efficient—it assumes a "readiness of the mind" necessary for attempting higher-level thinking. The method moves children from the path of a DLE to a particular problem situation in which they transfer concepts to new situations. This is the simplest problem-solving modification of regular textbook instruction; it requires only that the teacher adapt the textbook material by presenting a question or problem and then arranging for groups of children to explore solutions based on the content. It is an easy procedure to implement and could even be used as a transition phase from textbook-centered to inquiry-based programs.

Deductive closed-ended inquiry differs in that the strategy begins with a problem rather than the exposure to information. The children actively engage in gathering and working with data rather than having the data presented to them. The teacher does not systematically base the program on a textbook, but the textbook can be used like any other source of information in gathering data.

The Problem

In the process of inquiry, the teacher offers a unique, unfamiliar problem area to the children. The main concern is appeal—the children will not want to investigate something they do not care about. There are *two* basic ways to generate interest: (1) by asking a stimulating question or presenting a perplexing dilemma; or (2) by arranging the classroom environment and encouraging exploration of various pictures or objects in a display. The climate must be such that children are free to question and discuss the things in the display. Ask open-ended questions that encourage children to think, imagine, and explore. These questions do not require right or wrong answers and are not threatening to the child:

"What can you tell me about this?"

"What else can you do with that?"

"How do you suppose that is used?"

"What do you think those people are doing?"

"I wonder what will happen next. What do you think?"

These questions ask children to examine ordinary situations with a new perspective. With open-ended questions, teachers initiate the process of scientific inquiry.

From the initial spark provided by the question or display, the teacher calls the children together for further questioning and discussion. The teacher writes the questions on the chalkboard or a chart so the children can refer to them throughout their inquiry. From there, the teacher organizes the children into groups based on any of the criteria for group membership discussed in Chapter 4. After the groups are formed, the class is ready for action.

Solving the Problem

The groups need to understand that their task is to solve the problem and inform the class about their findings. What are possible sources of information for solving the problems? You should be fully prepared with answers to this question so the children will not be frustrated by a scarcity of resources. From the many sources of available information, the problem itself often dictates what is most appropriate. Teachers usually provide a number of suitable sources of information, including these:

Books	Guides and timetables	Music
Magazines	Reference books	Paintings
Encyclopedias	Trade books	Radio
Almanacs	Advertisements	Television
Catalogs	Posters	Records
Dictionaries	Guest speakers	Objects
Government publications	Field trips	Artifacts
Travel brochures	Filmstrips	Movies
Pamphlets	Slides	Museums
Atlases	Photographs	Natural environment

Before you provide any of these materials, be sure the children know how to use resources independently. In Table 5–1, Bush and Huebner contrast the independent study responsibilities children should be able to assume in doing their own research with the responsibilities teachers normally assume while leading children through the subject matter. During each work period you will need to check the children's success with independent study techniques.

When children attack problems and collect data, you must guide them through a thorough examination of the material so they can define and generalize accurately and objectively. Do this carefully and deliberately with questions such as these:

"What are some of the ways you've tried to find out about your problem?"

"How did you decide what to do to test your ideas?"

"Are there any other ways of testing that you might have tried?"

"How did you decide which ideas were correct?"

"Would you plan to do anything differently if we did this kind of lesson again?"

"How does your group feel about its findings? Are you satisfied?"

Children need to learn the skills for evaluating and extracting information from various sources:

- Identifying the main idea of a selection
- Selecting appropriate supporting data—major facts and details
- Recording relevant data
- Distinguishing between fact and opinion
- Comparing data from several sources looking for variations and inconsistencies
- Judging whether the data are useful or important

TABLE 5–1
Study Techniques

Effective study habits are developed when teachers . . .	*Independence in study techniques is achieved when students . . .*
1. Arouse curiosity by setting the stage with pictures, displays, visitors, and so on.	1. Turn naturally to reading to satisfy their curiosity, for pleasure, and so on.
2. Ask a motivating question to prepare children for a short reading selection (sentence, paragraph, or single page).	2. Ask themselves what they hope to learn from a reading selection; then concentrate on reading to find answers to the questions they themselves raise.
3. Relate the new lesson to children's experience or to previous lessons when applicable.	3. Note any relationships between the reading at hand and experience (personal or vicarious) that seem applicable.
4. Set a reading task that can be completed in an amount of time reasonable for the age and ability of the children.	4. Set a reasonable time for studying; then complete the task.
5. Raise additional questions to emphasize the main points, details, sequence of ideas, conclusions (if any).	5. Record in their own words the main ideas, supporting details, illustrations, conclusions, and so on.
6. Review at regular intervals for reinforcement to assure retention.	6. Review notes taken in step 5 immediately; review again before examinations, to aid retention.
7. Plan opportunities for students to use the information gained through reading (whenever possible).	7. Develop self-confidence through the use of information gained in reading; keep alert to situations in which new information may be put to use.
8. Alternate reading lessons with big muscle activity to prevent fatigue.	8. Develop psychologically varied approaches to homework—planning, spacing, and timing.
9. Make new sources available; encourage creativity.	9. Work on their own, or go beyond requirements in initiating a learning activity.

Reprinted with permission of Macmillan Publishing Co., Inc., from *Strategies for Reading in the Elementary School* by Clifford L. Bush and Mildred H. Huebner, p. 136. Copyright 1970 by Macmillan Publishing Co., Inc.

This phase of the problem-solving process, extracting and evaluating data, calls for the use of several higher-level skills. Perhaps the ultimate skill in the independent research process is to think critically. Children must check materials for bias, prejudice, opinions, accuracy, and logic. They begin to learn to ask questions such as: "Is the material relevant to what I am studying? Can the facts be verified? What are the writer's qualifications? Does the source seem to be omitting or suppressing any important facts? Are the statements expressions of facts or feelings? Should I revise my own ideas in light of what I have learned?"

As you move from group to group helping the children answer these questions, you will probably find yourself taking on the role of resource person, guide, or authority.

RESOURCE PERSON.   Children may often turn to you for help, especially when they have had limited experiences with inquiry. They may need someone to help them answer questions—"Where do you find material on seeds?" or "This book says the population of our state was 1,500,000 in 1980, but that magazine says 1,400,000. Which is right?" You may want to give direct help at times, but remember not to steer the process away from the children. Eventually you want children to make decisions themselves.

GUIDE.   As children search through information and begin to select the most suitable data for solving their problems, guide them toward some important considerations. For example, a common problem during inquiry episodes is a child's strong need to prove his predictions or hypotheses correct. Children often choose only data that supports their predictions; they tend to feel they have "failed" if their predictions prove wrong. Watch for situations that block good data collection and interpretation. If you discover a major problem, a short class discussion on how to find and use data may be helpful.

AUTHORITY.   If unresolved conflicts sometimes emerge, you must be on hand to furnish direct action. You must be especially aware of situations that impede positive group work, such as inability to work with others, failure to share ideas, or misuse of materials. The results of a group's efforts may well be determined by how the teacher diverts negative forces.

The importance of developing independent research to solve problems cannot be overestimated. Well-educated students are much like detectives; their minds are flexible, yet disciplined enough to search between the lines or to discern implications. Children need to learn several methods of original data collection.

DESCRIPTIVE RESEARCH

The purpose of descriptive research is to *describe* physical and social phenomena primarily through *observation*. The usual type of observation for descriptive research in elementary school classrooms is *direct observation*, as we discussed earlier in relation to "curiosity centers." When youngsters examine a chick breaking through a shell or look at an old photo album, they are using basic observational skills necessary for data collection. The observational experience itself, however, does not guarantee meaningful acquisition of the background information necessary for developing higher-order concepts and generalizations. Children need your skillful leadership and guiding questions or comments to help them gather and interpret data from the mysteries that confront them. With their relatively limited backgrounds of experience, young children often misinterpret new experiences. As Seefeldt says,

> Observing young children, talking to them, asking them questions about how they think engines work or why they think clouds move reveals to the adult the level of their scientific thinking. Often the children have misconceptions that need clarification and revision. They may believe, for example, that the

wind moves because it is happy or the shadows move to get out of their way. . . .Engines, air, the clouds, according to the young child, move because they want to. Often the young child's egocentricity influences his concepts: He may believe that the sun sets because he goes to bed or that the rain is falling because it does not want him to go outside.[3]

Skillful guidance can be an effective deterrent against formation of misconceptions when children observe new phenomena. You can guide their observations with questions like these:

"What do you see here?"

"How do you suppose it is used?"

"I wonder what would happen if. . . ."

"Let's try it again to see if the same thing happens."

"Is this like anything you've ever (used, seen, tried out) before?"

"How can we find out about. . .?"

"Maybe we can find out if we watch it carefully."

"What makes you think so?"

Some of these questions and comments help children look for specific things; others are more open-ended, to encourage higher thought processes such as predicting and discovering relationships. Through such experiences, children develop the rudimentary skills of scientific observation required for data collection in subsequent grades; your professional role continues to be that of guide as you stimulate thinking with questions like those above, but with adaptations to particular cultural items:

"Who do you think might use this?"

"Where do they live? What makes you think so?"

"What can you tell about the people who use this?"

"What do you think of the people who use this?"

Our goal during direct observation is to lead the children toward unbiased observations that result in clear, accurate descriptions. Your questions and comments lead to deeper observations, and the children discover and record evidence. The situation is described, and the research question is partly answered but open to further research.

Direct observation is not limited to examining *objects* brought into the classroom. Observing *people* and *processes,* such as how postal workers speed letters through the post office or how a craftsperson creates a patchwork quilt, also require guidance so that children can attach accurate meaning to their direct experiences. Likewise, pictures, artifacts, books, maps, paintings, slides, film, and hundreds of other sources of raw data call for intensive inquiry, as children find solutions to problems they consider important and interesting.

Observation of objects, people, or processes thus comprises one important segment of descriptive research for elementary school social studies programs. A second common descriptive research technique is the *interview*. In addition to observing the behavior of construction workers at a building site near the school, for example, the children might want to ask some questions of the workers to clarify some concepts. Children must use care in creating and asking questions that will give them the information they want; this mode of data collection requires skill and practice. Usually the interviewer determines a list of important questions to ask someone before the visit. Young children might decide they want to know how the back-hoe operator learns to do his job, for example. The teacher suggests arranging an interview, explaining that the children must first compose *specific questions* they want to ask. They would probably decide on something like this:

How did you learn to work the machine?

Where did you learn?

How long did it take?

What do you like about being a back-hoe operator?

Some teachers would ask the class to return to the construction site to interview the worker; others would invite the worker to school; still others might be able to encourage children to seek information by using telephones in the classroom. Whatever the approach, you *must* arrange for the children to carefully compose a sequence of questions as part of the interview so they can gather and record pertinent information. In the upper grades, teachers stress the process of composing good interview questions and structuring the interview, but with different content. Here is an upper-grade example:

''What is fifth grade like in France?''

''What do the boys and girls study?''

''What do the boys and girls do after school?''

''What kind of music, TV, or movies do they like best?''

Interviewing as a way of seeking information personalizes the social studies program and involves children in making decisions about what they learn. To be successful, however, teachers carefully guide the children in composing the questions they need to gather the necessary data for successful inquiry.

SURVEY RESEARCH

Surveys are a means of gathering information about the attitudes, opinions, or preferences of any particular group of people. Suppose children want to find out which lunch menu is most popular in their elementary school and which is least popular. They know they could *observe* the lunchroom each day for a week or so to gather their information, but they decide that process would take too long. Their teacher leads them into conducting a survey by asking them to make some predictions (hypotheses) about what they might find. A few predictions might be:

1. Pizza is the most popular lunch.
2. Boys like pizza best; girls like hamburgers best.
3. Goulash is the least favorite lunch.

After constructing the hypotheses, the children must construct the opinion survey. The questions must be precise so they will yield the exact information we want from the survey. A question such as, "What do you think of the lunches served in the lunchroom?" is too vague and would cause difficulty in categorizing the responses. On the other hand, "What is your favorite lunch served in the lunchroom?" and "What is your least favorite lunch served in the lunchroom?" target the responses and make the information easy to record. Once the questions are determined, the actual survey sheet must be constructed. Have the children write the lunches that are served most often in the lunchroom at the top of each column, as shown in Figure 5–5.

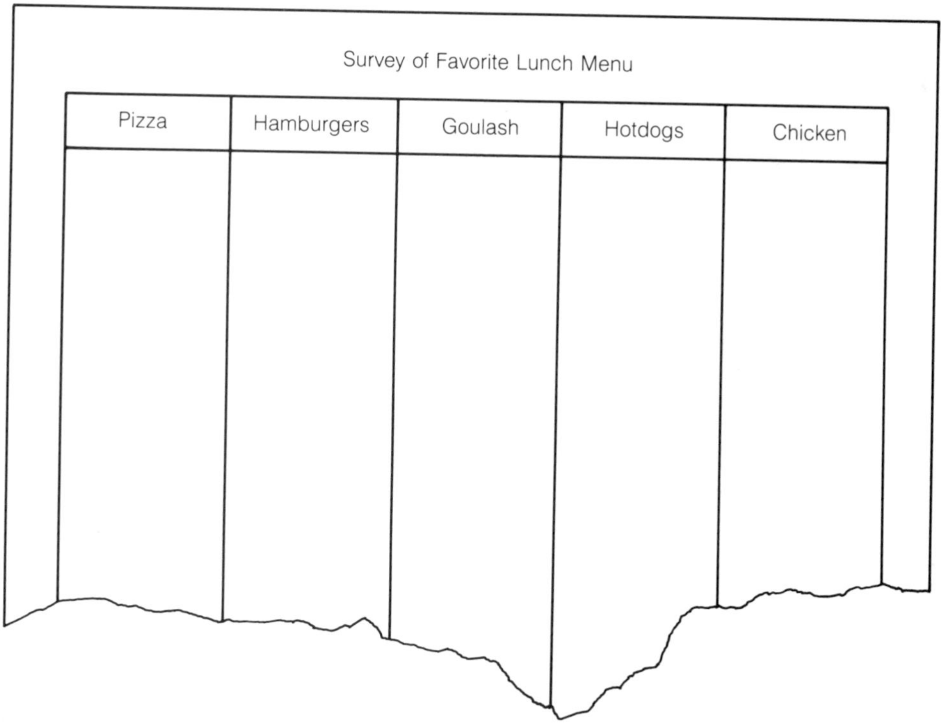

Survey of Favorite Lunch Menu				
Pizza	Hamburgers	Goulash	Hotdogs	Chicken

FIGURE 5–5
Sample Survey Sheet

After they construct the survey sheet, the children must decide who to interview to gather their data. Do they need to ask every child in school to develop valid conclusions? Most surveys utilize some type of *sampling method*. They might choose to interview every third student who goes through the lunch line; if they want a boy/girl representation, they might ask every third boy, every third girl, and so on. If the school has 300 students, they may choose to randomly select any 30 students. Whatever the choice, the children must be sure to provide "fairness" in selecting the sample. As each child interviews someone, she indicates the response by making a mark or signing a name in the appropriate column of the survey sheet.

When the surveys are completed, the children tally the responses and organize the data. They will count the responses in each survey category and, typically, record and communicate the findings on a bar graph. Young children may need to use blocks to make a concrete representation of the information (see Chapter 10), but older children can use a summary sheet to record results. Figure 5-6 shows a summary graph on which the children used a different-colored crayon for each column.

When they have recorded the information, the children must examine and analyze the data to draw accurate conclusions. Naturally, you don't impose a chi-square analysis on the children, or establish means, medians, and modes, or compute prob-

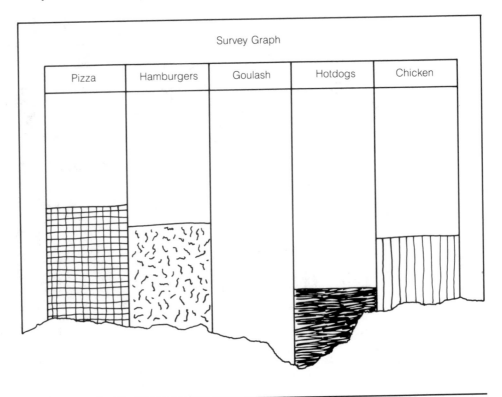

FIGURE 5-6
Sample Survey Graph

abilities, but you do want them to interpret the accuracy of their hypotheses on the basis of the recorded information. The findings of the lunchroom survey might include these *interpretations:*

1. Most of the children like pizza for lunch.
2. No one likes goulash best.
3. Few people like hot dogs best.

Each of the social science disciplines offers areas for survey research; for example:

What are the different religions in our class?

Should a shopping center be built near our school?

What form of exchange (credit card, cash, check) do our parents use most often?

What do our parents think of the nation's defense plans?

From what countries did our ancestors emigrate?

What is the most requested birthday present by fourth graders?

What kinds of books are most popular among the boys? The girls? Primary-grade children? Upper-grade children?

What is the most popular school subject?

The steps of the survey process are essentially the same at all grade levels; the teacher need only simplify the kind of problem and some aspects of the process (graphing, for example) for the younger or inexperienced child. The basic survey pattern includes these steps:

1. Predict or hypothesize
2. Write the questions and design the questionnaire
3. Determine a sampling method and administer the questionnaire
4. Organize the data
5. Analyze the data and form conclusions

HISTORICAL RESEARCH

Historical research is the attempt to explain the past by sifting through old documents, diaries, books, letters, and the like to search for answers to questions. This is a highly complex activity; the ability to acquire precise information from those sources is difficult in itself, and the skill of drawing inferences and conclusions is more so, even for professional social scientists. It is hard to imagine first- or second-graders meaningfully engrossed in historical research, but an emerging sense of historical inquiry can begin there, giving youngsters the realization that history is exciting.

Conducting their own historical research gives children a taste of how actual historians collect and interpret data.

Concept of Time

Basic to the study of history in elementary school classrooms is an understanding of the concept of time. Beginning with primary-graders, listen for evidence of time-related comments: "I learned to roller-skate today, and I couldn't do that a long time ago when I was little!" "My new shoes are one size bigger than last time."

Young children often face rapid changes in their lives. Although change is exciting, children are often confused when trying to place less personal occurrences into an organized time frame, such as, "It is time to go outdoors." "It's Washington's Birthday." "I'll tell you a story in just five minutes." How long is five minutes to a five-, six-, or seven-year-old? It might be a fleeting moment spent outdoors during recess or an eternity waiting in line to get a physical from the school doctor. How long is an hour, a day, a month, or a year to a child?

Time concepts are interesting and challenging to children, but difficult to teach. Most time concepts, beyond those normally taught with clocks and calendars, are taught within the context of history—events that happened in the past.

I've found that children are eager to learn about the past, providing their learning activities are concrete and meaningful. Children must be led to discover that the consequence and evidence of the passage of time is *change*. Seasons change, friends change, clothes change, weather changes, and skills and capabilities change. Focusing children's attention on these natural events will help them discover how change affects everyone. Personal changes like shedding a baby tooth or needing stronger eyeglasses are excellent opportunities to talk informally with children about physical changes that accompany the passage of time. Help children focus on other changes in their physical appearance by introducing simple comparisons. Ask parents to send their children's baby pictures, and have the children compare their appearances then and now. Have children bring their baby clothes, examine the clothes, and discuss why they do not wear similar clothing now. Compare baby food with food the children eat now. Keep a growth record on one classroom wall and mark the children's heights at the beginning, middle, and end of the school year. At the start of the year, when you first mark the children's heights, ask them to predict what their height will be at the end of the year. Record their predictions. At the end of the year, ask the children, "Did you grow as much as you thought? Why? Why not?"

Seasonal changes are the most obvious changes to talk about. When children notice the leaves turning red, ask, "Do you remember what color the leaves were in the summer? What will happen to the leaves in the winter?" Explore how seasonal changes affect clothing, plants, weather, and animals.

Emphasize that change can be regular, sudden, or unplanned—"If it's raining out, we'll have to play indoors" or "Jimmy has gone on a trip with his family and won't be back in school until next week." Comments like these help children learn that changes occur constantly whether or not we anticipate them.

The following activity helps students become familiar with the concept of passing time and the changes time brings. During the first week of school in September, have the children decorate a large box as a "Time Capsule." Discuss the concept of a time capsule and then follow with this series of activities:

1. Separate the children into three groups—tall, medium, and short—and take individual photos of the groups.

2. Have the children complete these individual tasks: writing their names, addresses, and phone numbers in their best handwriting; doing the "hardest" math problem they know how to do; spelling the hardest word they can spell; drawing a sample of their best art work; tracing their hands and feet on drawing paper.

3. Ask the children to write their answers to several of these questions on separate sheets of paper:
   - What is your favorite color?
   - What is your favorite food?

- Who is your best friend?
- What is your favorite TV show?
- What singer or singing group do you like best?
- What animal is your favorite pet?
- What is your favorite subject in school?
- What is your favorite free-time activity?
- If you could go anywhere in the world, where would it be?
- Of all the people in the world, who do you admire most?
- What is the one present you would like most for Christmas?
- What is your favorite sport?
- What do you like best about school?
- Do you ever cook? What is the best thing you ever made?
- What is one thing you are really good at doing?
- What time do you go to bed?
- Do you like school?
- Did you ever write a love note to a girl/boy?

4. Gather each child's work in separate manila envelopes, and have them sign their envelopes, seal them, and place them in the time capsule. Place the capsule somewhere obvious in the room and do not open it until the last week of school.

5. Repeat the first three activities during the last week of school. Have the children open the time capsule and lead them in comparing their initial work with their end-of-year work.

Children will react to the time capsule experiment in varying and exciting ways. Most will be amazed at how much they've grown physically or how much better they've become at math or spelling. There will also be discussions about who's missing from the capsule (newcomers to the class won't be in the original photo).

I remember one youngster looked at his work from the beginning of the year, crumpled it in his hands, and shouted, "This isn't mine. I was better than this before!" For some children change represents progress, for others it does not. Regardless, change surrounds children, and they should be led to an understanding that change is not something to fear.

Throughout the year, while you and your class wait to open the time capsule, provide other experiences that illustrate how things change with the passage of time.

Invite resource persons, especially senior citizens, to come to school to tell stories, share realia, or demonstrate skills that were important in the past.

Bring in objects from the past—butter churns, toys, clothes—and build an interest center around them. Encourage the class to manipulate the objects and discuss them.

Take a field trip to a local museum or an old building where children can observe things as they were long ago. Of course, the youngsters cannot completely comprehend the time period in which the objects were most commonly used, but they will be able to compare the use of objects with their newer versions.

Read or tell children stories of events that occurred long ago so they will learn about games of the past, occupations, jobs, challenges, and accomplishments.

Develop a scrapbook of the school year. Place photos, souvenirs from field trips, samples of work from special projects, and other materials in the book. Save the scrapbooks from year to year so that succeeding groups of children can compare scrapbooks from the past to their own.

Arrange a drama center with materials representative of the past. Encourage the children to use the items—long dresses, old tools, lanterns, and other historical artifacts—in their creative play.

Investigate games and activities that help children understand how youngsters played in the past. Jump-rope chants provide a real window into the past.

> House to let, inquire within
> Lady put out for drinking gin
> If she promises to drink no more
> Here's the key to her back door.

You can make the concept of time an exciting experience for young children by showing them that changing and growing are all a wonderful part of being alive.

History as Experience

As children mature and progress through the elementary grades, teachers must be careful to maintain the philosophy of history as experience rather than as facts. Events are bound by the child's experience—historical time is remote and unreal even for upper-elementary youngsters. We must constantly remember that historical "consciousness" does not develop for many individuals until nearly adulthood and is found only in rudimentary form in the elementary years. Jenkins and Shacter tell us that during the elementary years, children's concepts of historical time are usually limited to an understanding about days and months and years, and they are trying to relate themselves to a past and a future.[4] They show an interest in things that happened "long ago," although they are often extremely confused about just when events occurred. They may think that grandmother lived in the time of the Pilgrims, that she used a spinning wheel, and was afraid of Indians. But at least they realize there was a past in which people lived and did things. Upper-grade elementary children should be led to an awareness of the power of history in their own lives and of *themselves* as historical beings.

Biographies

Perhaps the most appropriate place to begin a search into the past is with the children themselves. After discussing the concept of *biographies* with her fifth-grade class, one teacher paired off the children and asked each to write the other's biography. Naturally, the children began asking each other questions that took them way into the past: "Where were you born? Did you always live in this town? Where are your grandparents? What do you remember about when you first went to school?" The teacher asked the children to bring old photographs to illustrate the biographies;

if children were not allowed to bring photographs, drawings were made. The result was a library of "historical biographies" that provided a year's worth of happy reading. This project provided a surprise for the teacher as the children became interested in moving from their biographies to the study of other cultures. One child from Vietnam stimulated initial interest and motivated other children to learn about the richness of Vietnamese culture, Vietnamese immigration into the United States, and the political events that shaped Vietnam.

Oral History

Oral history is often an interesting way to remove the remoteness of many historical concepts. Invite individuals, especially senior citizens, to spin tales of the old days. Don't be too surprised if those "old days" are all too clear to you, for the children will certainly consider things you grew up with to be old-fashioned. These items, for example, are real in my memory. How about you?

Lassie (or Uncle Miltie or Howdy Doody) on television

Green desk blotters with leather triangles on all four corners

Burma Shave road signs

Charm bracelets

Drugstores with a soda fountain

If these items are not familiar to you, you probably consider them "old-fashioned." They might be more interesting, however, if I were to share some of my experiences with them the way Mrs. Frazer, seventy-four years old, interested children in turn-of-the-century life. "When we got automobiles around here, you couldn't use them in the winter," Mrs. Frazer said. "My father had one of the first cars in town. It was one of those open cars with leather seats and brass lamps. I'll never forget one Sunday; we had eleven flats!"

Mrs. Frazer had the children in awe when she told what a dollar would buy in 1939: one dozen eggs, a loaf of bread, a pound of butter, and a half-pound of bacon. She also told the children about a whistle-stop campaign during which Teddy Roosevelt visited town in 1912 ("I can see him to this day") and the transfer of the Liberty Bell on flatbed car from Philadelphia to San Francisco for safekeeping during World War I. You should use such valuable sources of historical information both for the children's enjoyment and as a source for researching and recording details from the past. These experiences give them a clearer understanding of and appreciation for people and events of the past.

Historical Panorama

Moving from biographies and oral history experiences, the teacher might begin a historical panorama that would become a living history for classes to come. On one long, empty wall, secure a large sheet of tagboard, with the class name across the top of the sheet: "Fifth Grade Class, Main Elementary School (1987–88)." Beneath the title place individual class pictures of each child with the name beneath. In succeeding rows, ask the children to fill in information such as: This year's president was. . ., The most popular movie star of the year was. . ., The most popular song of the year was. . ., The winner of the World Series was. . ., The most popular hairstyle was. . ., The most popular clothing style was. . ., Our class officers were. . ., and so on and so on. Throughout the year, the children can complete the sentences with words or pictures. A teacher who used this panorama planned to have each succeeding year's fifth-grade class do the same and eventually have a growing history of the school and that particular room.

Field Trips and Historical Investigation

Children can increase their insight into history by taking field trips into the community to inspect buildings and other features from the past. By examining places of immediate historical interest, children can be led to use the method of inquiry often utilized by historians: identifying interesting problems, hypothesizing solutions to those problems, assembling data to support or reject their hypotheses, and forming conclusions based on the data. One enterprising teacher, for example, took a group of children on a walk through their community for the purpose of listing as many interesting historical places as they could. The children found the local cemetery particularly fascinating and decided it would be an interesting place to study.[5] The teacher knew their interests by listening to the children's questions and comments as they examined the gravestones: "What is an epitaph? Why were they put on gravestones? How long did people live back then? What did they die of? Why did so many young children die? Look at the different names." In this context, the children became involved in the first characteristic of historical investigation: *identifying interesting problems*.

When the class returned to school, the teacher encouraged further discussion and recorded the children's interests on the chalkboard as each contributed. Along the way, the teacher asked the children to offer guesses to their questions and made no judgment as to whether their guesses were right or wrong. Regardless of her own knowledge about the topic, the teacher listed each guess without a judgmental comment. In this context, the children carried out the second stage of historical investigation: *hypothesizing solutions to problems*.

The third stage of historical investigation, *assembling data to support or reject hypotheses*, began with hundreds of gravestone rubbings the children made by placing large sheets of newsprint against the gravestones and rubbing crayons over the paper. Everything on the gravestone (names, dates, epitaphs) transferred to the paper and provided excellent research material for the classroom. Children were grouped according to interests and used their rubbings along with a variety of library material to accomplish the fourth stage of historical investigation: *forming conclusions*. To achieve this aim, the teacher and children cooperatively planned the following activities:

Record the ages at death for any twenty men and twenty women. Determine the average for each group. Which group lived longer? Look through the material on this table (books and magazine articles were offered) and find as many reasons as you can.

Record the average age at death for any ten men who died during each of the following periods: (1800–49), (1850–99), (1900–49), (1950–present). During which period did they live longest? Think of some reasons why you feel this happened. Check the resources at this table to see if you were right.

Look at the gravestones for epitaphs. Record the longest, shortest, funniest, most interesting, most religious, and so on.

Examine the form of writing on the gravestones. Do any of the words or letters seem peculiar to you? List the ones that do.

Suppose you were appointed to design a gravestone for the President of the United States (or other popular figure). Draw a picture of the gravestone and display it on the large bulletin board.

How are the gravestones of the past like ours? How are they different? What changes can you predict for gravestones in the future? Use the large boxes to design a possible gravemarker of the future.

Make a list of the most popular names on the gravestones. Are they popular today? What nationalities seemed most prevalent at the time? Why?

After the groups gathered their data and pulled them together to form conclusions, they shared their findings with each other.

Sources of Historical Data

Children gradually realize that historians must find out about events of the past even when they cannot directly examine the evidence. If this happens, children can be encouraged to study different kinds of *written records* such as letters, diaries, wills, mortgages, and tax receipts, or interview either *primary witnesses* (those people who were part of an event) or *secondary witnesses* (people who got information secondhand). A spacecraft launching illustrates these three sources of historical data. Thousands, perhaps millions, of people watch the launching on television and become *secondary witnesses* to the event while newspapers carry accounts of the event and give us accurate *written records* for future reference. Who might be the *primary witnesses* to the event?

Children should understand that when secondary accounts must be examined, historians must carefully check the information. But even after they check their information for accuracy, problems remain. Like witnesses who offer conflicting testimony of a crime in court, even the most well-meaning primary witnesses interpret what they see differently. They tell what they *think* they saw, but did they *really* see what happened? To illustrate this point, one teacher arranged for a colleague to enter his room in the middle of the afternoon, disheveled, with the purpose of creating a minor disturbance while the children were quietly working at their desks. This fellow teacher was to simply enter the classroom to create a shock effect for the children by yelling, safely throwing a chalkboard eraser, etc. After the colleague played her role and left the room, the regular teacher asked the children to write about what they saw and heard. When the children were finished, they compared individual accounts of the incident. Finally the teacher asked: "What does this tell you about witnesses?" In the same way, historians must carefully examine written accounts to decide if witnesses have reported them well.

Children should learn to critically compare historical accounts. Consider the following accounts of the Russian Revolution, one written for young children by a Russian author and the other by an American.[6]

The Soviet Story. During 1917, a revolution took place in Russia. The working people overthrew the *czar* (zär), a Russian king. The czar and his family were killed. Everyone longed for freedom. They had never had it under the czar.

Under the slogan, "All power to the Soviets," a new government was formed. It was a dictatorship of the people. At last the people had their own government. All land was owned by the government. Since the government was the people, the people owned all the land.

The government also took over the banks, factories, mines, and stores. The people then owned everything.

The Communist (käm-yə-nəst) party was the wise leader of the working people. It led the people along the right path. It led them to liberty and a classless life. The Revolution was a people's revolution. It threw out those who would make slaves of the workers. It established the dictatorship of the people.

The Revolution brought a new life to all mankind. It brought them the victory of communism.

The American Story. In 1917 the Russians revolted against their czar. The Communists cruelly killed the czar and his family. The Russians hoped to win freedom.

Most of them hoped that the Russian Revolution would make their lives better. The Russian peasants hoped to divide the land among themselves. The workers wanted better wages. They wanted their living conditions improved.

After the bloody Revolution, a new government was set up. It was a government controlled by Communists. It took over all the property owned by the people. The property became the property of the government. It took over factories, banks, and stores.

The people did not get what they wanted. They did not control the government. The government was controlled by the Communist party. No one could disagree with the party. Those who tried to disagree were put in jail or killed.

The Revolution made the Soviet people slaves of their government. It took away their religion. It took away their property. It took away their freedom.

Do you notice the similarities and differences in these accounts? For one, they report the same facts: (1) the Russian Revolution took place in 1917; (2) the czar and his family were killed; (3) the government owned everything after the Revolution; (4) the government was led by the Communist party. But the Russian historian and the American historian disagree about what the facts mean. Who was right? Both writers are convinced they are right, and it is here, when writers try to explain what facts mean, that the historian gets into trouble.

When children begin to understand this concept, that a historian interprets facts by what he believes them to mean, it is fun to place them into open-ended problem situations. Here is what one student wrote when the teacher said: "Just suppose that an Indian wrote the acceptable account of the sale of Manhattan. What would it say?"

INDIANS GIVE US MAXI-HA-HA

A bunch of natives from Brooklyn paddled over to Manhattan in 1626 to eyeball the strange white guys who had landed and camped there. The Brooklyn Bridge wasn't built yet, but the natives of the land knew they had a bunch of yokels on the hook as soon as the settlers brought up the subject of buying an island no one was living on anyway.

Besides Manhatte's (that's what it was called back then) lousy reputation as a hunting land, the natives didn't have the white man's concept of land ownership—they figured the land was given by God to anyone who wanted to use it. So, when Peter Minuit kept heaping trinkets before them, the Canarsee Indians (the natives of Brooklyn), just stood straight-faced until they got enough loot to fill their canoes—about sixty guilders' (twenty-four dollars) worth of beads, needles, fabric, buttons, and fishhooks.

Then America's first fly-by-night real estate brokers paddled away hurriedly—probably to tell their friends about the easy "marks" the new neighbors were. It was later that Minuit realized he was swindled. Manhattan actually belonged to the Weckquaesgeeks who finally were paid for Manhattan, too. But, as businesspersons, the Canarsees had a way to go to catch the Raritan Indians. They sold Staten Island six times!

Notice that the creative experience was more than a "fanciful" activity. The student drew on his creative talents to produce something original, but still based his product on actual knowledge he had gained in the classroom. Through the use of historical research, teachers establish a basis of involvement that makes all inquiry an exciting learning process.

Reporting the Results

Children gain a great deal from their planning and research activities, but those phases do not complete the inquiry process. The children must also learn to share their findings with the class. They may choose to create illustrations, models, or replicas; deliver oral reports; construct charts, tables, graphs, or maps; plan skits, dramatic plays, or demonstrations; make bulletin-board or table displays; or develop murals or picture collections—there are many options for this phase of the inquiry process. It is important to remember, though, that inquiry is a cooperative, personalized venture, and children should have the opportunity to choose their own methods of sharing information. Be a trusting, flexible teacher who encourages "partnerships in learning" as a characteristic of the social studies program.

The Teacher's Role in Closed-Ended Inquiry

Your role in a closed-ended inquiry episode is one of planning within an outlined format:

1. Arouse curiosity and interest in a topic; make children aware of the problem.

2. Allow children to decide what special aspects of the problem they want to pursue. Assign group or individual projects.

3. Help children collect and analyze data.

4. Act in various roles while the children work so you can immediately address particular problems.

5. Encourage individuals or groups to plan and develop creative techniques of sharing their results with others.

Elementary school teachers can plan inquiry sessions that last from one or two days up to a week or two. How do teachers organize these two types of inquiry sessions? This first sample teaching episode illustrates how one third-grade teacher planned an inquiry lesson that lasted a single class period.

Mr. Jackson's third-grade class was involved in a series of lessons focusing on the principle of change relating to the passage of time. For this day, Mr. Jackson needed an activity to express the concept that as time passes, everyone learns to do more and different things. To prepare for today's activity, Mr. Jackson prearranged with two kindergarten and two fifth-grade teachers in his building to have several children spend some time observing children in each of their rooms. But before he sent the children to those rooms, Mr. Jackson asked the class these questions:

Mr. Jackson: What are some things you can do in school now that you couldn't do when you were in kindergarten?

Children: Read. Write. Tie our shoes. Draw better. Do harder math problems.

As the class continued to offer comments, Mr. Jackson recorded them on the chalkboard under the heading of *Third Grade, Present*.

Mr. Jackson: What are some things kindergartners might do in school that third- or fifth-graders would not do?

Children: Eat snacks. Rest on cots. Cry. Play with blocks.

Again, Mr. Jackson listed the children's comments on the chalkboard, this time under the heading of *Kindergarten, Past*.

Mr. Jackson: What are some of the things you think you might do in the future—in fifth grade?

Children: Learn harder things. Learn French. My sister said fifth-graders have more spelling words to learn each week.

Mr. Jackson continued to list the children's guesses, this time under the heading *Fifth Grade, Future*.

Mr. Jackson: Now I would like to divide the class into four groups—two groups will visit kindergarten rooms and two

> groups will visit fifth-grade rooms. Those of you going to the kindergarten rooms will need to copy the "past list" from the board and those who will visit the fifth-graders will copy the "future list." You will spend one-half hour watching what the children are doing. Try to be quiet while you're there, but whenever you see someone doing anything on our list, put a check next to it. Also, add anything to the list that we did not think of.

When the children returned from their visits, Mr. Jackson asked each group to transfer the findings from their checklist to the chalkboard. He then led the children through an examination of the data by asking questions that encouraged the children to compare the observed activities with what went on in their classroom.

This lesson shows how a teacher can motivate children with a personal problem, encourage them to hypothesize, organize them to collect data, and lead a discussion to examine the data for the purpose of developing the generalization stated at the beginning of the lesson. Many teachers, especially those in the earlier grades, choose single-day inquiry sessions as the first exposure because it is a compact way to introduce children to a new mode of social studies instruction.

As the children gain confidence and skill as inquirers, teachers gradually offer increasing freedom and time to pursue topics of interest. In the following episode, a fifth-grade teacher allows one week for collecting and reporting data.

> On the first day of a two-week study on China, Mrs. Levenson arranged areas of interest in the classroom with boxes, cartons, desks, tables, and bulletin boards. Many materials were evident in the classroom—pictures, objects, newspaper clippings, books, reproductions of Chinese art, writing samples, and Chinese symbols such as those for Yin and Yang. She put a sign on one of the boxes: "Travel Agency." Arranged at the Travel Agency were flyers and brochures about China. While the children browsed, a record of traditional Chinese music played in the background.
>
> This introductory activity took about thirty minutes. Mrs. Levenson provided this time because she knew that upper-grade children are often interested in contrasting cultures and spontaneously ask questions once their interest is stimulated. Mrs. Levenson encouraged questions and comments from the children and concluded that their major interest was: "How is life in China different from ours?" The children eagerly agreed to think of other questions that would help in solving the major problem. The next day the class met for a planning session. The teacher listed all the children's questions on the chalkboard:
>
> What are some Chinese legends?
>
> How are East Asian values like mine? Different?
>
> What is a dynasty? How is China ruled now?
>
> What do the writing symbols mean?
>
> Why are ancestors so powerful in Chinese culture?
>
> What are Yin and Yang?

What kind of family life would we find in China?

What kind of life did the peasants lead?

Who was Confucius? Why was he so important?

What is the Great Wall? Why was it built?

What role did the Buddhist religion play in China?

How did China become communist?

Who were Marco Polo and Genghis Khan?

As she listed the questions on a chart, Mrs. Levenson reworded them for clarity. The class compared and contrasted the questions, finding many that could be placed into categories—clothing, family style, government, religion, people, the landscape, and so on. Mrs. Levenson provided separate sheets of chart paper for each category of questions and a different colored marking pen for each chart. Committees were appointed to separate questions on the appropriate charts under the various headings: "food questions," "clothing questions," and so on.

The next day, the completed charts were displayed around the room. The children added new questions as they examined those from the previous day. Now the class was ready to explore means of solving the problems they had formulated. Mrs. Levenson informed the class that they were going on a simulated excursion to China to find answers to the questions. But to research the questions most effectively, the children would need to form committees. The teacher asked the children to decide what committees they wanted to work on and to sign their names on the appropriate charts.

"Our committees have been formed," announced Mrs. Levenson, "but before we go to China to find our answers, we need to find out a few things: How much will air fares, hotels, food, guides, tips, gifts, and other expenses cost? Do they use dollars in China? What clothing should we take? Where is China? How long will it take us to get there? Will we need shots?

China's geography and economic systems were brought into the study as the children prepared for these last-minute considerations. After "passports" were created, the decorated, brown-bag "luggage" was "packed" with pictures of clothing and other essentials, and "customs" processed the travelers, the children were ready to take off! Committees were assigned plane seats by color and everyone was welcomed aboard. The flight attendant (Mrs. Levenson) welcomed them and explained about the plane, the exits, and the oxygen masks. Then a tape-recorded jet roar signaled takeoff and the children settled back in their seats. The room darkened while a film about China was shown. When the film was over, the plane landed, and the children were ready to begin.

The next day, the children were taken to assigned meeting places in "China" to fulfill their research duties. Textbooks, trade books, films, filmstrips, slides, records, and other resources were available for each committee. Each committee knew that it had a responsibility to choose a chairperson, decide how to go about finding answers to its questions, and make plans to present what they found out to their classmates.

After three or four days, the committees were ready to return to the United States and their classroom to share their findings. One group made a scrapbook of pictures depicting China's terrain, architecture, and other physical features. Another group planned a program of Chinese songs and dances. A third group presented a dramatic skit involving Marco Polo and the

Mongols. To pull the entire learning experience together, Mrs. Levenson summarized what the class had learned on information retrieval charts next to each committee's question chart.

In these two inquiry examples, the children learned much more than subject matter. They learned to work together, to think critically, to accept responsibility, and to make individual contributions to a group's plans. An important facet of such experiences is their cooperative nature. Cooperative learning is an approach to solving problems that approximates democratic living, and thus reinforces an important purpose of social studies education. The goal of curiosity-stimulating experiences is to make children question and discover new ideas. Our intention is to motivate children to continually want to know about things and develop the logical thought processes they will use as functioning citizens in a democracy.

COGNITIVE STYLE AND THE INQUIRY PROCESS: ALTERNATIVES

In all inquiry episodes, children are, theoretically, researchers who independently solve problems much as a detective would. But in actual practice, few children approach a study topic with similar investigative methods. Consider these two student profiles: Bonnie examines data carefully, and seeks to organize bits and pieces of information together in a step-by-step fashion to come up with a logical pattern or a sound conclusion. Carlos, on the other hand, judges evidence intuitively; rather than piecing together bits of information, he looks at everything whether it fits together or not. He sifts through all the accumulated information and, rather than trying to establish a pattern, simply finds that an explanation falls into place.

Systematic or Intuitive Style

For a long time, we have known that individuals have a characteristic way of thinking, or *cognitive style*, that they call upon when they are confronted with problem-solving situations. The two styles are generally referred to as *systematic* (Bonnie) and *intuitive* (Carlos). Regardless of whether you are solving the problem of how to study for your next exam when a big party is scheduled for the night before, or where to get money for next year's tuition hike, you are likely to rely on one cognitive style to solve it. Think of a problem you faced recently and how you arrived at a solution. Now reread the two student profiles. Which style is closer to yours?

Where do these differences in style come from? Research into the human brain has revealed that there are two sides, or hemispheres, each capable of processing information in a unique way and, in effect, giving us two minds in our heads.[7] The *left side* of the brain controls the logical, rational thought processes (as well as the right side of the body); the *right side* controls functions of intuitive, abstract thought (and the left side of the body). In most people, then, logic resides in the left hemisphere, intuition in the right. Like handedness, in early childhood, one hemisphere eventually becomes dominant. So, when thrown a problem, most of us solve it in our preferred style. Before these breakthroughs, little was known about the right hemisphere. Since speech and language were functions of the left hemisphere, and most school work called upon systematic rather than intuitive thinking, there was no way of communicating with the right hemisphere to find out what its contributions were. Therefore schools (and society in general) tended to overemphasize left-hemisphere skills at the expense of right-hemisphere skills, giving our children an apparently "lopsided" education.

Bruner examined the research into brain hemisphere characteristics and informed educators of its importance in *On Knowing: Essays for the Left Hand*.[8] Bruner criticized the nearly exclusive emphasis on teaching toward systematic, rational (left-hemisphere) thinking in our schools and advocated teaching strategies that also encouraged exploration of innovative, experimental thinking (right-hemisphere). Edward de Bono looked at this "left-handed" (or right-hemisphere-controlled) thinking and found it to be quite distinct from logical thinking and more useful in generating new ideas.[9] He used the term *lateral thinking* to describe intuitive thinking and *vertical thinking* to denote conventional logical thought processes. De Bono explained that lateral thinking is easiest to appreciate when seen in action, as in the situation illustrated in Figure 5–7. While this problem looks deceptively simple, it is actually quite difficult. As a matter of fact, only about one person in a hundred is able to solve it the first time around. There are four volumes of Shakespeare's collected works on the shelf. The pages of each volume are exactly 2″ thick. The covers are each ⅛″ thick. A bookworm starts eating at page 1 of volume I and eats through to the last page of volume IV. What is the distance the bookworm covers? Try to work the problem before you look at the answer.

The answer is five inches. Remember that the bookworm started at page one of volume one. Put your finger on that point; do not count the back cover and all the pages in between. Are you catching on? Similarly, the bookworm ate only to the last page of the last volume; do not count the front cover and all the pages of the last volume. What causes so many of us to generate "correct" answers by look-

FIGURE 5–7
Bookworm Problem

ing only at obvious solutions to problems? Torrance feels that a great deal of blame should be placed on the schools:

> **Creative imagination during early childhood seems to reach a peak between four and four-and-a-half years, and is followed by a drop at about age five when the child enters school for the first time. This drop has generally been regarded as the inevitable phenomenon in nature. There are now indications, however, that this drop in five-year-olds is a man-made rather than a natural phenomenon.**[10]

Some argue that this phenomenon occurs because schools limit children's freedom from kindergarten on. "You're acting like a first-grader," or "Stop being so silly," and similar sarcastic put-downs often accompany original, adventuresome attempts at self-expression. Highly creative individuals like Einstein and Edison were considered dunces and were forced to leave elementary school because they would not (or could not) conform to the rigid behavioral expectations of their teachers. Albert Einstein once stressed his regard for creativity when he commented, "The gift of fantasy has meant more to me than my talent for absorbing positive knowledge." John Lennon, one of the great modern composers, was viewed by the headmaster at his school in England as a boy "up to all sorts of tricks, and didn't make life easy for the staff. I caned him once and he had been caned many times by my predecessor."[11] These men are only a few who had the persistence to "stick it out." But what has happened to the thousands of youngsters who surrendered their creative urges to conformity and were never encouraged or allowed to make significant creative contributions?

New, creative solutions to problems come from the ability to shift directions in thought; to move from the obvious to the subtle. The *vertical thinker* attacks a problem by first establishing a direction of thought and then digging deeper in that direction until he finds an answer or solution. The *lateral thinker* also attacks a problem by initiating a direction of thought, but when that direction appears to be leading nowhere, he feels comfortable taking new chances. Figure 5–8 characterizes the difference in vertical and lateral thinking.

Just as a person can become, with practice, more proficient with the non-dominant hand, so can children become more novel problem solvers by looking at situations in more ways than just the most probable—practicing with the right hemisphere of the brain in classroom activities. I do not mean to persuade you that *all* vertical thinking experiences are "bad," nor that *all* lateral thinking experiences are "good." The intention is to make you aware that a child's mind is capable of different thought processes, and that children may demonstrate greater skills in some processes than in others. Just as a child's physical realm may be characterized by greater skills in running than in hitting a ball, so his intellectual realm may be characterized by greater skills in lateral thinking than in vertical thinking. Teachers must be aware of this variability and plan classroom experiences that foster an assortment of thought processes. This perspective is especially important when we consider that the organization of the brain is quite plastic in young children. David Galin reports that lateralization is in flux up to about the age of ten.[12] Knowing this, we

THE VERTICAL THINKER

THE LATERAL THINKER

Digs one hole deeper to find
a solution.

Abandons one hole and digs
several experimental holes.

FIGURE 5–8

Vertical and Lateral Thinkers

must develop classroom practices that encourage interaction of both sides of the brain.

Robert Samples, who worked on hemispheric functioning with Bruner at Harvard, designed educational strategies that bring both brain hemispheres into equal partnership. He found three characteristics in the resulting learning process: (1) higher feelings of self-confidence, self-esteem, and compassion; (2) wider exploration of traditional content subjects and skills; and (3) higher levels of creative invention in content and skills.[13] We must encourage in the social studies classroom not only the systematic problem-solving experiences described in Dewey's inquiry process, but also the inventive, intuitive thinking associated with *creative discovery*.

PLANNING FOR OPEN-ENDED INQUIRY

Planning either type of problem-solving program takes more time, more materials, more effort, and more thinking by both the teacher and the children. Is the extra effort worth it? It depends on what we want from the learner.

Basically, we must place children into two major problem-solving situations: (1) closed-ended and (2) open-ended. In the closed-ended situation, we plan a teaching/learning episode based on Dewey's concept of inquiry and ask students to solve problems through research or other experiences that provide evidence to support or reject hypotheses. Children explore the information, analyze its worth, and draw conclusions. These situations, called *application* by Bloom, utilize the talents controlled by the left hemisphere of the brain. These are examples of directed problems:

- While studying the events that led to the American Revolution, students break up into three groups—Loyalists, Revolutionaries, and Neutrals—to gather information and to form an argument by which each solicits new members for their respective groups.

- Students investigate a number of resources and prepare their own newspaper describing the daily activities of a particular historical period, perhaps pre-revolutionary colonial life.

- Boys and girls learn the concept of specialization of labor by comparing the time used to prepare peanut butter individually and by an assembly line technique.

- Boys and girls trying to understand economics or the cost of providing for a family are allotted $200 or so and asked to prepare a weekly budget for a family of five.

- Children preparing to study a new country pretend they are going to make a trip there. What type of transportation would be best to get there? What type of clothing would they need when they arrived? What kind of people will they meet? Where is it, what is the climate like, what activities are popular?

- The class studies the effects of television advertising by polling students in the school to see how many buy a certain product because they have seen it advertised on television.

An *open-ended problem* differs from a directed problem in that children deliberately make themselves look at several solutions for each problem and offer their thoughts no matter how absurd. Open-ended problems correspond to Bloom's *synthesis* level: thinking abilities that help originate unique, *creative* solutions to problems. The characteristics of creative thought are identified in Table 5–2.

The social studies curriculum can encourage creative thinking in many ways, one of which is to offer stimulating discussion questions. When questioning, you must be aware of four basic steps:

1. Establish a creative climate in the classroom. You can stimulate creative thinking when you encourage children to think freely. Such an environment encourages a flow of ideas because it allows for the emotional characteristics of creative thinkers.

2. Present a challenging question or problem. Your role is to make children aware of a puzzling situation and to develop a personal concern for it. Pose challenges, puzzles, and problems that do not have a correct answer and thus stimulate a wide variety of responses. Use these types of questions:

TABLE 5-2

*Intellectual and Emotional Characteristics of Creative Individuals**

Intellectual Characteristics	Emotional Characteristics
1. *Fluent thinking abilities:* Can generate large quantities of ideas as possible solutions to problems. The child who responds to the question, "What things are red?" with "apple, book, car, beet, crayon, and shoes" is a more flexible thinker than the child who says, "fire engine and candy."	1. *Risk taking:* They have the courage to take wild guesses and expose themselves to criticism or failure. Creative thinkers are strong willed and eager to defend their own ideas.
2. *Flexible thinking abilities:* Can offer a variety of different categories of responses to problems. The child who indicates that a pencil may be used for such diverse purposes as writing, holding up a window, tapping on a drum, or leading a song is more flexible than the child who suggests it might be used to draw, write numbers, write words, or compose secret messages.	2. *Complexity:* They enjoy looking at the way things are and thinking about the way they should be. Creative thinkers delve into intricate problems and seek many alternatives so that order can be brought from chaos.
3. *Original thinking abilities:* Can offer highly unusual or clever responses to a problem. The child who finishes the incomplete sentence, "He opened the bag and found. . ." with "a giant spotted butterfly" is more original than the child who suggests "an orange."	3.*Curiosity:* They are inquisitive and full of wonder. They are open to puzzling problems and toy with many ideas as they ponder the mysteries of things that surround them.
4. *Elaborative thinking abilities:* Can add on to or expand simple ideas or responses to make them more "elegant." The child who responds to a teacher's invitation to add more information to the sentence, "The cat sat on the porch," with "The lazy black and white alley cat sat on the top of the rotten old porch," demonstrates greater elaborative ability than the child who says, "The black cat sat on the old porch."	4. *Imagination:* They dream about things. Creative thinkers often are "dreamers" who visualize and build mental images and reach beyond the boundaries of reality.

*With assistance from E. Riley Holman.

- Quantity questions

  List all the ways you can use an empty beverage can.

  How many ways can you come up with to encourage people to stop polluting the environment?

  If a garbage heap was the only thing left of a civilization, *what are all the possible* things you might learn about the people?

- Involvement questions

  How would you feel if you were the Mayflower?

  How would you feel if you were the football that scored the winning field goal in the Super Bowl?

  How would you have felt if you were one of the Wright brothers during the first airplane flight?

- Supposition questions

  Suppose only women had the right to vote. What would happen?

  Suppose insects were more intelligent than human beings. What are all the things that might happen?

- Viewpoint questions

  How would winter look to an Australian Aborigine?

  How would a ship look to the fish in the ocean?

  How would the lush grasslands look to a herd of starved cattle?

3. Allow time to consider alternatives. During this phase, encourage the children to produce a large number of possible responses to your question. It is especially important to defer judgment as to the worth of each suggestion until a solution is called for. *Brainstorming* is a popular technique for this phase of creative production, which we will discuss later. These are a few of the strategies that can be used when children consider alternatives to a situation:

   - Confront the children with the familiar
   - Turn the familiar into an ambiguity or uncertainty
   - Ask provocative questions that require the children to think about things in a new way
   - Invite the children to explore new possibilities
   - Preserve open-mindedness during discussion sessions
   - Call for a sharing of constructive responses
   - Encourage several solutions to the same problem
   - Ask children to project their thinking into the future

4. Encourage the children to put their ideas into use. The final stage of the creative process is to consider all possible consequences of each alternative and select the most acceptable. You can lead children to this goal through *attribute listing*. Table 5–3 is an example of an attribute listing activity. In this process, children list all the attributes of the problem in one column, generate ideas for improvement in the next, positive features next, and negative features in the final column. They can consider the positive and negative features of each alternative to reach a final solution.

TABLE 5–3
Attribute Listing Activity

Problem Area	Attribute	Possible Solutions	Positive Features	Negative Features
Swings on the playground	Too high for small kids	Lower them	Small kids can reach them	If too low, some kids can get hurt

Brainstorming

In the third step of encouraging creative thinking, you will find brainstorming an effective technique for helping children consider alternatives. Brainstorming works best in elementary classrooms when you limit the size of brainstorming groups to six or seven children. To begin, state the problem and encourage group members to think of as many new (and wild) ideas for possible solutions as fast as they can. One group member should record all ideas as they are offered. The children must be aware of the rules for brainstorming.

The main objective of the first part of the brainstorming session is to generate the greatest number of suggestions possible. Children should offer ideas for between five and fifteen minutes, depending on the size of the group and how long interest is sustained. After this suggestion period, critical evaluation of ideas begins with restating the problem and inviting each group to narrow down its list of solutions to about four or five. They must address concerns such as: Will it actually solve this problem or create new ones? Is it practical—will we be able to use it in the near future? What are the strengths and weaknesses of each? Can any of our ideas be combined into one useful solution?

After the list has been narrowed down, the group should work toward a final solution through discussion. The ultimate solution may contain one idea or a combination of ideas. Members are free to develop the ideas further so they can share them with the class as we discussed earlier: making diagrams, models, or designs of the idea or object; composing a letter to appropriate individuals or agencies; or offering a creative skit.

Perhaps your most valuable skill in guiding open-ended problem-solving experiences is to ask questions to spur the children's thinking while they are formulating ideas. Same sample questions follow:

New ideas
  Can it be used in new ways as it is?
  Can it be put to other uses if it is changed in some way?
Adaptation
  What else is like this?
  What other idea does this make me think of?
  What new twist could I add to the idea?
  Could I change the color, shape, sound, odor, etc.?
Enlargement
  What can I add?
  Should I make it longer, wider, heavier, faster, more numerous, thicker?
Condensation
  What can I take away?
  Should I make it smaller, shorter, narrower, lighter, slower, thinner?
Substitution
  What else can be used to do the same thing?
  What other materials or ingredients might be used?

One classroom teacher used brainstorming with his social studies class this way:

This brainstorming activity was intended to capitalize on an understanding of the concepts of past and future. The children had been investigating great inventions of the past and made comparisons between past and present ways of doing things. They were placed into a directed problem when Mr. Lacey, their teacher, asked them to spend some time looking through copies of an 1897 Sears, Roebuck catalog and a book of early American games for the purpose of arranging a turn-of-the-century birthday party for their room. The children were divided into groups to examine the resources and think about what they would have and do at their party. Mr. Lacey then led a discussion comparing and contrasting party activities in the past and in the present. The following day, he began the social studies class.

Mr. Lacey: In the front of the classroom, I have two pictures. Take a good look at them. Tell me what you are looking at.

Cindy: One picture shows men using old-fashioned saws to cut down trees and the other shows a modern chain saw.

Mr. Lacey: That's right, Cindy. Can anyone think of a way we can describe each picture?

Jacques: The men look like they're working a lot harder in the old picture.

Marcie: The man with the chain saw looks like he can cut more trees than the men with the saws.

Mr. Lacey: Does it seem like the *new* chain saw is better?

Children: Yes!

Mr. Lacey: Why?

Vernon: It makes the work easier.

Lucy: People can get a lot more done.

Mr. Lacey: That's exactly right. Most modern inventions are good because they make work easier and help us get a lot more done. Can you see things around you that are changing right now? Now, I'd like you to think about something. . .what would be an invention you would like for the *future* to make work easier for you when you become adults?

Mr. Lacey then divided the class into groups of six.

Mr. Lacey: It would be interesting to see what each group thinks it would like to see invented in the future. Spend a few minutes thinking up all the wild and interesting things you can.

The groups spent about fifteen minutes in uninterrupted brainstorming, after which Mr. Lacey asked them to narrow their choices to about five. Then he asked the recorder from each group to write its list on the chalkboard and led a discussion:

Mr. Lacey: How will it work? How fast will it go? How might it be made?

After the class discussed each other's "inventions," Mr. Lacey asked each group to illustrate (make a "blueprint") each of the things on the list of items it would like to see in the future. These were completed and displayed in an area of the room called "The Hall of Inventions."

Synectics

Rather than presenting children with a specific, completely described problem as we do in a brainstorming situation, Gordon's *synectics* approach is an interesting variation of the brainstorming approach, as it presents an initial abstraction of the problem instead of a clear, well-defined problem.[14] For example, we may wish to address the problem of finding suitable parking facilities for cars in a large city. Instead of telling the brainstorming group that this is the *specific problem*, Gordon would simply tell them that the problem is one of *storing things*. "How many ways can you think of for storing things?" the teacher might ask. Lefrancois asked this question in a number of his classes and received these responses: "Put them in bags," "Pile them up," "Can them," "Put them on hangers," "Put them in rows," "Convey them on belts to storage areas," "Cut them up," "Fold them," "Put them in your pocket," "Put them in boxes," "Disassemble them," "Put them on shelves."[15]

As the session evolves, the leader gradually narrows the problem. Initially, the leader may suggest that the objects are large; later, that they cannot be cut up or folded. Finally, the specific problem is given to the group. By now, interestingly, the group is often motivated to pursue solutions that it might have rejected if the specific problem had been originally described. Consider, for instance, the possibilities growing from the suggestion "putting things on hangers in large storage areas."

Open-ended problems thus differ from closed-ended problems in that they call for divergent, imaginative solutions to perplexing situations. They provide built-in motivation for achievement by children with right-hemisphere brain domination and essential practice for those who are left-hemisphere dominated. Both types of problems, however, are valuable additions to the social studies program in that they encourage children to dig into things, turn over ideas in their minds, try out fresh possibilities, search for new relationships, and struggle for new knowledge.

Table 5–4 summarizes children's thinking skills and the recommended practices for reinforcing and enriching those skills.

SUMMARY

The major purpose of inquiry-oriented learning is to develop in children the curiosity and skills necessary for becoming independent problem solvers. Inquiry-oriented learning is usually based on John Dewey's inquiry model and explained as a four-step process: (1) problem awareness, (2) hypothesis formation, (3) testing the

TABLE 5-4
Thinking Skills and Appropriate Teaching Practices

Thinking Level	Thought Process	Teaching Process
Synthesis	Child creates original solutions to problems (emphasis on process)	Open-ended inquiry and brainstorming
Analysis	Child classifies, composes, contrasts information (emphasis on process and product)	Explores data or ideas gathered through closed-ended or open-ended inquiry
Application	Child uses content or concepts to solve unique problems (emphasis on product and process)	1. Inductive closed-ended inquiry 2. Deductive closed-ended inquiry
Comprehension	Child forms concepts (emphasis on product and process)	1. Planned questioning (e.g., Taba) 2. Questions 3. Information retrieval charts 4. Webbing techniques
Knowledge	Child recalls exact facts or details (emphasis on product)	Providing information

hypothesis and gathering data, and (4) developing conclusions. This process involves questioning and hard thinking about observable events.

Special instructional experiences help create a "readiness" for inquiry in the primary grades: (1) directed lessons at the beginning of the school year; (2) grouping children for special purposes as they gain in confidence and ability to work with others; (3) offering exhibits, "mini-museums," and other curiosity-arousing areas around the room to present new adventures or stimulate interests; and (4) moving the children into situations involving rudimentary problem solving.

The two major types of inquiry are open-ended and closed-ended. When children are challenged to solve unique problems with specific evidence, we refer to closed-ended inquiry. It is closed-ended because the solution must be based on the application and analysis of concrete evidence for the solution of the problem. And, closed-ended inquiry may be of two different types: (1) *inductive closed-ended inquiry*, in which instruction proceeds from the specific to the general, and (2) *deductive closed-ended inquiry*, in which learning moves from the general to the specific. Whether they work with the inductive or deductive option, children attack problems and collect data through research techniques such as descriptive research, survey research, and historical research.

Open-ended inquiry differs from closed-ended in that children are not restricted to any particular set of data to solve their problem, but are encouraged to develop their own unique ideas as solutions. Given new scientific support as a teaching strategy by recent studies into brain-hemisphere functioning, open-ended inquiry is widely valued for its stimulation to creative thought. The social studies curriculum can encourage creating thinking in many ways, one of which is to offer stimulating questions that include these factors: (1) establishing a climate for creativity in the classroom; (2) presenting a challenging question or problem; (3) allowing time to consider alternatives, and (4) encouraging the children to put their ideas to use.

It is no exaggeration to say that today's knowledge explosion is but a mere puff compared to what we can anticipate for the future. The ability to solve problems and to create will certainly be more appropriate for dealing with unknowns than limiting thinking solely to the acqusition of knowledge. The purpose of this chapter is not to "sell" the inquiry method as the ultimate, nor as the preferred, instructional mode in social studies classrooms. It is presented as an option for teachers so that they can explore and promote all the levels of thinking needed by an educated citizenry.

ENDNOTES

1. Neil Postman and Charles Weingartner, in *Teaching Is. . .*, ed. Merrill Harmin and Tom Gregory (Chicago: Science Research Associates, 1974), p. 57.

2. Lori Fisk and Henry Clay Lindgren, *Learning Centers* (Glen Ridge, NJ: Exceptional Press, 1974), p. 58.

3. Carol Seefeldt, *A Curriculum For Child Care Centers* (Columbus, OH: Charles E. Merrill, 1974), pp. 176–177.

4. Gladys Gardner Jenkins and Helen S. Shacter, *These Are Your Children* (Glenview, IL: Scott, Foresman, 1966), p. 172.

5. See Edward Stranix, "The Cemetery: An Outdoor Classroom," *Teacher*, 93, no. 2 (October 1978): 66–67.

6. Frederick M. King et al., *Using the Social Studies* 1970, p. 262. By permission of Laidlaw Brothers, A Division of Doubleday & Company, Inc.

7. Robert E. Ornstein, *The Psychology of Consciousness* (New York: Viking, 1972).

8. Jerome Bruner, *On Knowing: Essays For the Left Hand* (New York: Atheneum, 1965).

9. Edward deBono, "The Searching Mind: Lateral Thinking," *Today's Education*, 58, no. 8 (November 1969): 20–24.

10. E. Paul Torrance, "Adventuring in Creativity," *Childhood Education*, 40, no. 2 (1963): 79.

11. William Popjoy, John Lennon's Schoolmaster at the Quarry Bank Comprehensive School. Comments made during a newspaper interview shortly after John Lennon's death in 1980.

12. David Galin, "Educating Both Halves of the Brain," *Childhood Education*, 53, no. 1 (October 1976): 20.

13. Robert Samples, "Mind Cycles and Learning," *Phi Delta Kappan*, 58, no. 9 (May 1977): 689–690.

14. W.J.J. Gordon, *Synectics: The Development of Creative Capacity* (New York: Harper & Row, 1961).

15. Guy R. Lefrancois, *Psychology for Teaching: A Bear Sometimes Faces the Front* (Belmont, CA: Wadsworth, 1980), p. 255.

Learning Centers

KEY CONCEPTS

☐ *Understanding what learning centers are and how they contribute to the elementary school social studies program*

☐ *Differentiating among the various purposes for which learning centers are created*

☐ *Encouraging children to make choices and assume responsibility for their own learning*

☐ *Arousing interest in the social studies by inviting children to plan and work cooperatively*

> The opening day of elementary school is like an opening night on Broadway, with celebrities gathered to look one another over and then to see what the play is all about. As an audience waits expectantly for the opening curtain, so children enter classrooms in September with the hope that something is going to happen.[1]

The elementary school social studies teacher uses movies, slides, books, bulletin boards, pictures, and many other teaching aids that all contribute to the overall learning process. The strongest emphasis, however, is on the use of real things. By whatever educational term you call it, your major consideration must be to take the children "where the action is" or to bring them a "happening." You search for situations that involve direct experience and stimulate the children to ask "What is that? Where did it come from? What is it used for? What is it made from?" The answers must not always come from us but from the children themselves as they explore and discover. We can make our classrooms places that provoke curiosity by nurturing children's natural responsiveness to life around them. The independence and activity of learning centers often meet this need.

PURPOSE

Different purposes determine what types of learning centers we find in a social studies classroom. The centers may be designed: (1) to reinforce skills previously learned; (2) to acquire information through problem solving and inquiry; (3) to stimulate creativity; or (4) to examine attitudes and values. Most learning centers, though, can serve more than one purpose at a time. For example, a creativity-oriented learning center may have been designed to focus on the colonial art of quilling, but because of the nature of the activities, the center provides for creative expression as well as for skills development (reading and following directions), research (finding out how the colonists used quilling in their lives), and attitude response (reacting emotionally to a part of early colonial culture). This multiple-purpose aspect of center design should be considered as you organize social studies learning centers.

TYPES

Of the many uses for learning centers, four possibilities include reinforcement, acquiring new information, encouraging creativity, and exploring attitudes.

Reinforcement Center

Teacher A wanted his students to have many follow-up experiences with map symbol recognition after he introduced several new symbols to the entire class. He designed independent learning activities to provide extra practice;

for example, one activity in his map skills reinforcement center consisted of a cigar box divided into two equal sections with a tagboard divider. In one section, he placed a number of "symbol cards"—cards on which map symbols were drawn. In the other section, he placed a number of "picture-word cards"—cards with drawings or photographs of each symbol along with the printed word. The teacher pasted two colorful hands on the inside cover of the cigar box, and put a drapery hook into each.

The children were to hang a "symbol card" on one hand and the corresponding "picture-word card" on the other.

New Information Center

Teacher B wanted her pupils to explore on their own the advantages and disadvantages of working individually versus working cooperatively at different kinds of jobs. She set up a center that instructed students to perform a variety of tasks such as erasing the chalkboard, illustrating a story, drawing a picture, and moving a desk, first alone, then with another classmate. The children first recorded how long it took to complete different tasks by themselves and then with a partner's help. Then they shared their reactions and conclusions.

Creativity Center

Teacher C wished to deepen her students' interest in poetry as an expressive medium of the Japanese culture. She introduced several forms of Japanese poetry to the class. They enjoyed interpreting the ideas and the techniques of each form. Then the teacher planned an independent learning center. She displayed pictures of Japan's scenic beauty and encouraged the children to compose Haikus or Tankas about them. The children drew their own illustrations for their poems and hung their finished products in the center.

Attitudes Center

Teacher D hoped to capitalize on the children's desire to talk about their personal wishes, hopes, and dreams. He constructed a "Wishing Well" by covering a large coffee can with construction paper and drawing lines to make the base look as though it were made of stone. He then made a canopy out of construction paper attached to dowel sticks that he taped inside the can. A series of sentence starters were written on slips of paper and placed inside the wishing well; for example, "When my friends talk about me, I wish they would say . . ." or "I wish the president of our country would. . . ."

The children were to reach into the well and pull out a wish, then complete the sentence with a story: serious stories, funny stories, fantasies, or anything the child chose. The children had a choice of posting their stories, signed or unsigned, on a Wishing Well Bulletin Board. Or, if they preferred, they put their stories into folders to show the teacher.

CONSTRUCTING LEARNING CENTERS

After establishing the purposes for a social studies learning center, you must plan the center. There is no magic formula for defining learning center patterns, but two key elements for establishing successful centers are the methods of putting together the center and presenting directions for students.

Pupils' Needs and Interests

Direct observation of children at work or play, some simple pretesting techniques (your own or standardized tests, skills analysis checklists, attitude surveys), and careful consideration of the children's cumulative records will help determine the children's needs and interests. Most important is direct feedback from the children in terms of their reactions to the materials you select for each learning center.

Activities and Materials

Appealing activities with *concrete materials* (realia) can provide exciting learning experiences for children (Figure 6–1). A variety of *audiovisual materials* can also be used to accomplish specific learning center purposes. Tape recorders, film loops, instructional kits, and so on may at times be the most appropriate means to present, reinforce, or enrich a concept. Children enjoy working with learning center materials such as these and, given proper instruction and guidance, can soon be trusted to use the machines independently.

Children prefer *manipulative activities* when they work independently. Materials for these activities may include commercial, teacher-made, or "junk" items. Teachers and children can find tools for learning in the home, school, and community. Some materials for designing various manipulative activities are tin cans or film containers with lids, tools (e.g., hammers, saws, nails), yarn and cloth scraps, broken appliances, styrofoam of all kinds, clean milk cartons, frozen food trays, egg cartons, lumber scraps, shoe boxes, old telephone directories, plastic buckets.

Game boards stimulate children; teachers frequently comment on how much children enjoy game-oriented center activities. Games give children the same practice they get through traditional drill or worksheet activity, but in a more enjoyable form. Therefore, game boards are generally used in reinforcement centers, since they involve activities that promote reinforcement of previously taught ideas or skills. You must carefully evaluate achievement levels within the class with respect to a particular skill so the game is neither too hard nor too easy. If the game is too easy, there was probably no need for practice in that skill (unless the purpose was to build independence or self-confidence). If the game is too hard, it will be frustrating, and constant failure will kill the children's motivation. Ideally, a game should be designed so that winning or losing depends on the children's ability to employ effective strategy to contend with the vagaries of chance. When games combine luck and skill, they keep competitiveness in balance; while motivating children to use their best skills, they also allow children to accept defeat graciously and realistically.

I will mention a few basic formats in board games that seem to be exceptionally popular with elementary school children. Each of these boards can be used for any area within the social studies curriculum. You can print the tasks on the game board squares or prepare a deck of cards with content questions or skills activities. For example, the cards may require the child to identify pictures, furnish definitions for

Experimenting

Interviewing

Constructing

Illustrating

HOW MANY BEANS IN THE BOTTLE?

Estimating

Collecting data

FIGURE 6–1

Appealing Activities with Concrete Materials

words, or associate states and capitals. To differentiate between easier and harder tasks, you can have the card specify the number of spaces a player can move, with answers to harder questions allowing children to move more spaces. Or place movement may be left to chance, and spinners or dice determine the number of spaces to be moved. For example, a child could roll a die and draw a card from a deck. If the child can do successfully what the card asks, he gets to move the number of spaces shown on the die. If he can't, the card is placed at the bottom of the deck and the child must remain where he is until his next move. The game continues until one player reaches the finishing point. In this way, that child or another player may get a chance to remember the right answer for the missed question if it comes up again later. To help sustain interest in game boards, you can include reward and punishment cards as well as skill cards in the deck; a spaceship race game board might contain cards like those shown in Figure 6–2.

Hundreds of start-finish game board ideas are possible for the imaginative teacher. How many can you add to this list?

Reach a pot of gold at the end of a rainbow

Have a cat catch the mouse

Shoot a rocket to the moon

Have a magnetized ladybug climb a stem to reach the flower

FIGURE 6–2

Sample Reward and Punishment Card

The same basic format can be followed to design game boards for soccer, football, baseball, tennis, volleyball, or other popular sports. Questions or tasks can be printed in the circles or squares on the board, which gives the game a limited life span, or the teacher can write rewards and punishments on the board and put questions and tasks on separate cards that can be changed as needed.

Imaginative teachers have created interest and enthusiasm among their children by designing novel independent *written activities* as shown in Figure 6–3. *Commercially prepared materials* can also be used in learning centers. Many good learning center games and activities are being marketed. Take advantage of them.

NUMBER OF ACTIVITIES.   The particular content, as well as the special needs and interests of your students, dictates the number of activities you will need for the center. Don't overwhelm the children by planning more than they can handle and don't provide them with such unattractive or unchallenging activities that

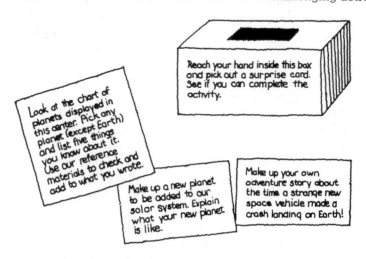

FIGURE 6–3

Sample Surprise Cards

interest in the center soon wanes. Don't hesitate to change or drop an activity if it seems indicated. Experience in using a learning center approach and observing children at work in centers will show you what constitutes an appropriate number and variety of activities.

SUCCESSFULLY COMPLETING A TASK. Build into the learning center some means or device so the children can tell immediately whether they have completed a task successfully. Provide a special answer key at the center for immediate reference, or place the answers on the reverse side of the activity card. Another approach to feedback is to use a code. Letters or numerals can be placed on the reverse side of the activity cards, and matching symbols on the bottoms of cans, cartons, or boxes into which the cards are to be sorted. *Symbol or color codes* can also be used. Children match colors or pictures to check their answers. Some activities are self-correcting by design; for example, when puzzle pieces fit together, they show the student he is correct.

Center directors may correct the children's work. Teacher's aides, parent volunteers, older students, or classmates who have completed the activity can do this. Teacher-student conferences are often used in addition to self-evaluation. They are especially useful as feedback for creative activities that have no one correct answer, or when the teacher wants to know more about the children's attitudes toward the activities in the centers. Of course, diagnostic information about the child's growth in skill or concept development also emerges as the teacher asks questions or observes pupil performance in activities.

DIRECTIONS. Giving clear directions enables the children to use the learning center activities independently. In addition to carefully introducing the children to each center activity and thoroughly explaining how to use it, clear directions should be displayed so the children will be constantly aware of the center's organizational pattern and can function independently.

Carefully print or type the directions. Be economical with your words. The nature of a learning center requires that children work independently, so make sure all of them understand the vocabulary. Avoid unnecessary words; for example, don't say, "Get some crayons. Find the stack of drawing paper. Take a piece of paper and draw a winter scene." Instead, say "Draw a winter scene." The materials should be provided right at the center. Underline or highlight key words that are essential for completing an activity; for example, "*Draw* a picture of. . . ." Whenever possible, use action words to begin directions; for example, "*Look* carefully at the picture. . . ."

Enumerate the directions in proper sequence; for example, "*First*, ask fifteen classmates to name their favorite rock stars. *Second*, list the names of the stars in order so that the most popular star is first, etc. *Third*, compare your list with a classmate's list. Are your lists the same or different? Why do you think this is so?" Include pictures or hand-drawn illustrations to help students who may have difficulty reading printed directions. A drawing of a pencil can illustrate a writing task or a picture of scissors a cutting task. Tape record the learning center directions for the very young child or the child who has extreme reading difficulties.

Providing examples in the directions is helpful. Whenever possible, try to make the directions open-ended; that is, encourage the child to extend the activity into a new area of interest: "How would the results be different if. . ." or "Compare your results with a friend. Why are they the same? Different?"

Explain in the directions how the finished work will be evaluated: an answer key? answers on the reverse side of the material? covered answers? Tell them what will be done with the finished work.

ATTRACTIVE BACKGROUNDS.   Children respond favorably to unique packaging techniques. Capitalize on this by providing a colorful background picture accompanied by a catchy caption to attract attention. Place the directions in a strategic spot on the center background. If you are not a great artist, don't despair; you can obtain pictures for center backgrounds from several sources. Commercially prepared transparencies can be projected on a sheet of oaktag. Trace around the image with a marking pen and color in the areas with other marking pens, crayons, or paint. You can also prepare your own transparencies by running a favorite picture through a thermofax machine or tracing it on a sheet of clear acetate. Use an overhead projector and follow the preceding procedure. Pictures can also be projected onto a sheet of oaktag with an opaque projector. Instead of projecting an image for tracing to create your center background, you can simply cut out illustrations from magazines and newspapers, store displays, advertising circulars, and coloring books and paste the pictures on heavy tagboard.

In addition, plan to create centers in a variety of shapes and place them in different spots in the classroom. (See Figure 6–4.) Learning centers should contain a number of activities necessary to complete an objective, that are multilevel in nature when the children differ in achievement levels. Three decisions you face in using a learning center format in the social studies classroom are: (1) familiarizing students with the organization and management patterns; (2) deciding when the centers will be used; and (3) assigning students to the centers.

INTRODUCING CENTERS

Since children need careful guidance with any new classroom procedure, an introduction to learning centers is no place to hurry. Introducing children to this new classroom learning arrangement all at once by setting up a room full of centers and expecting each child to work independently with little or no introduction may be devastating to both teacher and child. The analogy of the tortoise and the hare is apropos; starting out quickly with learning centers, you may find that the children do not understand what to do with them, even though they are enthusiastic and all too willing to rush headlong into them—just like the hare in the race. At this point, slow the children down and give more careful introduction to guide them in crossing the bridge between what may have been a formal classroom environment and the new learning center environment.

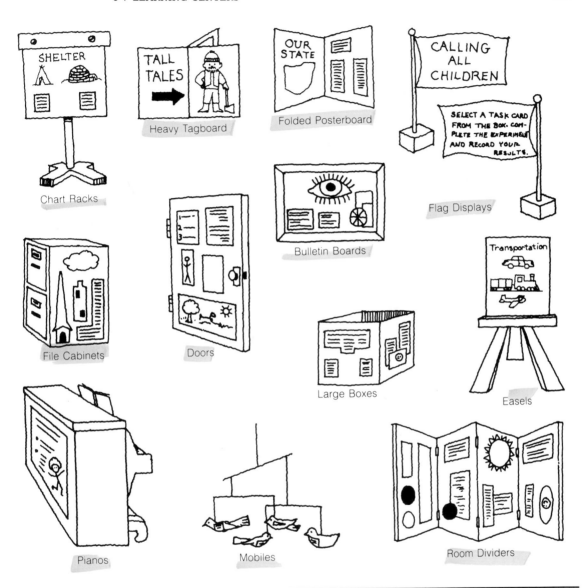

FIGURE 6–4

Sample of Shapes and Locations

To introduce learning centers, it is better to adopt the tortoise's gait rather than the hare's, establishing a starting point and proceeding very slowly while clearly explaining every step to the children. Gradually, you will find that your classroom is operating smoothly and efficiently, without the setbacks that befall an impulsive and hasty teacher.

Inform students about how the learning centers are to be used. Don't get involved with detailed educational jargon, but explain these points simply:

- What kinds of activities are available at our centers?
- When are the centers to be used?
- How is each center to be used?
- How are the children to be assigned to the various centers?
- What responsibilities do the children who are working at the centers have?
- What is to be done with the work that has been completed?

Tell the children of your availability for the social studies time slot. You will need to divide your time among activities such as giving individual or group assistance, holding conferences, special teaching to small groups, and guiding whole-group projects. Making your plans known to the children helps them in self-direction and in formulating their own plans for the class time.

Since no single way of introducing learning centers has proven best, all decisions should reflect the children's needs as well as the teacher's experience. Howes suggests three possible variations of introduction:

1. The teacher introduced and explained the new way of working to a few of the more mature students. Others were invited to participate as the teacher formed new groups with the experienced children serving as leaders. Gradually, the entire class made the change to the open classroom.

2. The teacher divided the class into four equal groups on a heterogeneous basis. The fourth group was introduced to the new program as the other three pursued their usual studies. The teacher rotated the pattern so that each group worked part of the day in the new pattern and part in the old pattern. Gradually, the time was lengthened for each group to work in the new program.

3. The whole class was introduced to the new way of working and the teacher continued the normal studies for those children who were more comfortable continuing in the traditional pattern. Gradually, more and more children began to spend more time in the new way of working until a complete change was made.[2]

USING THE CENTERS

Along with deciding *how* to introduce the new centers, you must identify *when* to use them most advantageously. Again, many different patterns have been tried successfully. You may decide, for example, to use the centers as a supplement to the social studies curriculum. Remember that slower-paced students are often unable to complete assigned work in time to work with the centers and may feel frustrated when they don't have a chance to participate because of time constraints. By assigning realistic follow-up activities for meeting individual differences, however, the teacher can alleviate this problem. Your schedule might look like this:

9:00–9:20   Teacher-guided, whole-class activities (textbook assignment, resource person, film, etc.)

9:20–   Follow-up activities (workbook pages, special projects, etc.)

10:00–   Children work in learning centers

With this pattern, the children who finish their follow-up activities most quickly have more time to work in the learning centers. If you want all the children to work in the learning centers, you might schedule only teacher-guided activities for half an hour, then have all the children go to learning centers. Another alternative is to use the centers as the basis for all instruction in the social studies curriculum. A certain time of the day can be scheduled for the students to work individually or in small groups with concepts and skills introduced and reinforced in learning centers. One word of caution: do not use learning centers as designated areas in which activities are isolated only for those who finish their assigned "seat work" before the other children or for those who are ready for advanced enrichment activities. This limited interpretation contradicts the belief that children should take responsibility for their own learning. Pupil participation in the social studies learning centers should not be restricted to special times or only for enrichment for the able learners. We risk a damaging blow to any interest the children may show to the approach by abusing centers this way.

The rate at which you can extend the use of learning centers will become apparent by the time you have followed some of these procedures. By thoroughly evaluating the children's capabilities for working with the centers, as well as observing their desire to work in a new classroom environment, you will begin to sense the amount of guidance necessary to move toward a completely decentralized approach to instruction.

When you have begun to introduce new centers and decentralize the surroundings, finding adequate space may pose a formidable problem. As shown in Figure 6–5, grouping desks may alleviate this problem and help you move to a less formal classroom setting. The transition from rows of desks to functional groupings of materials and equipment can be achieved in stages. Gradually, your room may evolve into an environment that encourages children to experience more and more physical and academic freedom. By removing some student desks, grouping others, bringing in tables, placing bookcases and screens to serve as partitions, introducing a couch or pillows in a reading/research corner, the classroom atmosphere changes from a formal environment to an informal activity-oriented place where children have opportunities to work independently, by themselves or in small groups.

Organizing Routines and Student Assignments

The way you organize your classroom often affects to what extent the children will become absorbed in the learning center activities. It also determines the effectiveness of classroom management. You should:

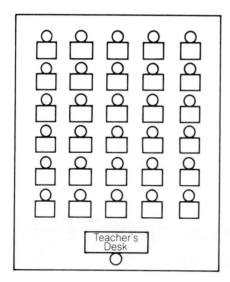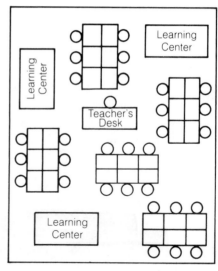

FIGURE 6-5
Formal to Informal

Separate areas that involve quiet activities from those that involve noisy activity

Provide areas for individual work and areas for group interaction

Reserve areas for displaying the children's work

Make provisions for neat storage of supplies and materials

Arrange adequate procedures for moving pupils to and from learning centers

The method of movement you decide on will closely reflect your personal educational philosophy, which will probably follow one of these patterns:

- Teacher makes all learning center assignments
- Teacher provides child with two or three alternatives and the child chooses from among them
- Teacher and children choose jointly from among all possible choices
- Children have free choice of all learning possibilities; teacher serves as a source for verification, classification, and evaluation

Scheduling

Among the scheduling procedures to consider are manipulative techniques, charts, and contracts.

MANIPULATIVES. For younger children, planning guides should be as concrete as possible to help them understand what they are to do in the various centers.

Having a manipulative visual plan also helps children use their work time appropriately. These are several concrete planning devices:

Coding. Each center has an assigned number, color, or shape. Assigning a child to a center can be done with a ticket, necklace, badge, or other device that corresponds to the code.

Pictures. Photographs of the children can be extremely useful in making center assignments. Take a picture of each child, mount it on a clothespin, and clip each to the center in which the child is to work.

Name Tags. Write learning center titles on a large, sturdy cardboard circle. Place clothespins with the children's names on the corresponding centers for each time of the day.

Tickets. Color code the centers. Use construction paper in corresponding colors to make tickets for admission to each center. The children match the colors of their tickets to the color symbol at the learning center.

CHARTS.   As seen in Figure 6–6, charts are useful tools. Attach library book pockets to a firm sheet of tagboard. Place a child's name on each pocket. Print the names of the learning centers on card strips. Put the cards into the pockets to indicate the learning center at which each child is to work.

CONTRACTS OR AGREEMENTS.   Contracts (some educators call them agreements) require students to sign up for the activities with which they will be working each day. With young children, the initial contract form should include pictorial symbols coordinated to symbols placed near or on the learning center. Gradually, the contract forms can become more abstract. Whatever the format for drawing contracts, the important outcome is that the children gain a sense of responsibility for following a daily or weekly planning guide.

Various formats for contracts progress from concrete to abstract representation of centers and from limited to greater student choice of which center to work in and

FIGURE 6–6
Sample Chart

of activities within a center. Also, as children gain experience in choosing and completing activities, they can take on greater responsibilities for organizing their own time.

In Figure 6–7, the teacher assigns each child to a center. The child colors the circle with crayon to identify the center to which he has been assigned. The centers are color coded.

In Figure 6–8, the teacher puts checks in the circles to specify the one or two centers at which a child is to work. The child is free to choose one or two additional centers she would like to work in. The Meeting Box indicates a teacher- or pupil-initiated conference period.

The contract forms in Figure 6–9 are especially useful for project-oriented learning centers and call on the children to make long-range commitments to complete work in a chosen area of interest.

Record Keeping

Effective record keeping is essential to the success of learning-center-based instruction. With concise record-keeping forms, excessive paper work and hours of extensive review can be minimized. Forms of various design can be used to keep track of children's interests, involvement, skills, and deficiencies. Some of these forms can be completed by the children; others will have to be maintained by the teacher. A complete description of the many different individual and whole-class record-keeping instruments is beyond the scope of this book; however, a few general suggestions will stimulate your thinking toward formulating alternative models.

Table 6–1 illustrates a whole-class record form. The *1* indicates that a child has contracted for the activity, while the + indicates that the activity has been satisfactorily completed.

Individual record sheets help the teacher develop a clear picture of each child's growth. Simple record forms prevent accumulation of volumes of information. Most of the data you record on the sheets are gathered from individual conferences. The conferences should be part of the teacher's daily work plan, with a definite time set aside for discussing each individual's progress.

In addition to formal conferences, a great deal of evaluation in the informal classroom occurs during planned group discussions. The teacher should schedule a short period (ten to fifteen minutes) to follow the use of learning centers for sharing ideas,

TABLE 6–1
Whole-Class Record Form

Name	Map Center	Research	Construction	Games
Joe	1			+
Myra		1		+
Tom	1	+		
Jane			1	

FIGURE 6–7
Color-coded Contract

FIGURE 6–8
Check-coded Contract

CONTRACT

I am interested in doing the following work in the

_____ learning center.

_____

_____

_____

I will spend about _____ minutes each day in
the center. It will take me about _____ days to
finish my work

SEAL
OF
APPROVAL

My signature

_____

Ye Olde Contract

I, _____ do hereby agree to work in
_____ learning center and com-
plete the activities listed below. It will take
me about _____ days to finish my work

Activities and Projects
☐ Charts and graphs
☐ Scrapbooks
☐ Cartoon or editorial

FIGURE 6–9
Project-oriented Contract

comparing projects, talking about how children feel about the centers, and so on.
Open discussion is an important and valuable experience in the classroom.

Besides planned and informal conferences with the children, various types of
student record forms can be used to gather information about how meaningful, interesting, enjoyable, or appropriate the children find the centers. A sample student

checklist is presented in Figure 6–10 for primary-grade youngsters; for older children, you can use index cards and have them fill them in in a format like this:

Another Day in the Life of _____		Date: _____
Center	Activity	My Personal Reaction

Giving It a Try

Trying something new is always a bit frightening. But you will know how effective you have been when you observe whether you are more relaxed, more stimulated, more excited about teaching and whether your children are more interested, more involved, and happier in school.

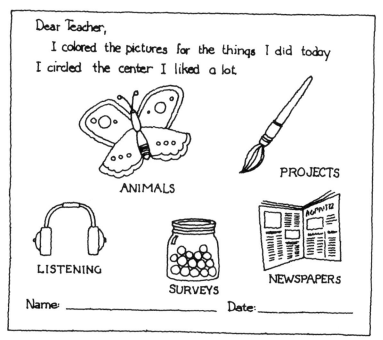

FIGURE 6–10
Primary-grade Student Checklist

You will know whether it has been a profitable experience when you observe whether the children are developing proficiencies and skills in subject areas and whether they seem to be gaining self-confidence, initiative, and independence. You will know by their test scores, comments from their parents, and their motivation whether their achievement is the same, poorer, or better than it had been in a more formal learning environment. You will judge the impact of this approach on individual children. You will know which ones flourish in an environment that encourages responsibility for self-learning and which ones need more structure, more instruction, more outer controls. Eventually, you will be able to design a classroom flexible enough to meet almost all the children's needs.

Two learning center plans will help you begin to implement an informal approach to social studies instruction in your classroom.

TRAVELING THROUGH TIME.   This learning center promotes concepts of colonial America. The center, designed to place the children in the role of problem solvers, requires them to research stimulating questions about colonial life. They record the information they uncover and design ways to creatively share their findings. The center should be stocked with a variety of books, maps, photographs, audiovisual aids, and any other learning resources that will help the students in their investigations (Figure 6–11).

FIGURE 6–11
Traveling Through Time

Games and Activities

Newspaper Notebook: Stock the center with appropriate reference materials about colonial America. Instruct the children to imagine that they have been taken back in history to the period of colonial America. To report back to their newspaper, they are to keep an accurate account of what happened on their time travels. The first four activities stimulate the creation of a newspaper story.

Map It Out: In your time capsule, there is a map that shows you how America looked in the 1700s. Write the name of each of the thirteen English colonies on the map.

Take a Good Look: Children act as reporters and fill in the statement, "I landed at _____. This is what I saw. . . ." Choose any place in colonial America where you imagine your time capsule landed. Draw the first four things you saw after you emerged from the time capsule.

Photo Album: You met a boy whose father was an important man in colonial history. Many people came to his house to meet with him. Draw a picture of the four most unforgettable people you met during your stay. Beneath each picture, describe the work that person was most famous for (Figure 6–12).

Newspaper Report: While your friend was doing his chores, he gave you a newspaper to look at. You realized that many important events were occurring in our country at that time. What events did you read about in the newspaper dur-

FIGURE 6–12
Photo Album

ing your time visit? Write the stories that go with the headlines and draw the picture (Figure 6–13).

Colonial Parade: Provide boxes, crêpe paper, tagboard, construction paper, clay, and other construction materials. The child is to select a scene, person, object, or event important in colonial history. She decorates a box with crêpe paper and construction paper to look like a parade float, as in Figure 6–14. She identifies her selection and constructs, mounts, or draws appropriate items on the box. Arrange the floats in parade fashion near the learning center display.

Colonial Hall of Fame: Create pedestals out of boxes mounted on heavy tagboard and display them at the learning center (Figure 6–15). The children each select a person who contributed a great deal to colonial life. They draw his or her picture, glue a tongue depressor to the back of the picture, and stick it in a pedestal. They write a short description of the chosen person's contributions and paste it on the pedestal below the picture. Add members to the "Hall of Fame" as children contribute their choices.

2087: Draw a large crystal ball on construction paper and mount it near the learning center (Figure 6–16). Instruct the children to imagine what their homes, city, or country will be like one hundred years from now. They write their ideas on circles cut out of construction paper and paste them on the crystal ball. Questions like these will spur their thinking:

What will be the greatest invention?
Where will be the farthest place to which we will travel?
What will your school be like?
What will be the most popular sport?
What kind of transportation will be most popular?
What kinds of jobs will people be doing?

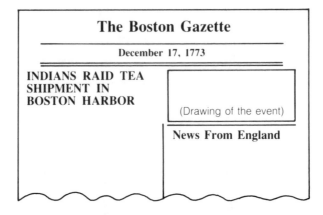

FIGURE 6–13
Newspaper Headlines

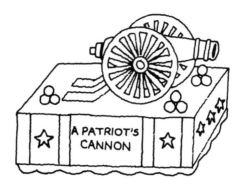

FIGURE 6–14

Parade Float

FIGURE 6–15

Pedestals

FIGURE 6–16
Crystal Ball

What kinds of foods will people eat?
What will be done to cure hunger? illness? conflict among humans?

LOOK AT ME!   A center like this one promotes creative self-expression and growth in values and attitudes. The activities at this center help children get to know themselves and each other better. They share facts, feelings, and experiences and become aware of how they see themselves, how they see others, and how others see them. They develop a sense of and a respect for the uniqueness of each human

FIGURE 6–17
Look At Me!

being. Some of the material that emerges becomes highly personal, and the teacher must exercise judgment about how to use and share it (Figure 6–17).

Games and Activities

I Am Me: Take a photograph of each child. Provide copies of a data sheet, as shown in Figure 6–18. Each child completes the information on the data sheet and pastes his picture at the top. The children hang their completed data sheets in the classroom for others to read and discuss. This activity must be completed before beginning the second activity.

Who Am I? Provide a supply of white construction paper and marking pens. Instruct the children to use a strong flashlight or the light from the overhead projector to make a silhouette. To do this, one child sits in a chair between the strong light and a wall to which the construction paper has been tacked. Another child traces the silhouetted profile on the construction paper. Then they switch positions. When both have a profile, they draw or paste pictures on them to represent the information from their data sheets in the previous activity (Figure 6–19). Each day, display three or four completed silhouettes on the center background. Number them and have the children examine the silhouettes and guess who each one is. Guesses may be written on voting sheets. At the end of the day, reveal whose silhouettes were displayed and see how many correct guesses were made.

My Mood Book: In a box or envelope, put strips of paper identifying many differ-

I am _____ .
I am _____ years old.
My address is _____ .
My phone number is _____ .
My favorites:
Hobby _____ Color _____
Sport _____ Book _____
Food _____ Animal _____
My pet peeve is _____ .

FIGURE 6–18
Photograph and Data Sheet

FIGURE 6–19
Who Am I?

ent moods: happy, sad, angry, silly, afraid, disappointed, excited, nervous, frustrated. In another box, put a supply of white paper and cardboard picture frames. The child chooses a mood word and draws a picture of himself showing how he looks when he is in that mood. He pastes the picture in the frame, then writes a little story telling about a time he was in that mood. After the child has done a few mood stories, he can combine them into a book by punching holes and using paper fasteners or yarn, and making a cover, title page, and table of contents. Display the children's books in the classroom for everybody to read (Figure 6–20).

My Coat of Arms: Prepare dittoed coats of arms, as illustrated in Figure 6–21. In each section, have children draw pictures or symbols, or write words, phrases, or sentences in response to questions you suggest. Display the finished products on an attractive bulletin board. Possible questions are: What three things are

FIGURE 6–20
My Moods

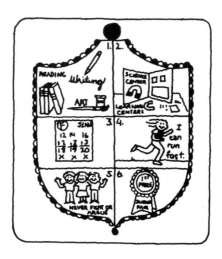

FIGURE 6–21
Coat of Arms

you good at in school? What is one thing you like to do most in our school? What would you like most to change or improve about yourself at school? What is one thing your classmates admire about you? What one thing can your friends do to make you happy in school? What has been your greatest accomplishment in school?

SUMMARY

There is not one common definition that explains the term "learning center." Perhaps a major reason for this problem of definition is that learning centers are designed primarily to meet children's needs in unique ways. Because of this personalization, learning centers differ from one another much as children do, and it is as difficult to describe a typical learning center as it is to describe a typical child.

As they apply to the ideas in this book, learning centers are activities that organize individualized instruction in ways that encourage children to assume major responsibility for their own learning; thus, any independent activity in which the children provide major direction for their own learning is considered a learning center.

Different purposes determine what types of learning centers we find in a social studies classroom. The centers may be designed (1) to reinforce skills previously learned, (2) to acquire information through problem solving and inquiry, (3) to stimulate creativity, and (4) to examine attitudes and values. After establishing the purposes for the centers, the teacher must plan their design. These guidelines will help in designing a social studies center: (1) analyze pupils' needs and interests; (2) choose effective, attractive activities and materials; (3) provide clear directions; and (4) create an attractive background display.

The activities and suggestions in this chapter reflect a step-by-step approach to changing the classroom setting; however, the sequence need not be followed slavishly. Choose the elements that are most appropriate to your children's needs and interests, and adapt or ignore those that do not appear to adequately address individual needs.

ENDNOTES

1. Albert Cullum, *Push Back the Desks* (New York: Citation Press, 1967), p. 13.

2. Virgil M. Howes, *Informal Teaching in the Open Classroom* (New York: Macmillan, 1974), pp. 197–98.

Valuing Processes

KEY CONCEPTS

- ☐ *Understanding the requisite classroom atmosphere for conducting effective values programs in the elementary school*
- ☐ *Identifying some general social values as they derive from our legal system, our traditions, and our heritage*
- ☐ *Planning and utilizing* indirect *methods of teaching values to elementary school children in situations that occur naturally in the classroom*
- ☐ *Planning and utilizing* direct *methods of values instruction in situations that encourage children to examine values choices and understand how decisions are made*

> I have rarely been able to pinpoint an unequivocal right or wrong on my own, but at least when I was a child I felt secure that my mother and Franklin Delano Roosevelt could. Even as an adolescent, when almost all issues seemed up for re-examination, there were some moral truths which seemed unambivalent: .... you shouldn't steal song sheets and makeup from the 5 & 10, and you shouldn't copy on an exam. (This last was becoming confusing because so many of my friends, of otherwise impeccable character, were doing it.)
>
> In college, where a lot of useful un-learning takes place, my friends and I spent many long nights in passionate discussion of such old saws as who is permitted into the crowded lifeboat and whether *any* war is justifiable. ...
>
> I'm not sure whether my present moral uncertainties are the product of age or circumstance; but lately the issues seem infinitely more complex, and the people in decision-making positions are no help in clarifying where the [values] imperative lies.[1]

In a simpler culture, societal issues seemed clear-cut; there was usually only one side for a "good citizen" to take on any issue. Schools, too, operated on the assumption that absolute values could be identified, so they carefully controlled teaching methodology and subject matter selection so as to transmit the values identified as "right," "desirable," or "good." Educators assumed that the best technique for transmitting values was *inculcation*, or direct instruction of specific values. In the 1800s emphasis was on reading, memorizing, and repeating value-laden materials, often of a religious flavor, as we see in this selection from the *Boston Primer* of 1808:

Let Children who would fear the LORD,
  Hear what their Teachers say,
With rev'rence meet their Parents' word,
  And with Delight obey.[2]

Values training also occurred in teachers' verbal interaction with the children, as in this recitation:

T: You must obey your parents.
S: I must obey my parents. (The pupils, at each repetition, place the right hand, opened, upon the breast.)
T: You must obey your teachers.
S: I must obey my teachers.[3]

At those rare times that children questioned their superiors about a behavior, the dialogue might have gone like this:

Master: You must not do so.
  Child: And why must I not do so?
Master: Because it is naughty.
  Child: Naughty! Why is that being naughty?

Master: Doing what you are forbid.

Child: And what harm is there in doing what one is forbid?

Master: The harm is, you will be whipped for disobedience.

Child: Then I will do it so that nobody will know anything of the matter.

Master: O, but you will be watched.

Child: Ah! But then I will hide myself.

Master: Then you will be examined.

Child: Then I will tell a fib.

Master: But you must not tell fibs.

Child: Why must not I?

Master: Because it is naughty.[4]

Educators of the time justified the process of inculcation with arguments like this: "Thus, we go round the circle: and yet, if we go out of it, the child understands us no longer. . . .I could be very curious to know what could be substituted in the place of this fine dialogue. . . .To distinguish between good and evil, to perceive the reasons on which our moral obligations are founded, is not the business, as it is not within the capacity, of a child."[5]

Young children were considered incapable of making personal decisions because they had not yet acquired the ability to think rationally. The most popular practice thus required manipulating the environment or the experiences to which students were exposed so as to promote certain values outcomes.

Today's issues, however, are much more complex; the contrasts and changes we must deal with are overwhelming. Contemporary youth often reject traditional values, and as a result, become confused about what values *to* accept. They are not convinced they will have any personal use for the knowledge they acquire in school. What should teachers do? Should they ignore questions of values? Should they teach specific values, as in the past, or should they try to encourage the development of personal values in some other way?

Sanford A. Lakoff feels the central problem of values education lies not in whether values should be part of the curriculum, but only *how* they should be dealt with. At one extreme are people who believe that citizens' failure to understand certain democratic values would undermine the American political system. Proponents of this position do not give teachers license to project their own value preferences, but recommend direct instruction of certain values; they seem afraid to entrust the future to an emerging generation that is not completely instilled with unwavering pride in the American way of life. At the other extreme are those who believe all values are subjective, nothing is truly right or wrong, and all values are exclusively a matter of personal taste. More moderate types like Lakoff feel the first position borders on totalitarian teaching—at best, an inconsistent approach to teaching democratic values: "How can you perpetuate democratic values such as *freedom of choice* without offering opportunities to examine and choose?" The other end of the continuum appears naive: "How can one generation expect to pass on its ideals to the next when, by definition of this approach, it has nothing to transmit?" Education has settled more toward the center position than at either of the extremes.

This is certainly the position of the National Council for the Social Studies, as we discussed in Chapter 1. Review their *Democratic Beliefs;* you will find that some democratic tenets (justice, equality, responsibility, freedom, diversity, and privacy) are considered sufficiently basic that schools should treat them as instructional necessities. The NCSS advises that "As a matter of policy, the public clearly expects schools to inculcate those values on which there is consensus. . . .The main thrust of democratic beliefs and values is to guarantee the continuance of respect for human dignity and freedom."

How should we teach these beliefs and values in the social studies curriculum? Both *indirect* and *direct* methods are appropriate. Indirect methods have to do with the classroom environment and the example set by the teacher. Direct methods include identification and examination of specific values for intensive study and analysis.

INDIRECT METHODS FOR TEACHING VALUES

The instructional climate of the classroom should mirror the beliefs promoted in the social studies program. Merely by the fact that teachers "live" with the children each school year makes them an important influence on their students' values. Undoubtedly, the value system you communicate to the children during interpersonal situations each day sways them as much as any other single factor. What do you communicate, for example, if you openly scold a child in front of others for accidentally spilling a jar of paint? Could it be that you value the paint more than the child's feelings? What do you seem to prize if you openly criticize a child's "sloppy paper" when the child has tried her best to be neat? Worse, what will these interactions eventually do to children who must first feel capable as individuals before they can participate effectively in situations that call for free, autonomous thinking?

When teachers demonstrate a disregard for individual worth by consistently communicating "There's something wrong with you" messages, students internalize an image of inadequacy and will eventually resist or withdraw from situations that require independent thought. The overall influence you have on value development is far from clear, but it should be apparent that the extent to which your own value system permeates interpersonal relationships with children provides either a model of consistency or a model of confusion to the child. Ask yourself, "Does my classroom encourage initiative and individuality or does it emphasize blind conformity?" Your answer determines whether you believe it is appropriate to raise questions that call on children to reflect on and clarify their values.

In the primary grades, children need many formal and informal activities that help develop an adequate "ego strength" that is prerequisite to personal decision making. We discussed some of these activities in Chapter 4 in regard to the personal and social factors that influence effective group work. These activities help youngsters distinguish themselves from others and promote the self-confidence required to defend a personal choice against peers when they must reconcile contradictory value positions. The socialization tasks recommended in Chapter 4 extend the concepts of individuality to accepting one's place in a group. From such experiences, children learn to understand a basic principle that underlies the rights and responsibilities of individuals in a democratic society: establishing and maintaining rules and order with cooperation and mutual respect.

Establishing Rules

Learning about rules and their role in helping govern personal conduct is an appropriate and convenient way to begin. Instead of making a rules chart or stating a set of predetermined, teacher-made rules, however, your program might begin with an understanding that rules are necessary for people's safe, orderly interaction. Unstructured literature experiences can help children establish concrete referents for that complex understanding. Marie Winn's book *Shiver, Gobble, and Snore* is a particularly useful resource.[6] The story focuses upon a funny king who made silly rules. In his kingdom lived three unhappy subjects: Shiver, who was always cold; Gobble, who was always hungry; and Snore. Guess what he liked to do. Many of the king's rules adversely affected these characters, so they decided to move away to a place where there would be no rules. Alas, the three friends discovered that disputes could not be resolved in their new land—because they had no rules. They finally decided that to live peacefully, they must make rules. After reading them the story, you can lead the children through a discussion: What are rules? Who made the rules in the kingdom? Did the rules make sense or were they foolish? Did all the people want to obey the rules? Why or why not? What did they decide to do? What else could they have done? What have you learned about rules?

Another excellent literature resource is one of the episodes from *The Tale of Peter Rabbit* by Beatrix Potter in which Peter is instructed not to go into Mr. McGregor's garden. Discuss the following: What rule did Peter's mother give him? Why do you suppose she made it? Did Peter obey the rule? What happened to Peter because he did not follow the rule? Who makes rules in your family? Why are those rules made? What happens when those rules are not obeyed?

The purpose of these questions is to encourage children to realize that rules are necessary to protect people's rights and safety from others' unacceptable behaviors. At this point, you may wish to introduce a classroom "Guardian of Rules"—perhaps a stuffed animal or a colorfully illustrated character—to help the children discuss these questions: Do *we* need rules? Why? What are some problems we might have if there were no rules? Who should make the rules? What are some rules that are important for our classroom?

Design a colorful display of these rules and place it in a prominent classroom location. When problems arise, you can pretend to consult your "Guardian of Rules" and let the character lead the children in an exchange of opinions about how to solve the conflict.

You can introduce older children to the need for rules and lead them to understand the essential nature of rules in the lives of citizens in a democracy through a game sequence like this one:

- Phase 1   Divide your class into equal-size groups. Give each group member a wooden block and tell them to play a game. Watch the children as they try to figure out what to do. When you notice the groups reaching a point of frustration, stop them and lead a discussion with these questions: What took place when you started to design the game? Did you have any problems? Why? How did you decide to make the rules? Who made up the rules?

- Phase 2   Ask each group to pass its blocks to one member. Declare that person the winner. Then discuss these questions: Did this rule bother anyone? Is it important for you to share in making the rules? Why? How can we all share in decisions?

- Phase 3   Follow the suggestions the children offer in their response to Phase 2 and create rules for a game using the blocks distributed to each group. After the rules are written, have them play the game. Many will have designed a good sequence to follow, but some groups may have created rules that contradict each other or are too difficult to follow. Frustration will certainly result. At this point, the children can eagerly discuss their feelings about the problems that arise from unclear rules or too many rules.

After this game sequence, you may want to focus on these concepts:

1. What is a rule?
   (a guide that helps us know how to act)

2. Where are rules?
   (everywhere—home, school, community, etc.)

3. Why do we need rules?
   (they protect us and help us to live together in groups)

4. Who makes rules?
   (everyone can help make rules in our country)

5. Why should we follow rules?
   (people will find it hard to get along; it may be dangerous or unsafe; someone might be punished)

Following this discussion, let the students help develop a list of classroom rules. Emphasize the need for good, clear, concise rules to help the classroom run smoothly. These rules should be appealingly illustrated and placed around the room for reinforcement. The hope is that with this personalized input from the children, they will follow the rules voluntarily. But when they do not, how do we handle *conflicts* in the classroom? Generally, teachers have these options:

1. Be a dictator. When conflicts arise, the teacher's position always prevails. You make the decision and the children follow your wishes. This teacher takes the position that "I'll never let these kids run over me; they've got to know who's boss."

2. Be permissive. These teachers feel that children should have total freedom in their actions. They dislike confrontation so much that they look the other way and pretend that a problem has not happened. Through freedom of action, permissive teachers hope that children will maintain their self-respect and learn to like their teacher even more.

3. Be democratic. This pattern of teacher-child conflict resolution is based upon mutual respect. The democratic teacher employs a number of interpersonal interactions to encourage joint solutions to conflict situations.

Teacher Effectiveness Training

The democratic approach to conflict resolution is explicated in Thomas Gordon's Teacher Effectiveness Training (TET). Gordon's program is based on the resolution of two types of situations that often contribute to conflict in the classroom: (1) when the child has a problem, and (2) when the teacher has a problem.

A CHILD'S PROBLEM. Gordon believes the most useful skill for helping solve another person's problem is the technique of *active listening.* TET claims that when children are upset or troubled, most teachers don't listen at all; instead, they tend to moralize, preach, criticize, or give advice. When children appear upset, a teacher's tendency is to talk: "Oh, come on. If at first you don't succeed, try, try again," or "Stop crying, you're no baby," or "That wouldn't have happened if only you were more careful." Gordon refers to these statements as "roadblocks to communication." The responses teachers make when children are troubled often block further communication by making children feel "bad," "stupid," or "untrustworthy." As a result they often withdraw completely, fight back, or become resentful and angry. These are some roadblocks Gordon describes:

1. Ordering, Commanding, Directing   By giving children direct, forceful orders ("I don't care if it's snowing; sit down and finish your work") teachers often produce fear of their power.

2. Warning, Threatening   These messages are like commands, but consequences are added: "If you don't finish your work I'm going to keep you in for recess all week." Again, we allude to the teacher's use of power.

3. Moralizing, Preaching   These messages communicate to students that the teacher is always "right" and because of this wisdom, the children should rely on their judgment: "You have to learn one important thing; good boys never tell lies."

4. Lecturing, Arguing, Giving logical arguments   These messages try to influence the student with lengthy, one-sided interpretations of facts or opinions.

5. Judging, Criticizing   Characterized as put-down messages, these statements denigrate the student and chip away at self-esteem: "You're acting like a bunch of wild animals today" or "You are always the one who starts trouble around here."

6. Praising, Agreeing, Giving positive evaluations. While most teachers understand the terrible power of *negative* statements, they are often shocked to hear that praise is not always beneficial to children. A positive statement that does not match a child's self-image is often interpreted as a subtle attempt to manipulate; absence of praise in a classroom normally loaded with it may be interpreted as punishment; praise is sometimes embarrassing when given publicly ("Janie is the *only* one who got a perfect paper"). Students who are praised a lot may become overdependent upon it.

7. Name-calling, Ridiculing   These are forms of negative evaluation that have a devastating effect on children: "I never taught a class of babies before."

8. Probing, Questioning   Sometimes questions convey lack of trust or have the effect of putting a child in a corner: "How long did you work on that report? Only two class periods? Well, no wonder it was not what I expected."

9. Sarcasm, Humoring   When children have a problem, they need to talk about it and are generally serious about it. They need respect; if faced with distractions, they will take their problems elsewhere: "Are you a clown today, Al? Well, fold up your tent and take your act elsewhere."[7]

Instead of roadblocks, Gordon recommends that teachers demonstrate *acceptance* through a willingness to relate to and listen to the children. When children have problems, they need and want to share them; they need teachers to *listen*— not talk—to them. "But I *do* listen to my children," most teachers claim. Surely, listening does help children open up and share their inner feelings, but TET promotes an even more effective strategy: *active listening*, a way of responding to a child that is new and at first strange to many teachers. To understand active listening, we must first examine the communication process.

For instance, any message emitted by an individual can be interpreted as a coded effort to describe his inner state. What the listener hears is the listener's *personal interpretation* (decoding) of the sender's message.

In Figure 7–1, the teacher "hears" the child's statement as a neutral request for information. Actually, however, this student is feeling anxiety because he fears alligators and realizes he may have to look at the reptiles. Obviously, he must communicate this fear by going through the process of encoding, or selecting verbal symbols to describe an inner state. We are supposing he chose the verbal code represented in Figure 7–1a, the direct question: "Are we going to the zoo today?" The receiver of the coded message must then attempt to decode it—to understand the meaning of the message and respond accordingly (Figure 7–1b). While the receiver *infers* the meaning of the message, he cannot be sure whether he is right or wrong because the receiver "cannot read the sender's mind." Therefore, you need to determine the accuracy of your decoding effort. This determination is the heart of active listening. All you need to do is *feed back* the results of your decoding, as in Figure 7–1c. Paraphrased "feedback" of the child's message is intended to open up lines of communication by creating a safe psychological environment in which children realize their needs are heard, you want to hear more, and the concern will be dealt with. Hearing feedback, the child would probably say, "That's right, but

FIGURE 7–1
Message Codes

I'm afraid of alligators." Feedback, then, helped clarify the child's original reason for asking the question and might have led to a conversation like this:

Teacher: Oh, you're worried that we'll stop at the alligators.

Child: Yes. I don't like to look at them. They're scary.

Teacher: When we get to the alligator house you can stay with Mrs. Martin at the tigers. Is that okay?

Child: What a relief! I'm not worried now.

The skill of active listening takes much practice but is an extremely valuable technique of conflict resolution. It provides a model of joint problem solving within a democratic environment where people are free to think, explore, and share feelings.

A TEACHER'S PROBLEM.   It is one thing to become effective in helping children deal with *their* problems, but what should be the democratic teacher's role when children give *her* problems—when children are being noisy or disruptive, for example. When children have a problem, you communicate your willingness to relate to and listen to them. Now, when *you* have a problem—when your needs or rights are being violated—you must communicate to the children what you are feeling without sending a message of condemnation. The *wrong* way to communicate your feelings is by what Gordon calls "You-Messages":

"*You're* a real bunch of monkeys today."

"*You* better stop that right now!"

"*You* act so foolish when you do that."

"*You* better grow up and act your age."

These messages are predictably useless—they make the child resist change, damage self-esteem, and often lead to resentment. With TET, teachers learn to send different messages that maintain leadership responsibility, get the point across, and avoid hurting the child's feelings. Gordon calls these messages "I-Messages." Effective I-Messages have three basic elements:

1. Stating *what* (specific behavior) is creating a problem for the teacher: "*When the work materials are not returned to their proper places . . .*"
2. Clearly identifying the effect of the specific behavior on the teacher: "When the work materials are not returned to their proper places, *I have to waste a lot of my time putting them away . . .*"
3. Communicating the teacher's feelings that result from the condition or behavior: "When the work materials are not returned to their proper places, I have to waste a lot of my time putting them away and *often get frustrated.*"[8]

The sequence is important but not rigid. An I-Message in any order (or even with a part missing), if sincere, stands a good chance of being heard by the child as an honest and open statement. The intent is not to hurt or embarrass the child, but only to alert the child that you have a problem and are asking for help rather than inviting a confrontation. It demonstrates your trust in children and your acceptance of them as worthwhile individuals. And, as children understood your desire to help them with their problems through your active listening technique, they will learn to alter their problem behaviors out of consideration for your needs.

The techniques of active listening and I-Messages are foreign to teachers who view conflict resolution as win-lose confrontations. This approach implies a power struggle that builds resentment between teacher and children. One type of win-lose format is the teacher's constant use of a power-based authority role to reward or punish student behaviors; resentment flows from student to teacher as the teacher "wins" and child "loses." Other win-lose–oriented teachers look at conflict resolution as giving in to the children; teachers like this are manipulated and controlled by the children. When teachers, for whatever reason, are so permissive, they can be considered "losers" and the children "winners." Resentment then flows from teacher to children. These teachers eventually develop coping behaviors such as escape (perhaps through heavy eating or drinking), not associating with peers, or resigning. Instead of these two potentially damaging win-lose confrontations, Gordon proposes a *no-lose* conflict resolution method.

No-lose methods are employed whenever the I-Message or active listening techniques fail. When this happens, the temptation is often to moralize or lecture; instead, the teacher must change the approach. Gordon calls this approach Method III, or the no-lose *process* of working through a conflict from beginning to end during which teacher and children put their heads together to search for possible solutions.

In this example, Mr. Marshall and his student, Alice, use Method III to resolve a classroom conflict:

Mr. Marshall: Alice, when your group talks so loudly it makes it difficult for me to concentrate on helping Gary with his model, and I feel it's unfair to him. (I-Message because teacher owns problem)

Alice: But you asked us to finish our project by next week and we have to talk so we can get our plans straight. (Expresses own problem)

Mr. Marshall: I see. You're talking so loudly because you're concerned about the time you have left for completing your project. (Active listening)

Alice: Yes. We have to finish up our research by Tuesday or we won't have time to plan our skit to show the rest of the class on Thursday.

Mr. Marshall: It sounds like you're under some real pressure, but I also feel pressure to help Gary. We have a real problem. Do you have any ideas about how we can solve it?

Alice: Well . . . would it be okay for our group to work in the library? It's always empty during this hour and the librarian said she is willing to let us work there by ourselves if she's there.

Mr. Marshall: That would sure solve the problem. Alice, you go down the hall and check with Miss Lawrence to see if it's okay with her.

Notice how the teacher used all the skills of democratic conflict resolution we have talked about so far. When both needs were known, it was not difficult for Alice and Mr. Marshall to find a solution without forcing either party to resort to power. They both "won." Method III of conflict resolution is a six-step problem-solving process:

1. Define the problem (make sure both parties understand it)

2. Generate possible solutions (be open-ended; do not evaluate proposed solutions yet)

3. Evaluate the solutions (both parties state their opinions and preferences)

4. Make the decision (if steps 1, 2, and 3 are followed, step 4 usually results in a solution; if it does not, do not vote, but try to work toward consensus—invite both parties to try things out and, if they do not work, to reconsider and change)

5. Implement the decision (determine *who* does *what* and *when*; the failure of problem-solving efforts is usually attributable to lack of sound implementation)

6. Assess the solution (check on the effectiveness of your efforts: Has the problem gone away? Are we happy with our decision? How did our decision work out?)[9]

Skills in positive conflict resolution will help you as a teacher not only in the ways they contribute to effective classroom management but also in how they model the highest ideals of humanitarianism and democracy. You may want to do further reading into Teacher Effectiveness Training or other techniques for developing your skills as a democratic teacher. Become aware of workshops that teach these skills and explain their uses and abuses. Strive to become a model of the democratic processes you profess to your children. It will help you gain a new perspective on children and help your children gain a new perspective of their world.

A democratic system gives us freedoms and, at the same time, limits our freedoms—rules and laws balance and protect personal or group interests and rights. To clarify children's ideas about democratic functioning, the classroom must reflect "regulated freedom." An appreciation for regulation within a democratic framework presupposes acceptance of the principles that underlie those regulations: (1) rules reflect social values; (2) rules are created to regulate human behavior; and (3) rules assume voluntary compliance. Elementary school social studies programs should encourage examination of those principles through both direct activities and informal interactions.

Carl R. Rogers emphasizes that any values program must begin by establishing supportive social environments where children are encouraged to tune into their own and others' feelings, where they are taught communication skills that maximize interpersonal understanding, and where they are given opportunities to make informed decisions. It is in such an environment that values can be meaningfully examined and that individuals can come to appreciate the fundamental democratic beliefs of justice, equality, responsibility, freedom, diversity, and privacy.

VALUES

Rogers says the term *value* can be used in several ways:

1. *Operative values*—the tendency of individuals to show preference for one kind of objects or objectives rather than another. For example, a young child reaches out for a red ball instead of a blue one. The value choice, many times unconscious, is made simply by selecting one object and rejecting another.
2. *Conceived values*—the tendency of individuals to show preference for a symbolized object. Usually the individual involves conceptual thinking as he anticipates the outcome of such a symbolized object. For example, a choice such as "an eye for an eye" is considered a conceived value.[10]

Even the infant has a clear approach to values:

Hunger is negatively valued. His expression of this often comes through loud and clear.

Food is positively valued. But when he is satisfied, food is negatively valued, and the same milk he responded to so eagerly is now spit out . . .

All of this is commonplace, but let us look at these facts in terms of what they tell us about the infant's approach to values. . . . What is going on seems best described as an organismic valuing process in which each element, each moment of what he is experiencing, is somehow weighed and selected or rejected. . . . This complicated weighing of experience is clearly an organismic, not a conscious or symbolic function. These are operative, not conceived values.[11]

Rogers views operative valuing as a sound process because the infant evaluates and decides strictly within himself. He is not yet influenced by parents, peers, churches, teachers, or other "experts" in the field. Eventually, we lose this highly efficient system and move toward actions that bring us social approval, affection, or esteem.

Humanistic Classrooms

A major concern of educators is to determine how teachers can develop valuing maturity in children while maintaining many of the unbridled decision-making characteristics of the child at infancy. They feel the process is best carried out in an environment where the child is prized as an individual, where his feelings are understood and valued, and where he is given freedom to experience his own feelings and those of others without being threatened.

Teachers in this kind of humanistic environment look at children as unique individuals and accept them for what they are. The teacher may say, for example, "Angela really helped her social studies group today with all the nice pictures she found." Children feel accepted and know they belong to the group. They realize the teacher is happy to see them. For example, the teacher might say, "I'm glad you are back in school today, Warren. We missed you yesterday." The humanistic teacher allows children to learn by experience, sometimes by making mistakes, but mostly through successes. The child can say, "My adobe brick didn't harden because I didn't have enough dirt," and not feel threatened with punishment or ridicule. The teacher also helps children realize the effects of their actions on others: "Janie's tower tumbled because you bumped it. Is there something you could do to help her feel better?"

Openness to experience and acceptance leads naturally to value directions such as sincerity, independence, self-direction, self-knowledge, social responsivity, social responsibility, and loving interpersonal relationships.

In a humanistic classroom, open, flexible teachers or "facilitators" provide intensive group experiences that allow for freedom of personal expression, interpersonal communication, and exploration of feelings. Each child is encouraged to put aside defenses and façades and to relate directly and openly to everyone in the classroom. According to Rogers, the experience produces significant benefits:

> **Individuals come to know themselves and each other more fully than is possible in the usual social or working relationships; the climate of openness, risk-taking, and honesty generates trust, which enables the person to recognize and change self-defeating attitudes, test out and adopt more innovative and constructive behaviors, and subsequently to relate more adequately and effectively to others in his everyday life situation.**[12]

The effect of the experience for teachers is to convey a sense of new directions in performing professional duties:

They are more able to listen to students.

They accept innovative, "troublesome" ideas from students, rather than insisting on conformity.

They pay as much attention to their relationships with students as they do to course content.

They work out problems with students rather than responding in a disciplinary and punitive manner.

They develop an equalitarian and democratic classroom climate.

The effects of the humanistic orientation on children's self-esteem and values acquisition skills have been demonstrated:

They feel freer to express both positive and negative feelings in class.

They work through these feelings toward a realistic solution.

They have more energy for learning because they have less fear of constant evaluation and punishment.

Their awe and fear of authority diminish as they find that teachers and administrators are fallible human beings.

They find that the learning process helps them deal with daily problems.

DIRECT METHODS FOR TEACHING VALUES

Direct methods of values education include any of the teaching approaches used to examine specific values in a variety of contexts, usually those related to the normal social studies program. Table 7–1 illustrates how the National Council for the Social Studies has organized various democratic beliefs for inclusion in the program of each of the grade levels. Some examples reflect indirect methods; others relate directly to the subject matter. The NCSS cautions that these are examples only and should not be construed as a recommended curriculum. Within each area, we must encourage open discussion of issues to build support for democratic values and develop the skills needed to function in a free society. There are special programs designed to help teach values; each program is based on developing social competence becoming involved in decision making.

The frequent references to Bloom's taxonomy throughout chapters 3, 4, and 5 emphasized that thinking is not a single or simple task. Instead, we have seen that social studies content can be a source through which children can carry out numbers of interrelated thinking processes; lower-order thinking tasks relate to acquiring knowledge and forming concepts, while higher-order tasks call for solving problems through the application of subject matter or creative thinking. Another higher-level thought process that helps individuals bring deeper personal associations to the examination of social studies content is Bloom's *evaluation level*. At this level, children make personal judgments about right and wrong, good and bad, significant and insignificant, and other polar extremes as they relate to analysis of human behavior.

The different viewpoints as to the process people go through to form value judgments share these factors: (1) they urge students to examine alternatives; (2) they

TABLE 7–1

Illustrative Examples of Applications of Democratic Beliefs and Values

	Central Focus	Democratic Rights, Freedoms, Responsibilities, or Beliefs Addressed	Illustrations of Opportunities
KINDERGARTEN	Awareness of self in a social setting	1. Right to security 2. Right to equal opportunity 3. Respect of others' rights 4. Honesty	1. Explore how rules make a room safe for everyone. 2. Schedule every child to be a leader for a day. 3. Emphasize that when someone speaks we should all listen. 4. As teacher, reinforce honesty as exhibited by children.
GRADE 1	The individual in primary social groups	1. Impartiality 2. Freedom of worship 3. Consideration for others	1. When an altercation is reported, the teacher tries to find out exactly what happened before taking action. 2. Stress that each family decides whether or not or how to worship. 3. Make clear that everyone has a right to his/her turn.
GRADE 2	Meeting basic needs in nearby social groups	1. Respect for property 2. Respect for laws 3. Values personal integrity	1. Discuss vandalism in neighborhoods. 2. Demonstrate how laws protect the safety of people. 3. Explore the importance of keeping promises.
GRADE 3	Sharing earthspace with others	1. Pursuing individual and group goals 2. Government works for the common good	1. Explain how goods are exchanged with other places in order to meet the needs of people. 2. Discuss how government is concerned about the unemployed and works to reduce unemployment.
GRADE 4	Human life in varied environments	1. Respect for the rights of others 2. Respect for different ways of life	1. Stress the importance of respecting the right of individuals from other cultures to have different values. 2. Help appreciate that lifestyles of people in other places are different from ours.
GRADE 5	People of the Americas	1. Freedom to worship 2. Right of privacy	1. Point out that people came to the Americas because of religious persecution. 2. Explain that a home cannot be searched without a warrant except under most unusual circumstances.

TABLE 7–1
(continued)

Central Focus	Democratic Rights, Freedoms, Responsibilities, or Beliefs Addressed	Illustrations of Opportunities
GRADE 5 (cont'd)	3. Freedom of assembly	3. Make clear that there are no laws prohibiting people from getting together in groups for any lawful purpose.
GRADE 6 People and cultures	1. Governments respect and protect individual freedoms 2. Right to life 3. Right to justice	1. Compare the record of various governments in protecting individual freedoms. 2. Study societies in which individual human rights are not respected. 3. Examine various types of judicial systems.
GRADE 7 A changing world of many nations	1. Freedom to participate in the political process 2. Right to equality of opportunity 3. Government guarantees civil liberties	1. Discuss the anticolonial movement in parts of the world. 2. Discuss social class systems in various parts of the world. 3. Debate the status of civil liberties in various developing nations.
GRADE 8 Building a strong and free nation	1. Right to liberty 2. Participation in the democratic process 3. Freedom of expression	1. Discuss the injustices of slavery. 2. Analyze the voting record of Americans and particularly that of young people. 3. Study the debates and compromises reached in the development of the Constitution.

Source: Task Force on Scope and Sequence, "In Search of a Scope and Sequence for Social Studies," *Social Education* 48 (April 1984): 258.

encourage exploration of the consequences of the alternatives; and (3) they help children to reach their own decisions.

Climbing a Decision Tree

One of the most effective programs for encouraging decision making in the development of values is that of Richard Remy and others at the Mershon Center of Ohio State University. The program, *Making Political Decisions*, was planned as a supplement to a teacher's regular social studies program.[13] Several creative techniques help youngsters make political decisions, of which one of the most imaginative and applicable forms is *Climbing a Decision Tree*.

To begin the Decision Tree, ask how many students notice that they make decisions as they climb a tree or wall. Do they plan their attack by looking over the obstacle or seek alternative routes should their first choice fail? Do they foresee the consequences of a weak branch or a sharp point? Inform them that they are going to use their ability to see alternatives and consequences that grow out of an occasion for decision—they are going to help Sir Lottalance make a decision about fighting Dingbat the Dragon.

Tell the children to put themselves in the place of the knight, Sir Lottalance, as they listen to this story:

> One day very long ago, Sir Lottalance was riding along on his white horse minding his own business when he came across some very sad townspeople. They were sad because the mean old dragon, Dingbat the Dimwitted, had lumbered out of his deep, dark cave and carried off the beautiful princess from the king's castle. The king had offered a huge reward for anyone who could destroy the dragon and save his daughter's life. But the first knight to try had been barbecued by Dingbat's fiery breath. The second knight to try had tripped over his own sword and became the dragon's shish kabob. Sir Lottalance could hear the princess beating her fists fiercely against the dragon and calling him the nastiest names you ever heard. He could hear Dingbat's tummy rumbling as the dragon eyed Lottalance and eagerly waited for another tasty meal of fried knight. Sir Lottalance was the fastest, strongest, and bravest knight in the kingdom but he wasn't sure about Dingbat. What could he do?

Now point to a large construction-paper decision tree on the wall as in Figure 7–2 so that the sign "Occasion for Decision," portraying Dingbat the Dragon, is exposed to view. For the children to climb the tree, they will have to think of Sir Lottalance's alternatives. Ask them for alternatives. When they have described fighting or fleeing, write the responses on the alternative branches on the tree and congratulate the children for doing such a good job of climbing a decision tree.

Lead the students to climb higher into the branches of the tree to look at the consequences of Sir Lottalance's decision by asking: "What would be a *good* (or positive) consequence of getting out of there fast?" and "What would be a *bad* (or negative) consequence of getting out of there fast?"

When the students have suggested ideas corresponding to "stay alive" and "be called Lottalance the Sissy," add them to the blank pieces of paper above the "getting out of here fast" alternative. Again, congratulate your students for a good job of climbing and remind them they still have an alternative branch to explore. Ask, "What would be a bad (or negative) consequence of fighting Dingbat the Dragon?" and "What would be some good (or positive) consequences of fighting Dingbat the Dragon?"

Again, list each contribution as it is offered. Examine the whole tree and look for the students' sense of accomplishment. Then, weighing the consequences, ask the class to vote on a decision. Then, place their decision high on the top of the decision tree.

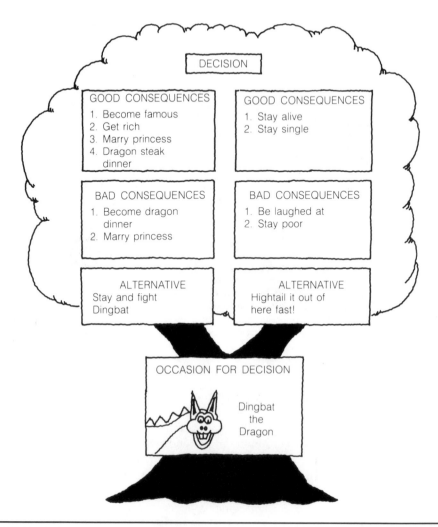

FIGURE 7–2
Decision Tree

The decision tree technique is useful whenever individuals or small groups face important decisions: what to do with friends on a free afternoon; who to invite to a birthday party; where to go on a field trip; what to do if your friends don't like each other; rules for a game with few players; who gets to play with what equipment or toys; how to raise money for a group; who's team captain; who gets to play. The teacher's role in a decision tree strategy is to:

1. Decide what question to examine and label it at the base of the tree
2. Abbreviate the decision in the "Occasion for Decision" sign

3. Encourage children to think up alternatives and write them in the boxes on the branches of the decision tree

4. Discuss positive and negative consequences of each alternative, *one at a time*

5. Write in the consequences, ask the children to weigh each, and write in their goal

6. Congratulate the children as successful decision makers

From these early decision tree experiences, you can lead children to examine more pressing social concerns: Should the planned sewage plant be built despite the taxpayers' protests? Should the new tuna nets be outlawed because they are killing so many friendly porpoises? Should America's space program be escalated at the expense of federal programs for the poor? Should Congress continue the Social Security system? Should our community legislate leash laws for dogs? How should our class enforce the new regulations we added to the Classroom Constitution?

You are the individual who will determine how values will be handled in the social studies curriculum. There is no absolute way to deal with values education. Children will face many different problems in their future that will call for different intellectual operations. You must thus consider alternatives for teaching values just as the children will need to examine alternatives while making decisions in your classroom. Learn about the alternatives, the consequences of using each alternative, and then put your choices into action. We will talk about two of the most popular valuing strategies.

STAGE THEORIES OF MORAL DEVELOPMENT

In recent years, educators have been guided by various stage theories of moral development. Although various degrees of compatibility appear among these theories, they all share the assumption that social behavior can be categorized in terms of a predetermined sequence of stages, referred to as *cognitive developmental stages*—cognitive because they recognize that moral education, like cognitive education, requires stimulation of active thinking about moral issues; developmental because each stage is a new structure that includes elements of earlier structures but transforms them to represent a more stable and sophisticated level of thinking.

Piaget's Theory

Jean Piaget suggested the first widely accepted stage theory of moral development after he observed children in a variety of conflict situations. The first part of his proposal describes children's concepts of rules. Piaget believed development progressed along these lines:

1. Egocentric stage. This stage occurs when children do not know or follow rules, but insist that they do. The child centers on himself and fails to take into account another person's point of view. Children view right and wrong according to what adult authority figures permit or forbid them to do.

2. Stage of incipient cooperation. This level is characterized by acquisition of a genuinely social character. The child at this stage both cooperates and competes with others and realizes that rules help solve interpersonal conflicts.

3. Stage of genuine cooperation. At this stage, the child completely understands the purpose of rules and enjoys inventing new rules or elaborating upon old ones. He even tries to understand all the consequences that may arise from accepting or rejecting rules.[14]

To summarize, children initially pattern their behavior according to parental or other adult demands. After that point, as a result of spending increasing amounts of time with other adults and with peers, they gradually assume greater awareness. Eventually, children learn to make decisions for themselves and do not necessarily accept others' authoritative views without reflection. In other words, children move from a unilateral respect of authority toward a position of mutual consideration of others.

The second part of Piaget's theory of moral development moves from a description of moral behavior to children's judgments of the goodness or badness of actions in explicitly moral situations. To study this, he told children a pair of stories in which characters differed in two characteristics: (1) in terms of the intentions guiding their actions, and (2) in terms of the amount of damage they caused by their actions. In one story, the main character performed an act that unintentionally resulted in large damage; in the other, the child caused very little damage as a result of a deliberately improper act. The task of the child being studied was to determine which of the central characters was good and which was bad.

This example illustrates the first type of story:

> John was playing outdoors when his mother called him for lunch. When he went to the table, he noticed his mother was on the phone and that his milk glass was empty. He thought of filling the glass to help his mother so that she would not need to hurry. But while he was opening the milk carton, it spilled and made a big puddle on the tablecloth.

And the second story:

> There was a young boy named David. One day his mother was out shopping, and David thought it might be fun to secretly take some cookies and milk. First he got the cookies from the cookie jar, and then he poured the milk. But while he was drinking the milk, a few drops spilled from the glass and made a little stain on the tablecloth.

After hearing the pair of stories, children were asked to explain whether one of the children was naughtier than the other or whether both were equally guilty. Piaget found that until the age of ten, responses fell into two categories: *moral realism* and *subjective responsibility*. In this stage of moral realism, the child argues that the amount of damage determines the character's guilt. To this child, motives for particular actions do not enter the picture. John, the boy who wished to help his mother, is guilty because he made a large puddle, whereas David, the boy secretly taking cookies and milk, is not guilty because the stain was small. Piaget calls this stage moral realism because the child's decision is realistic—that is, the criterion of guilt is not subjective (the intent) but material or real (the amount of damage). In the stage of subjective responsibility, the child determines a character's guilt by the nature of his motives. To this child, the boy who wanted to help his mother but caused a great deal of damage is less guilty than the boy who participated in an improper act that resulted in little damage. Piaget calls this subjective responsibility because the child takes into account the motives (the intent) of the character in the story.

Piaget determined that the great majority of responses from children of elementary school age fall into the category of moral realism. He gave two reasons for this occurrence. First, parents and teachers are usually "realistic" themselves. Some adults punish a child more severely for breaking five glasses unintentionally than for breaking one intentionally, and since adults are respected, so are their rules. An implication of this moral viewpoint seems to be that if adults (teachers and parents) move away from "realistic" methods of disciplining children toward methods of subjective discussions, so will the child move more easily toward subjective moral reasoning. Second, many children of elementary school age have egocentric thought patterns, and since they find it difficult to assume points of view different from their own, they cannot see the other's need for truth; consequently, they are not aware that their "lies" are deceiving the listener.

Piaget contends that, while the stages are loosely age-determined, two major factors may provide the necessary ingredients for altering children's moral orientation: maturation and experience. There are not many specific suggestions for classroom applications of Piaget's theory of moral development because they were not part of his original goals. The major purpose of his work was to stimulate further research and experimentation, and moral reasoning has now become one of the most popular topics in social studies educational literature. Piaget's theories have been built upon by Lawrence Kohlberg, who has incorporated several Piagetian concepts into his own work—particularly the ideas of stage sequence and moral reasoning.

Kohlberg's Cognitive-Developmental Model of Moral Reasoning

Kohlberg became interested in the Piagetian scheme of moral development in 1955 and sought to validate Piaget's ideas by carrying out intensive studies throughout the world. Despite differences in cultural, social, economic, and religious backgrounds, Kohlberg found that all individuals move through the stages of moral development as described in Table 7–2.

Although Kohlberg does not assign age designations to any level, his theory is so closely identified with Piaget's that we can assume primary-grade children operate at the Preconventional Level, while most middle- and upper-grade elementary school children function at the Conventional Level. Surprisingly, Kohlberg found that over eighty percent of the adult population becomes frozen at the Conventional Level—"law and order." How can we encourage the moral growth of our future adults?

TABLE 7–2
Kohlberg's Stages of Moral Development

Preconventional Level: Egocentric in Nature

Stage 1: To be "well behaved" means unquestioned obedience to an adult authority figure. The child considers actions to be either good or bad solely because of the physical consequences involved (punishment, reward) or because of the desires of authority figures (teacher, parent, etc.).

Stage 2: The child is basically egocentric (self-centered) at this stage and regards goodness or badness on the basis of whether it satisfies personal needs. Children at this stage begin to consider the feelings of others, but elements of fairness and equal sharing are interpreted in a manner of "what's in it for me?" Children are out to make the best "deal" for themselves. Being "right" is viewed in a context of fairness: "You scratch my back and I'll scratch yours."

Conventional Level: Orientation to Conformity

Stage 3: Good behavior is that which pleases or helps others. Children conform to what they imagine to be a "good" or "nice" person and begin to see things from another's viewpoint for the first time (put themselves into the shoes of another person). Behavior begins to be judged on the basis of intent—a conscience is beginning to form. Children are strongly oriented to being labeled "good boy/nice girl."

Stage 4: The individual is oriented to obeying authority and following fixed rules for reasons of law and order. A good person does one's duty, shows respect for authority, and maintains the given social order for its own sake. One earns respect by performing dutifully, living up to one's socially defined role, and maintaining existing social order for the good of all.

Postconventional Level: Individual Moral Principles

Stage 5: Since laws have been critically examined and agreed upon by the whole society, they continue to guide decisions regarding goodness or badness. However, right and wrong begins to become characterized by personal feelings; the result is an emphasis upon the "legal point of view," but with an emphasis upon the possibility of changing laws, rather than obeying them as in Stage 4. One makes an internal commitment to principles of "conscience"; individuals are guided by a respect for the rights, life, and dignity of all persons.

Adapted from Lawrence Kohlberg, "The Claim to Moral Adequacy of a Highest State of Moral Judgment," *The Journal of Philosophy* 70, no. 18 (October 25, 1973): 631–32.

First let us examine some considerations of Kohlberg's stages:

The stages always occur in the same order. Moral reasoning of the preconventional kind always takes place before conventional thought.

All movement through the stages is forward in sequence. Once a child has begun to reason on the conventional level, for example, he or she will never return to the reasoning patterns associated with the preconventional level. Of course, often children will be half in and half out of a certain stage and will seem to be moving backward, but this characteristic only indicates a pattern of growth from one stage to the next.

The stages cannot be skipped. They represent an "invariant developmental sequence," which means they come one at a time and always in the same order.

Some individuals move farther and faster through the stages than other individuals. Differences in achieving various levels of moral reasoning can be compared to the differences in achieving various levels of cognitive skills.

The movement from stage to stage is not an automatic process. Individuals may stop at any given stage and apply the related reasoning processes to all moral situations encountered throughout their lives.

Kohlberg's approach to affective education is based on the assumption that growth through the stages can be stimulated by involving children in "moral dilemmas"—stories in which individuals face situations that involve issues of trust, fairness, or taking advantage. Children are encouraged to examine situations and make judgments about the various actions the characters might take.

An example of a moral dilemma suitable for upper-grade elementary school children is the case of Rosa Parks, a black woman in Montgomery, Alabama, who refused to give up her seat on a bus in defiance of the prevailing segregation customs in 1955. Here is a teaching plan to encourage children to think about the difficult decision Rosa Parks faced.

WARM-UP QUESTIONS.   These questions should orient children to the situation. "How many of you have ever ridden on a bus? Were you able to sit anywhere you liked when you got on the bus? Did you ever hear of people being told that they couldn't sit on any section of the bus because of the color of their skin? their height? their sex? their religious persuasion?"

PRESENTATION.   Explain to the students that they are to read a short story about a woman who was told she could not sit on a particular seat on a bus because of the color of her skin. She must decide whether to sit in that seat. Her name is Rosa Parks and the city in which the decision took place was Montgomery, Alabama. Tell the children to decide what they would do if they were faced with Rosa Parks's decision. Supply them with an account of the incident.

FOLLOW-UP DECISION.   The first questions should help clarify the story. "Where was Rosa Parks before she got on the bus? How did she feel? Why was she asked to leave her seat? When did the story take place?"

GROUP DIALOGUE.   Split the children into groups and ask them to decide what Rosa Parks should do. Move from group to group and offer questions to guide the children's thinking: "Why do you think some cities had rules establishing separate facilities for blacks and whites? Does Rosa Parks have a right to break those rules? Were the rules fair? What could happen if she did not give up her seat to the white person?"

FOLLOW-UP ACTIVITY.   In this case, each group can be encouraged to role play the scene on the bus, stopping at the point of Rosa's decision. Then, they should portray what Rosa should have done and what the consequences would have been. What other follow-up activities might be appropriate?

ENRICHMENT.   The children will naturally be curious about the real outcome of this dilemma, and their questions will flow spontaneously: "What did Rosa Parks do? What happened to her?" The questions will indicate a perfect starting point for an inquiry session. You may wish to offer the information yourself or encourage the children to search for the answers in material you have collected for them. For your information, Rosa Parks refused to give up her seat and was arrested. Her arrest touched off a bus boycott in Montgomery and was one of the major events in launching the campaign for black civil rights. In 1980, Mrs. Parks received the Martin Luther King Peace Award for the inspiration she provided to resolve racial differences through nonviolent means.[15]

When the children share their responses to story situations, they provide you with insight into the different levels of moral reasoning at which they are operating. The stages of moral reasoning are not defined by the nature of the decision itself, but on the basis of the reasons they give for each decision. For example,

Stage 1: "Rosa Parks should get up from her seat because she would be in real trouble if she didn't. The bus driver would probably throw her off the bus." (People *cannot* disobey authorities or they will be punished.)

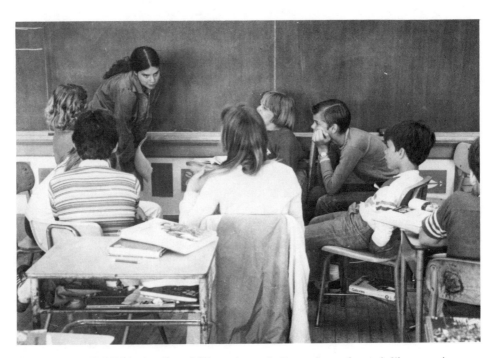

According to Kohlberg, leading children through discussions of moral dilemmas is the key to improving their moral reasoning.

Stage 2: "Rosa Parks should not go to the back of the bus because she is aw-fully tired and there wouldn't be anywhere else for her to sit." (Everyone has a right to do what he wants to fulfill legitimate needs.)

Stage 3: "Rosa Parks should start to move to the back of the bus because if the white man finds out how tired she is, he will be sure to understand and let her stay in her seat." (Children have a sense of fair play at this stage—what would a *good* person do?)

Stage 4: "Rosa Parks should move to the back of the bus because she would be breaking the law if she didn't. People are expected to follow society's rules." (Established law emerges as a central value.)

Most elementary school children will not have gone beyond Stage 4 in their think-ing. What do you think would be responses of individuals functioning at Stage 5 or Stage 6?

SMOOTH CLASSROOM MANAGEMENT

These suggestions ensure smooth classroom management of any moral dilemma:

1. Focus on reasons.
   Decisions are important, but they are not enough. Children need to examine their reasoning and the reasoning of others as they justify their solutions. "The process of stating, challenging, being challenged, defending, explaining, criti-cizing, and comparing highlights the existence of a gap between one's own stage of reasoning and the reasoning at the next higher stage. In time, students be-come conscious of this gap and move to close it."[16]

2. Choose discussion groups with care.
   Mix children at different stages of moral development in each group so that chil-dren at the lower stages of moral reasoning will benefit from exposure to the thinking of children operating at higher levels.

3. Give direction and guidance.
   Allow as many students as possible to respond to the dilemma. When shy stu-dents are reluctant to do so, simply ask students to react to another's comment: "Harold, do you agree with Marge, or do you have another idea?" or "Jane, many of your classmates think the boys should keep the kitten. What do you think?"

4. Encourage undecided children.
   Moral issues can be thoroughly perplexing, and decisions are not easily reached. Other children may attempt to exert peer pressure to win over the undecided child to their side, and it becomes extremely difficult for some children to with-stand the pressure. They fear that hesitation will be interpreted as a sign of weak-ness. To prevent children from "going along with the crowd," you should attempt to convince them that it's okay to remain uncertain until they have had enough time to make up their minds.

5. Avoid giving your own opinion.

To move children away from Stage 1 reasoning, they must be encouraged to see right and wrong from a point of view other than that of authority and must be led to understand that the most important products of moral discussions are personal ideas and feelings.

6. Provide variety.

Children need a variety of conditions in which to consider moral issues. Use a variety of puppetry or other creative dramatics situations to improve and invigorate your program. Children develop a great sensitivity to others by ''becoming'' another person. Their imaginations take over and allow them to verbalize and act in ways they would not normally consider.

A strategy for guiding moral discussions, summarizing the roles of teacher and child, is presented in Figure 7–3.

Perhaps the teacher's most important role is to identify the children's reasoning levels and make sure the children are exposed to the next reasoning stage higher than their own. Children can easily understand the reasoning below their own level and reject it as simplistic. But they grow in their abilities to reason only by listening to the arguments of those reasoning one stage above their own. They cannot under-

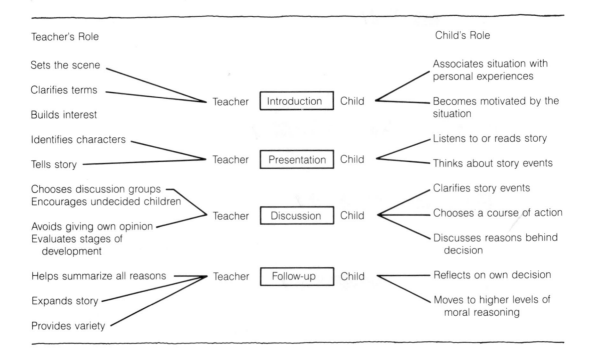

FIGURE 7–3
Strategy for Guiding Moral Dilemmas

stand the arguments of those who are reasoning more than one stage above their own. Figure 7–4 illustrates these concepts.

Young children enjoy a variety of stories containing moral dilemmas from their social studies program. Look for commercial materials such as films, filmstrips, and audiotapes or records, too. One company that specializes in the production of commercial materials appropriate for use with children of elementary school age is Guidance Associates. *First Things: Values* (Pleasantville, N.Y.: Guidance Associates, 1972) is a filmstrip and record program presenting young children in various situations of moral conflict.

The type of control to which you expose children in normal classroom management needs careful consideration. Consider the typical scene in which two children are sent into the classroom for fighting on the playground. The first question usually fired at the children is, "Okay, who started it?" And to the guilty party, "Well, how would you like to have this sort of thing happen to you?" Her question is met with a slight shrug and downward turn of the eyes. "Look at me when I'm talking!" demands the teacher. "Answer my question."

Tears well in the eyes of the "winner" as he desperately tries to answer the teacher's question, managing only a barely audible, "I don't know."

Frantic by this time, the teacher shakes the child and blurts, "Okay, Smartie, you just sit in for one week during your outdoor recess periods and think about it!"

If we analyze that fabricated situation according to Kohlberg's ideas, we might assume that the "winner" was operating at Stage 1 of moral reasoning. He knows

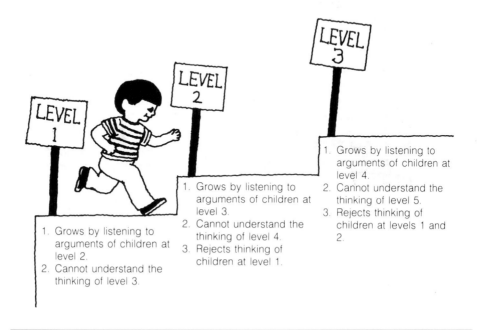

FIGURE 7–4

Principles of Movement Through Kohlberg's Stages of Moral Development

he has done wrong, but only because he has broken a rule established by the teacher—no fighting on the playground. In her disciplinary action, however, the teacher asked the child to reason at Stage 3—to put himself in another's shoes. Therefore, the child becomes frustrated and cries because he truly cannot understand the type of response the teacher wants. An important part of the teacher's use of Kohlberg's ideas is to help the child re-examine his actions before engaging him in new reasoning patterns that require reordering of thinking processes and seeking new ways to organize feelings. Every child needs to be aware that he is a member of a group and has a responsibility toward the group. For that reason, we usually have only a few restrictions in preschool settings, but they should be rigidly enforced. Prohibited acts are usually those that endanger the welfare or restrict the rights of others. The child must be aware that there are things he can and cannot do if the environment is to be safe. You must explain the reasons to him, at the same time understanding that his comprehension of your explanation may be extremely limited. He will usually listen and obey because you are the authority figure in the classroom and have gained his basic trust (Stage 1). In many instances, the child *demands* your limits.

Handling feelings is an extremely sensitive area. Guiding a child entails a great deal of personal insight. "Overdirection may distort his development; so may lack of direction. He needs time to learn through suitable experiences. He is sure to make some mistakes in the process of learning. . . . if we deal calmly and confidently with unacceptable behavior, we will create the kind of climate in which the child is helped to master his impulses and to direct his own behavior. We will be using authority in constructive ways."[17]

THE VALUES CLARIFICATION APPROACH

Values clarification is an alternative approach to affective education. The values clarification approach is most often associated with Louis Raths, Merrill Harmin, and Sidney Simon, authors of *Values and Teaching*. They believe that children acquire values only as they progress through the processes of choosing, prizing, and acting.

To Raths, Harmin, and Simon, a value is defined when seven subprocesses are satisfied:

Choosing
1. freely
2. from alternatives
3. after thoughtful consideration of the consequences of each alternative

Prizing
4. cherishing, being happy with the choice
5. willing to affirm the choice publicly, when appropriate

Acting
6. doing something with the choice
7. repeatedly, in some pattern of life[18]

CHOOSING FREELY. If something is in fact to guide one's life whether or not authority is watching, it must be a result of free choice. If there is coercion, the result is not likely to stay with one for long, especially when out of the range of the source of that coercion. Values must be freely selected for the individual to truly ascribe to them.

CHOOSING FROM AMONG ALTERNATIVES. This subprocess concerns things that are chosen by the individual; obviously, there can be no choice if there are no alternatives from which to choose. It makes no sense, for example, to say that one values eating. One really has no choice in the matter. One may value certain types of food or certain forms of eating, but not eating itself. Only when a choice is possible, when there is more than one alternative from which to choose, can a value result.

CHOOSING AFTER THOUGHTFUL CONSIDERATION OF THE CONSEQUENCES OF EACH ALTERNATIVE. Impulsive or thoughtless choices do not lead to values as we define them. For something intelligently and meaningfully to guide one's life, it must emerge from weighing and understanding. Only when one clearly understands the consequences of each alternative can one make intelligent choices. There is an important cognitive factor here: a value can emerge only with thoughtful consideration of the range of alternatives and consequences in a choice.

PRIZING AND CHERISHING. When we value something, it has a positive tone. We prize it, cherish it, esteem it, respect it, hold it dear. We are happy with our values. A choice, even when we have made it freely and thoughtfully, may be one we are not happy to make. We may choose to fight in a war, but be sorry that circumstances make that choice reasonable. In our definition, values flow from choices we are glad to make.

AFFIRMING. When we have chosen something freely, after considering alternatives, and when we are proud of our choice, we are likely to affirm the choice when asked about it. We are willing to publicly affirm our values. We may even be willing to champion them. If we are ashamed of a choice, if we would not make our position known when appropriately asked, we would not be dealing with values but something else.

ACTING UPON CHOICES. A value shows up in aspects of our living. We may do some reading about things we value. We are likely to form friendships or join organizations that nourish our values. We may spend money on a choice we value. We budget time or energy for our values. Nothing can be a value that does not, in fact, give direction to actual living. Someone who talks about something but never does anything about it is dealing with something other than a value.

REPEATING. Where something reaches the stage of value, it is likely to reappear on a number of occasions in one's life. Values tend to have a persistency, to make a pattern in life.

The question of what the teacher must do to help children develop values according to the values clarification theory now arises. Raths, Harmin, and Simon say the process flows naturally from the described definition of values; that is, the teacher should:

1. Encourage children to make choices freely.
2. Help them discover and examine available alternatives when faced with choices.
3. Help children weigh alternatives thoughtfully, reflecting on the consequences of each.
4. Encourage children to consider what it is that they prize and cherish.
5. Give them opportunities to make public affirmations of their choices.
6. Encourage them to act, behave, live in accordance with their choices.
7. Help them to examine repeated behaviors or patterns in their life.[19]

The basic technique of the values clarification approach involves a "clarifying response"—a way of responding to children that results in their considering what they have chosen, what they prize, or what they are doing. The comments should merely prod the child to think. Here are three classroom situations illustrating the use of a clarifying response.

Maurice: I'd like to be President some day.

Teacher: How long have you felt this way?

Maurice: Gee, I'm not sure. I guess I felt that way after I read a story about John F. Kennedy.

Teacher: What was there about the story that made you come to your decision?

Maurice: I liked the way he fought for the rights of all people.

Teacher: That's very interesting. Thank you for telling me, Maurice.

Charles complained to his teacher that it was too confusing in the classroom when groups were working on their social studies projects. When the class was all together for group time, the teacher guided this discussion: "How do you like our room when you're trying to work in groups? Should it be like that all the time?"

One morning, during a planning period at the start of a social studies unit, the teacher asked: "When you came to school in the morning and had a chance to look over all the things placed around the room, did you get an idea of what items interested you most? What do you like best? Why? What do you like least? Why? Would you like to work alone or with other children? All of the time?"

You may by now sense some criteria for effective clarifying responses. These are among the essential elements:

- Do not criticize or evaluate the child's response.

- Put the responsibility on the child to look at his ideas and think about what he wants for himself.

- Do not try to do big things. The purpose of a clarifying response is to set a mood. Each response is only one of many; its effect is cumulative.

- Do not intend for the clarifying response to develop into an extended discussion. The idea is for the child to think, and he usually does that best alone. Allow for two or three rounds of dialogue and then offer to break off the conversation with some honest phrase, such as "Nice talking with you," or "I see what you mean now," or "Your idea was very interesting. Let's talk about it again some other time."

- Do not respond to everything everyone says or does in the classroom.

- Direct clarifying responses to *individuals* whenever possible. A topic in which Henry needs clarification may be of no interest to Mae. Issues of general concern may warrant a general response to the entire class, but even here the individual must ultimately do the reflecting for himself.

- Use clarifying responses in situations where there are no "right" answers, such as those involving feelings, attitudes, or beliefs. They should *never* be used to draw a child's thinking toward a predetermined answer.[20]

Clarifying responses are not designed to follow any mechanical formula, but must be used creatively and with insight. There are several responses, however, that experienced teachers have found useful with children. As you read through the list that follows, try to elaborate upon the items and add to the suggestions.

"Are you proud of that?"

"Do you really like that idea?"

"Does that make you feel good?"

"Are you happy about your choice?"

"How did you feel when that happened?"

"Did you think of any other way to do it?"

"When did you first get such an idea?"

"Have you felt this way for a long time?"

"Did you do it yourself?"

"When might you use that idea?"

"What other choices did (do) you have?"

"Should everyone go along with your idea?"

"Is that important to you?"

"Do you do that often?"

"Would you like to tell others about your idea?"

"Do you have a reason for doing (or saying) that?"

"Would you do the same thing again?"

"How do you know it's right (or good)?"

"Is that something that you like very much?"

"What do you mean?"

"What would happen if your ideas worked out?"

"Would you really do that?"

"Would other people believe that?"

"Is this what I understood you to say?"

"Would you do that again?"

As you read through the list, you should have related each comment to the seven components of the Raths valuing process. Those seven criteria are valuable guides as you think of other useful clarifying responses. In one way or another, all clarifying responses should encourage children to choose, prize, or act as outlined by the value theory.

Raths recommends that the teacher (1) establish a climate of psychological safety, and (2) apply a clarification procedure.[21] These procedures help establish a climate of psychological safety:

Nonjudgmental attitudes. Teachers must refrain from unnecessary comments, such as "That's good" or "That's bad," while responding to a child's idea.

Manifestations of concern. Teachers should show interest in the children's ideas by listening carefully and remembering what they say. The student will feel flattered by this recognition.

Opportunities for sharing ideas. Teachers should encourage children to share their ideas and feelings in many different situations during the school day.

Values Clarification and Social Studies Content

You may draw from among these general situations to select strategies to help children think more deeply about their attitudes toward social studies content, about prevailing social conditions, or about their own lives. Raths, Harmin, and Simon suggest curriculum techniques:

1. *The Picture Without a Caption:* The teacher brings in a picture which involves a story of some kind. . .Students are asked to supply a caption describing what is going on. After various captions are examined in the light of the available evidence, an attempt is made to see what the students would have done in the same situation. As example, photographs of a street fight were used.

2. *A Scene from a Play or Movie:* A teacher obtains the script from a play, TV show, or a movie and duplicates a small part of it. Students act it out, but it is cut off before there is any solution to the problem. The students then take over and discuss what should have been done, how this situation was like something in their own lives, etc. Showing films which are cut prematurely can also lead to interesting discussions.

3. *Other Idea Sources*
   Briefly, here are other suggestions for sources of materials to spur discussion having a values clarification focus.
   a. Editorials
   b. Letters to the editor
   c. Literature passed around at election time
   d. Popular song lyrics

    e. Tape recordings of news broadcasts and other programs
    f. Tape recordings of interviews students have obtained from various persons in the community with strong viewpoints
    g. Excerpts from speeches
    h. Materials from embassies or foreign countries
    i. Advertising
    j. Cartoons, comic strips, etc.
    k. Films[22]

4. *Open-ended Questions:* An open-ended question is dictated or written on the board and students are asked to write responses either in class or at home. For example, "If I had twenty-four hours to live . . ." or "The purposes of my life are . . ." What comes out of such writing, usually, is a rather fruitful list of some of the child's interests, hopes, fears, the people he likes the most, and some things in his life which he considers worthy or unworthy. Here are some other open-ended questions which have been productive:
    a. With a gift of $100, I would. . . .
    b. If this next weekend were a three-day weekend, I would want to. . . .
    c. My best friend can be counted on to. . . .
    d. My bluest days are. . . .

5. *The Values Continuum:* The class or the teacher identifies an issue to be discussed in class. Then two polar positions are identified . . . (and) placed at opposite ends of a line on the board. . . . The task of the class, then, is to identify other positions in the issue and try to place them on the continuum, both in relationship to the poles and to the positions already placed. For example,

            Strongly   Strongly
            Agree   ⌊___,___,___,___,___⌋ Disagree
        There should be strict federal control of education.

6. *Voting:* To use the voting strategy, the teacher poses a list of questions . . . and students state a position by a show of hands. For example, the teacher might ask the following sequence of questions, pausing after each for a vote, the recording of the vote on the board, and a moment to reflect on the ideas generated by the question:
    a. How many of you have ever been seriously burned?
    b. Anyone here ever own a horse?
    c. How many think sometimes of dying or what death might be like?
    d. I'd like to see how much loneliness is in this group. Vote either that you feel lonely often, sometimes, or seldom. How many feel lonely often? Sometimes? Seldom?

7. *Devil's Advocate:* Too many discussions in value-related areas suffer from having only two positions in the room: a consensus and a "don't care" position. Especially in certain political and social topics, dissension is often absent. What often is needed is persuasive argument *against* civil rights, *for* the use of profanity, *against* respect for elders, *for* revolution, *against* patriotism, and so on. . . .
    Each teacher does well to announce to the class that, from time to time, he will play a role that is not his real one, that he will do it merely to present a position that has not otherwise arisen. It is often fun to label this role as that of the devil's advocate and to announce what one is doing when it is played, but usually that is unnecessary. The extreme and dogmatic statements that characterize the devil's advocate signal that something is afoot.
    "I want to play the devil with you. I'll screw on my horns and get ready to jab you with my pitchfork. Watch out."

You know all of that stuff you've been reading about these heroes who go up in space ships? Well, this devil thinks they're not heroes at all. What's so heroic about going up in a space ship? Why they have those things so carefully figured out that nothing can go wrong. With all of those movie cameras grinding and all of those TV cameras focused on them, you don't think our government could afford to have the bad publicity of anything going wrong do you? This devil thinks that your walk to school every morning has about as much danger in it as the danger those so-called heroes had to risk. And to ride in a car without seat belts is twice as dangerous as that. But no one calls you a hero when you do that.

Anyhow, if there is such risk, what kind of man would leave his wife and children to do something a monkey could have done? Finally, you foolish children, this devil wants to raise the question about all that money that goes into this man-on-the-moon project. Did you know that we spend over a billion bucks a year, and that money could easily wipe out the slums, build new colleges, work productively on cancer and mental illness research.

So spoke the devil.[23]

What a lively class session followed the devil's discourse. Few students take that kind of confrontation lying down, and the alternatives to consider filled the room.

Simon and Goodman have used a values clarification activity called ''The Coat of Arms'' to help children explore the issue of death in an unthreatening way. The procedure calls for the teacher to prepare an outline of a coat of arms, as shown in Figure 7–5. The students should draw a picture for each segment in response to a topic you suggest; for example, the contributions of Ronald Reagan as President of the United States:

1. Draw a picture to show what Ronald Reagan would most miss about not being President.
2. Draw a picture to show a time Ronald Reagan really laughed.
3. Draw a picture of the time when Ronald Reagan lost his temper.
4. Draw a picture to show Ronald Reagan's greatest accomplishment.
5. Draw what you think is important to Ronald Reagan.
6. Draw something to represent what Ronald Reagan would do if he were your age.

FIGURE 7–5
''The Coat of Arms'' for Values Clarification

Students can share, in small groups, the drawings on their coats of arms, explaining the significance of the symbols. A variation of the exercise might involve construction of coats of arms of popular news figures, figures from the past, or the teacher.

While values clarification strategies are recommended for use in all school situations, several materials have been developed specifically for social studies topics. Some resources for materials are:

Casteel and Stahl, *Value Clarification in the Classroom: A Primer* (Pacific Palisades, Calif.: Goodyear Publishing Co., 1975)

Raths, Harmin, and Simon, *Values and Teaching*, 2nd ed. (Columbus, Ohio: Charles E. Merrill, 1978)

Simon, Howe, and Kirschenbaum, *Values Clarification* (New York: Hart, 1972); seventy-nine strategies to help students build the seven valuing processes into their lives

Volkmor, Pasanella, and Raths, *Values in the Classroom* (Columbus, Ohio: Charles E. Merrill, 1977); a multimedia program providing activities in values clarification; components include six sound filmstrips and text

A LOOK AT BOTH APPROACHES

Both theories of moral stages and values clarification may appeal to you, thus causing confusion as you prepare to choose one for your own teaching. For that reason, we need to examine some of the weaknesses of each approach.

Critique of the Moral Stages Approach

Some educators question Kohlberg's argument that his six stages describe moral development for *all* people in *all* cultures. While Kohlberg's supporters believe that all morality is based on the concept of justice, critics question whether this is a universal and valued concept. Kohlberg stresses that higher stage reasoning is not only different, but better. This notion (higher is better) is difficult for some individuals to accept. Fraenkel argues:

> If higher-stage reasoning is better it should contain or possess something that lower-stage reasoning does not. And if this is true it is difficult to see how those reasoning at lower stages would be able to understand the arguments of those at the higher stages. And if they cannot understand the arguments, it is difficult to see why those at the lower stages would be inclined to accept such reasoning as better than their own as a justification for various actions. If "higher" is not "better" then there doesn't seem to be any justification for trying to "improve" the reasoning of children by helping them to move through the stages.[24]

Some critics challenge the notion of stages. Walter and Harriet Mischel argue that children's moral judgments change not because of movement through stages but because adults react differently to children as they grow older. Because adults talk differently to young children than they do to adolescents, children's responses are naturally different than those of teenagers.[25]

Critique of the Values Clarification Approach

Some authors question the "theory" underlying the values clarification approach. They claim that because the ideas of Raths and his associates are not based on careful research, they can be considered no more than an unsupported set of assumptions. Other critics argue that values clarification activities can result in great peer pressure and in a tendency to neutralize all opinions because of that pressure. Stewart, for example, claims, "Only the most popular or the strongest dare express their honest opinions and feelings about values/moral issues publicly without fear of ridicule or rejection."[26] He feels it is unrealistic to believe that all seven requirements must be met before a value can be developed:

> One of the most frequently used strategies is the "Values Continuum," which involves having students take positions on issues presented on a continuum from one extreme to its opposite. One of the items in this strategy asks, "How do you feel about premarital sex?" The two ends of the continuum are (1) Virginal Virginia (sometimes called Gloves Gladys) and (2) Mattress Millie. Virginal Virginia "wears white gloves on every date" and Mattress Millie "wears a mattress strapped to her back." Now consider the very shy, sensitive, and fearful girl in the class as an example—the girl who's tremendously concerned about her standing with the other girls, or the boys, or the teacher. Suppose that her position on this issue is clear, even as the result of having applied the principles of Values Clarification, and that she truly believes in either one of the two extreme positions. Would she be likely to affirm publicly such a position in this situation? I would think not.[27]

SUMMARY

To teach attitudes and values is perhaps the most perplexing area of social studies instruction. So many factors influence the development of values in young children—parents, relatives, peers, significant others, religious leaders, television, and movies. Obviously, the teacher is only partially responsible for developing young people's attitudes and values.

How should attitudes and values be taught in the elementary school classroom? Both *direct* and *indirect* methods are appropriate. Indirect methods have to do with the classroom environment and the example set by a teacher. In the early grades, for example, children need many formal and informal activities that help develop an adequate "ego strength" for making personal decisions. From there, they must have opportunities for group work to gain confidence in defending personal choices.

Eventually the children should be led into situations where they learn to accept the basic rights and responsibilities of individuals in a democratic society. Experiences in which children establish rules for the classroom or the teacher uses a democratic approach to conflict resolution, such as Gordon's Teacher Effectiveness Training program, help build the feelings of mutual respect necessary for a satisfactory program dealing with attitudes and values.

Direct methods of values education include any of the teaching approaches used to examine any of the specific values derived from our legal and judicial system, great documents, or other cultural traditions. Some of these values are taught naturally during daily classroom routines, but they must often be treated in specific teaching situations. Richard Remy's Decision Tree is an effective program for helping children make political decisions. Lawrence Kohlberg's cognitive-developmental model of reasoning is based on the premise that children progress through stages of moral maturity, movement through which is stimulated by active involvement in situations called "moral dilemmas." Raths, Harmin, and Simon present yet another alternative, the Values Clarification approach, through which a value is developed as seven subprocesses are satisfied. Raths, Harmin, and Simon encourage teachers to help children choose freely and thoughtfully from among alternatives, to be happy with their choice and affirm it publicly, and repeatedly do something with the choice.

The major approaches to affective education seem to identify as their major goals:

- Giving children experiences in thinking critically about issues
- Giving them opportunities to share feelings with others
- Giving them a chance to develop cooperative problem-solving skills
- Giving them a chance to apply value skills in their own lives

They approach the development of valuing from a personal perspective. They are based on the idea that if children are put into a supportive social environment and encouraged to tune into their feelings and the feelings of others, and if they are taught communication skills that maximize interpersonal understanding, they will naturally tend to make wise judgments and will use their experiences to correct unwise judgments. A key implication is that teachers should become more honest, warm, and empathetic. From that base, children achieve the personal strength to address issues involving controversy and commitment.

ENDNOTES

1. Lois Lamdin, "Moral Uncertainty," *Great Valley News* (Malvern, PA: Business Development and Training Center) 2, no. 2 (October 1985): 3.

2. The Boston Primer (1808), cited in Richard H. Hersh et al., *Models of Moral Education* (New York: Longman, 1980), p. 16.

3. *A Manual of the System of Discipline and Instruction* (New York: Longman, 1980), p. 16.

4. Jean Jacques Rousseau, Selections from Emilius in Robert Ulich, ed., *Three Thousand Years of Educational Wisdom* (Cambridge, Mass.: Harvard University Press, 1971), p. 397.

5. Rousseau, p. 397.

6. Marie Winn, *Shiver, Gobble, and Snore* (New York: Simon and Schuster, 1972).

7. Thomas Gordon, *T.E.T. Teacher Effectiveness Training* (New York: Peter H. Wyden/Publisher, 1974), pp. 80–87.

8. Gordon, pp. 142–44.

9. Gordon, pp. 227–34.

10. Carl R. Rogers, "Toward a Modern Approach to Values: The Valuing Process in the Mature Person," in *Reading in Values Clarification*, ed. Howard Kirschenbaum and Sidney B. Simon (Minneapolis, MN: Winston Press, 1973), pp. 75–91.

11. Rogers, in *Readings in Values Clarification*, pp. 77–78.

12. Carl R. Rogers, "A Plan for Self-Directed Change in an Educational System," *Educational Leadership* (May 1967): 718.

13. Richard C. Remy et al., *Skills in Making Political Decisions* (Columbus: Mershon Center, Ohio State University, n.d.).

14. Herbert Ginsburg and Sylvia Opper, *Piaget's Theory of Intellectual Development* (Englewood Cliffs, NJ: Prentice-Hall, 1969), pp. 100–102.

15. Ronald E. Galbraith and Thomas M. Jones, *Moral Reasoning: A Teaching Handbook for Adapting Kohlberg to the Classroom* (Minneapolis, MN: Greenhaven Press, 1967), pp. 172–80.

16. Barry K. Beyer, "Conducting Moral Discussions in the Classroom," *Social Education* (April 1976): 197.

17. Katherine H. Read, *The Nursery School: A Human Relations Laboratory* (Philadelphia: W. B. Saunders, 1971), pp. 108–109.

18. Louis E. Raths, Merrill Harmin, and Sidney B. Simon, *Values and Teaching* (Columbus, OH: Merrill, 1966), p. 30.

19. Raths, Harmin and Simon, *Values and Teaching*, pp. 38–39.

20. Based on Raths, Harmin, and Simon, *Values and Teaching*, pp. 53–54.

21. James Raths, "A Strategy for Developing Values," *Readings for Social Studies in Elementary Education*, ed. John Jarolimek and Huber M. Walsh (New York: Macmillan, 1974), pp. 252–54.

22. Raths, Harmin, and Simon, *Values and Teaching*, pp. 117–20.

23. Raths, Harmin, and Simon, *Values and Teaching*, pp. 127–55.

24. Jack R. Fraenkel, *How to Teach About Values* (Englewood Cliffs, NJ: Prentice-Hall, 1977), p. 72.

25. Walter and Harriet Mischel, "A Cognitive Social Learning Approach to Morality and Self-Regulation," in *Morality: Theory, Research, and Social Issues*, ed. Thomas Likona (New York: Holt, Rinehart, and Winston, 1976).

26. John S. Stewart, "Clarifying Values Clarification: A Critique," *Phi Delta Kappan* (June 1975): 684–685.

27. Stewart, p. 685.

Selecting Instructional Resources

KEY CONCEPTS

☐ Choosing from among the abundance of social studies instructional resources those most likely to achieve your objectives

☐ Understanding the proper techniques to use with various instructional resources

☐ Appreciating the importance of providing varied resources so that learning is interesting and meaningful

☐ Realizing that effective social studies programs are products of two interrelated factors: choosing appropriate instructional resources and using a variety of strategies and techniques

When you are ready to teach this child geography, you get together your globes and your maps; and what machines they are! Why, instead of using all these representations, do you not begin by showing him the object itself, so as to let him know what you are talking of? . . . he will examine every new object for a long time. . . . He is thoughtful. . . . Be satisfied, therefore, with presenting objects at appropriate times and in appropriate ways. [Then, when] you see his curiosity fairly at work, ask him some . . . question which will suggest its own answer. . . . Leave him to himself, and he will be certain to think the matter over. . . .

In general, never show the representation of a thing unless it be impossible to show the thing itself.

–Rousseau

This advice, offered by Rousseau hundreds of years ago, underscores the fervent interest people have maintained toward providing meaningful learning experiences for young children. That interest is still expressed in professional literature in words so similar to Rousseau's that it would be easy to surmise that his advice came from a current periodical.

Hedin and Conrad, interested in children's 1980s lifestyle and the influences of computers, television, electronic games, and other fast-paced media, interviewed 300 teachers and administrators in a suburban school district in Minnesota to compare children of today to those of the 1960s.[1] There was no question that today's youngsters have a stronger need to be entertained and expect instant gratification for their educational desires. Typical teacher comments were ''Kids have become passive receptors. They are less able to think, reason, and respond creatively. Less problem-solving ability is displayed,'' and ''TV has had a strong influence. They're more insatiable. They demand instant information.''

Elementary teachers felt that, despite the fact that children are passive learners, they were more aware, knowledgeable, sophisticated, and worldly. So, children are perceived as coming to school ''knowing more'' than they did in the past, but also showing less inherent interest in becoming involved in the educational process—''information rich but action poor.'' Children find school repetitious and monotonous—a place to pass the time until they are able to get back to the TV or their electronic games. The challenge to teachers is to choose, organize, and present learning materials in a way that approaches the stimulation they encounter outside the classroom. To address this challenge, teachers must examine the influence of two interrelated components in effective social studies programs: (1) the *subject matter* and (2) the available *learning activities*. As Fraenkel explains, ''One cannot learn something about economics, for example, unless one learns it *in some way*. One cannot learn to think unless one thinks about *something*. One does not become skilled in working with people unless one works with them on *some task* involving *some data*.''[2]

We have so far considered the professional responsibility to choose teaching approaches through which children can best *learn something in some way*, but have not yet examined the multitude of learning resources available for teachers who might, by now, visualize themselves as becoming a directed teacher, an inquiry teacher, or some combination of the two.

Learning resources provide the data, or subject matter, that teachers use to motivate children and to maximize their learning. It is difficult to prescribe exactly which kind of learning activity or resource is most appropriate for elementary school children, because learning activities must be chosen according to the objectives teachers wish to accomplish and the subject matter they wish students to attain. Teachers think in terms of history, geography, inquiry, directed learning; children build, dance, cook, or read. In their minds, skilled teachers recognize the learnings or skills associated with learning activities or resources and "pull out" significant outcomes "without the children realizing it." James L. Hymes describes the subject matter learnings elicited during a field trip to a farm:

> A group of [children] takes a trip to a farm to learn where milk comes from. If you make the teacher put one label on the experience, she will probably call it science. Or if that is too general, biology. Or if not specific enough, animal biology. But what about the conversation in connection with the trip: before, during, and after? That should be called the language arts. The stories before and after the trip are literature. The singing—"Old MacDonald Had a Farm" is fated to be sung!—must be called music. Rules for conduct are developed. This is what civics, government, and politics are all about. The teacher recalls what happened the last time the group took a trip: "You remember how we all crowded around and some people could not see." The lessons of the past are usually labeled history. A child misbehaves; the teacher's response is a lesson in psychology. Someone counts the children to be sure no one is left at the farm: arithmetic. The trip costs money; that is when the [children] take a brief course in economics. The cow is probably pretty, even if the farmer and the highway are not. The presence of beauty and the absence of it are matters of aesthetics. When the teacher soothes a disappointed child—"Things don't always work out the way we want"—the lesson is one in philosophy. And if, on such a trip, the children drink some milk, that experience is labeled nutrition. Yet the whole trip was labeled Science![3]

Whether designed to promote knowledge, skills, or values objectives, learning experiences can be classified into two major types:

Intake-of-information activities—children must be able to take in and process data before we can expect them to do anything with it. Activities such as reading, listening to recordings, viewing films, or tasting ethnic foods are thus essential to young learners' success in social studies.

Expressive activities—children must organize, make sense of, personalize, demonstrate, and attach feelings to what they learn. Activities such as charting, graphing, mapmaking, constructing time lines, designing murals, participating in role-playing activities, or writing an original story give children opportunities to *do things* with the information they receive.

Although there is probably no instructional resource that falls exclusively into the realm of *intake* or *expressive* activity, we will discuss *intake* activities in this chapter and *expressive* activities in Chapter 9.

INTAKE OF INFORMATION

Preparing children to cope with contemporary and future problems is a frightening educational responsibility. An integral part of that responsibility is to help them develop the thinking skills necessary to take in, interpret, analyze, and evaluate social studies content. Learning materials help the teacher attain those goals by offering avenues for involving students in the instructional process. Figure 8–1 organizes the types of materials available for social studies classrooms into a Cone of Classroom Experiences. The cone shows the most concrete, lifelike experiences at its base and

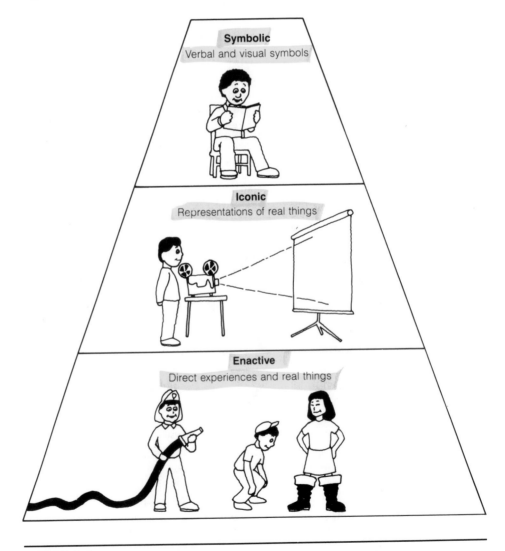

FIGURE 8–1

Cone of Classroom Experiences

the most abstract at the summit. Social studies teachers usually begin instruction at the base—they provide many opportunities to examine the real and actual. Younger children especially need opportunities within this category, to see and do and explore. As they experience the concrete, the real, they begin to develop the solid base necessary for associating new ideas as they come along. With this foundation, children eagerly seek new ideas through alternative sources, and classroom teachers introduce learning experiences that move toward the top of the cone. With a concrete base, children gain a sense of more abstract learning experiences, including those that involve symbols, and are no longer locked into the world of their own experience. The urge to learn from others or from books quickly blossoms. A good social studies classroom, therefore, focuses on *balance*—the children see, hear, talk, taste, touch—*and* listen *and* read.

Most quality school districts encourage teachers to use varieties of materials in the social studies program because not all pupils learn in the same way, and different media appeal to different learning styles; reading ranges among children in elementary classrooms are great, averaging three to five years in the lower grades and five to ten years in the middle and upper grades; each of the media has particular strengths and limitations in the way it conveys messages; the impact of a message is likely to be stronger if more than one sensory system is involved in receiving it; using a variety of media motivates and generates interest; and different sources can provide different insights on the same subject, while some discrepancies or inaccuracies may go undetected if a single source is used.[4]

Ways of Knowing

Jerome Bruner and his associates have identified three ways of knowing upon which I have based the Cone of Classroom Experiences. These levels, *enactive, iconic,* and *symbolic,* describe the modes by which children organize and store concepts.[5] Children may need to have one type of experience as opposed to another for any given topic, or may need to use two or more of them together.

ENACTIVE MODE.   This mode of knowing involves all methods of *doing something,* whether making a recipe from Spain or playing a game from China. For some children, enactment is the best way of knowing. For example, if your objective is to develop concepts of how some Mexicans construct their homes from adobe brick, then the experience may begin with children actually mixing clay, straw, and water to make real adobe bricks (rather than using a less direct approach such as watching a film of the process).

ICONIC MODE.   This knowing involves "imagery," or using representations of real objects when the objects themselves cannot be experienced directly. For example, your objective may be the same as with the creative mode, but you realize that the children's concepts of an actual adobe house will not be accurately developed unless they can actually see a house constructed from the brick. Unable to travel to one, you may decide to bring in a scale model of an adobe home or even a picture, or show a movie of an adobe home being constructed. *Copies* help children form concepts when real things are not available.

SYMBOLIC MODE.   This mode involves arbitrary symbols in written or oral form to communicate and store concepts. For example, the teacher might choose to further reinforce the concept of an adobe home by asking the children to read a selection from their textbook that describes the advantages of living in an adobe home.

Understanding these three ways of knowing is important for planning and organizing learning activities for your social studies program. They help you recognize the need for *balance* among the activities you choose, so that there is not too much symbolism (workbooks, practice sheets, reading) and not enough enactment (or vice versa) in your program.

Enactive Learning

Young children learn by doing; they "mess about" and naturally get into or try out everything. They do whatever it takes to discover things—they strive to see, hear, touch, smell, and taste all the special things around them. They want to know all about the mysterious people, places, and things that confront them each day. They may come to elementary school knowing a little bit about a lot of things, but one characteristic they all share is a thirst for experiences that will help them find out more. When these enthusiastic, energetic youngsters come to school they *expect* to learn about all that interests them in much the same way, through activity and involvement. They are not greatly interested in memorizing information or in confining activities such as completing ditto sheets or workbook pages. They want to try things out. To understand how much direct involvement and personal activity affect us, take a few minutes to think about the three most powerful learning experiences you can recall from any context in your life. In other words, when did you learn three things that have had a significant impact on your life? Write down the three incidents and consider these questions: Where did each occur? Was any in a school setting? Did you have a special need to learn at the time of each experience? What elements of the learning experiences made them so meaningful? Did any of the learnings fall under a "subject matter" heading or were they more personal in nature? If possible, share your answers with classmates. What generalizations can your group make about the conditions under which individuals learn best? Are "personal need" and "active involvement" mentioned?

Children may receive direct, meaningful information in the social studies classroom from four major sources: (1) activities within the classroom, (2) realia, (3) field trips, and (4) resource persons. Regardless of the source, they are directly involved in actually *doing something real*—a learning principle so aptly described in the old Chinese proverb: "I hear and I forget. I see and I remember. I do and I understand."

Activities within the School

A number of opportunities for direct experience are available in the school. Direct involvement in concrete experiences such as churning butter or making fabric dyes from berries enhances a child's understanding of life in colonial America. The election of classroom officials is an important experience for developing a rudimentary understanding of national election processes. Writing letters to the mayor or other elected officials helps children develop a positive attitude toward social action. By assuming classroom duties, such as running errands or feeding the pets, young children develop job responsibility and an appreciation for an individual's contribution to the overall good of a social group.

Here are additional samples of real, direct experiences. Can you add to the list?

Having the children break a piñata and scamper for the prizes

Collecting cans and bottles for a recycling center

Polling children throughout the school to determine what new piece of equipment is most needed for the playground

Designing a school or classroom flag

Dancing the Virginia Reel

Cooking a favorite ethnic recipe

Making a compost pile to produce soil for the class garden plot

Visiting a senior citizens' home during a holiday season to sing songs and exchange gifts

REALIA. In addition to providing experiences in which children actually participate in doing something real, you should consider sharing real items or artifacts (*realia*) to elucidate difficult concepts. Typical items of realia might include:

Clothing (police uniform, Mexican serape, Alaskan parka)

Money (rubles, yen, marks, Confederate money)

Documents (wills, letters, mortgages, newspapers)

Household items (old candleholders, antique eating utensils, old furniture, butter churns, cooking supplies)

Tools (farming tools, blacksmith's tools, community helper's tools)

Weapons (old rifles—be sure they *cannot* work, powder horns, clubs)

Foods (authentic cultural, national, or ethnic foods)

Toys (toys of ethnic, cultural, or historical interest)

School items (books from other nations or time periods, hornbook, globes or maps from the past)

Sports items (hockey equipment, soccer ball, bullfighting equipment)

These materials are excellent learning resources to help children more easily understand what life is like in other places or at other times. Of course, it is impossible to expect teachers to provide realia for every social studies topic; however, that does not excuse you from trying to provide as many real objects for your children as possible. Three resources will probably provide an abundance of real material for your classroom.

You will often find items related to specific topics of study at your local public library or museum. Some libraries and museums allow teachers to borrow items for short periods of time. If not, a field trip to the library or museum may be appropriate, especially if provisions are made for a tour guide to explain special items of interest.

Check your own materials for possible classroom value. If you have taken trips, reexamine souvenirs and other memorabilia that you may have stashed away or forgotten. Seashells, rock or mineral samples, surfboards, old clothing, records, and the like are often taken for granted; think about those things and also about bringing back interesting items from future trips.

In most instances, parents or other adults in the community will be your greatest asset for realia. Parents especially are willing and often eager to lend things once they know what you need and that their items will be properly cared for. A letter sent home with the children a few days before beginning study on a new topic will often result in a wealth of real classroom materials. A sample letter of this type is shown in Figure 8–2.

Don't shirk from bringing real items into the classroom. It is your job to search out items and get them into the classroom where they can be put to good use.

Field Trips

The world outside the classroom is rich in direct learning experiences. By organizing *field trips* outside the classroom, you help children explore and deal with the real world rather than representations of it. Trips are an important part of children's social studies learnings—children love the excitement, adventure, and new awareness of the world around them.

Young kindergarten or first-grade children need to be in school for awhile (at least a week in most instances) and become familiar with their classroom environment and their teacher before taking trips. As they become accustomed to these new features in their lives, a short exploratory walk around the school building will help the children place their room in relationship to the other rooms in the building and familiarize them with your expectations in such settings. They can learn about their school by visiting the principal's office, kitchen, nurse's office, storerooms, heating plant, library, and gymnasium. After this first trip experience, you can take the children on a walk around the block, even though the sights may already be familiar to them. Point out even the most obvious things, as your goals should be to develop awareness of the environment and to help the children articulate about what they see and hear.

During one episode, for example, a rabbit hopped out from among some short bushes as the children walked by. "Look at it hop," "Look how long the back legs are," and other comments ensued. The teacher encouraged their animated discussion and occasionally inserted questions to guide their observation: "Did you see its fluffy tail?" The children's interest was evident as several youngsters began "hopping" along the street to their next adventure. It is important to encourage dialogue at this age because it establishes the groundwork for active thinking about what the children will see on future trips. As you expand the walking trips, you will notice traffic lights, fire hydrants, mail boxes, bus stops, telephone booths, parking meters—

March 14, 1987

Dear Parents/Guardians,

Our next topic of study in social studies will be *The Western States* (Washington, Oregon, California, and Arizona). In order to help the children learn about these places and about the people who live there, I am trying to locate and collect as many real items as possible in order to organize a classroom display. If you have any real items from those states that we could borrow, would you please let me know by returning this note to me?

Thank you for your help in this matter.

With appreciation,

Mr. Woodburn

Parent/Guardian Signature _____

Phone Number _____

_____ Sorry, but I cannot help at this time.

_____ I have items you can borrow, and

      _____ they are fragile so please do not allow the children to handle them.

      _____ they may be handled with care by the children.

      _____ I will be glad to visit your classroom to show how the items are used.

FIGURE 8–2

Sample Letter Requesting Realia from Parents

all the sights and sounds of the streets. Loading and unloading of trucks, repair work on streets involving exposed pipes, open manholes, or large cranes are exciting to see. During the spring or fall months, pick a "class tree" or "class plant" and follow its progress for a few months. You might follow the route some of the children take to go home, stop and talk to a police officer, see the buildings where the children live, and on your return, try to find the windows of the classroom from the street.

You can visit, shop at, or just look at (1) stores (supermarket, pet shop, bakery, shoe-repair shop, florist, hardware store, open air market, automatic laundry), (2) building construction sites, and (3) community services (post office, fire station, police station, public library, subway station, health center, parks, factories, garages, lumber yards, housing projects).

Handle these first experiences away from the classroom carefully. You should be familiar with the location and be sure your visit has a distinct purpose. Be sure to establish a secure feeling by telling the children where they will be going, what they will see, and what they will hear or taste or smell. Don't be too informative, though, because you will want the trip to be a learning experience in itself. After you prepare the children for the trip, consider these precautions:

Adequate supervision (at most a 5:1 child-adult ratio)

Toileting (everyone goes before you leave)

Emergency materials (bandages, tissues, safety pins, change for the phone)

Clothing (extra clothing for winter, rain gear)

Rules (walk in pairs, hold hands, walk with the teacher, stay on the sidewalk, cross streets on signal from the teacher, don't run)

When the children have had walking experiences of this type and feel comfortable in settings outside the school, you can begin to locate worthwhile places that require transportation. Some school systems provide buses for transportation or offer a subsidy for trips. The same basic considerations for walking trips apply to transportation trips: finding a good place to visit, having a good purpose to visit, informing the children, and being aware of prerequisites. However, transportation trips require a great deal more preparation:

Arranging transportation

Scheduling the visit with those at the other end

Securing written parental permission (usually on a form provided by the school)

Planning for lunch (either packed at home or at school)

Arranging for admission costs to places such as the zoo

Maintaining a 5:1 child-adult ratio (parents are usually willing to volunteer)

Establishing rules for behavior

Trips vary in kind, as we have seen, but regardless of the type, take a camera. Some young children may never have seen pictures of themselves, so take individual as well as group shots at the places you visit. If you mount them on a classroom wall at the children's eye level or use them for a group scrapbook, they will be a tremendous source of satisfaction as well as an important learning experience. The pictures come in handy to stimulate discussion long after the trip has been taken.

You can maximize the value of trips if you follow them up with a related activity after the children return to the classroom. An experience story is one good approach; illustrations, discussions, creative skits, and comparing the experience with information from reference books are others. Whatever you choose, the trip will not be valuable unless you lead the children through activities that help to summarize their experience and apply it to the topic of study. You and the children should also evaluate the trip by asking questions like these: "Were we able to answer our questions? Did we develop any new interests (e.g., hobbies, ideas)? In what ways did our behavior affect the trip? Would we recommend this trip for others? Why? What suggestions could we give to make the next field trip better?''

In addition to careful planning of all phases of a field trip, it is advisable to extend courtesy and appreciation by sending group-dictated letters of thanks to everyone involved—chaperones, resource people, bus driver, school nurse, and principal. You can handle letter writing in the early years by asking the children to express their thoughts to you; as they dictate their message, write it on a chart. If any of the children are able to write, they can copy the letter and send it to the designated person. People especially enjoy receiving letters the children have handwritten.

An additional point to remember is that it is helpful to compile a schoolwide file of successful field trips. This file can be kept in the supervisor's office or in the teacher's room for reference. Information should be compiled in summary form and stored on a file card like the one in Figure 8–3.

These are good sites for field trips in the elementary years:

Farm	City Hall	Public library
Museum	Supermarket	Truck terminal
Department store	Post Office	Concerts
Historical sites	Camping	Cultural events
Airport	Public buildings	Zoo
Railroad station	Bus terminal	Repair shop
Factories	Shopping center	Bakery
Newspaper building	Planetarium	Construction projects
Fire station	Children's theater	

Place name:

Address:

Phone:

Name of person to contact:

Best time to call:

Admission charge:

Number of people accommodated:

Time required:

Experiences available:

FIGURE 8–3
Field Trip Information Form

This checklist summarizes the major considerations to address before, during, and after field trips.

Pretrip evaluation

I am familiar with the location to be visited.

This trip is suitable for the maturity level of my children.

Teacher preparation

My principal has been notified of the trip.

Administrative approval has been secured in writing.

Parental permission slips have been signed.

Transportation has been arranged.

Proper supervision has been planned (a 1:5 adult-child ratio is ideal).

Toilet facilities are present at the location to be visited.

Clothing requirements have been communicated to the parents.

Safety rules were communicated to the children:

  Stay together in a group
  Walk with a friend
  Stay on the sidewalk
  Cross only with the direction of your teacher

Teacher-child planning

The children are familiar (but not *too* familiar) with where they are going.

Points of interest have been shared.

Individual and group responsibilities have been assigned.

The trip

All children can see and hear.

I offer cues and comments to stimulate the children's interest.

I am constantly aware of special problems or emergency situations.

Follow-up activity

Informal discussion of the trip

Art projects related to the trip

Group experience charts

Creative dramatics

Bulletin board display

Resource Persons

Resource persons are individuals within or outside the school who have certain expertise, experience, skill, or knowledge in a field of special interest to the class. Generally, children enjoy contact with outside visitors and the interesting materials they share. In studying topics related to the neighborhood or community, for example, much insight can be gained from people who provide goods or services in the area—police officer, firefighter, farmer, delivery person, construction worker, doctor, nurse, and so on. When introducing children to different cultures or ethnic groups, people with appropriate backgrounds can provide information and answer questions. When studying remote cities, countries, or regions, people who live or have traveled there are good resources. As with field trips, careful planning is essential for a successful visit by a resource person:

1. Determine whether inviting a visitor is the best way to get the intended knowledge and information

2. Determine whether the speaker's topic and style of delivery are suitable to the children's maturity level

3. Inform the speaker about the children's age level, their needs, the time alloted for the presentation, and the facilities available

4. Provide follow-up and discussion related to the speaker's presentation; discussion, reporting, art projects, dramatization, creative writing, and further reading will summarize and extend the information

5. A joint evaluation is a means of judging the effectiveness of the speaker and the audience

6. Write a letter of thanks

Merely having someone visit your classroom does not guarantee a successful learning experience. Two examples will show the benefits of thoughtful planning.

One day Mr. Perry overheard a spirited discussion about construction machinery among a small group of children as they examined books on the reading shelf. He listened as the children expressed wonder at the size and power of backhoes, bulldozers, and other machines. Seizing the moment, Mr. Perry suggested inviting a construction worker to come to school to talk about his work.

"Would he really come to see us?" asked Michael.

"I'd like to see him come here," added Meghan. "Can we ask him to come?"

Mr. Perry had no doubt that the children's intentions were sincere, so later that day, he called the local construction company to see if a visit could be arranged. Learning that the company was working on a project nearby and was not only willing to send out a worker but also a piece of heavy equipment, Mr. Perry prepared the entire class for what would take place the next day. He told the children about what they were going to see, why they were going to see it, and how to conduct themselves safely.

The next day the children eagerly waited at the school parking lot for the construction machinery to arrive. Their anticipation grew into excitement as a bright yellow loader motored up the winding entrance. Keeping the children well in control, Mr. Perry reminded them to stay behind him until the vehicle came to a complete halt. When it did, the children gingerly approached the huge piece of machinery. The construction worker came out to show the children how the loader worked and to explain his related job responsibilities.

"The loader is so big," remarked Michael.

"Yeah, and listen to it beep when it goes backwards!" shouted Jeffrey.

"The construction worker is a lady. Wow, a lady loader driver," commented Ashley, all agog.

The children watched, listened, commented, and asked questions as they sat on the stopped loader, touched its huge tires, and tried on the worker's hard hat. All of this wonderful activity culminated in a well-supervised, short trip around the parking lot on the loader as the children took turns sitting in the high seat with the driver. Mr. Perry was rewarded by the children's enjoyment and by their learning a great deal about heavy construction machinery.

After the construction worker left the school, Mr. Perry gathered the children together and invited them to share their thoughts. As the children spoke in turn, he recorded their comments on an experience chart. Later, the children dictated a thank-you note to the worker.

Mrs. Orlando, on the other hand, assumed quite a different posture in providing her class with a visit by a resource person. To deepen the children's study of colonial America, Mrs. Orlando invited a personal friend to the classroom who was particularly skilled at weaving. When the weaver arrived at school, Mrs. Orlando quickly called for the children to put away their math papers and focus their attention on the front of the room.

"Quickly and quietly, children, put away your math work and clear your desks. Show Mr. Quinlan what good boys and girls you are."

Promptly and efficiently, the children put away their materials, folded their hands on the tops of their desks, and directed their attention to the front of the room.

"Weren't they just terrific?" commented Mrs. Orlando, as if attempting to convince her friend of her superlative classroom control. The children, not prepared beforehand, listened to a lengthy introduction of the visitor without completely understanding why he was there. When the resource person eventually got a chance to speak, he explained his craft in such minute detail that even the most mature child's attention wandered. Nervous glances from Mrs. Orlando informed each fidgety child of her displeasure over their actions. At the end of the long presentation, Mrs. Orlando eagerly thanked the speaker for visiting and warned the children of the danger of going too close to his weaving loom for fear of damaging it.

"Stay in your seats, children," she admonished. "Work on your math papers until our speaker packs up his materials. First we'll all show him how much we enjoyed his visit. Everyone clap now." Dutifully, the children followed Mrs. Orlando's instructions.

Compare Mr. Perry's and Mrs. Orlando's techniques. What were the apparent strengths in Mr. Perry's approach? What were the obvious flaws in Mrs. Orlando's technique?

Schools or parent-teacher organizations often keep a centralized card file of community members who are willing to share their expertise and people who can help break down stereotypes—senior citizens with special skills or hobbies, women carpenters, male nurses, and so on. The card file can be organized by subject for teachers to use as a ready reference (see Figure 8–4). Care must be exercised, though, in soliciting possible classroom speakers. The practice of sending request forms throughout the community, for example, is a questionable procedure since a small number of persons who have little or no immediate usefulness may volunteer. Undesirable public relations problems can result if these persons are never called upon to speak.

Area of knowledge:
Preferred age level:

Name:
Address:
Phone:

Days available:
Hours available:
Is it best for us to visit you, or are you willing to come to our classroom?

FIGURE 8–4
Special Speaker Questionnaire

The safest approach seems to be to request recommendations from other teachers, involved parents, and other school personnel. This will enable you to select speakers who will inform and motivate your children about a variety of new jobs and experiences.

ICONIC LEARNING

Models or Replicas

There are many instances when you will not be able to bring realia to the classroom or take your children on a trip to see it. For example, in studying modes of transportation during the Westward Movement, it's unlikely that you can provide an experience with a real covered wagon. But you could bring in a *scale model* of a covered wagon. The model may be authentic in every detail except size. Similarly, *replicas* are actual reproductions of realia that duplicate the original object in every way, including size. Use these items when problems of size (the original item may not be transportable), time (many original historical items are too fragile), or expense (the original may be too valuable) prohibit sharing a real thing.

Collections of models or replicas can be displayed in the classroom in special *exhibit areas*. In a study of Mexico, you might arrange replicas, models, and realia on a large table for the children to see and touch. You can stimulate the children's attention to the exhibit area with a large, attractive bulletin board displaying pictures and documents. Exhibits not only help clarify desired concepts, but bring authenticity and motivation to any topic of study.

When choosing models or replicas, be aware of their many uses:

■ To introduce a topic of study
  1. Allow children to view and handle the materials to motivate interest in further investigation

2. Encourage the childen to ask questions and make comments about the materials
-   To enrich understanding during development of the topic
    1. Use the materials as models to clarify vocabulary or build concepts
    2. Use as a guide for construction activities
    3. Use as a stimulant for discussion either before or after reading assignments, films, field trips, or other learning activities
    4. Encourage children to use the materials to add realism to skits or other dramatizations
    5. Prepare an arrangement so the children can view the materials in a realistic setting
-   To culminate a topic of study
    1. Encourage children to show real objects as they deliver oral summaries
    2. A display of real objects in realistic settings can summarize major learnings

Simulation Games

Simulation games are realistic representations of actual life situations that involve the children's ability to consider alternatives while making decisions people actually face under similar conditions. Roles, rules, and material for simulation games present a simplified representation of reality. In simulation games, scoring and reward systems are used to evaluate the *correctness* of a player's decisions. These results closely approximate those in real life situations and form the element that determines winners and losers. In other creative dramatics exercises, the player merely acts as he thinks the person being portrayed would act and does not directly experience the immediate consequences of the actions. The "Stores and Shoppers" game illustrates the major features of simulation.

> *Stores and Shoppers* is probably best used to teach the following social studies objectives to primary pupils.
>
> 1. To help the children discover that people may prefer to buy for any of several reasons—lower prices, better goods or services, convenient location, customer confidence.
> 2. To help children understand that owners of stores earn income from the production and sales of services and goods, and that from income they must pay for goods and materials to replace what they have sold, wages for their workers and selves, rent and utilities, repair and replacement of tools and equipment, taxes.
> 3. To help children understand that the income left after the business owner has paid his expenses is his profit. He earns this profit by the risks he takes since he can't be sure that his customers will buy the goods and services he sells.
> 4. To help the child discover that business owners compete to attract customers with better goods and services or prices.
> 5. To show how stores use advertising to tell what they are selling and what are their prices, and to help children understand how advertising can help people make choices.

The Situation.

The players are divided into two groups: shoppers and store owners. In a class of thirty, there might be four stores with three owners per store. Each store selects an owner to be the treasurer. Pupils are score keeper, resource keeper, and card dealer. Others are shoppers.

Resources for Players.

Each shopper has some sort of medium of exchange, which can be play money or a simulated medium such as red paper circles. Each shopper receives an equal amount of "money," and all shoppers receive identical shopping lists of items to be obtained at the stores. All the stores have equal amounts of the exchange medium, but their amounts are not equal to that of the shoppers. The stores are also provided with goods for the shoppers to buy, but the quantity and prices vary among the stores. Goods are represented by different colored paper squares, triangles, and rectangles. Prices are set by the teacher; for example:

> Store 1:—2 green triangles sell for 3 circles;
> Store 2:—6 green triangles sell for 1 circle;
> Store 3:—1 green triangle sells for 5 circles;
> Store 4:—1 green triangle sells for 5 circles.

The card dealer has small cards which designate amounts of exchange medium that must be paid by store owners at different intervals. For example, "Pay rent—5 circles."

The resource keeper is only used in a more complex game for a middle grade. He sells goods to stores when they want to use their profit to buy more goods.

Goals for Actors.

The shoppers try to buy all the things on their shopping lists. The shopper who completes or comes closest to completing his list in the given time is the winner. If two shoppers tie, the shopper with the most exchange medium left is the winner.

The store owners try to sell all their goods at the prices the teacher has set. The store with the most profit is the winner.

The score keeper is in charge of counting the stores' profits and determining the winner among the shoppers.

Special Rules and Limits.

1. When the card dealer blows the whistle, each treasurer of a store must draw a card and pay to the dealer what the card says.

2. All sales are final.

3. Shoppers cannot resell goods.

4. Stores cannot trade goods; shoppers cannot trade.

5. Playing time is set by the teacher—approximately twenty minutes to one-half hour.

Follow-up.

The most important part of a simulation game is the follow-up. Leading questions asked by the teacher help children verbalize the objectives of the game and the meaning of the game symbols. Such a question for this game might be, "Why did you buy green triangles at Store 2 instead of Store 1?" Hopefully the answer would be that the price was lower at Store 2.[6]

Teachers often wish to construct simulation games that more closely address particular concepts than do commercially prepared games. To do so, follow these key construction guidelines:

1. *Decide what you want the game to teach.* Clearly define the skills, concepts, or attitudes that will be reflected in the objectives.

2. *Identify the real life situation you want the game to simulate.* Be sure the situation involves competition or conflict.

3. *Outline the broad details of the situation to be simulated.*

4. *Specify the roles of the players.* All players must be faced with decisions so that he or she has an effect on the outcome.

5. *Identify the resources* (money, raw materials, machinery, military arms) *available to each player.* Determine the relative value of each resource and its influence on the outcome of the game. Specify the method of resource distribution to each player.

6. *Determine the interactions of the participants.* Players may face interactions based on group or individual actions; for example, if store owners group together to limit the amount of a product to be sold, individual consumers will be faced with higher prices. Consumers then have a choice to boycott or to buy anyway.

7. *Determine the sequence of events.* A simulation game is normally played in well-defined cycles. Action in each cycle begins with a crisis of some kind. Cycles may be defined in terms of a certain amount of time (hours, days, months), a certain number of repetitions, or in terms of achieving a certain score.

8. *Write the directions for carrying out each phase of the simulation game.*

A simulation game in the social studies classroom is easy to play. Its success or failure depends upon your preparation. Sound preparation involves these strategies:

1. *Preplanning.* Know the game yourself by carefully studying the rules and materials. If possible, play the game with several students in advance. Divide and organize game materials in advance, and introduce the game by *briefly* telling the students what it's all about. Divide the players and assign roles, giving students a clear description of each role.

2. *Playing the game.* Do not help the players with their strategies, but be available to answer questions concerning rules. Keep the players informed of the scores throughout. Permit students to play the game several times, since they may be interested in trying alternate strategies or other roles.

3. *Follow-up discussion.* Discuss decisions the players faced and the strategies each chose. What were their reasons for choosing specific strategies? How can the decisions and strategies be applied to real life? Discuss how the game could be modified to make it better.

Simulation games have a number of strengths and weaknesses. They vary greatly in style and appeal, so what works for one group of children may fail with another.

The key to success is to follow the suggestions on these pages and give the game a chance to show what it can contribute to your social studies classroom.

Because children have a natural love for games, simulation games capitalize on a child's self-motivation. They actively involve children in social studies learning. Also, because the game situations represent real-life circumstances, the students view the games as relevant. An advantage for teachers is that many concepts can be developed with one activity. In addition, the slow learner or emotionally upset child has an equal chance to compete with faster learners in the same activity. A final advantage of simulation games is that children work cooperatively.

Most simulation games are too expensive for the classroom. Commercially prepared games cost from $15 to $100. Yet constructing one's own game requires an overwhelming amount of time. The games can be lengthy; many take at least a half day to play completely, and some children may lose interest toward the end of an exceptionally long game.

MOTION PICTURES.   Like many of the activities treated in this chapter, motion pictures are representations of reality. But because children are generally not *directly* involved in preparing motion picture films and are mainly passive viewers, the medium is considered less concrete than other learning experiences we have discussed. The motion picture film, however, does have many unique contributions to offer social studies teachers. Among the special advantages of using a motion picture are these described by Hartley:

1. **It moves.** When movement is essential to the concept being taught, then a good film can help the teacher get the idea across. With the aid of a film, the steps in a process may be readily followed, or cause and effect may be readily shown.
2. Through the use of animation, slow motion, time-lapse photography, and microphotography, the film may depict scenes otherwise unobservable.
3. Through the use of historical reenactments, the motion picture can give the students a sense of the continuity, the setting, and the mood of the past, which is difficult to catch in any other way.
4. Through dramatic incidents, stirring music, and wisely edited scenes, the motion picture can build up attitudes toward outstanding problems.
5. The film lends variety and interest to teaching. Properly used, it can make other classroom activities more meaningful and educationally significant.[7]

The success of a film in a social studies classroom depends on how you use it.

1. *Preplanning.* Preview the film so you can analyze it. As a result of previewing the material, you can create questions to guide discussion before and following the class viewing, thus establishing a *purpose* for viewing, and relating your follow-up questions to that purpose, as we discussed regarding the DLE in Chapter 3.

    Another important aspect of preplanning is to determine the most advantageous place in the unit for showing the film. You can introduce the topic or theme with the film, use the film as the study progresses to supply or clarify related details and concepts, or summarize or review the material at the end of a topic.

2. *Class preparation.* Prepare the class to view a film by asking a few key questions that the film will answer. Without clear *purposes* to guide them as they view a film, children may wonder why the teacher expects them to sit and watch. Guiding questions remove that doubt and establish thought direction. Don't ask too much questions, however; too many questions may be as confusing as not asking any at all. Three or four questions should be a maximum. Vary the types of questions; the most appropriate are those that ask the student to identify main ideas, analyze thoughts and feelings of others, look for relationships, or evaluate the film's truthfulness. Purpose-setting questions that ask the student to recall facts and details should rarely, if ever, be used. Discourage notetaking during the film; overemphasis on factual purpose-setting questions may lead students to take notes during the film and perplex and distract them from the continuity of the presentation.

3. *Showing the film.* Prepare the class for viewing the film as an *educational experience* rather than as a "movie show." Children should look forward to each and every learning experience in the social studies classroom as a specific educational outcome.

4. *Follow-up.* The follow-up portion of the lesson evaluates how successful the viewers were in finding answers to the purpose-setting questions. Encourage the students to relate their film experience to a discussion of the previously established purpose.

Some films may be interesting to view for a second time. The second showing can be made during the same period if the film is short, or on another day if the film is especially lengthy. When showing the film the second time, you could have the students explain the action as the film plays silently, or students could supply the voices of characters in each scene. Use stop-action or slow motion to emphasize certain points.

Films can be used in a variety of creative ways. You can use a motion picture camera or videotape machine to record the major characteristics of your local environment and set up an exchange program of films or tapes with schools in other areas.

Films can also be used to record and present dramatizations. Learning experiences become more concrete if students are directly involved. Have a group dramatize a process, historical event, or the like, and record it on film or videotape to show to the rest of the class.

NARRATED SLIDES AND FILMSTRIPS. The instruction pattern used in conjunction with motion picture films can be applied to narrated slides and filmstrips. Many commercially-produced filmstrips and slides are accompanied by sound tapes or recordings. Generally, these materials are much less expensive than motion picture films, and filmstrips and slides are easier to stop at individual frames for discussion or analysis.

Most teachers use filmstrips or slides during whole class instruction, but several group or individual projects offer excellent possibilities. Individuals may view the filmstrips or slides in an isolated section of the room to achieve special independent study goals. On group research projects, children can select pertinent frames for a class presentation. In class, children can view the first five frames of a filmstrip or slide presentation and speculate about what will follow, then view the rest of the filmstrip and compare their speculations to the actual outcomes. Original filmstrips can also be created. Children can photograph things on field trips and then cooperatively prepare the narration to accompany each slide.

COMPUTERS. In addition to all the possibilities for traditional learning materials, you must become aware of a powerful new force on the educational scene—the computer. With its general acceptance as an important teaching tool, the computer will enter all of your lives as an ally for social studies instruction. Teachers use computers primarily to teach programming, for drill and practice, and for educational games. With the rapid spread of computer usage in the schools, new uses such as simulation and problem solving are supplementing those activities.

Computer technology appears to have a good possibility of altering the character of instruction in our schools. Commercial developers have begun producing computer-based instructional materials and some textbook publishers supplement their textbooks with materials for computer use.

Basics of Operation. The computer is an electronic device that cannot operate by itself. It must follow carefully prepared commands; these step-by-step procedures comprise instructional sequences called *programs* that are written in special computer languages. Although there are more than 150 computer languages, BASIC (Beginner's All-Purpose Symbolic Instruction Code) appears to be most popular for school-related materials. The purpose of this discussion is not to teach you computer programming, but an example of BASIC language would be: PRINT 2 + 1. The word PRINT is called a *command* because it signals the computer, in a complex way, to take the result of whatever follows and put it on the screen. The computer follows the command, adds the two numbers, and prints the result. The series of commands are stored in three forms: (1) *disks* (or floppy disks, or "floppies"), which are 5¼" square magnetic devices resembling 45 RPM records; (2) *cartridges*, small, plastic devices resembling cartridges used in audiotape recorders; and (3) *cassettes*, similar to tape recorder cassettes. The disks, cartridges, and cassettes are referred to as the computer's *software*.

Children learn to use computer software quickly because program operation is fairly simple. You can make a picture chart showing the operational steps and guide the children through the appropriate sequence, as in this typical procedure:

1. Take the disk out of the paper jacket and hold it so that the label faces up.
2. Put the disk into the slot on the disk drive and give a gentle push.
3. Close the door on the disk drive.
4. Turn on the computer.
5. Type LOAD "PROGRAM NAME", 8 and hit the RETURN key.
6. The disk will make a whirring noise and the screen will say READY.

7. When READY comes on, type RUN on the keyboard.
8. Play the game.
9. Take the disk out of the disk drive and place it in its jacket.
10. Turn off the computer.

You do not need to know how to write programs to use the computer in your classroom. All you need to know is how to carry through the sequence for the specific computer.

In the most common type of computer program, the child begins by typing in her name from a keyboard. The machine usually responds with some kind of welcome, such as a smile face and the word "hello" printed on the screen. Problems—perhaps matching capitals and states—appear on the screen, and the child works them out. If the decision is correct, the smile face appears and enters the next problem or task on the screen. If the response is incorrect, the machine notifies the child in either script or an alternate symbol and invites the child to select another response. If the child gives a second incorrect response, the computer automatically shows the correct answer. This type of program, designed primarily to teach social studies content, would normally take 10 to 15 minutes to complete.

Some educators criticize this pattern of computer-aided instruction as nothing more than an expensive form of teaching with a drill-and-practice emphasis. Proponents of computer-aided instruction counter that computers were never meant to replace teachers, but simply as a tool to help them in their teaching. For students who need remediation, or learn best from an individually paced program, or lack the background for understanding new material, or for those who simply enjoy the stimulation of electronic games, judicious use of drill-and-practice programs may be the key to effective instruction.

Computer usage in the social studies, although primarily drill-and-practice, has other valuable uses as well. Glenn and Rawitsch identify these uses for the social studies instructional program[8]:

1. *To deliver content.* Types of activities for delivering content include *tutorial,* in which new information is imparted; *drill,* in which knowledge of previously imparted information is tested; and *simulation,* in which students learn by experiencing a model of a real-life situation.

   An examplary *tutorial* program in geography is *States and Traits,* developed by Designware. In one learning option, the outline of a state appears on the right of the screen, and the child must move the state to its correct position on an outline map of the United States. Students learn a great deal about the states, including their capitals and major products.

   One of the most noteworthy simulations available for elementary school children is *Oregon Trail,* developed by the Minnesota Educational Computer Consortium (MECC). It presents a series of decisions pioneers faced in 1847 as they set out in wagon trains to find new homes in the Oregon Territory. They stock up with provisions at the beginning of the five- to six-month journey, but heavy rains, wagon breakdowns, illness, and robberies eventually deplete their supplies. Children must make decisions along the way, but if they choose to hunt for food or stop at a fort, for example, they lose precious time and could cause starvation or illness, or fail to pass the western mountains before the freeze and blizzards. The computer mathematically determines the outcome of the children's decisions and gives the decision makers immediate feedback about the consequences of their choices. Although most simulations involve only one user per computer, *Oregon Trail* assumes a small group approach by engaging a student family of four or five children to make the difficult decisions.

2. *To receive and analyze information.* Computers can tally numerical amounts, as in analysis of a sample opinion survey. They can select information based upon chosen characteristics. For example, a data collection for all countries can be created showing location, type of political and economic system, and so on. Students can then use the computer to investigate questions such as, ''Are there common characteristics among countries that have dictatorial governments?''

3. *As an example of the use of technology in society.* In a world increasingly dependent on technology, understanding social implications becomes more important. Computers are at the heart of this new information technology. Having computers available facilitates teaching students about the technology that will influence their lives and helps them more directly comprehend conflicting issues related to a technological society.

4. *To develop thinking skills.* Most subject areas are concerned with developing children's thinking skills, but the goals of logic and problem solving appear to apply most directly to social studies learning. Computer activities can contribute directly to the development of these skills. A relatively new computer language, *Logo,* was developed specifically for educational purposes. Logo was designed to move from the rote learning aspects of other computer-aided instruction toward problem solving and active learning. Its developer, Seymour Papert, was influenced by Piaget's theories.

Although Logo can be used to do almost everything other computer languages can do (from controlling a robot to designing a simple word-processing program), it is best known for its graphics environment, *turtle geometry.* Logo's turtle is a small white triangle that appears on the center of the screen. Users make the turtle move by typing in simple commands such as FORWARD (to make the turtle draw a straight line in the direction it is headed) or RIGHT (to make the turtle head in a new direction). When each command is followed by a number, the turtle knows just how far to go in any particular direction. Beginning students are often given those two commands (forward and right) and a chance to see what they can do. They may figure out how to make the turtle draw geometric shapes, such as a square, by typing:

```
TO    SQUARE
      FORWARD 50
      RIGHT 90
```

```
                    FORWARD 50
                    RIGHT 90
                    FORWARD 50
                    RIGHT 90
                    FORWARD 50
                    RIGHT 90
        END
```

From this point on, the computer will draw a square whenever someone types the command SQUARE.

As the children experiment with the commands and create exciting new designs, they experience the process of problem solving that is essential to upper-level thinking abilities. Some other motivational programs available for elementary school studies are:

Oh Deer! (Grades 5–9)   Students become members of a town council charged with the responsibility of dealing with a swiftly growing herd of deer in a residential area. How can they maintain a herd size that is in balance with the natural environment and human tolerance? Should they shoot some of the deer? Poison them? Ship them to another area? This simulation allows children to experience the social pressures of dealing with such a real-life dilemma. (Minnesota Computer Consortium)

Elementary Volume 6 (Grades 2–6)   In each program, children take a trip to a different time and place where they must develop whole new sets of survival skills. "Furs," for example, is a simulation of the North American fur trade of the 1770s. "Voyageur" transforms students into early eighteenth century woodsmen in the forests of northern Minnesota. This is a fascinating "time machine" in which children experience history. (Minnesota Computer Consortium)

Meet the Presidents (Grades 6–12)   A series of portraits of American Presidents is "painted" on the screen as the child is given brief factual statements at the bottom of the screen. The object of the game is to identify each President by typing his name on the keyboard before the portrait is complete. The teacher has an option of changing or adding to the facts presented. (Versa Computing)

U.S. Atlas Action (Grades 4–8)   Children learn place location, state abbreviations, birthplaces of famous people, names of rivers, mountains, and cities. (Educational Information Systems)

RECORDINGS.   Tape recorders and record players are adaptable instruments that produce interest and vitality in many phases of the social studies program. Records and tapes are relatively inexpensive and are available for a variety of topics. The possibilities for use in the social studies classroom are limited only by a teacher's imagination and originality. These are some uses; you can add others of your own:

"You Are There" recordings that transcribe actual events offer unlimited possibilities. The children can listen to speeches by past presidents; to accounts of historical events, such as the explosion of the *Hindenberg;* to sounds of places, such as an airport; or to unique sounds from other lands.

Recordings of literature or music from a culture or era under study can deepen understanding. Dance expression can be encouraged as the children associate movement with rhythm.

Dufty and Scott offer general principles for using musical recordings in the social studies classroom:

1. Select authentic creations of the people who composed them rather than "simplified" or "improved" versions.
2. Actively involve the children; encourage them to think about questions such as: "What kind of instrument is being played? What viewpoint is being expressed? What conditions are being described? What is the mood or purpose of this song? Why did people choose to express themselves this way?"[9]

To obtain maximum value from recordings, avoid common misuses. Some teachers limit their effectiveness by selecting recordings that are too long. Others fail to provide the children with a clear purpose for listening. Some try to cover too much information at one time or select materials that are unsuitable to the children's level of appreciation. An effective teacher avoids such pitfalls by carefully selecting appropriate listening materials and presenting them in the proper way at the most appropriate time.

OPAQUE PROJECTION.   Opaque projectors can be used to share diagrams, maps, tables, pictures, charts, paper money or coins, printed pages, and other *nontransparent materials* that are not available in classroom quantities. Since the opaque projector is rather large, not easily portable, and requires a darkened room, teachers use it less than the overhead projector.

OVERHEAD PROJECTION.   The overhead projector does not have the disadvantages of the opaque projector. The overhead projector uses a *transparency,* which may be manufactured commercially, drawn by the teacher with magic markers or grease pencils, or produced by a thermofax copying machine.

An overhead projector allows everyone to see concrete illustrations of main points. Cartoons, pictures, designs, diagrams can be analyzed. Step-be-step relationships in a sequence of events can be shown, such as the expansion of the United States at different periods of history. Sizes of territories can be compared in the same way. In addition, rainfall, product, or population figures can be superimposed on a regional map to illustrate specific geographical relationships. Opaque objects can be projected as silhouettes on the screen and children can try to identify the silhouetted shape. If a map or figure is projected onto a large sheet of paper, children can trace around the shape to reproduce figures that need to be detailed and accurate. Students can also create their own transparencies to illustrate an oral presentation.

FILM LOOPS.   The film loop is a short, super 8-mm film, either silent or with sound, usually without captions, sealed in a plastic cartridge that is inserted into a film loop viewer. The film loop deals with a single concept (such as ''latitude'' or ''transportation'') and normally lasts less than four minutes. It is designed for individual use, but the teacher usually provides the student with a question guide or viewing purpose. The major advantage of this medium is that the student assumes an active role in personally interpreting the material.

PICTURES AND STUDY PRINTS.   A valuable project all beginning teachers should initiate as early as possible is collecting a picture file for each topic they will teach, from many sources such as magazines, newspapers, calendars, and advertising brochures. Pictures help children visualize people, places, processes, or feelings they cannot experience directly. The dress, home, and family composition of people in different regions of the world can be clarified and enlarged through pictures. Geographical terms, such as *plateau, tundra,* and *desert,* can be visualized much more clearly. The processes of irrigation, moving through canal locks, extracting ore from a mine, making bread, and so on become more meaningful through pictures. Abstract concepts, such as fear, trust, or love, can be perceived more tangibly by examining pictures that reflect selected moods and feelings.

Teachers at the various elementary-grade levels should realize that children vary in their ability to read and interpret pictures just as they vary in their ability to read and interpret verbal symbols. Chase and John describe pupils at the *low level* as being able to name, list, and enumerate objects being viewed.[10] Children at this stage tend to focus on the upper left-hand quadrant of the picture until they are encouraged to do otherwise. The pupils at the *middle level* are able to detail meaning and describe what is happening. The students at the *high level* are able to draw inferences, see relationships, interpret, and think critically. You should strive to provide questioning and discussion at each of the levels to give children of varying abilities the chance for success at their individual levels at the same time they are exposed to higher levels of interpretation through the comments and observations of their peers.

Graham and Persky contrast effective and ineffective ways to initiate discussions of pictures and study prints:

> The untrained person . . . will show a book to a child and ask, ''Do you like the pretty pictures?'' She does not realize that a question asked in this way boxes the child into a ''yes'' or ''no'' response. The person who understands that there is a relationship between thought and language and that verbal interaction can promote thinking skills will word her comments so that they evoke a more thoughtful and complex response—e.g., ''Why do you think the puppy is running after the little boy?'' This can be the beginning of a conversation and an exchange of ideas rather than a simple question and answer episode.[11]

You can encourage children to look for different things in a picture by guiding their observations:

- Low level: "Tell how many. . ."
                "Tell me what you see. . ."

- Middle level: "What are _____ doing?"
                "What kind of _____ do you see?"
                "Describe the _____ ."
                "What color (how large, how far, etc.) is the _____ ?"

- High level: "What kind of _____ do you think _____ is?"
                "What will _____ do next?"
                "Why did _____ happen?"
                "What title can you give this picture?"

Some publishing companies have organized sets of pictures around central themes or problems for study and discussion. The study prints are placed on dur-

To lead a group picture discussion, design a sequence of questions appropriate for the range of the children's interpretation abilities.

able, attractive mounts and indexed for easy reference. They include a teacher's guide in the form of a manual or printed on the backs of the pictures for ease in guiding discussion. You should examine catalogs and samples of study prints since they vary a great deal in quality and price.

NEWSPAPERS.   Children should learn to examine the various sections of the newspaper (world news, sports, community events, etc.) with special attention to the sources of material for these sections—wire services, local writers, syndicated columns, and so on. Children can understand that a good news article answers four basic questions (*who, what, where,* and *when*) in the first paragraph or two and then may go on to explain *why* and *how.* Lead the children through the *literal* interpretation of news articles by making copies of an article, distributing it to each child, allowing them sufficient time to read it (for a *purpose* of course), and then guiding their interpretation with questions such as these: Who is the story about? What did the person do? When did the event take place? Where did the event take place? Why did the event come about? How can this event be extended, prevented from happening again, teach us a lesson, etc.?

News items are objective; they present the facts without personal reaction. Encourage the children to share their feelings about a particular news article with questions such as: How did you feel about the situation? What would you have done? Would you be willing to do the same thing? Do you agree with the central character? Is there any information you can add to the article? Do you think the story was written fairly (accurately)?

After the children learn to interpret objective news articles, they should be led to distinguish among factual accounts (such as articles on the front page) and opinionated accounts (such as those on the editorial pages). Select sentences like the following pair and ask the children to analyze whether they are fact-oriented or opinion-oriented:

The incredibly tiny 11-week-old infant entered the world weighing just 15 ounces.

The death penalty would have a deterrent effect in certain criminal cases.

After the children understand the differences between factual and opinionated articles, have them bring in editorials or letters-to-the-editor and use them to support or reject feelings about contemporary events. Political cartoons can also be used for this purpose. You may want to extend their understanding by inviting the children to write their own editorials and letters-to-the-editor or draw political cartoons, all for classroom display.

Cartoons are special ways of communicating ideas or feelings. Sometimes the message of a cartoon is just plain fun—an illustrated joke. Other times, however, cartoons carry serious messages intended to change a reader's opinion about an important issue, even though they use humor or sarcasm to make their point. The humor or sarcasm usually condones or rejects a stance on an issue by forcefully presenting a single point of view.

Most cartoons deal with one central idea and are fairly uncomplicated. Cartoons use few words to express ideas because the illustrations communicate most of the message. Cartoons often emphasize outstanding physical characteristics; George Washington's hair or Abe Lincoln's beard have been popular distinguishing characteristics used by cartoonists. Cartoons also use standard, quickly recognized symbols—Uncle Sam, the Russian bear, dollar signs, the Republican elephant, the Democratic donkey, the hawk, and the dove quickly communicate an idea or feeling. Cartoons also use exaggeration and satire. This characteristic can be a problem for social studies classes for, if not handled properly, it can inspire unfair stereotypes of other people or other lands.

In a study by Lawrence F. Shaffer, children in grades four to twelve were asked to interpret ten cartoons.[12] Children in grades four through six tended to describe the cartoon literally rather than to interpret its implied message. Not until later grades were children able to interpret cartoon symbolism. The researchers pointed out that this age (eleven to thirteen) corresponds to Piaget's stage of formal thinking—the age at which abstract problem solving begins to emerge. For this reason, it is probably better not to introduce cartoons into the social studies program until the intermediate grades.

You should select only cartoons that convey the simplest of ideas in as uncomplicated a fashion as possible and allow time to analyze them. Have the children learn to identify the standard symbols and central characters; recognize the activity in which the characters are engaged; analyze the cartoonist's point of view; determine the cartoonist's purpose; and decide whether they agree or disagree with the cartoonist.

Figure 8–5 is a political cartoon. These are some questions you could ask children about this particular cartoon to help them understand the purposes of political cartoons in general:

1. This cartoon contains illustrations of people you may know. Are these real people? Can you recognize any of the people in the cartoon?
2. Who are the men in the dark suits? Who are the others? Why are four of the presidents in dark suits while the others are in the clouds?
3. What is happening in the cartoon? Why are the presidents pointing to each other? Is there anything in the cartoon that can help you answer my question? What kind of a problem is an economic problem?
4. What are some economic problems faced by our nation today?
5. What point is the cartoonist making about those problems?
6. Do you agree or disagree with the cartoonist? Why?

Once children understand the nature of cartoons as a learning medium, they may want to draw their own cartoons in an effort to influence opinions on matters of immediate interest to the class.

FIGURE 8–5

Political Cartoon (Paul Conrad, © 1982, Los Angeles Times. Reprinted with permission.)

Through questioning strategies, we help youngsters understand that cartoons are tools of communication that focus on one person's point of view and his attempt to sway others toward that line of thinking. Can you think of a time when you had a strong urge to communicate your feelings about an issue? Could that situation have been turned into a cartoon? Think of an issue in social studies education that you presently have strong feelings about. Make a serious point about that issue in a funny or sarcastic way by drawing a cartoon. Share your cartoon with your classmates.

Sharing News Items

Voluntary participation begins when children gain interest in the newspaper and wish to share news at regular or irregular intervals. Frequently, the teacher sets aside a fifteen-minute period early in the day for children to report on and discuss items of interest. Children in the early grades normally report on events that affect them personally, but as they mature, they expand their interests to broader topics. The quality of the sharing period depends on the teacher's skill. If you can generate the children's interest and enthusiasm during the sharing period, they will learn to:

Develop an awareness of some of the most important news stories

Provide support for an individual's position on a current issue

Compare news sources that present conflicting points of view

Develop interest in current events

Several activities can help supplement and extend sharing of current news items.

- News bulletin board
  Separate areas can be set up for local, state, national, and world events, or for front-page, sports, weather, and entertainment news. Using a world map as a focal point, news items can be connected to their appropriate geographical locations with colorful yarn. Use catchy phrases, such as "A Nose for the News," to attract children to a general display of news items.
- Class newspaper
  Assign reporters to different classifications of news topics: school news; gossip column; cartoon page; sports news; local, state, and national news.

There are also many general ways to use newspapers; for example:

1. Fictionalize a story about what happened just before and just after the moment captured in a newspaper picture.
2. Give students a newspaper headline and ask them to write a news story based on it.
3. Take a student survey to find out what part of the newspaper interests them most. Divide the class into groups, each with a variety of interests. Each week assign a group to report to the class. Urge each "reporter" to read all he can find in the newspaper each day concerning his field. Each "reporter" then reads to the class one item in his field that especially interested him that week.
4. Read only the first paragraph of a news article, then make up the rest. Be original! Compare with the original article if you want.
5. Have each student study newspaper articles about different well-known personalities and each day pantomime personality sketches as other students try to guess who is being portrayed. As students become skilled in mime techniques, have them scan the newspaper for simple situations to play out in pairs or small groups. Other students will enjoy guessing the actions.
6. Have a student assume the personality of a favorite cartoon character, such as Charlie Brown, and have classmates interview him. Remember, the student who assumes the character's personality must answer questions using the character's observed speech, attitudes, and mannerisms.

7. Have students write a nursery rhyme as a news story and give it an appropriate headline; for example, *Mr. Egg Fractures Skull.*

8. Have your students write letters to their favorite comic strip or newsmaking characters. Stress proper letter form and originality.

9. Let your students be advice columnists. Have them read Ann Landers or Dear Abby. Pupils write their own advice. Check student replies with answers given by advice columnists.

10. Clip headlines from stories, but keep one newspaper intact. Students read news stories and write their own headlines. Did students discover the main idea of the story expressed in the headline? Compare student headlines with the headline in the uncut issue.

11. After identifying the main topic of an editorial, scan the paper to locate stories related to the topic and read them. Study how the editorial was developed and then have students write their own editorial on the same issue.

12. Children can write to other newspapers for a copy for a specific date, like October 18th. When the newspapers arrive, pupils can compare major stories on the same event as reported in the different newspapers. What were the headlines? Where were news stories placed in the newspaper? What people were mentioned? What background interpretative data were included in the story? What can you conclude from this activity?

13. Most students know that the highest government official is the president. How many students can name the highest elected officials in your community? For one week, have students clip newspaper articles that mention government officials. Urge them to watch for officials of national, state, and local agencies, and cabinet members and members of the judiciary. Have them label three sheets of paper with titles: "Executive Branch," "Legislative Branch," "Judicial Branch." Students list each official they find and whether he (she) is a local, county, regional, state, or national official and to what department (executive, legislative, judicial) he or she belongs.

14. When Columbus discovered America, no reporters stood by to herald the event. Tell your students to pretend they are news reporters in 1492 and write a headlined story of Columbus's discovery of the New World. Have students also write editorials on the importance of Columbus's voyages and discoveries.

These are a few of the reasons newspapers are an excellent classroom resource:

They are an adult medium. No big fifth-grader with a reading problem likes to be seen carrying around "Six Ducks in a Pond," but he's proud to be seen reading the newspaper.

They bridge the gap between the classroom and the "real" world.

They contain something for every student: comics for the slow reader, editorials for the bright youngster; real math problems for the child who hates textbooks; science as it happens.

This current events learning center encouraged children to pursue newspaper articles independently and guided their associated reading.

They contain practical vocabulary, the words students will use over and over throughout their lives.

They can be marked, cut, pasted, colored—important to young children who learn by doing and seeing.

They contain in their news stories the best models for clear, concise, simple writing.

They are the perfect model for teaching students to write for a purpose and for a particular audience.

They are the only really up-to-date social studies text there is.

They are the only text the majority of children will continue to read throughout their lives.

They are an influential and integral part of our free society. Freedom of the press is guaranteed under the Constitution; some have said that freedom is "less the right of the newspaper to print than it is the right of the citizen to read."

Current Affairs Periodicals

Teachers often rely on current events magazines or newspapers published especially for elementary school children for most of their program in current affairs. This approach has several advantages and disadvantages.

ADVANTAGES.   They are graded; news items reflect varied developmental interests; material is presented objectively; they are available to each child. By developing a common background of experience, children are better able to contribute to class discussions. Periodicals offer teaching suggestions as well as recommendations for follow-up questioning and activities.

DISADVANTAGES.   Some teachers become tied to a formal reading-reciting technique; some periodicals fail to relate articles to social studies topics under study; periodicals present articles of world, national, or regional scope and cannot deal with important local events.

In effect, the classroom news periodical is a textbook of current affairs and should be used with the same guidelines established for textbook use in the social studies (see Chapter 3.) I find current affairs periodicals an important educational tool. For one, these periodicals can motivate. They are written especially for children, and even reluctant readers respond positively to the nontext format and the comfortable reading levels. Second, the periodicals select interesting, contemporary topics. This week's big news, a special TV presentation, or the latest technological breakthrough help to make the classroom more current. Finally, periodicals are accompanied by comprehensive teacher's guides that describe creative teaching strategies. The magazines are used in thousands of schools around the country and are a valuable resource material. A sample page from one popular news periodical, *My Weekly Reader*, is shown in Figure 8–6.

Supplementing the Regular Program

Some teachers prefer to use current affairs as an integral part of regular social studies instruction. For studying a unit on "Highway Safety Problems," for example, one teacher asked the children to be on the watch for news items relating to highway safety. They would share and display the items on a bulletin board. It was hoped the children would be better able to associate classroom learning to the "real world" outside the classroom. This kind of teacher concern and implementation is excellent; however, if this technique of current events instruction excludes other techniques, children rarely become motivated to examine current events that have no immediate bearing on the unit.

MAPS, GLOBES, GRAPHS, AND OTHER GRAPHIC MATERIALS.   Materials in this category include information sources that summarize and represent data, such as maps, globes, graphs, and timelines. Whether organized by someone else or by the children themselves, these materials allow children to secure information and

Weekly Reader
NEWS PATROL® EDITION 3 • VOL. 55 • ISSUE 10 • NOV. 15, 1985

Page 2
MIKE'S
MUSCLE POWER

Underwater Robots
Help Scientists

Drawing shows a ship towing an underwater robot to a shipwreck.

They don't need air to live. They don't mind icy cold water. And they travel thousands of feet deep into the ocean. What are they? Underwater robots!

Underwater robots are being used for important jobs in deep, icy cold water. Humans can't travel or work there.

One robot went 2½ miles deep into the ocean to find and take photos of a famous ship called the *Titanic*. It's the first time the ship has been seen in 73 years. On its first trip across the ocean the *Titanic* hit an iceberg and sank. The ship carried 2,200 passengers. Nearly 1,500 passengers died.

Another robot went 6,000 feet underwater to a jet plane. The plane had crashed in the ocean. The robot was sent to get a metal box from the wreck. The box had tape recordings in it. The tapes helped scientists learn what had happened on the plane just before it crashed.

These robots, which are as big as cars, have become our "eyes" in deep oceans.

FIGURE 8–6

Sample Weekly Reader Page (*Special permission granted by* Weekly Reader, *published by* Field Publications © 1985, Weekly Reader.)

make informed decisions about everyday phenomena. Because use of these learning materials involves complex developmental skills, we will discuss them in Chapter 9.

Symbolic Learning

Symbolic learning deals with the different kinds of abstract experiences teachers provide to communicate social studies concepts: textbooks, reference books, trade books, magazines, and lecture. Each of these forms of communication is an integral part of our daily lives, but they may be considered the most highly abstract means of sharing ideas because they involve a system of arbitrary, abstract *symbols* (printed and spoken words) that stand for *real* ideas or objects. Each is a social instrument to help people understand things they want to communicate to each other. The written and spoken word are the foundation of the school curriculum, and teaching these two abstract forms of communication is perhaps your most important task as a social studies teacher. We discussed the proper way to share books with young children and examined ways to encourage oral expression in Chapter 5; now, we will talk about the positive and negative features of these two symbolic learning experiences so we can determine their proper roles in the social studies classroom.

Using Social Studies Textbooks

Skill in selecting instructional activities and resources for your social studies program and using them to greatest advantage is an important professional competency. For some purposes, such as learning about community helpers, no classroom activity would be as valuable as a trip to the firehouse or post office. You should bring materials, such as a doctor's kit or worker's hard hat, into the classroom to make learning activities concrete. Bricklayers, community leaders, airline pilots, or other resource people can visit the classroom to offer information or answer children's questions. Many kinds of audiovisual experiences such as movies or slide-tape presentations offer valuable sources of purposeful learning experiences. But the most popular materials in elementary schools today are the most familiar: *textbooks*. It is estimated that up to 90 percent of all elementary school instruction is tied into textbook use. Do you remember how social studies textbooks have been used and abused by some teachers in the past?

All children read silently from the same book.

The teacher sits at a desk (perhaps correcting math papers or counting lunch money?) while the children read.

Some children have difficulty reading the pages so the teacher asks the better readers to read the selection aloud while the others look at the book (while few actually listen).

When the reading selection is completed, the children are directed to write the answers to questions or to do related workbook pages.

CRITICISMS. Despite negative criticisms, none of the abuses could be directly attributable to the textbook itself, only to the teacher. Textbooks are actually valuable teaching tools if used properly, and most abuses are not inherent in the textbook approach. For example, one criticism of the approach is that it stifles teacher creativity by causing dependence on the teacher's manual; however, manuals are not designed to be followed exactly, but merely to guide teachers.

Another criticism is some teacher's tendencies to treat the material in the textbook as the only reading material to which the child should be exposed. Obviously, children at all grade levels should have opportunities to explore many reference materials suitable to each individual's reading ability. Most children's texts even provide lists of materials for further reading, reinforcement, or enrichment. (We will discuss this kind of material later in the chapter.)

The tendency of some teachers to expect all children at a certain grade level to be able to read a particular textbook is another criticism of the approach. This tendency certainly accounts for children's becoming disinterested in the social studies material and frustrated in the process of developing related skills and abilities.

A further criticism is the amount of material covered in the textbook. The teacher should realize that the textbook is not meant to be covered page-for-page and cover-to-cover throughout the school year, but to serve as a unifying force for whatever content is deemed appropriate for a given group of children.

Finally, critics point out that textbooks quickly become outdated. Since school districts find it too expensive to buy sets of new texts regularly, children may acquire outmoded interpretations of social issues.

ADVANTAGES. Because textbook use is and will remain popular, you should learn how to make the best use of them. With all the criticism of textbooks, why does this method continue to remain so popular? The main reason is that, when teachers must cover art, math, reading, science, and spelling, textbooks greatly lighten the number of instructional decisions and reduce the pressures associated with comprehensive preparations in each subject area. A further advantage of textbooks is that they present an orderly sequence of material from one grade level to the next. Each teacher from kindergarten through grade eight knows what the children have covered in earlier grades and what they will experience in successive grades, eliminating gaps or repetition. Additionally, textbook programs are accompanied by comprehensive teachers' manuals that contain a wealth of recommendations for instructional activities. Elementary school teachers are often grateful for valuable suggestions for introducing concepts or following up lessons. Also, textbook publishers have recently redesigned their materials to reflect fairer treatment of the contributions of various ethnic and minority groups; the past practice of concentrating wholly on the white, middle-class individual has been tempered so that the textbook no longer represents a fantasy never-never land for many readers. Finally, new textbooks have adopted conceptual-inquiry approaches to social studies teaching. They encourage active exploration into problem situations and organize learning experiences so that the text is but one of many sources of data for finding solutions to problems. Thus, social studies textbooks have remained popular over the years because they supply busy teachers with a sound, organized program and many suggestions for instructional activities to carry it out. Figures 8–7 and 8–8 will

Some people earn identity for the way they act. Did you ever say about someone, "He's a grouch" or "She's stuck up"? Have you ever heard someone described as friendly or outgoing? Grouch, stuck up, friendly, and outgoing are all kinds of earned identity.

Think About It

1. What two kinds of identity are there? How are they different from each other?
2. Which kind of identity do you think is more important? Why?
3. Take the "Who Am I?" quiz. Copy the quiz on paper and fill in the blanks. The quiz should be private.

Who Am I?

My name is _____

I live at _____

My favorite people are _____

My favorite things are _____

I like to play _____

I like to study _____

I would like to earn identity as _____

_____

As a **challenging activity**, students may divide the clippings into several file categories such as sports, bravery, social, business, government, and unlawful activities. (Students should learn that negative identities may be earned too.) Discuss why newspapers identify a person by giving information about the person as well as a report of what was done that was newsworthy.

Interested students could interview someone who has earned a special identity, such as an award. After the interview the students should report to the class on such things as what the earned identity is, how it was earned, and how the earner feels about it.

Have the **whole class** read and make reports on books about famous people. Ask the librarian to arrange a special display of books with content about "earned" identities.

As a **challenging activity,** have students look in the local newspapers for people in the community who are receiving recognition for contributions to community life. Then have students make reports to the class on the people being recognized and their achievements.

Answers to <u>Think About It</u>
1. Earned identity and given identity. Given identity is things a person is born with such as birth order and nationality. Earned identity is things a person must work to achieve such as good artist, nice person, or being stuck-up.
2. Responses will vary. Accept each response.
3. The "Who Am I?" quiz should be a private activity for students.

Related Materials
Have pupils complete page 42 of the workbook.

169

FIGURE 8–7

Sample from a Social Studies Teacher's Manual (From SCOTT, FORESMAN SOCIAL STUDIES, Book 4, Barbara Parramore and Dan D'Amelio. Copyright © 1982, 1979 Scott, Foresman and Company. Reprinted by permission.)

NAME _____

Your Earned Identity

You earn identity for the things that you do. Your hobbies and interests are part of your identity. The way you do things is part of your identity too.

Get to know yourself better. Think about what identity you have earned in the different ways shown below. Choose one and draw a picture of some part of your earned identity.

IDENTITY EARNED AT HOME    HOBBIES AND INTERESTS    IDENTITY EARNED AT SCHOOL

Drawings will vary.

© Scott, Foresman and Company

PART OF MY EARNED IDENTITY

FIGURE 8–8

Sample from a Social Studies Workbook (From SCOTT, FORESMAN SOCIAL STUDIES, Book 4, Workbook, Randee Blair et al. Copyright © 1982, 1979 Scott, Foresman and Company. Reprinted by permission.)

help you conceptualize the major components of contemporary social studies textbook-based programs.

So, as a beginning teacher, you must realize that although there are certain weaknesses in any material we use to instruct children, there are many good elementary school social studies textbooks, and you should exploit their strengths. These are some strengths of textbooks:

The material is written and produced by reputable individuals.

Concepts, style of presentation, and reading material are usually appropriate to the capabilities of the children who will use them.

The type size, spacing, format, and other technical qualities are appealing.

The material contributes to problem-solving and inquiry skills.

Large numbers of pictures and illustrations are attractive and appealing to children.

Illustrative materials—maps, pictures, drawings—are purposeful in that they contribute to the content rather than serve as "decoration."

The manual suggests practical and appealing activities.

The various social studies skills are introduced and developed in an interdisciplinary manner.

On the whole, minority groups and alternative life styles are treated fairly and adequately.

If controversial issues are included, they are generally presented on a level that the children can grasp.

Because teachers are aware that reading and interest levels may vary greatly, they often choose to use two or more textbooks in their classrooms. When teachers use a multiple text approach, they select three or four textbooks that vary in the amount or type of information they present and in the levels of reading difficulty. The sample textbook pages in Figures 8–9 and 8–10 show how two textbook series treat similar information. Also, although elementary school social studies texts are carefully checked by editors for readability levels, they often vary from publisher to publisher on their actual grade-level target. For example, one publisher's text targeted for a fifth-grade classroom may actually be written at that reading level, while a second publisher's text may measure out at the sixth-grade readability level. Therefore, if you are concerned about individual differences in reading ability in your classroom (as you should be), you might supplement your grade-level social studies text with one that measures at a lower reading level for those children below average in reading ability and a text that is above grade level for those who are above average. An easy way to judge whether a social studies text is written at, below, or over the actual grade level designated by the publisher is to use the simple readability formula constructed by Edward Fry (Figure 8–11).

Another point to consider in choosing multiple texts for your social studies program is that textbook series today vary widely in the content they cover within each grade level. In the past, the expanding-environment approach to content selection

Lesson 5 Around the World . . .

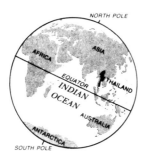

The United States is a nation of immigrants. The immigrants came from all over the world. They came from many different backgrounds. They brought with them and kept alive a variety of different customs.

Some other countries are different. They were not founded by immigrants, but are made up of people whose families have lived there for generations. They share the same backgrounds and the same customs. Thailand is a country like that. Let's look at some of its customs.

What happens when you greet a friend? "Hello, Tom," or, "Hi, Linda," you might say. You might wave. What happens when grown-ups say "hello"? They often shake hands.

Now try this. Press your hands together. Hold them up in front of your face. Now, bow your head way down. That's how people often say "hello" in Thailand. It's called the *wai*.

Now, say "hello" to Lamai Patibatsarakich. She lives in Thonburi, a city across the river from Bangkok, the capital of Thailand. If you have trouble saying her name, you're not alone. Most people in Thailand have long last names like Lamai's. So almost everybody just goes by first names.

FIGURE 8-9

Sample Textbook Page (From SCOTT, FORESMAN SOCIAL STUDIES, Book 3, Richard K. Jantz. Copyright © 1982, 1979 Scott, Foresman and Company. Reprinted by permission.)

and placement resulted in nearly identical coverage at each grade level, from series to series, of school, neighborhood, community, and so on. A second-grade teacher in California could expect his counterpart in Vermont to be teaching "communities"

3

Our country's people

Who we are   Our country is sometimes called a nation of **immigrants.** Immigrants are people who come from another continent or country to live in our country. We are all Americans. Yet every American is an immigrant or is an offspring of someone who came from another place.

The first groups of people in what is now the United States came from Asia thousands of years ago. These groups of people are now known as American Indians and Eskimos. At a much later time European people began to come to our country. And many black people were brought here from Africa to work as slaves.

We are one people, but we have many different backgrounds. Look at the circle graph on this page. It will help you understand where our people came from. Where did most United States immigrants come from?

Today our country is made up of people from almost every continent. And immigrants still come to the United States. They follow our way of life, but they also have their own ideas and ways of doing things. How do you think these groups of people have added to the American way of life?

UNITED STATES IMMIGRANTS BY PLACE OF ORIGIN, 1820–1974

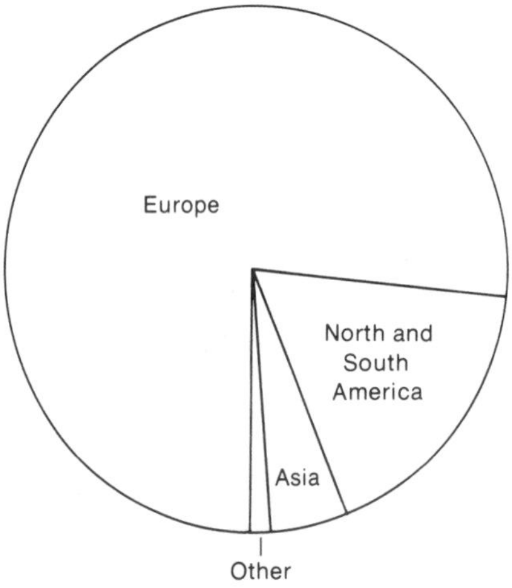

Europe

North and South America

Asia

Other

FIGURE 8–10

Sample Textbook Page (From Understanding Our Country, *Frederick M. King et al., Grade 5, 1979. By permission of LAIDLAW BROTHERS, A Division of Doubleday and Company, Inc.)*

just as he was. With today's emphasis on concepts and generalizations, however, we often find that the content of text series from two different publishers varies widely from grade to grade and that some topics presented at a higher grade in one program may be offered at a lower grade in another. That feature can help you present

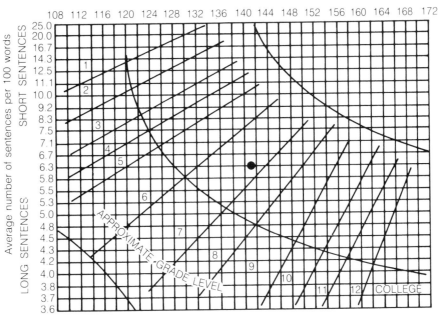

Average number of syllables per 100 words

SHORT WORDS   LONG WORDS

DIRECTIONS: Randomly select 3 one hundred word passages from a book or
an article. Plot average number of syllables and average number of sentences per 100 words on graph to determine the
grade level of the material. Choose more passages per book if
great variability is observed and conclude that the book has
uneven readability. Few books will fall in gray area but when they
do grade-level scores are invalid.

EXAMPLE:		SYLLABLES	SENTENCES
	1st Hundred Words	124	6.6
	2nd Hundred Words	141	5.5
	3rd Hundred Words	158	6.8
	AVERAGE	141	6.3

READABILITY 7th GRADE (see dot plotted on graph)

FIGURE 8–11

Fry's Readability Graph

similar information to advanced or slower learners by offering the appropriate text
to either learner. Examine the two selections from separate textbooks shown in
Figures 8–9 and 8–10. The reading levels of the two selections are dramatically different and, if both texts were chosen for use in your classroom, would certainly meet
children's individual needs.

When using multiple texts, teachers operate with a conviction that, at least during early phases of study, the entire class should be grouped together so as to acquire a common background of information. But they also realize that individual differences must be accounted for, so you will find that children are given texts at their individual reading ability levels at the beginning of a topic of study. The teacher will introduce the topic for study and motivate the children by using artifacts, pictures, bulletin board displays, and the like. Then she will guide the class for two or three days as they read their respective textbooks to search for information related to the purposes she has established or to learn about the artifacts she organized for them. Following this common exposure to basic information, the teacher normally groups the children into smaller interest or research groups for the purpose of discovering further information. You will find a sample classroom teaching episode patterned after this multiple text design later in the chapter.

Trade Books

As you become less restrictive in selecting instructional materials for the social studies classroom, you will certainly want to include a variety of *trade books*. Trade books, often referred to as children's literature, include books written for libraries or bookstores rather than for textbook use. These books, fiction or nonfiction, are available for every imaginable topic.

For those with experience working with children, few characteristics are as evident as their curiosity. They want to know: "Why? What is it? How does it work? Where does it come from?" This drive to know and understand is a need that trade books help satisfy. You need only to discover or stimulate your children's interests and help them locate books that answer questions reliably, stimulate new curiosities, and motivate further exploration to satisfy personal needs. Successful and pleasant experiences with trade books will obviously extend children's knowledge.

ADVENTURE STORIES.   Children should explore many types of trade books for social studies, not only the biographical or informational types we normally associate with social studies teaching. Adventure stories, for example, are enjoyable because of their emphasis on action, suspense, danger, and intrigue. Children thrust themselves into these stories as a substitute for personal experiences, thereby gaining insights into people, places, and standards of behavior impossible to obtain through other means. Imagine the reaction of a child reading about the surprising adventures of Professor Sherman on the Island of Krakatoa as described by William Pene du Bois in *The Twenty-one Balloons* or the problems faced by Andy in Americana as he develops a friendship with Onion John in Joseph Krumgold's *Onion John*. Books such as Ivan Southall's *Hill's End* describe courage and excitement among children in other lands (Australia).

REALISTIC STORIES.   These stories may be as exciting as adventure stories, but are about plausible events. Even early primary-grade children have a special need for factual stories. Lucy Sprague Mitchell in *Here and Now Story Book* notes that this consideration was not met prior to the 1920s[13]; instead, youngsters were given "Red Riding Hood," "Three Little Pigs," "Gingerbread Boy," and the like. Of course, they liked these stories, but they should also have been exposed to stories about themselves and about the objects and events of their everyday world. Two books that appeared shortly after Mitchell expressed her concerns were *The Poppy Seed Cakes* (1924) by Margery Clark, a collection of stories with a Russian atmosphere involving the lively adventures of a young boy named Andrewshek, and *Pelle's New Suit* (1929) by Elsa Beskow, telling how a little Swedish boy (Pelle) worked so hard to get a new suit. The early stories of this type about people in other lands tended to present the interesting and picturesque side of life rather than the usual—the Japan of kimonos, the Holland of wooden shoes, and other stereotypes. For that reason, we must carefully examine each book of this type and judge whether it accurately presents everyday life. Also, we must point out to the children that the special customs of people all around the world should not be used as a single description of their lives. How would children in other countries characterize Americans if they used, for example, the Halloween customs as their basis? We are moving toward interesting stories that give young children simple plots and understandable, fair accounts of people's activities throughout the world. Prominent authors in this area include Margaret Wise Brown, Lois Lenski, Marjorie Flack, Robert McClosky, Mark Twain, Leo Politi, Taro Yashima, Charlotte Zolotow, Armstrong Sperry, Marguerite DeAngeli, Elizabeth Enright, Meindert DeJong, Beverly Cleary, and Virginia Hamilton.

FOLKTALES. These are wildly imaginative stories in which heroes or heroines perform nearly impossible tasks in order to survive. The conflict is always between good and evil; goodness always triumphs because it is backed by wisdom and courage. Usually referred to as *folklore,* these stories provide interesting insight into culture; folklore is often called the "mirror of a people" because it explains efforts to describe strange phenomena of nature. For early primary-grade children, stories such as "Cinderella," "Three Little Pigs," "Three Billy Goats Gruff," and "The House That Jack Built," dramatize the conflict of good versus evil. For older children, folktales such as *Grimms' Fairy Tales,* Uncle Remus stories (Joel Chandler Harris), *Drummer Hoff,* and "Rumpelstiltskin" move children at times to joyful laughter and at other times to tender pity. Reread some of the folktales you remember as a child, then search for folktale collections from other nations so that, as children study other lands and people, they will more easily understand the universal concern about selfishness, wickedness, exploitation, poverty, and other discouraging facets of life.

BIOGRAPHIES. Children meet Paul Revere, Sam Houston, Abe Lincoln, George Washington Carver, or Maria Tallchief in their social studies texts, but reading about their "real lives" presents a realism difficult to attain through other means. Biographies impress children with a sense of reality of older days. Even early primary-grade children can become interested in biographies if you give them picture biographies such as those by Ingri and Edgar Parin d'Aulaire (*Abraham Lincoln, Benjamin Franklin, George Washington, Pocahontas, Columbus, Buffalo Bill*). Gradually, you can move on to many excellent biographies suitable for children at each age level: Fernando Monjo's *The One Bad Thing About Father* gives a son's view of Teddy Roosevelt, James T. DeKay's *Meet Martin Luther King, Jr.* is a picture essay describing King's early childhood and growth into adulthood, Dan D'Amelio's *Taller Than Bandai Mountain: The Story of Hideyo Noguchi* tells of a Japanese doctor's efforts to combat serious obstacles while achieving success in bacteriological research, and Evelyn Lampman's *Wheels West: The Story of Tabitha Brown* describes a sixty-six-year-old woman's trip to Oregon by wagon train where she became a famed educational pioneer.

INFORMATION BOOKS.   Information books deal with almost any subject, from the birth process to space exploration to cooking or ecology, with brilliant formats and imaginative writing. Handbooks, experiment books, how-to books, and others fulfill the child's need to know. You must help children choose appropriate informational books so they will not become confused or frustrated while searching through them for appropriate information. Guide the children so that they do not miss a valuable reading experience by being overwhelmed with numbers.

Most teacher's guides or curriculum guides recommend appropriate trade books to accompany a topic. You may wish to discuss your needs with the school librarian so that he or she can help you and your children select appropriate trade books for a particular area. Finally, reexamine professional books written especially on the topic of children's literature.

Language Experience Charts

Language experience is often initiated with kindergarten or first-grade children or with upper-grade children who are experiencing reading difficulties. In this approach, the teacher capitalizes on some common experience the children share and writes about it on large chart paper as the children dictate. *What* is done and *how* it is done are two considerations of language experience charts.

1. Capitalize on an in-school or out-of-school experience that interests the children by stimulating them to talk informally.
2. Write the children's ideas on chart paper (18″ × 36″) exactly as they are spoken, as in Figure 8–12.

> The Zoo
> Arthur said, "We went to the zoo."
> Mary said, "The elephant was huge."

FIGURE 8–12

Beginning a Language Experience Chart

3. Say each word as you write it.

4. You may or may not indicate the name of the child who offers an idea.

5. After each child has had an opportunity to contribute, read the entire account, pointing to each word as you read.

6. You may invite the children to read, too. Some may be able to read only the title or one or two words; others may be able to read entire sentences. Move your hand across each line as it is read.

7. Follow these reading activities with comprehension checks:
"What animal did Ramon tell us about?"
"What word in James's sentence is the same as in Carrie's sentence?"

8. Invite the children to illustrate the story and copy the sentence from the chart to show the part they are illustrating.

9. Some children may want to tell a related story as they make their illustrations. Write down the words on an extra piece of drawing paper and ask the child to illustrate it.

10. Illustrated experience stories, from either the group account or individual illustrations, make interesting "library books." Give them attractive covers and place them in an area readily available to the children.

A page from an experience story composed by a group of children following a visit to a post office is shown in Figure 8–13. Notice that they "wrote" this book using their thoughts of the trip to describe the photographs. Here is a sample classroom scene showing how one teacher utilized the language experience approach to summarize the children's interests after a visit from a police officer.

Mrs. Jonas:	We really liked Officer Miller's visit this morning, didn't we? Let's see if we can think of some things that we especially remember about it. When you think of something, I'll write it down on this large sheet of paper with the words Officer Miller at the top. What do these words say? [Points to *Officer Miller* at the top of the chart.]
Children:	Officer Miller.
Mrs. Jonas:	That's good. What do you remember about Officer Miller?
Tanya:	She wore a badge on her suit.
Mrs. Jonas:	Yes. She wore a badge on her suit. Now watch me write what Tanya just said. [When finished with the sentence, she reads it back to the class while pointing to each word.] Can you think of something about Officer Miller's visit?
Alan:	Officer Miller worked the police siren for us.
Mrs. Jonas:	That's good. I'll write what Alan said while the rest of you listen to see if I remembered. Ready—here I go. [Again, Mrs. Jonas says each word as she writes it and then reads back the entire sentence.] Would someone like to tell us about the siren?

FIGURE 8–13

Experience Story

Louise:	It was so loud it hurt our ears.
Mrs. Jonas:	It sure was. Now watch as I write what Louise just told us.

Eventually, the chart looked like the one in Figure 8–14. Following the story, Mrs. Jonas involved the children this way:

Mrs. Jonas:	Let me tell you what this word says. (Points to *Officer* and says it; then points to *Miller*) What does this word say?
Carmen:	Miller . . . Officer Miller.
Mrs. Jonas:	Very good. Now I'll say something about Officer Miller . . . she wore a badge on her suit. Who can point to the words I just said? (Children volunteer.)
Mrs. Jonas:	You're excellent today. Now, I really have something for you to try. See if you can read Alan's sentence with me as I point to the words.

The dialogue continued in this way until Mrs. Jonas was satisfied that each child contributed what he or she wished to. She then invited the class to copy the sentence they wished to illustrate or to give their new ideas on the same topic to her to write on a piece of drawing paper while they illustrated them.

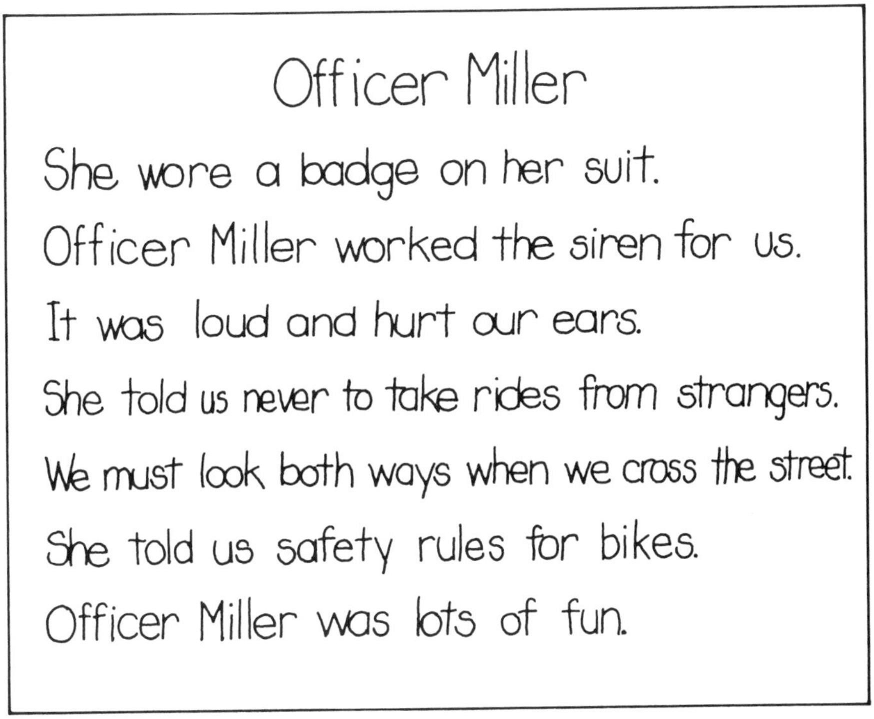

> # Officer Miller
>
> She wore a badge on her suit.
>
> Officer Miller worked the siren for us.
>
> It was loud and hurt our ears.
>
> She told us never to take rides from strangers.
>
> We must look both ways when we cross the street.
>
> She told us safety rules for bikes.
>
> Officer Miller was lots of fun.

FIGURE 8–14
Sample Chart

Teachers who use language experience charts often find that children respond positively to seeing their "talk being written down." With this built-in motivation, a chart has value far beyond that of the one day it is used in the classroom.

Lecture

Lecturing is the oldest instructional technique. Before the invention of the printing press, those few individuals fortunate enough to read and own a book would share their knowledge by reading from their book while others listened. (The word *lecture* derives from the Latin word *lego (legere, lectus)*, "to read," and the process of teaching others by reading to them became generally described by the term *lego*.) Because the technique eventually became so popular, the word *lego* took on the expanded meaning, "to teach." Even when books became more readily available after the invention of the printing press, teachers continued to base instruction on their reading text materials to students. After years of abuse, the technique fell into disfavor among critics of social studies education, who characterized the teacher as a stern autocrat lecturing in front of a class with his or her words going into the student's notes without passing through the minds of either. Despite these negative connotations, the lecture method, when used correctly, can be a valuable addition to the social studies program, because the weaknesses attributed to verbal instruction are not inherent in the method itself.

Although the lecture technique (or any other technique) should never be used as the exclusive instructional method, there are occasions when it can be used to advantage.

INTRODUCING A TOPIC.   Your enthusiasm can be contagious, so a major use of the lecture might be to arouse interest in a topic. Transferring enthusiasm to students, however, is a difficult skill for teachers to attain.

PRESENTING INFORMATION.   You will sometimes find the books and other reference materials used in class do not present major points that need to be developed or lack up-to-date information. A lecture can fill in gaps and smooth over rough surfaces. In these cases, the teacher must be careful to emphasize that the lecture is only one viewpoint and must be evaluated as critically as any other source of information used to gather data.

INTEGRATING INFORMATION.   You will sometimes find it necessary to explain difficult ideas to the children. In this type of lecture, the teacher shows the students the process of logically ordering information to arrive at a clear explanation. Students can be encouraged to repeat the process in explaining individual areas of interest.

GIVING AN OVERVIEW.   You may wish to use the lecture technique to relate a new topic of study to a previous topic or to place a topic in perspective. This type of lecture is not as concerned with providing specific information as with providing an overall idea or general picture of a topic.

SHARING PERSONAL EXPERIENCES.   If you or a fellow teacher have had an interesting experience such as a trip to an important place or a visit with a popular personality, you will want to share it with the children. They are interested in their teachers' lives and may be motivated to find out more about the people or places associated with your experiences.

If you find that a lecture is the only or best possible technique to achieve your goal, then you must present the lecture articulately, enthusiastically, and interestingly. Often, beginning teachers are tempted to memorize the content they wish to share with the children. Try not to do that, because it often leads to a stiff and stilted performance. Of course, you should know the content well and organize the important points in your mind. From there, you must realize that lecturing is a very personal skill; there is no special formula to ensure its success. The technique one person uses may work magic, whereas the same technique might fail terribly for someone else. Nevertheless, some general guidelines will help you deliver an effective lecture.

Guidelines

PLAN A GOOD INTRODUCTION. Give the children an idea of what your presentation is going to be about, but don't get too involved with highly detailed descriptions of people or events. Avoid statements such as, "Today I want to tell you about oil drilling." Try to capture their attention with statements such as: "How many of you have ever thought a grasshopper can be used to pump oil? Let me tell you."

USE YOUR VOICE EFFECTIVELY. Speak naturally, but be aware of the ways loudness or softness and fastness or slowness can affect the mood of your presentation. Your voice can add surprise, sadness, question, or fear to the presentation, but do not get overdramatic. If you do, you will shift the focus from the content of the presentation to yourself and interrupt the children's interest and concentration.

ESTABLISH GOOD EYE CONTACT WITH THE CHILDREN. A good oral communicator looks directly at the audience to establish and maintain their interest. A few facial or body gestures will add to the vividness of your presentation.

ANTICIPATE QUESTIONS AND MINOR INTERRUPTIONS. Handle these situations tactfully so that the trend of the content is not interrupted. For example, a child may become so involved in a lecture that he may unconsciously blurt out, "Oh, I wonder how the aborigine boy will be saved." Another child might insightfully offer the actual solution and seemingly spoil the suspense you were generating. Although it is easy to become flustered at such a time, remember to remain composed and bring the children back with a simple comment such as, "Your idea was very good, Loren, but let's all listen to the end and see if you were right."

USE AUDIOVISUAL AIDS. Illustration of major points helps the children understand what you are telling them and brings realism to information that might otherwise be difficult to imagine. A photograph of an oil pumping "grasshopper," for example, shows children how this large pump got its name from its resemblance to an insect. In short, remember that "A picture (or other audiovisual aid) is worth a thousand words."

DISCUSS THE MAIN POINTS. After your presentation, ask children to summarize the content or share their feelings about it.

Finally, at least for beginning teachers, rehearse your lecture several times before delivering it to the children. In the "rehearsal" stage, consider these suggestions:

Rehash it silently to get an overall idea of the presentation.

Say it aloud so you can develop a "feel" for its mood. Read it on a tape recorder and analyze your style. Be especially watchful for "uhs," "ahs," and "ya-knows."

Sit or stand in front of a mirror. Try to use body gestures and facial expressions to emphasize major points or to communicate moods and feelings.

If you possibly can, practice your presentation in front of a friend and ask for an honest critique of your technique.

Determine how long your presentation will take. Children's attention spans vary from topic to topic, but a good rule of thumb is to stay within a time frame of five to fifteen minutes.

Using a Variety of Activities

The following episode describes one fifth-grade teacher's approach to using many of the activities suggested in this chapter. Of course, there are many possible variations to this approach. What are some *you* would suggest?

Ms. Lawrence's social studies program reached the point where her children were ready to move from a single-text approach to one that would present information from several sources, still using the basic text as one of those sources. So, for this unit on Africa, Ms. Lawrence chose to use *three* textbooks for exposure to basic information before branching out into individual or group projects. Also, individual differences could be met and the reading might lead to good class discussion comparing the different accounts.

Ms. Lawrence, realizing that some *vocabulary building* was needed before good reading could be expected, addressed this concern by examining new terms during the initial phases of reading on the topic of the Ibo culture of Africa. She wrote words such as *tunic* on the board and pronounced them. Ms. Lawrence had prepared a display of pictures and artifacts so the children could read for the purpose of identifying each item on the table. Lois found a paragraph in her book describing *tunics* which she read to the rest of the class who were not using the same text: "A tunic is a long slip-on robe or gown." Lois took a card with the word *tunic* printed on it and placed it by a robe at the display. This, however, was only a partial definition, and further reading would enlarge the concept of *tunic.* Rose and Jerome discovered that their book described much more elaborate tunics: "The king of Mali wears a fancy red tunic made of expensive foreign cloth." Rose and Jerome found the picture at the display that illustrated the fancy red tunics and contributed their part to a growing concept. In the same manner, the children identified the rest of the items at the display.

Following this introduction, Ms. Lawrence encouraged the children to discuss things they might like to learn about the Ibo culture. They suggested some ideas, and Ms. Lawrence wrote them on the chalkboard. Typical queries were: "What kind of clothes did they wear?" "How did they live?" and "What did they eat?" Ms. Lawrence used these questions as the purpose-setting part of her teaching procedure and directed the children to read further in their texts to see if they could locate appropriate information.

After two days of studying their texts, Ms. Lawrence demonstrated to the children how a trade book could help them find even more information about the ideas they had listed on the chalkboard. She read a short selection about ceremonies, from Sonia Bleeker's *The Ibo of Biafra* to show the beautiful rituals that are part of the Ibo culture. The children expressed strong interest in finding out more about ceremonies and traditions celebrated by Africans and Afro-Americans, so Ms. Lawrence pointed to a table of other trade books, magazine articles, newspaper stories, and pictures and suggested to the class that these resources might help them find information about their interests.

One group was motivated to study *Kwanzaa*, a relatively new black-American holiday, which means celebration of the "first fruits of harvest" in Swahili. It is described as the only true African-American holiday and lasts for seven days at a period of time coinciding with the Christmas holidays. After much reading, planning, and locating information, the Kwanzaa group was ready to begin the actual work of collecting and constructing materials to help them tell their story. The search for information gave the children practice in considering many sources of information, evaluating each source, and selecting the most important for their purposes. Once the information was collected, the groups were responsible for reporting their discoveries to their classmates. The boys and girls found that Kwanzaa activities begin on December 26 with a *mkeka* (straw mat) on which all items for the celebration are placed. Ms. Lawrence helped the children make the mkeka and listened as the children explained to their classmates that the mkeka is placed on a low table or on the floor because it represents the land. The children had built a *kinara* (candleholder) to hold seven candles, and brought *muhindi* (fruit and corn) from home to place on the mkeka. They then presented the story of Kwanzaa.

One candle is lit each day until the seventh, when the center and final candle is lit. Each one is labeled with one of the seven principles of *nguzo saba* (blackness) that serve as guidelines to follow all year:

- 1st day (*Umoja*—unity)
- 2nd day (*Kujichagulia*—self-determination)
- 3rd day (*Ujima*—collective work)
- 4th day (*Ujamaa*—cooperative economics)
- 5th day (*Nia*—purpose)
- 6th day (*Kuumba*—creativity)
- 7th day (*Imani*—faith)

The kinara represents the original stalk from which all people spread, and each muhindi represents a child. The kernels are the children and the stalk represents the father. At each meal during Kwanzaa, a candle is lit, its meaning is discussed, and everyone drinks from a unity cup.

Kwanzaa is primarily a children's holiday begun during the 1970s as a way to help them gain a true value of their cultural heritage and to prepare them for adult responsibilities.

Pleasurable experiences like this fostered deeper interest in cultural celebrations. Ms. Lawrence, with help from the school librarian, located other reading material that, when arranged with books, artifacts, and other materials already discovered, comprised an attractive exhibit of the things the children had all enjoyed learning about.

SUMMARY

An abundance of materials and activities is essential for successful teaching in the social studies. Most school districts encourage teachers to use a variety of media for instruction. Obviously, though, they reward teachers not only for the materials they use, but also for using them skillfully. Whether they are intended to promote knowledge, skills, or values objectives, learning experiences can be classified into two major types: (1) information intake activities and (2) expressive activities. Although probably no single material or activity falls exclusively into either realm, this chapter has dealt primarily with those that promote intake of information.

One method of describing reliable social studies learning resources is the Cone of Classroom Experiences. Based on Bruner's theory of how children organize and store concepts, the Cone specifies three categories into which all learning materials can be classified:

1. Enactive mode (involves all methods of doing something)
   Activities within the school
   Realia
   Field trips
   Resource persons

2. Iconic mode (involves representations of real objects)
   Models or replicas
   Simulation games
   Motion pictures
   Narrated slides and filmstrips
   Computers
   Recordings
   Opaque projection
   Overhead projection
   Film loops
   Pictures and study prints
   Newspapers
   Current affairs periodicals
   Maps, globes, graphs, and other graphic material

3. Symbolic mode (written or oral symbols to communicate concepts)
   Social studies textbooks
   Trade books
   Language experience charts
   Lecture

Whereas teachers should use a variety of activities for the social studies program, the overwhelming practice is to rely primarily on the textbook. This is not to imply that textbook usage is bad and that a multimedia approach is good, for you do not want to engage children in activities simply for the sake of making it appear as if the children are "doing something." Have a specific purpose for your social studies lesson and, if a textbook best helps achieve that purpose, fine. But if the specific purpose can best be achieved by taking a field trip, choose that experience for your children. What is important is that you identify the desired outcomes of your lesson beforehand and consciously select and offer the most practical and valuable learning material to ensure that outcome.

ENDNOTES

1. Diane Hedin and Dan Conrad, "Changes in Children and Youth over Two Decades: The Perceptions of Teachers," *Phi Delta Kappan*, 61, no. 10 (June 1980): 702–703.

2. Fraenkel, Jack R., "The Importance of Learning Activities," in *Social Studies and the Elementary Teacher: Promises and Practices*, ed. William W. Joyce and Frank L. Ryan (Washington, DC: National Council for the Social Studies, 1977), p. 38.

3. James Hymes, *Teaching the Child Under Six*, 3rd ed. (Columbus, OH: Merrill, 1981), pp. 80–81.

4. John Jarolimek, *Social Studies Competencies and Skills* (New York: Macmillan, 1977), p. 32.

5. Jerome Bruner et al., *Studies in Cognitive Growth* (New York: John Wiley, 1966).

6. John Twoler, Lisa Montgomery, and Judy Waid, "Simulation Games: How to Use," *Instructor* 68, no. 7 (March 1970). Reprinted from *Instructor*, copyright March 1970 by the Instructor Publications, Inc., used by permission.

7. William H. Hartley, "How to Use a Motion Picture," in *How To Do It Series*, no. 1. Washington, D.C.: National Council for the Social Studies, 1965, p. 1.

8. Allen Glenn and Don Rawitsch, *Computing in the Social Studies Classroom*. (Eugene, OR: International Council for Computers in Education, 1984), pp. 8–12.

9. David Dufty and John Anthony Scott, "How to Use Folk Songs," *How To Do It Series*, no. 25 (Washington DC: National Council for the Social Studies, 1969).

10. Linwood Chase and Martha Tyler John, *A Guide for the Elementary School Teacher* (Boston: Allyn and Bacon, 1972), p. 195.

11. L. B. Graham and B. A. Persky, "Who Should Work with Young Children?" in *Early Childhood*, ed. L. B. Graham and B. A. Persky (Wayne, NJ: Avery, 1977), p. 336.

12. Ralph C. Preston and Wayne L. Herman, *Teaching Social Studies in the Elementary School* (New York: Holt, Rinehart, and Winston, 1974).

13. Lucy Sprague Mitchell, *Here and Now Story Book* (New York: E. P. Dutton, 1948).

9

Understanding Graphic Representations

KEY CONCEPTS

- ☐ *Understanding the essential graphic skills that can be communicated to children at the elementary school level*
- ☐ *Planning and using learning episodes that help children learn graphic skills*
- ☐ *Realizing the importance of a developmental progression of graphic skills instruction*
- ☐ *Appreciating that interpreting graphic information is a lifelong skill*

> I'm not very good in geography. . . . They call it economic geography this year. We've been studying the imports and exports of Chile all week, but I couldn't tell you what they are. Maybe the reason is I had to miss school yesterday because my uncle took me and his big trailer truck downstate about 200 miles, and we brought almost 10 tons of stock to the Chicago market.
>
> He had told me where we were going and I had to figure out the highways to take and also the mileage. He didn't do anything but drive and turn where I told him to. Was that fun! I sat with a map in my lap and told him to turn south, or southeast, or even some other direction.
>
> . . . Dad says I can quit school when I am fifteen and I am sort of anxious to because there are a lot of things I want to learn how to do and as my uncle says, I'm not getting any younger![1]

This youngster's ability to use maps is clearly a direct outgrowth of concrete experiences. Riding with his uncle and interpreting map symbols resulted in a successful and stimulating experience. All of your education training has certainly underscored the significance of concrete learning experiences; spoken or written words cannot approach their value. To understand why direct experiences are important in developing map reading skills, though, one must have a clear idea of what a map is. Essentially, maps are symbolic representations of objects or ideas. Instead of using lengthy verbal explanations to get from one place to another or to describe a particular geographic area, we communicate with a special symbol system.

Learning to read maps, much like learning to read other special symbol systems (such as the printed word), depends on an individual's ability to assimilate previous life experiences into an established mental schema (concept) and to attach arbitrary labels to those mental schemas so as to communicate them to others. For example, when learning to read the printed word *chicken*, the child associates the arbitrary printed symbol, "chicken," with the actual animal only after she has first encountered a chicken in some way and has examined the actual printed word a number of times. The child is able to form a mental schema of the chicken because of her life experience; then she understands that the printed word represents that mental image.

All cultures have devised their own symbol systems to communicate ideas. In Spain, children learn to use the printed symbol "pollo" (po-yo) instead of "chicken" to represent the common domestic fowl whose flesh is used for food. Symbols are thus *arbitrary representations* that stand for other things. Basically, reading printed words is the process of attaching meaning derived from previous life experiences to a special printed symbol. Likewise, reading maps involves a similar process, but instead of attaching meaning to words, individuals must attach meaning to arbitrary symbols that represent spatial concepts such as direction, distance, and area.

PRE-MAPPING ACTIVITIES

Inherent in the acquisition of map reading skills is the acquisition of basic mental images to which map symbols can later be associated. Preschool and kindergarten children acquire these images as they explore and manipulate objects in their environment. As they use their senses and muscles in direct experiences, they are continually gathering, sorting, and storing the kind of information that subsequent map reading processes demand. Three important pre-mapping learning areas must be emphasized as children gather and assimilate knowledge about their physical world: (1) physical features, (2) the earth, and (3) representation.

Physical Features

Children continually "read their environment" for clues as to what the still undefined people, places, and objects in their young lives are all about. Teachers help children begin to make sense of their surroundings by directing them toward certain data or significant discoveries. This guidance does not stifle a child's interest in the experience, but provides the necessary direction to make the most of it. There are a variety of ways to help children inspect and identify physical features in their environment:

> If your playground is comprised of several different surfaces (sand, dirt, grass, asphalt, concrete, etc.), have the children observe each carefully and decide which is best for riding a trike or running in bare feet. Discuss why the hardest surface is easiest for some tasks and the softest is easiest for others. Ask the children to find the area that would be best for digging, for tumbling, for resting, or for other uses.

> Sand and water play can be used to help the children build model rivers, lakes, roads, mountains, farms, cities, and the like. Toy vehicles add additional fantasy to free play and help develop an awareness of the different types of geographical features on the earth's surface and how people use those features in their daily lives.

> Take a walk outside the school and locate various physical features. Churches, houses, apartment buildings, trailers, row homes, stores, parking lots, and parks can be identified. You should lead discussions to help the children compare and contrast the ways people use these neighborhood features.

> Take a trip to a more remote area than the one in which your school is located—to a rural area, for example. Encourage the children to look for different land formations and buildings, such as rivers, ponds, mountains, valleys, fields, farm houses, or barns. Lead a discussion of the ways this environment differs from their own, especially regarding clothing, work, play, and living arrangements.

THE EARTH.   Complete understanding of the earth and its features is certainly impossible for young children—consider, for example, the youngster who busily burrows with his shovel because he wants to "dig all the way to the bottom of the world." Despite maturational limitations, it is important for children to participate in experiences that focus on apparent features of the earth's surface:

> When standing in the sun, ask the children to find their shadows. Explain that the sun's strong light makes the shadow. Move to the shade and talk about the differences.
>
> Digging in the dirt and playing with water introduce children to the two basic features of the earth. Take the children to a lake or pond to help them more fully understand large bodies of water. Have the children classify objects or pictures that belong primarily on land or on the water.
>
> Have the children look at the many varieties of cloud formations to learn that large, puffy, white clouds mean fair weather and large, dark, thick clouds warn of rain or snow.
>
> During a windy day, point out the nature of the wind by asking the children to run into the wind and then turn away from the wind and run. Discuss the differences experienced during each effort.

Representation

The actual symbolic representations on maps are too abstract for preschool and kindergarten children to use. This does not mean, however, that young children are incapable of using symbols of any kind; their oral language skills show that they have begun to acquire symbolic thought. For that reason, a variety of informal representational activities will help children discover relationships between some physical aspect of their environment and its arbitrary symbol. These activities help promote initial instruction in representation:

> Encourage free play in the sand or water play areas with trucks, cars, boats, and the like. As children "build" roads, bridges, canals, and other geographic features, they begin to develop an understanding of how their miniature environment simulates the larger world.
>
> Take a class trip around the neighborhood and photograph the buildings as you go. Mount the pictures on blocks of wood and encourage the children to use them as they would use regular blocks in their play.
>
> Use photographs of the children to illustrate that familiar things can be represented by scale models—the picture shows you, "but the picture is very small and you are really much bigger." Take photographs or draw pictures of a variety of classroom features and ask the children to point to or pick up the real object. This leads children to understand that symbols represent real things or real places, but in much smaller ways.

Provide picture puzzles and map puzzles to help children develop accurate conceptualizations of real objects.

Some children use these experiences as springboards to successful map and globe consciousness, while others derive little benefit. What accounts for the variability? Perhaps the most reasonable explanation is that many children have not yet developed the ability to perceive the various spatial relationships required for understanding maps.

PERCEPTUAL FACTORS

Perceptual skills involve a child's ability to receive sensory input, interpret it, and respond to it. When the child receives stimulation from either of three basic sensory channels (auditory, visual, kinesthetic/tactile), he is able to interpret it only on the basis of how well his native neural capabilities and experiential background allow him to. If both areas are adequate, the child forms accurate perceptions and the map reading process develops normally. If, however, either area is inadequate, development of map reading skills will be delayed.

Egocentrism and Conservation

Two perceptual factors—Piaget's mental operations of egocentrism and conservation—are also important to successful map reading. *Egocentrism* refers to childrens' ability to see the world only from their point of view and their belief that everyone else sees it the same way. Children have difficulty imagining that a view of any physical feature changes if it is examined from a position other than their own. To test this characteristic, Piaget devised a square board with three distinctly different model mountains, arranged as shown in Figure 9–1. Interviewers would ask children to sit at a table so that they saw the view as shown in Figure 9–1. Then

FIGURE 9–1

Piaget's Arrangement of Mountains on a Square Board

the interviewers showed the children drawings of the mountains as viewed from several different perspectives and asked the children to select the view they presently saw. Next, the interviewers introduced a doll who "strolled" about the table along the outer edges of the model of the mountains, stopping at each side of the square. The children were to remain seated and select pictures showing how the doll saw the mountains at each stop. Results showed that some children were able to make firm choices before the age of eight or ten, but not until the age of eight or ten could most children make their choices with confidence.

In addition to egocentrism, Piaget told us that children younger than about seven or eight have difficulty counterbalancing the effects of how things look now as opposed to how they looked a short while ago (*conservation*). Details of the concept of conservation are illustrated in Figure 9–2.

Informal Play with Blocks

Because children before age eight are egocentric in their view of the environment and have difficulty conserving, teachers of young children should learn to work *with* and not against these natural tendencies. If we ignore these early developmental characteristics, children will have difficulty in the future matching what they should already know to new learning tasks. Teachers of children three to seven years old provide the foundation for helping the child conceptualize space by arranging blocks, boxes, and other construction materials in a variety of informal play situations. Children can build structures, large enough to play in, that represent neighborhood, school, shopping area, or airport. Although the emphasis is on creative play and not on constructing accurate representations, the children are making a symbolic representation of some real part of their environment, and in essence, that is what a map is.

Blocks are exciting materials for youngsters to work with. With blocks, children can make "real" things to touch, move, reach through, go around, and even to crash into an occasion. Children build, play, destroy, and build again as they gain mastery not only of their physical capabilities but also of their ability to represent some real place. Watch a group of kindergartners or first-graders strive to build a neighborhood with their blocks; cars, buses, and trucks maneuver up and down the streets, reacting to pedestrians and traffic signals or coming into a service station for a fill-up. The active involvement, role playing, and mental exercise help make this a valuable initial learning experience.

Your role during this kind of activity is to *observe* and *encourage*. You may offer support and encouragement, but do not build or participate in the actual block construction. Maintain a lookout for safety reasons and interfere only if there is continued disarray or confusion or seeming physical danger. The atmosphere is one of independence and responsibility, encouraging the children to work hard toward their own purposes.

In addition to informal learning with block play, what specific map and globe skills can the teacher help encourage in a more planned way? We can best answer this question if we think of a small group of children building with blocks who become aware they have made some structures and what appear to be streets or roads.

	Have the children agree that there are:	Then make this change:	And ask the children:
CONSERVATION OF LIQUIDS	two equal glasses of liquid. 	Pour one into a taller, thinner glass. 	Do the glasses contain more, less, or the same amount? Why do you think so?
CONSERVATION OF NUMBER	two equal lines of coins. 	Lengthen the spaces between the coins on one line. 	Do both lines have the same number of checkers or does one line have more? Why do you think so?
CONSERVATION OF MATTER	two equal balls of clay. 	Squeeze one ball into a long thin shape. 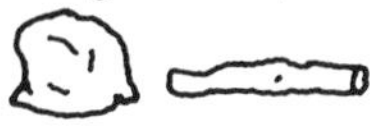	Which piece has more clay—the ball or the snake? Why do you think so?
CONSERVATION OF LENGTH	two pencils of equal length. 	Move one pencil. 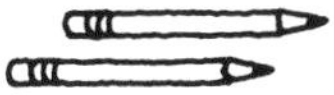	Would two ants starting a hike at this end of the pencils and walking at the same speed both travel the same distance? Why do you think so?
CONSERVATION OF AREA	two identical pieces of green construction paper representing a field of grass on which are placed the same number of red blocks representing barns. Add a toy cow to each field. Establish that both cows have same amount of grass to eat. 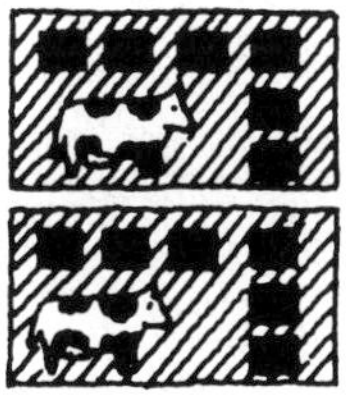	Rearrange the barns. 	Do the cows still have the same amount of grass to eat? Which has more? Why do you think so?

FIGURE 9–2

Piagetian Tests to Estimate Children's Ability to Conceptualize Space

They have included toy people, animals, cars, and other "props" that were near the block area. Skillful teachers will interact with the children, asking questions that lead to the development of specific perceptual skills necessary for successful map reading. These are appropriate questions and comments:

"Which automobile will fit through the garage door?"

"How can you make this road longer?"

"Does your road have curves or is it straight?"

"Where would that car go if this road was closed?"

"What made your building fall down?"

"Let's see if that building is as tall as this tower."

"Jimmy's foot is two blocks long. How many blocks long is my foot?"

"How can you build a bridge so that the truck can get to the other side of the river?"

"Are these blocks the same size?"

"I wonder what would happen if you put a round block here."

By interacting this way, teachers can lead to expansion of perceptual concepts such as size, shape, weight, measurement, classification, symbols, and categorization. These concepts, according to Piaget, are essential before formal map instruction begins.

Teachers can learn much about children by listening and watching. As the children investigate and discuss, the teacher may wish to unobtrusively introduce new materials or pull together random ideas. Do this carefully, because children's free experimentation and creativity can be stifled by teachers who fail to maintain the delicate balance between informal guidance and formal direction. The teacher's creativity, added in proper proportion to the children's, will bring interesting new aspects to the play. The teacher's role during this initial map reading experience includes these aspects:

- *Arranging the environment:* Provide blocks, boxes, boards, barrels, cardboard, spools from telephone cable, ramps, rugs, trucks, cars, fire engines, trains, boats, wagons, tractors, airplanes, rope, gas pump, traffic signs, barn, animals, family dolls, community worker dolls, and a variety of other equipment.

- *Informal guidance:* Allow children to experience the materials and to discover their dramatic possibilities. Creative play provides the necessary foundation for developing more sophisticated understandings.

- *Evaluation:* Observe the childen at dramatic play to pick up clues as to what areas need strengthening or which children are becoming ready for more formalized map instruction.

BEGINNING MAP INSTRUCTION

During children's experience with pre-mapping activities, their maturation will evolve at different rates. If you are in the process of building a truly developmental map reading program in the primary grades, children who do not have adequate experiential and perceptual characteristics should be given more opportunities for readiness-type activities. Children who are able to move ahead should be encouraged to do so with directed learning experiences that promote confidence and motivation to succeed, and that develop these map reading skills:

map reading skills

Locating places

Recognizing and expressing relative location

Interpreting map symbols

Developing a basic idea of relative size and scale

Reading directions

Understanding that the globe is the most accurate representation of the earth's surface

Planned instruction in map and globe skills is easy to begin with children identified as ready because of *direct involvement* and *concrete experiences*, two essential components of a program. According to Piaget, children learn best when they experiment with challenging materials that stimulate mental processes to organize and integrate new information into already present mental perceptions. This means that children can learn only if they have previously developed the perceptions necessary to make a logical progression to a new task.

Beginning Map Activities

Because of the importance of providing a continual, developmental approach to instruction, the experiences in the initial phases of planned instruction should remain concrete and not vary greatly from those of the pre-mapping period. Therefore, activities similar to those in dramatic play are used in this phase, but the emphasis changes from unstructured creativity to that of planning and developing accurate representations of some real observed environment.

Siegel and Schadler warn us that the environments should be thoroughly familiar to the children.[2] To support this point, the researchers conducted an experiment to determine whether familiarity with the environment enhances young children's ability to produce spatial representations (map constructions) and found that increased experience in the environment to be represented (a classroom, in this instance) significantly facilitated the accuracy of the representations. Perhaps the most desirable environment in which to begin, then, is the classroom. In this way, children are able to constantly observe the environment they are to represent, enabling them to more readily make direct comparisons and contrasts.

THREE-DIMENSIONAL MAPS. Begin this initial mapmaking project by asking the children to bring back from lunch their empty half-pint milk containers. Cut off the tops of the containers at a point below where they meet so that you have a square-shaped, open-top box. Turn the box over and cut away parts of the sides with scissors so that the cartons appear to have legs and begin to represent the forms of the children's desks (see Figure 9–3). Discuss the representation with the

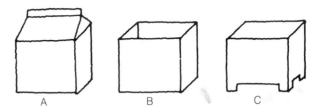

A   B   C

FIGURE 9–3

Stages of Constructing Milk Carton Desks

children, pointing out that these model desks are to look like their real desks. Encourage the children to paint the desks with tempera paint, to glue construction paper books or pencils on top, and to put their name cards on the fronts of the desks.

When the desks are completed, ask one child to place his desk on a large sheet of cardboard or paper that has been placed on a worktable or on the floor. Show the child that the large cardboard represents the classroom on a smaller scale. Let him observe the room and then the cardboard to see where the desk should be placed. Once satisfied, you may ask for the child who "sits next to Mike" to place her desk. Actually three basic map reading skills are being introduced as you continue to have the children place their desks on the cardboard.

1. Recognizing that their milk carton desks *stand for* their real desks (interpreting map symbols)
2. Finding where their desks should be placed (locating places)
3. Locating the placement of individual desks in relationship to the other desks (recognizing and expressing relative location)

At this point, ask the children to bring to school the next day empty boxes they might have around the house, from small jewelry boxes to boxes about the size of a toaster. Divide the members of the class who are able to work together into committees, each of which is responsible for constructing a classroom feature such as the piano, teacher's desk, learning center, and so on. Keep a careful eye on the children as they select the boxes most appropriate for their particular models. Often, the group responsible for the teacher's desk will select the largest box, even though that box is much larger than the relative size of the desk, because children view the teacher as an extremely important person in their lives and thus deserving the largest available box. But encourage the children to observe their own real desks in comparison to the teacher's so they can eventually select boxes that represent the true relationship. Individuals who work on smaller projects also experience similar relative-size problems. For example, one teacher found that everyone in her class had completed their assigned tasks and were ready to place their features on the growing three-dimensional map, while Alice was still busy at the back of the room finishing her model wastebasket. When the teacher went back to watch, Alice was busily folding and cutting dozens of tiny pieces of paper for her wastebasket—wanting to make sure the relative size was as accurate as possible!

When all classroom features are represented, they are decorated, painted, and ready for placement on the floor or table map. This phase of map reading instruction is crucial for its contribution to what Preston and Herman describe as the "bird's-eye-view" concept.[3] They found that a major reason for children's failure to read maps in the upper grades is the lack of ability to mentally view the environment as it would look from above, the way a map is constructed. You can help develop this key ability by encouraging the children to place their classroom features on the map and view them from above. That way, they will see only the tops of the desks, tables, file cabinet, and so on, and begin to understand that this is how a real map is constructed.

Notice that during this phase of construction, the three previous map reading skills are extended and reinforced, *and* a new skill is introduced: developing an idea of relative size and scale.

Once the classroom has been properly arranged, you can further extend and reinforce map skills with questions and tasks such as these:

Locating places
"Place your desk on the spot where it is located in our classroom."
"Where would you place the piano? The file cabinet?"
"Point to the box that shows the puppet stage . . . the work table . . . the teacher's desk."
"James, can you find Michelle's desk? Put your finger on it."
"Put your finger on the aquarium. Someone knocked on the door. Trace the path you would take to answer the door."

Recognizing and expressing relative location
"Whose desk is closest to the coatrack?"
"Trace the shortest path from the reading corner to the door."
"Which is closer to the door, the science learning center or the teacher's desk?"

Interpreting map symbols
"Pick up the box that stands for the learning center table."
"What does the red box stand for?"
"How can we show the coatrack on our map?"

Developing an idea of relative size and scale
"Which is larger, the spelling center or the piano?"
"Which box should be smaller, the teacher's desk or the worktable?"
"Point to the smallest (or largest) piece of classroom furniture."

Class discussion of their three-dimensional representation affords children opportunities to understand that objects can be used to symbolize other objects. This skill is vitally important in a developmental plan of instruction, since Piaget tells us that children most effectively acquire understandings according to the three levels of representation illustrated in Figure 9–4.

Our beginning map activity moves through these levels by giving opportunities to construct symbols that represent real objects (index and symbol levels of representation) and to put their experiences into words (sign)—whereby we have provided an accurate language base for newer ideas.

MAP SYMBOL ACTIVITY.   After the three-dimensional classroom representation has been properly used, begin a transition from this concrete experience to one that is slightly more abstract. To move to the construction of a simple flat map, have the children look at their 3-D map from directly above and discuss their perceptions. Then ask them to put a piece of construction paper beneath each feature and trace around the outside of each with a crayon. As the features are removed, the children should label the remaining outline, "file cabinet," "Bart's desk," and glue the outline in its appropriate place. The 3-D map gradually becomes a flat map as outlines replace the models. For the children to accurately perceive how the flat map is similar to the 3-D map, you should ask questions like those suggested for the 3-D map. Effective discussion is as important for this flat map phase as for the 3-D phase.

To reinforce the concept of map symbol through activities that go beyond classroom maps, present the children with a few easily recognized symbols they might see every day, such as those in Figure 9–5. Ask the children what each symbol or sign means to them. What do they stand for? Emphasize that symbols represent real people, places, things, or ideas. Following the discussion, ask the children to pair up and each draw a secret symbol without allowing the partner to see. Then have each pair try to guess each other's picture. If they have difficulty getting started, offer suggestions such as road signs, punctuation marks, math symbols, and the like. Prepare a bulletin board display of their efforts after they have shared the symbols with each other.

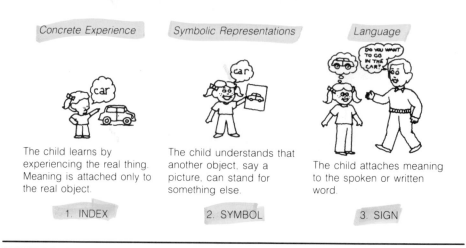

FIGURE 9–4

Piaget's Three Levels of Representation

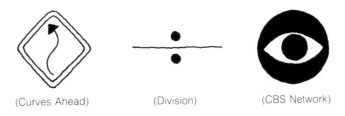

(Curves Ahead)   (Division)   (CBS Network)

FIGURE 9-5
Recognized Symbols

Explain that a symbol is a sign that stands for something. Illustrate this idea by sharing a familiar object, such as a toy airplane. Ask the children to draw an airplane, say the word, and write it on the chalkboard. Help children understand that some sounds are symbols, pictures are symbols, and printed words are symbols. The children should now be ready to understand that the special set of symbols a group of people commonly uses to communicate ideas is called a *language*. In the United States, most citizens use the English language to communicate orally and in print. In school, we learn English as our main language, but we also learn other languages, such as the language of maps.

To move from this introductory lesson on symbols, write the word *tree* on the chalkboard, and ask the children what a tree looks like. After discussing their many interpretations, emphasize that the written *tree* stands for a real thing the same way a map symbol does. Ask the children to suggest what the word for *tree* would be in the special language of maps. Follow this procedure while helping the children make up their own symbols for houses, factories, stores, libraries, lakes, roads, mountains, and so on. Don't be overly concerned if their symbols are not the same as standard symbols for these things; at this point you are most concerned not with accuracy of representation, but with the overall concept of symbolization.

The children can practice their ability to make symbols and place them on "maps" with the following activity. Clear a large area of your classroom or take the children outdoors (or to a multipurpose room). Outline the area as a diamond shape with a long piece of yarn, tape, or string. Have the children stand above the yarn and observe it from eye level. Show them a rough outline of this shape that you have previously drawn on a large sheet of paper. Discuss how the drawn outline is similar to their earlier classroom map construction because it shows a real area as it would look from the ceiling. Then ask the childern to draw their own copies with crayon on sheets of drawing paper—a simple diamond is fine. Place a box on the floor near one corner of the large quadrangle and invite the children to stand over it and look at it carefully. Then, ask them to draw a picture of what they saw as they observed it from above and put a word label on it. Add several more objects to this activity, each time following the same procedure. Use objects such as books, chairs, blocks, toys, and so on. Compare the relative size and distance of each item so children will see how position and proportion affect the accuracy of maps. Now split the class into groups of three or four. Have each group draw a special "map" showing how

Translating their three-dimensional model into a flat map helps children visualize the process of representing a location on paper.

they would arrange the objects. The groups then challenge each other by exchanging and determining where the real objects should be placed on the floor within the large diamond. Now invite the groups to further challenge each other by having one group rearrange the objects on the floor and asking the others to make the map of the resulting configuration.

Standard map symbols can gradually be introduced now that the children are more familiar with the concept of "symbol." Remind the children that maps are symbols on paper—that they stand for real things. Show them photographs or slides of a railroad, a bridge, and a building. Then show the children the three corresponding map symbols. Ask them to match the symbols to their corresponding pictures and add the word labels. Follow this progression (photo or picture—symbol—word label) whenever new map symbols are introduced in your classroom. After the entire map transfer and symbol recognition procedure has been completed, the children will be ready for an introduction to a new map skill—reading directions.

DIRECTION.   The best method of introducing children to direction is to make the learning experience meaningful. Primary-grade children enjoy going outdoors with simple compasses to find the cardinal directions (north, south, east, and west). After they locate north on the compass, the children will soon learn that south is behind them, east to the right, and west to the left. If the children are outside at *noon* on a sunny day, they will find a new clue for determining direction—that their shadows will point in a northerly direction. Once they determine north this way, the other directions will be easy to find. To help them remember the other directions, help the children search for outstanding physical landmarks. Have one child face north and select the first obvious feature, such as a large building. Give him a card labeled "north" and ask him to stand facing north with the card in his hands. Then select a second child to stand back-to-back to the northerly child. Ask the children what direction this child is facing. If no one says "south," tell them. Ask this child to find an outstanding physical feature to the south (such as a large tree) and give her a labeled card to hold. Repeat this procedure when explaining the east and west directions. The children can be encouraged to plot the position of the sun in the sky from morning through afternoon. By associating landmarks with directions, the children begin to understand that directions help us locate places in our environment. You may ask, for example, "In what direction must I walk if I wanted to go to that large hill?" To help reinforce these directional skills, provide a number of follow-up activities; for example, "Simon Says" can be adapted to a directional format—"Simon says, 'Take three steps west.' " "Simon says, 'Turn to the south.' "

After the children have had this fundamental introduction to direction, extend the learnings to their classroom maps. Ask the children to place their direction labels on the appropriate walls in the classroom after the outdoor experience is completed. Do not label the front of the room "North" and the back of the room "South" if these are not the true directions. After checking the classroom directions by using the compass or checking with the previously established reference points, teach the children to always orient their maps in the proper direction whenever they use them. This may involve turning chairs or sitting on the floor, but by always turning themselves and their maps in the direction of true north, children avoid the common misconception that "north" is the direction toward the front of the room.

The skill of reading cardinal directions can then be extended with the use of the children's classroom map and these questions or requests. "Point to the south wall." "Put your finger on the work table. Someone dropped a pencil near the chalkboard on the west wall. Show the path you would take to pick it up." "Put your finger on the puppet stage. In which direction should you walk to get to the teacher's desk?" "In what direction would you go to get from your desk to the drinking fountain?" "True or false—Richard's desk is north of Marie's desk." You may also use the children's textbook maps to reinforce directions. Use "Who am I?" riddles such as, "I am north of California and south of Washington. Who am I?"

SCALE.   The idea of scale should be introduced in a relative way rather than in a mathematical sense in the primary grades. Children should be led to realize that maps need to be small enough to be easily carried and readily used. Give the children sheets of drawing paper in shapes that approximate their classroom and tell them to construct their own maps using the 3–D map as a model. Some children will immediately reduce the size of the classroom features proportionately. Others will have greater difficulty trying to reproduce the large classroom features on their smaller papers.

Children move toward an understanding of maps as they master the skills of locating places, recognizing and expressing relative location, interpreting map symbols, reading directions, and developing an idea of relative size and scale. These skills are best developed in a program that stresses activity and concrete experience.

The Globe

Since the early primary-grade child's view of the earth may be fairly restricted, planned instruction in globe-reading skills is usually not recommended. But you should not totally omit globe-related activities from the primary classroom. With simplified twelve-inch globes, the children can understand that the globe is a visualization of the earth much as their map was a model of their classroom. The globe should have a minimum amount of detail on it and preferably should show the land masses in no more than three colors and the bodies of water in a consistent shade of blue. Only the names of the continents, countries, largest cities, and largest bodies of water should be indicated. Globes that show more detail can confuse and perplex the very young child.

You should use the globe as a valuable, informal teaching tool. When reading stories, children may wish to find where their favorite characters live, and you can show them the geographical location. For example, if your second-grade class is in Philadelphia and you are reading the children a story about Los Posados in the city of Los Angeles, you may want to show them where Los Angeles is in relationship to Philadelphia. However, even this would be a meaningless activity unless we relate it to the child's own experiences. We may ask, for example, "How many of you have ever taken a trip for a whole day in a car? Were you tired? If you wanted to go to Los Angeles by car, you would need to spend about eight days in a row riding in a car. That's how far Los Angeles is." Children who hear about the North Pole at Christmastime may want to know where this cold place is located. Television stories or newspaper articles may suggest places the children wish to find. The teacher can use instances like these to familiarize young children with characteristics of the globe and with the fact they can use the globe to find special places. The basic globe concepts for development in the primary grades are:

- To understand the basic roundness of the earth
- To understand the differences between land and water areas
- To begin to locate the poles, major cities, and the United States

These are some teaching suggestions:

> Use the names of large bodies of water and land masses, such as Atlantic Ocean, Pacific Ocean, North America, Africa, Pennsylvania, or the equator.
>
> Have the children locate large land areas and bodies of water.
>
> Talk about how it would feel to be an astronaut and to be able to look at the earth from a satellite. Discuss how the land masses and bodies of water would look.
>
> Have the children discover that the earth is composed of much more water than land. Also, most of the land is located north of the equator.
>
> When studying about families around the world, tape small pictures of people in traditional dress to their corresponding countries on a large papier-mâché globe constructed by the children. Discussion of the need for different types of clothing can lead to an awareness of warm and cold regions of the earth.

This list summarizes the teacher's role in developing map and globe skills in the primary grades.

- *Prepare the environment.* Encourage the children to carefully observe the environment and compare the physical features of objects in the classroom for use in their map.
- *Plan a developmental sequence.* Reproduce the environment with an accurate three-dimensional model. Gradually transform this model to a flat map, substituting outlines for each feature. Finally, construct individual maps from the larger models. Make large ''yarn maps'' for the purpose of understanding map symbols. Use compasses and the position of the sun to teach directions.
- *Stimulate thinking.* Develop a sound questioning strategy that encourages children to think concretely and creatively throughout the entire map instruction sequence.
- *Evaluate progress.* Observe the children at all times to see who is frustrated and who is bored. If either symptom is evident, you need to find the cause and adjust your instruction accordingly. Frustration occurs if you move too quickly with some children or present them with tasks for which they are not ready. If you fail to challenge gifted students or move too slowly for them, chances are they will become bored or apathetic. Remember that map instruction, like any other learning in the primary grades, must be developmental in nature and geared to individual needs.

Map and Globe Reinforcement

At the beginning of instruction, some teachers reinforce and extend map reading skills through commercially prepared map materials found either in social studies texts or practice booklets. Sample maps are illustrated in Figures 9–6, 9–7, and 9–8. What skills are being reinforced by each?

These activities supplement and enrich early map activities:

The children can find hidden surprises in a "treasure hunt" in the classroom. Hide a special prize somewhere in the room and encourage the children to find it by giving them map directions. Include directions such as, "Walk north to the file cabinet. Turn in the direction of where the sun rises and take three steps. Look under the book for your next direction."

In the primary grades, the globe should be used only as an informal learning tool. This teacher is pointing out the setting of a story she will read to the class.

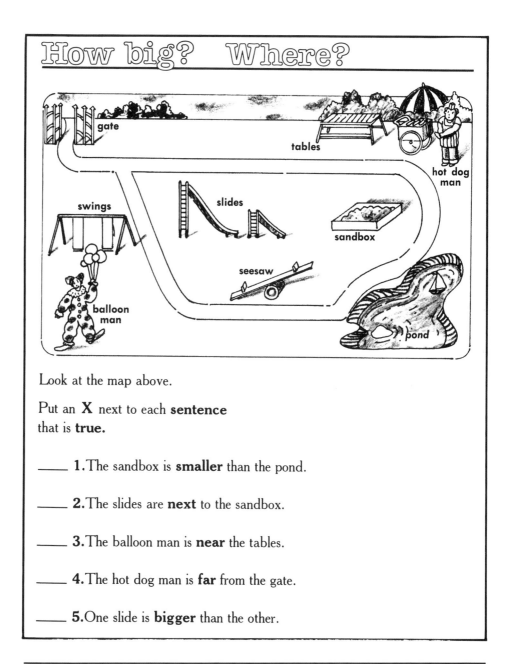

Look at the map above.

Put an **X** next to each **sentence**
that is **true.**

_____ **1.** The sandbox is **smaller** than the pond.

_____ **2.** The slides are **next** to the sandbox.

_____ **3.** The balloon man is **near** the tables.

_____ **4.** The hot dog man is **far** from the gate.

_____ **5.** One slide is **bigger** than the other.

FIGURE 9–6

Sample Map *(Reprinted by permission of Scholastic Inc. from* Scholastic Map Skills Book A *by Barbara Christensen. Copyright © 1978 by Scholastic Inc.)*

Maps use symbols

Here is another map of Pat's town.
This one has **shapes** or **symbols** on it.
The **symbols** stand for **different things**
on the map.

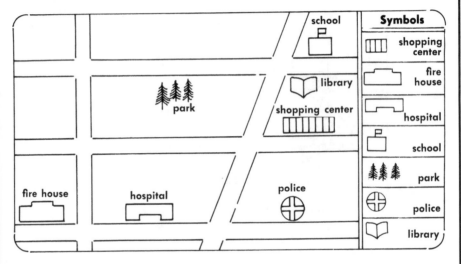

Look at the **symbols.** Look at the map.

1. Find the **hospital** on the map.
   Draw a **line under** it.

2. Put a **circle** around the **park** on the map.

3. Put an **X** on the **school** on the map.

4. Put a ✔ on the **fire house** on the map.

5. Put a **line over** the **library** on the map.

FIGURE 9–7

Sample Map (Reprinted by permission of Scholastic Inc. from Scholastic Map Skills Book A
by Barbara Christensen. Copyright © 1978 by Scholastic Inc.)

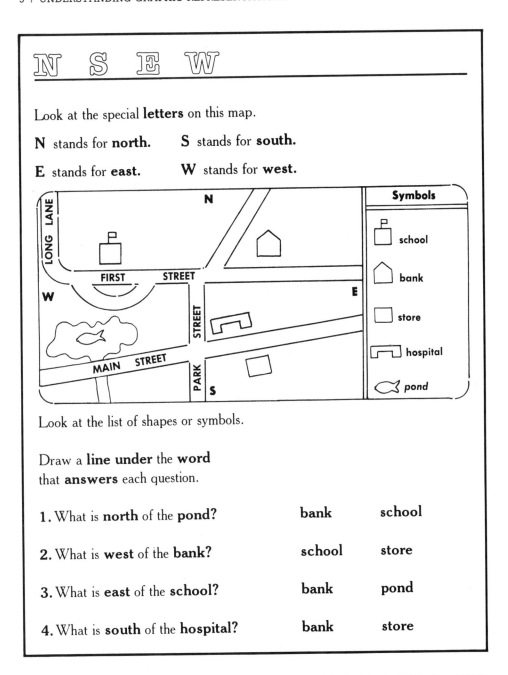

N S E W

Look at the special **letters** on this map.

N stands for **north.**   **S** stands for **south.**

E stands for **east.**   **W** stands for **west.**

Look at the list of shapes or symbols.

Draw a **line under** the **word**
that **answers** each question.

1. What is **north** of the **pond?**   bank   school

2. What is **west** of the **bank?**   school   store

3. What is **east** of the **school?**   bank   pond

4. What is **south** of the **hospital?**   bank   store

FIGURE 9–8

Sample Map (Reprinted by permission of Scholastic Inc. from Scholastic Map Skills Book A
by Barbara Christensen. Copyright © 1978 by Scholastic Inc.)

Because children have difficulty visualizing new map symbols when they move to representations of new, more remote areas, you should consider generous use of pictures, slides, and other visual aids. Otherwise, rich imaginations often distort the true meaning of "snow-capped mountains," "rich pastureland," etc.

Use a game to reinforce directional skills. Give each child a sheet of primary graph paper and read these directions: "Start at the large dot on your graph paper and place your own dot at each location that I give you. Move 7 spaces east and place your first dot. Connect the two dots. Next, go north 10 squares and connect those two dots. Then, east 1 square. Then, north 4 squares . . . west 5 squares . . . south 3 squares . . .west 3 squares . . . north 2 squares . . . west 2 squares . . . south 2 squares . . . west 3 squares . . . north 2 squares . . . west 2 squares . . . south 2 squares . . . west 3 squares . . . north 3 squares . . . west 2 squares . . . south 1 square . . . west 2 squares . . . north 1 square . . . west 2 squares . . . south 4 squares . . . east 1 square . . . south 10 squares . . . east 7 squares . . . north 7 squares . . . east 8 squares . . . and south 7 squares." The result should be a castle outline. You can ask the children to draw a flag in the tower farthest west, damsel in distress in the tower farthest east, etc.

To arouse enthusiasm, use the children's names as labels for map features. Duplicate the map and add a sheet of questions covering the related map skills.

Use building blocks to help the children measure the distance from one classroom feature to another—the number of blocks from the teacher's desk to the file cabinet, the sink, bulletin board, and so on. How many miles would this distance be if each block were 1 mile? Most youngsters aren't sure how far a mile is. Take them on a walk and actually measure it out.

Provide two bags, one containing map symbol terms and the other containing the associated word labels. Divide the class into two teams. Team 1 picks a symbol from its bag. Team 2 must then locate the word label within a specified time (10–20 seconds).

Divide the class into three groups. Have each group form a single-file line facing the front of the room. Three desks are in the front of the room, one for each group. Place a stack of cards on each desk, each card illustrated with a common map symbol. The children walk to the desk, pick up a card, and write what

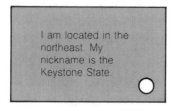
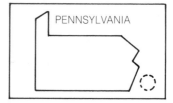

FIGURE 9–9
Sample Cards

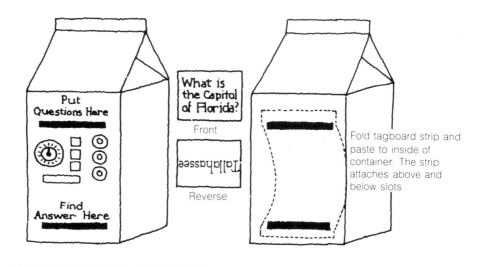

FIGURE 9–10

Construction of Computer

it represents on the board. The first group to go through all the cards correctly is the winner.

Prepare two sets of index cards (2 different colors are best), one set with riddles and one with state outlines. Punch a hole in the riddle card and trace the hole on the matching state card. Be sure the holes are in different places for each of the different pairs. The child reads each riddle and tries to identify the state. If the match is correct, the circle and hole will match (Figure 9–9).

Make up a set of cards with map questions on the front and the answers on the back. Write the answer and question upside down in relation to one another. When students insert the question into the computer, the answer will come out the bottom slot. (See Figure 9–10 for how to construct the computer.)

MAPS AND GLOBES IN THE SUBSEQUENT ELEMENTARY GRADES

The six basic map and globe skills introduced and reinforced during the early grades are used in the later grades in more highly sophisticated contexts and for different purposes. Children in the early grades, developing concepts of what a map is and how to read one, primarily use maps that (1) are fanciful in nature (usually depicting *familiar places* such as a zoo, park, or neighborhood; and *imaginary places* such as Playland, Fantasyland, or Spaceland), (2) contain mostly pictorial or semipictorial symbols, (3) often represent a real environment shared by all the children, and (4) begin to introduce children to the locations of people or places under study in other contexts, such as in literature or reading books. In later grades, the skills are refined to include using maps to gather information and to solve problems. Children are expected to extend their basic skills to using detailed maps of areas well beyond their immediate location and direct observation. In short, the direction changes from *learning to read maps* to *reading maps to learn.*

Place Location

As the children progress through the elementary grades, they are still required to examine a map to find a place. The major difference, however, is the level of sophistication of the map itself. Comparing this process to reading a book, you might say that children are taught to recognize words in first grade but only at a level appropriate for their stage of development. Later, as the children's skills mature, they are introduced to newer, more difficult words. Likewise, the maps early primary-grade children read gradually evolve into more specialized maps that require a greater skill to read. Look at the street map in Figure 9–11. Notice the abstract symbols depicting the physical features of an imaginary city. The children are asked not only to locate places by interpreting symbols, but also to use a sophisticated grid system (numerals and letters along the margins) to make the location process easier. For example, they may be asked to name the feature closest to the juncture of C-1. Experiences like this enable children to move toward the functional use of maps—employing maps, such as road maps, to acquire information for a specific purpose. As with the primary grades, children should be provided with varieties of activities that go beyond workbook or ditto maps designed to reinforce specific map reading skills.

GUESS WHAT? Give the children graph paper similar to that in Figure 9–12. Give them a clue, such as, ''I take you where you want to go.'' Encourage the children to find out by coloring in squares; for example, the squares at points E-3, E-4, D-8, etc. would emerge as a bus figure.

TIC-TAC-TOE. Divide your class into groups of three. For each of the following phases, designate two players and an umpire. During Phase 1, the umpire draws a regular tic-tac-toe grid and places *X*'s or *O*'s into the squares for each player. The players indicate the squares they want by pointing to the spaces only. Discourage any other form of communication. Play three games during Phase 1, alternating responsibilities so that each child has an opportunity to be an umpire and a player. For Phase 2, the umpire draws a regular tic-tac-toe grid but adds a new feature. On each row, she places the numerals *1, 2,* and *3.* Again playing three games, the players now indicate the *X*'s and *O*'s to the umpire by calling the numeral and then pointing to the appropriate square. The umpire writes in the proper mark. Finally, in Phase 3, the traditional tic-tac-toe grid is drawn with numerals for each row, and an added feature—letters for each column. Allow the children to play at least three games again, this time indicating their moves to the umpire by stating the row *and* column.

TAP-TAP. Arrange desks or chairs into rows. Tape a sheet of construction paper labeled with a different letter of the alphabet for each row to the first desk of each row so that it can be easily seen by someone standing in the front of the

Using a street map

A **street map** can be a great help to you in an unfamiliar city.
The map below shows part of a large city in the United States.

Look at the **compass rose** that shows **directions**.

- In what directions do most of the **named** streets run? _____

- In what directions do the **numbered** streets run? _____

Look at the **scale** of **miles** and **kilometers**.

- Into what **divisions** of **distance** is the scale of **miles** divided? _____

- Into what **divisions** of **distance** is the scale of **kilometers** divided? _____

Use this map to help you answer the questions on **page 7**.

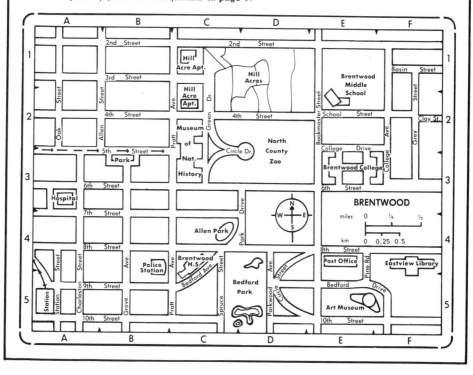

FIGURE 9–11

Sample Street Map (Reprinted by permission of Scholastic Inc. from Scholastic Map Skills
Book F by Barbara Christensen. Copyright © 1978 by Scholastic Inc.)

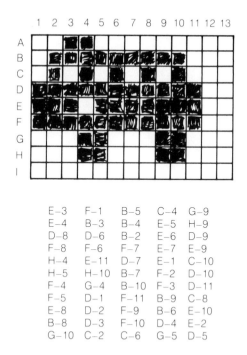

E–3	F–1	B–5	C–4	G–9
E–4	B–3	B–4	E–5	H–9
D–8	D–6	B–2	E–6	D–9
F–8	F–6	F–7	E–7	E–9
H–4	E–11	D–7	E–1	C–10
H–5	H–10	B–7	F–2	D–10
F–4	G–4	B–10	F–3	D–11
F–5	D–1	F–11	B–9	C–8
E–8	D–2	F–9	B–6	E–10
B–8	D–3	F–10	D–4	E–2
G–10	C–2	C–6	G–5	D–5

FIGURE 9–12

Guess What?

room. For each column, label a sheet of construction paper with a different numeral. Draw the names of five children from a hat and ask them to go to the front of the room and stand with their backs turned and eyes closed. Select five more children to sneak to the front, tap each child lightly, and return to their seats. Opening their eyes and facing the class, the original group of five must try to guess who tapped each of them by calling out the appropriate grid placement; for example, "The one who tapped me is seated at C-4." Alternate places so that everyone has a chance to participate.

ODD TOWN. Creative story writing and map skills instruction can be combined as an extension of the preceding activities. For example, encourage each child to look at a road map index and determine the oddest sounding name of a town or city in the state. In Pennsylvania, for example, children have many from which to choose—Snowshoe, Bird-in-Hand, Potato City, and Conshohocken, to name a few. Using the coordinates specified in the index, the location of the city should be made and marked with an X on the map so it cannot be used again by someone else. The children are then encouraged to write an original story telling how the town they selected got its name.

SPORTS MAP. Get a large map of the United States and glue small metal washers near each city that has a professional football team. Buy a set of miniature magnetized NFL plastic football helmets (available in most mail-order catalogs for a reasonable price) and have the children attach the appropriate helmet to each metal washer. If you cannot get the plastic helmets, cut out the helmets from the catalog ads, paste them onto sturdy tagboard, and glue a small magnetic strip on the back of each. To extend this activity, supply the current season's schedule of the most popular professional football team in your area. Ask questions such as: "Where do the Giants play their closest away game? What is the largest city the Giants visit? Going south from New York, what is the first city with a professional football team? What team must travel the farthest to play the Giants? What city on the Giants' schedule is farthest west?" Using the energy conservation concern as a focal point, ask your children to consider the current alignment of divisions within the NFL. For example, San Francisco, Los Angeles, Atlanta, and New Orleans comprise one division. Ask whether divisions could be realigned so that teams in one region could be grouped together. One group of fifth-graders eliminated New Orleans and Atlanta from the grouping above and came up with a Western Division of Seattle, San Francisco, Oakland, Los Angeles, and San Diego. As groups of children offer their alignment plans, many geographical concepts are brought out as support. The key idea, though, is that the children are beginning to understand how maps help us understand how people and the environment are so closely dependent upon each other.

MAP DISPLAY.   Display a large, colorful map on the bulletin board. Encourage the children to collect postmarks, business cards, matchbook covers, newspaper mastheads, clothing labels, etc. Pin them on the board and attach a piece of string to the location.

Latitude and Longitude

In the upper elementary grades, children extend their knowledge of grids as a place location device to the system of latitude and longitude. This system is comprised of east-west lines called *parallels of latitude* and north-south lines called *meridians* of longitude (see Figure 9–13).

The parallels of latitude, imaginary lines encircling the earth, measure distances in degrees north and south of the equator (designated as zero degrees latitude). The parallels grow smaller in circumference as they approach both poles. The meridians

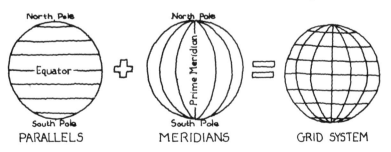

FIGURE 9–13
The Earth's Grid System

of longitude, also imaginary lines encircling the earth, converge at the poles and measure distances in degrees east and west of the prime meridian (designated as zero degrees longitude).

The importance of grids as a means of locating places can be illustrated with a large, unmarked ball. Lead a discussion comparing the similarities of the large ball and the earth as represented by the classroom globe. Glue a small plastic ship to the ball and ask the children to describe its exact location, imagining themselves shipwrecked and needing to radio their location to be rescued (the ship marks their wreck). They will discover that this is nearly impossible, since there is no point of reference from which to describe an exact location. For example, if the children say the ship is located on the front side of the ball, you can turn the ball and the statement will be incorrect. If they say the ship is on the top of the ball, turn it back again to the original position. Gradually, the students will experience the frustration of locating places on a globe without agreed-upon reference points. After some deliberation, they will most likely suggest the addition of parallel east-west lines, and instruct the rescue squad to search an area ''three lines down from the middle line.''

On closer examination of this arrangement, and after prodding from the teacher, they will discover that the rescuers need to travel all around the world along the ''third line down from the middle line'' to find them unless given even more precise locations by devising *meridians,* or north-south lines. Then, the rescue squad only needs to find where the two points meet. Eventually, the children can be led to locate many well-known places in the world using latitude and longitude. Exact locations by actual *degrees* of latitude and longitude may be beyond the mental development of most fourth- and fifth-grade children. Guide them, however, in using latitude and longitude for locating general areas, such as the low latitudes (23½ degrees north and south of the equator), the middle latitudes (between 23½ and 66½ degrees north and south of the equator), and the high latitudes (between 66½ degrees north and the North Pole and 66½ degrees south and the South Pole). Children can generalize about the climatic similarities within these areas. In which latitudes are most cities located? Where is the weather warm (or cold) throughout most of the year? They should be shown how to find places east or west or north or south of their location by using meridians. Also, after careful scrutiny, they may be surprised to find such interesting facts as that Rome, Italy is *nearer* the North Pole than New York is; Detroit is actually *north* of Windsor, Ontario; Reno, Nevada is actually farther *west* than Los Angeles; the Gulf of California *does not touch* California at any point; and the Pacific Ocean is actually *east* of the Atlantic Ocean at Panama. All early grid instruction should be general and avoid as much as possible the use of degrees in place location.

In the sixth grade, after grid concepts have been firmly developed, children can begin to make increasingly precise locations. They can locate places they are studying, such as, ''If you were at twenty degrees south latitude and twenty degrees east longitude, you would be in _____ .''

In addition to these activities, teachers may wish to reinforce the understanding of grid systems with other activities.

FOLLOW DIRECTIONS GAME.   The teacher gives each child a sheet of paper that has a marked grid, as shown in Figure 9–14. The children start at the dot placed on the graph paper by the teacher. They make their own dots at each location given, such as, ''Place a dot at the point ten degrees west.'' As they place the dot locations, the children connect them. An outline of an object, state, country, or continent results.

DESTROY A MONSTER.   The object of this game is for the player to capture an opponent's sea monster and to protect his or her own monster. Prepare two large tagboard squares as shown in Figure 9–15. Each large square is divided into a grid pattern. The rows and columns are numbered to represent degrees of latitude and longitude. Each player puts his game board in such a position that it cannot be seen by the other player. The players then place their monsters on the board in any position. Players take turns shooting at each other's monster in rounds. In the first round, each player may shoot at an opponent's monster ten times. A ''shot'' is taken by naming the square where a child thinks his or her opponent might be. For example, a child might guess the location ten degrees south latitude and twenty-five degrees west longitude. The opponent must tell whether the shot was a hit or miss. Every time a shot is taken, it is marked on the game boards. The rounds continue until one player has ''shot'' any part of his or her opponent's sea monster five times.

COORDINATE TIC-TAC-TOE.   Draw the diagram shown in Figure 9–16 on the chalkboard; use whatever successive numbers you wish to represent latitude and longitude. A child on one team gives a set of coordinates, for example, ''ten

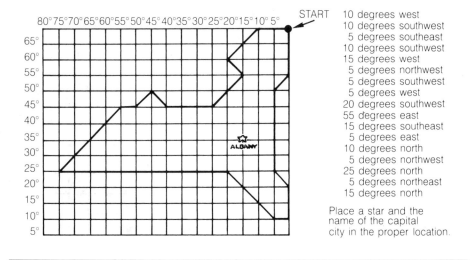

FIGURE 9–14
Follow Directions Game

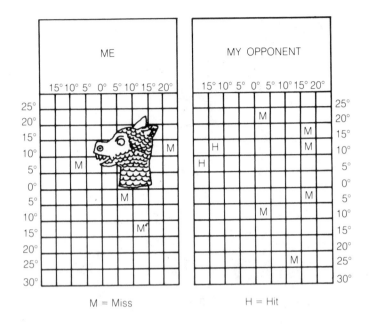

FIGURE 9-15

Destroy A Monster Game

degrees east longitude and twenty degrees north latitude" and places an *X* in that location. A child on another team gives another series of numbers. An *O* is placed on that spot. The teams continue in the same fashion as tic-tac-toe.

Relative Location

Place location, a significant map reading skill, must be expanded so that children achieve greater meanings from maps. Children must understand the influence of location on people's lives and how one physical feature may influence another. Recognizing and expressing relative location is a more sophisticated map skill because it involves not only finding places, but also interpreting the interrelationships among

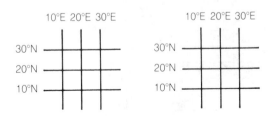

FIGURE 9-16

Coordinate Tic-Tac-Toe

geographical features, such as location, topography, and climate. For example, upon examining a rainfall map of an area such as that of Africa, shown in Figure 9–17, children should be able to determine the type of vegetation that might grow there and how its inhabitants use the land.

In the early primary grades, children can develop concepts of relative location by relating different places in the classroom ("Why do you think the science center is next to the sink?"). The concept is expanded in the intermediate grades as children develop the ability to interpret the significance of physical factors, such as mountains, deserts, valleys, and oceans, on human life. The effects of these geographic features should be discussed, along with humans' attempts to change conditions for their own benefit.

One way of doing this is to ask the children to participate in a simulation activity. Distribute a map of a community's downtown business section through which a new highway must be constructed. Assign each student a building in the section through which the highway must pass (bakery, florist shop, hospital, church, historic house, apartment building, department store, pizza parlor, movie theater, YMCA, auto dealership, supermarket, and so on). Construct a large master map and ask the children to write their names next to their respective businesses. Tell them that the highway must be completed with minimal delay, so the entire business community must meet to decide where to put the final route. How complex you get at this point is your decision, but insist that the children arrive at one solution. Tunnels or bridges are acceptable alternatives, but don't encourage children to choose them before they contribute those ideas by themselves. In similar ways, children can learn about other environmental interactions between humans and nature, such as the effect of a large shopping mall on an undeveloped rural area or the effect of a housing project on what was farmland.

These experiences further develop concepts of recognizing and expressing relative location:

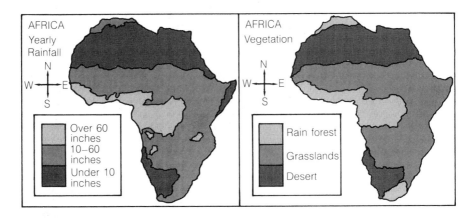

FIGURE 9–17
Yearly Rainfall and Vegetation Maps of Africa

Discuss the relationships among latitude and climate, temperature, and land use.

Discuss the relationships among latitude and climate, temperature, land use, and living conditions.

Discuss people's attempts to modify the physical characteristics of their environment. Locate dams, highways, cities, communications networks, and so on.

Have children locate areas of high population density in our country and cite possible reasons for growth.

Note relationships among topography and natural resources, population, vegetation, climate, and transportation.

Map Symbols

Maps and globes use symbols to represent a region's characteristics. In the primary grades, pictorial or semipictorial symbols are recommended; as a rule, the younger the child, the less abstract the symbols should be. As children move into the upper grades, conventional map symbols, as illustrated in Figure 9–18, can be used. Be careful to provide children with clear interpretation and visualization of newer map symbols. Present a picture of pictorial symbols (or the real thing). After discussing a new symbol, provide for review of the symbol without its label so children will learn the symbol and not rely on the label. Emphasize the importance of looking at the legend before using a map.

Many maps and globes use color or shading as a symbol, most commonly to show elevation of land from sea level. Color should be taught as a special kind of symbol. Children should understand that elevation is measured from sea level and that colors show the height above sea level. Discuss profiles of mountains and explain that color used in this way helps us determine elevation.

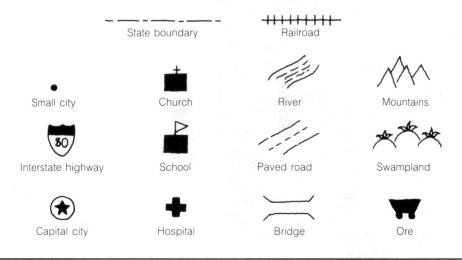

FIGURE 9–18
Common Map Symbols for Legends

Additional activities to help children grow in their ability to understand and use map symbols include these:

Provide a blank "profile drawing" of the United States. Have children plan a trip from Philadelphia to the Pacific Coast. As they proceed west, the children use crayons to color in mountains, valleys, and plains to represent proper elevations.

Encourage children to look through magazines you provide for them, select pictures of outstanding physical features, and paste them next to the labels and map symbols you have organized on a chart.

Examine *aerial photographs* to illustrate the relationship between an area's actual conditions and the symbols used to represent them.

When studying world regions, children should be supplied with outline maps and encouraged to provide symbols to represent features such as main products, vegetation, population trends, elevation, and rainfall.

Direction

In the early grades, children learn the cardinal directions and participate in related map reading experiences. As they become more mature and learn to grasp the concept of cardinal direction, they can begin more complex map work such as intermediate directions (northeast, southwest, etc.). The ability to use directional skills is often combined with latitude and longitude skills for locating places on maps. Reexamine the reinforcement activities for place location, and notice that each activity includes directional knowledge that would also be appropriate reinforcement of latitude and longitude concepts.

An even more sophisticated skill than *interpreting* maps is the ability to *communicate* directions. An illustrative activity is to divide your classroom into teams of three. One student thinks of an easily accessible place somewhere in the school or around the school grounds but cannot tell the other members of the group what that place is. She must then take an easily carried object, hide it there, and then tell her second group member (while the third cannot hear) how to get to where she's hidden the object. The "teller" describes which directions to go (north, south, northeast, etc.), what features he will pass (lavatory, drinking fountain), and how far he should go. Child 2, the "translator," translates the directions into a map showing the location chosen by Child 1. The map is given to the third team member who must find the hidden object. Each team that finds the hidden object is a winner. When the activity is completed, discuss the problems encountered in translating verbal directions into accurate maps.

Scale

To portray geographic features of the earth on a globe or flat map, the concept of scale must be utilized to ensure accurate size and space relationships among the features. This is accomplished by reducing the size of every real feature in an equal percentage. Very young children have difficulty conceptualizing that sizes and distances on maps actually represent some large, real geographical area. Therefore, the formal use of scales should not begin until a child is past grade three, and then, instruction should be gradual. The children can be introduced to the concept of scale by comparing a class picture to the actual size of class members. They can be led to realize that the picture represents a real group of children, but in a much smaller way.

You must be careful to move forward gradually. Have the children measure the distances between prominent landmarks on walking trips aorund the school. They can make maps of their experiences and discuss the actual distances between the landmarks and the amount of space on their maps. Although their scale will probably not be accurate, have the children discover that although the walking trip covered a distance of 2,000 feet, it is represented by only twenty inches on their map.

Perhaps the most appropriate formal map scale to use at the elementary school level is the graphic scale. A scale of miles may be placed at the bottom of the child's map. Children can place a cardboard marker between any two points (Los Angeles and San Francisco) on their maps, place a dot for each city, and then lay the edge of the marker along the scale. The segments of the scale on Figure 9–19 are of equal length and represent miles on the map. Comparing the marks on their cardboard marker to the scale, children will see that the distance between Los Angeles and San Francisco is approximately 350 miles.

These additional activities will help children grow in their ability to understand scale:

Show an aerial photograph of their city or neighborhood and have the children pick out recognizable landmarks. This will help them visualize that a small map can represent a large area on the ground.

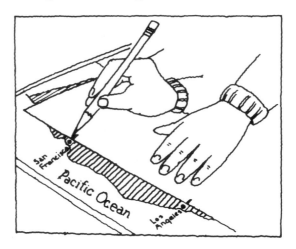

FIGURE 9–19
A Graphic Map Scale

Using a camera, take a close picture of an object and then take another at a greater distance. Compare the amount of detail shown in each picture to develop the concept of scale.

Have children compare two maps of the same area drawn to different scales. Discuss the likenesses and differences.

Reading A Globe

Recall the basic globe reading skills we discussed for the primary grades. Informal instruction aimed mainly at helping the children realize that the globe is a model that represents the earth. Their major formal map reading experiences up to this time dealt with flat maps on which they located cities and other places of interest. They learned how to tell direction and how to compute the distance between one place and another. Now, they must learn that a globe, round like the earth, is the only accurate map of it and an even better tool for studying locations, directions, or distances than is a flat map. To emphasize this fact, you may want to show a satellite photograph of the earth and compare it to a classroom globe. It is fairly easy to find satellite photographs, especially if you request them through the United States Weather Service.

After you compare satellite photographs to a classroom globe, illustrate just why the globe is more accurate than flat maps. Using a large, thin rubber ball or a globe made from papier-mâché, cut the ball in half and draw an outline of North America or any random shape on the ball. Have the children apply hand pressure to flatten the ball and discuss the resulting distortions. Then use scissors to cut through the ball along lines that represent longitude lines. Have the children try to flatten the ball again. Although the ball flattens more easily, the drawn outline still becomes distorted. Help the children discover that this is a major problem faced by mapmakers (cartographers) when they attempt to make flat maps of places on the earth (see Figure 9–20).

Globes help to show shapes of areas exactly as they would appear on the earth's surface. Unfortunately, maps are not able to do this. An example of how shapes of continents become distorted as cartographers attempt to transfer them from globes to flat maps is shown in Figure 9–21. A land area like North America takes a variety

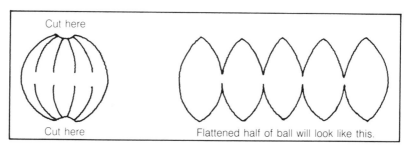

FIGURE 9–20

Globe as a Flattened Ball

FIGURE 9–21

Cartographic Distortions of a Land Mass (Reprinted with permission of Macmillan Publishing Co., Inc. from Social Studies in Elementary Education by John Jarolimek. Copyright © 1982 by John Jarolimek.)

of shapes on maps, depending on the projection used. A classroom globe shows shapes and areas more accurately than maps and should be used in conjunction with the study of wall maps. Because of this major problem, globes and maps should be used reciprocally while developing the skills outlined in this chapter.

As a third step in establishing the true characteristics of globes, lead the children to realize that the earth, a planet, is a large, spherical, solid body that moves through space around the sun and that it is from the sun that the earth receives its heat and light. Accompanying the earth as components of our solar system are eight other planets, the largest of which is Jupiter and the smallest Mercury. Earth, the third planet from the sun, is a relatively small planet which houses the only life of which we are aware. Establish that the earth *revolves* around the sun, making one complete revolution each 365¼ days. At the same time it is revolving, the earth makes another movement—it turns around or *rotates* in a west to east direction once every twenty-four hours. Point out that the earth turns on an *axis* which always leans a little (23½°) from a true vertical line. The axis is an imaginary line that runs through the earth from North Pole to South Pole. Show how the earth rotates on an axis by spinning a gyroscope and having the children observe how it tilts to one side as it moves.

After familiarizing the children with these basic globe concepts, they should learn that the earth can be divided into *hemispheres (hemi,* a prefix meaning ''half of''; *hemisphere* meaning ''half of a sphere''). If we live in the United States, we live in the northern half of the globe, or the Northern Hemisphere. At the same time, we live in the western half of the globe, or the Western Hemisphere. The *equator* and the *prime meridian* split the earth in half in each direction to form the hemisphere. Other significant lines that encircle the earth and run parallel to the equator are called parallels of latitude. Two important latitudes are the tropic of Cancer and the tropic of Capricorn. The region between these two lines, including the equator, is called the tropics. The tropic of Cancer is north of the equator; the tropic of Capricorn is south of the equator. Lead the children to discover that a combination of all these factors accounts for seasons. They have learned that the earth is tilted 23½° on its axis and that the axis always tilts in the same direction. Note the angle shown on the four positions of the earth illustrated in Figure 9–22. As the earth moves around the sun, there are certain times when the Northern Hemisphere leans toward the sun and receives its direct rays and times when it leans away from the sun and receives less direct rays. This gives us the summer season (when the direct rays are between the equator and the tropic of Cancer) and our winter season (when the direct rays are between the equator and tropic of Capricorn). On what major parallel of latitude do the direct rays shine on March 21 and September 21? What seasons do we have in the Northern Hemisphere at those times? Why? It should be apparent to you at this time why the tropic of Cancer and the tropic of Capricorn are each located 23½° on each side of the equator. How could you explain this fact to your children? Regardless of the season, though, it is always hot in the tropics. The two zones that lie on each side of the tropics receive less direct rays from the sun and have a more moderate climate. It is in these regions that the seasons change. These

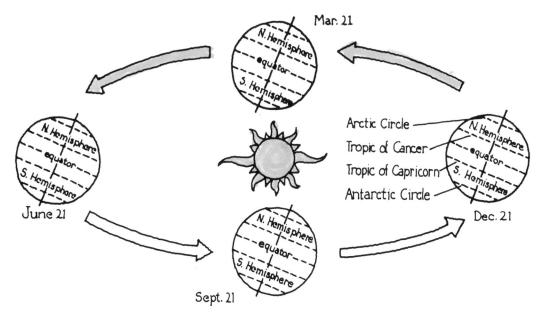

FIGURE 9–22

Position of the Earth During the Four Seasons

are the Northern mid-Latitude Region and the Southern mid-Latitude Region. Seasons in the two regions are the opposite of the other because of the tilt of the earth's axis. As we move toward the North and South Poles, we encounter the Polar Regions which receive little direct sun and are cold all year around.

MAP SELECTION FOR THE CLASSROOM

Selection of appropriate maps and globes for the children's developmental levels is essential. Every school should be equipped with a large variety of maps, including wall maps, special purpose maps, outline maps, atlases, and globes. A variety of information can be shown on these maps, as in Figure 9–23. The *relief map* gives information about land elevation, the *vegetation map* shows what grows naturally, the *export map* shows what products are sold to other countries, and the *rainfall map* shows how much rain falls yearly in a region. These materials should be available in schools: physical-political maps of the home state, United States, each continent, and the world; plastic-coated washable maps of the United States and the world; plastic raised relief maps of the United States and each continent; outline maps of the home state, United States, each continent, and the world; physical-political globes; large markable globes; world atlas; pictorial chart of geographic terms; special purpose maps; and satellite photographs.

Besides using commercial maps in the classroom, children should also make their own maps. To be of value, however, these maps should directly relate to a specific topic or unit of study and suit the children's developmental level. As mentioned, initial mapmaking experiences should relate to the child's immediate environment and should be realistic and concrete. As children develop maturity, these activities can be extended to include areas beyond their immediate environment.

Outline Maps

Having children produce freehand map drawings of specific locations can be an unnecessary, time-consuming activity. When the need arises for an outline map, you should provide one as quickly and efficiently as possible. The opaque projector is one good source to use in constructing outline maps. Enlargements can be projected from textbooks, magazines, newspapers, atlases, or similar reference materials, and their outlines can be traced on the chalkboard or large poster paper. You can use an overhead projector if the necessary transparencies are available. If transparencies are not available, you can make tracings on clear plastic or glass. In the proportional squares technique, one covers the map to be enlarged with small squares. The same number of squares is then drawn on a much larger piece of paper, resulting in much larger squares. Match the outline shown in each small square with the corresponding large square, as shown in Figure 9–24.

Chalkboard outline maps can be made by punching large pin holes approximately one inch apart on an outline map. Hold the map up against the chalkboard and dust

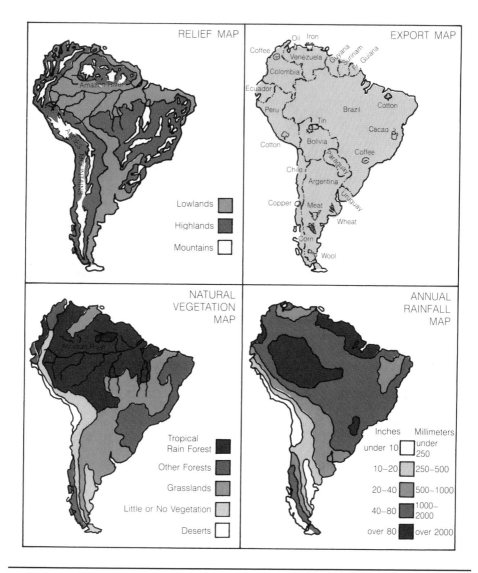

FIGURE 9–23

Special Subject Maps (Reprinted by permission of Scholastic Inc. from Scholastic Map Skills
Book E *by Barbara Christensen. Copyright © 1978 by Scholastic Inc.)*

an eraser full of chalk over the holes. An outline of the map will appear on the
chalkboard, which you can trace over with chalk.

Small outline maps can be made for individual student use by tracing original
maps on a master for reproduction on a duplication machine. Commercial publishers
also produce inexpensive printed outline maps.

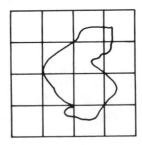

FIGURE 9-24
The Proportional Squares Technique

Relief Maps

Maps that incorporate raised features are useful aids for visualizing topographic features and for determining the effects of those features on distance, travel, weather, terrain, and other conditions. One of the problems in constructing relief maps is the distorted vertical-horizontal relationship. Children must understand that the relationship of height to distance is highly exaggerated to show the topographic features more clearly. If true height-distance relationships were shown while scaling the earth down to the size of a large beach ball, the beach-ball model would actually be smooth, and no actual topographical features could be shown. If relief maps are used, it must be understood that they show vertical distortion of topographical features.

Relief maps should be constructed on a firm base, such as plywood. Posterboard or similar materials are not strong enough to support wet modeling materials and can buckle and curl as the materials dry. An accurate outline for the relief map should be prepared carefully, and a second map should always be near to serve as a working guide as the modeling material is being placed over the outline. Rivers, lakes, mountains, valleys, and other features should be sketched where needed. After elevation and other land features have been identified, nails, pins, brads, and other materials can serve as supports for mountains, peaks, ranges, and hills. Color can be added to represent changes in elevation, to identify lakes and rivers, and to highlight other natural phenomena.

Several different recipes can be used to produce modeling materials; among the most popular are:

Papier-mâché. Cut newspaper or paper towels into strips about one-half to three-fourths of an inch wide and soak them overnight. Drain off excess water and crush the soaked paper into a fine texture. Add wheat paste until the mixture assumes the consistency of dough. Surface features can be built by applying this mixture to the modeling surface. After drying for three to six days, the surface becomes extremely hard and is ready for painting.

Paste and paper strips. Cut paper towels into half-inch strips and dip them into wheat paste. Place them over crumpled paper used to build up the surface features. Cover the entire surface with two layers of material. After this has been done, apply a coat of wheat paste over the surface. After the material is dry, paint can be applied.

Salt and flour. Mix equal parts of salt and flour with enough water to ensure a plastic consistency. The mixture can be added to a map outline and the terrain molded according to specifications.

Modeling dough. Mix together three cups flour and one cup salt. Stir and knead these materials together, gradually adding water until the mixture attains the consistency of dough. Dry tempera paint can be added to produce a bright-colored product.

Puzzle Maps

Puzzle maps can be made from cardboard, posterboard, or plywood. Trace the major features as you would on an outline map. Color in rivers, lakes, mountains, and other significant topographical features. Cut the map into a variety of shapes and encourage the children to reconstruct it.

Topographic Maps

Nearly everyone, at one time or another, has used a topographic map. In fact, the U.S. Geological Survey distributes more than seven million topographic maps annually. Chances are the children you teach will eventually have contact with a topographic map—as adults in jobs as diverse as fishing or engineering. Older children may use the maps for a variety of purposes in the classroom, including simulations involving highway and airport planning, selecting industrial sites and pipeline and powerline routes, making property surveys, managing natural resources, agricultural research, and planning recreation areas.

Topographic maps provide a detailed record of a land area, showing geographic positions and elevations of both natural and man-made features. They show the shape of the land (mountains, valleys, and plains) with brown contour lines; water features are shown in blue; woodland features are shown in green; roads, buildings, railroads, and powerlines are designated by black markings; and urbanized areas are shown in a red tint. Other special features are shown by appropriate symbols.

The physical and cultural characteristics of the terrain are determined by precise engineering surveys and field inspections by United States Geological Survey personnel, who then record the data on a map. Topographic maps are published for each state and are free upon request from: Branch of Distribution, U.S. Geological Survey, 1200 South Eads Street, Arlington, VA 22202.

Outdoor Maps

Some schools will allow construction of maps on hard-surfaced sections of the playground. Prepare the class by having them construct a paper model. Outlines, parallels, meridians, and/or significant topographical features can be drawn on the hard surface using the model as a guide. Many gallons of paint will be used to mark the selected countries as well as to designate the selected cities.

This list summarizes the teacher's role in developing and reinforcing map skills in the upper-elementary grades.

- *Prepare the environment.* Provide a wide variety of maps and globes, both commercially produced and child-constructed.

- *Plan an instructional sequence.* Continue with the developmental sequence begun during the primary grades. Reinforce and extend those skills with increasingly sophisticated maps such as relief maps or special purpose maps. Use concrete experiences to teach new concepts such as grids or those related to the globe. The emphasis has changed from learning to read maps to reading maps to learn.

- *Stimulate thinking.* Encourage youngsters to think logically and creatively while constructing and interpreting maps. Help them see how maps summarize and explain geographical phenomena and their influence on humankind.

- *Evaluate progress.* Remember that map instruction, like any other teaching task in the elementary grades, must be geared to each individual. Failure to challenge the gifted or meet the special needs of the slow learner will result in a classroom of disinterested, dissatisfied youngsters. Be constantly aware of the children's progress and adjust your teaching strategies accordingly.

Upper-grade children constructed this large outline map of the United States on the asphalt playground surface as a map reading project.

GRAPHIC MATERIALS

Tables, graphs, and time lines represent lengthy information in summary form, allowing students to gather information, visualize relationships, and make comparisons much more easily than with narrative materials. All forms of graphics appear in social studies materials, but to make maximum use of graphic materials, children must be able to comprehend on three levels: literal, inferential, and critical.

At the level of literal comprehension, one leads children in locating specific factual data with questions such as "How many . . .?" or "What are . . .?" Literal comprehension is the basic level of understanding and is essential to the thinking required on the next two levels.

At the inferential level, children compare and contrast factual data to form generalizations and draw conclusions. Guided interpretation of the graphic material through thoughtful questions is the best way to develop inferential comprehension: "In what ways is _____ similar to (or different from) _____ ?" "Explain what is meant by . . ." or "Why did _____ happen?" These questions require the student to project beyond the immediate factual data in more abstract ways than in answering literal questions.

Developing critical comprehension of graphic materials helps children examine and recognize biased or inaccurate information. Questions that guide critical thinking might be in these forms: "For what reasons would you favor . . ."? or "Which of these _____ would you consider to be of greatest value?" or "Do you agree with these conclusions?" or "Is this information useful or valuable?" In all cases, the student must indicate the basic criteria and supply the appropriate data that caused her to make a decision.

Just as we apply developmental learning principles to all phases of children's skills acquisition, we must also introduce graphic materials to a child by means of something he has experienced. Young children grasp the relationships shown in graphic representations only if they first go through the process of representing things graphically themselves.

TABLES.   Tables present numerical data concisely in columns and rows for quick comparisons. Tables in social studies materials may represent comparative data on exports, imports, rainfall, income, mountain elevations, population, and dozens of other concepts. Since children need to become familiar with tables before they can understand and interpret other graphic materials, the teacher should plan early learning experiences that will help the child clearly understand how to make them.

The children's first tables, like those in Tables 9–1 and 9–2, should be short lists of figures related to daily classroom experiences. For example, the children may compare the number of boys and girls in the three second-grade classrooms, favorite pets, favorite colors, favorite times of the day, attendance for each day of the week, etc.

Gradually, children will move to tables similar to Table 9–3 that are common in social studies materials. Be sure, though, that the children can read large numbers before they meet them in social studies tables.

TABLE 9–1
Boys and Girls in Second Grade

Room	Boys	Girls
2-A	17	10
2-B	12	15
2-C	11	15

TABLE 9–2
Class Attendance

Day	Absent	Present
Monday	3	21
Tuesday	2	22
Wednesday	4	20
Thursday	3	21
Friday	1	23

TABLE 9–3
Growth of White and Black Population in the U.S., 1800–1960

Year	White	Black	Total
1800	4,306,446	1,002,037	5,308,483
1820	7,866,797	1,771,656	9,638,453
1840	14,195,805	2,873,648	17,069,453
1860	26,922,537	4,441,830	31,443,321
1880	43,402,970	6,580,793	50,155,783
1900	66,809,196	8,833,994	75,994,575
1920	94,820,915	10,463,131	105,710,620
1940	118,214,870	12,865,518	131,669,275
1960	158,831,732	18,871,831	179,323,175

GRAPHS.   Graphs present quantitative information that can be read and interpreted quickly. In elementary school social studies, this is accomplished with pictorial graphs; bar graphs; circle, pie, or area graphs; and line graphs. Generally, the pictorial and bar graphs are the easiest to interpret; the others may be more difficult for elementary school children.

In the children's earliest experiences with graphs, you should make instruction as concrete as possible. Use blocks, books, or other stackable materials to help children understand how factual data can be represented with graphs. Bring an empty table to the front of the room and choose a topic on which the children might have a variety of responses—favorite foods, sports teams, flavors, colors, and so on. Construct labels for about four of the most apparent choices and tape them on the edge of the table so all can see. Then ask the children to name their preference and, one by one, place their blocks above the appropriate label. When everyone has done so, you can easily compare and contrast columns by asking, "Which food has the most blocks? What does our class enjoy as its favorite food? Which food has the least blocks? What is our least favorite food? Do any foods have the same number of blocks? Do you think the results would change if we asked the children next door to tell us *their* favorite foods?" You may want to repeat this experience several times using different categories.

From these initial experiences, provide a transition activity before the children try to interpret graphs in books or other sources. This transitional activity begins by once more choosing a topic of personal interest for the children. Rather than pass out blocks, give each child a rectangular piece of colored construction paper (about 1″ × 2″). Following a procedure similar to the concrete graphing experience, ask the children to make their choices and to glue their rectangles on a large sheet of chart paper (or tack to the bulletin board) above their choices. Children can see summaries of data in a graph that evolves before their eyes (Figure 9–25). Follow the graph construction with questions like those in the concrete graph discussion. End your questioning sequence with an evaluative-type question to encourage *critical comprehension* of graphs: "How might our graph be different if it were done in Pittsburgh rather than Denver?"

Now, you can begin to show children how closely graphs and tables are tied together. For example, you might use your table of class absences and ask the children to transform it into a graph by placing pictorial symbols on corresponding sections of the graph (a *pictorial graph*), as in Figure 9–26.

In the later grades, picture graphs can be used to illustrate such factual data as natural resources, exports, imports, manufactured goods, population, methods

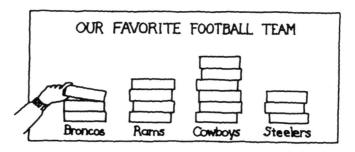

FIGURE 9–25
Transitional Graph Activity

Monday	3
Tuesday	2
Wednesday	4
Thursday	3
Friday	1

Monday	⚥ ⚥ ⚥
Tuesday	⚥ ⚥
Wednesday	⚥ ⚥ ⚥ ⚥
Thursday	⚥ ⚥ ⚥
Friday	⚥

FIGURE 9–26
Numerical and Pictorial Graphs Showing Class Absences

Centerville   🧍🧍🧍🧍

Mayville   🧍🧍🧍

Quarryville   🧍🧍

🧍 = 1,000 people

FIGURE 9-27

Comparison of Populations in Three Cities

of transportation, comparisons of population, and so on, like the graph in Figure 9–27.

Picture graphs appeal to children because of their simple presentation of data. The symbols are more concrete than those of any other graphic form, and the children can interpret their meaning fairly easily. They must learn to construct them carefully; carelessness in counting may account for inconsistencies in the data, especially when large numbers of symbols are necessary. In addition, picture graphs can be ineffective either because the information is difficult to illustrate pictorially or because pictorial symbols give an inexact representation of certain data.

As the children progress, they will encounter increasingly sophisticated bar graphs. To read these data successfully, children must have had prior experiences. Eventually they will be able to quickly comprehend the summary information presented in graphs and use more sophisticated thought processes to compare two or more graphs, as in Figure 9–28. Questions you might ask about the graphs in Figure

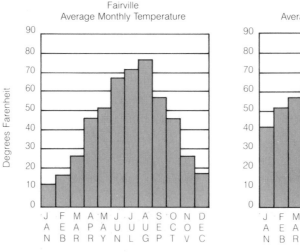
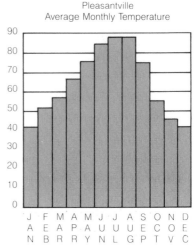

FIGURE 9-28

Two Bar Graphs for Comparison

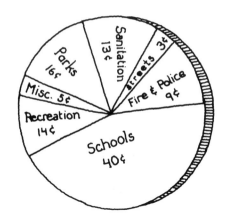

FIGURE 9-29

A Pie Graph Showing How Much of Every City Tax Dollar Is Spent for Different Services

9-28 include: Which city has a warm climate? A cool climate? How do you know? Why do you think people might choose to live in Fairville? Pleasantville? Where in the United States do you think each city might be located? Why?

Circle, pie, or area graphs are most appropriate for showing how a total amount is divided into parts. Because children have a difficult time interpreting fractional parts or percentage of area in the primary grades, circle, pie, or area graphs are recommended for use later in the intermediate grades. Figure 9-29 illustrates the typical use of area graphs in elementary school social studies materials.

Line graphs constitute the most accurate form of graphing. They are especially useful for showing changes that occur over a period of time. Because young children have relatively poor time concepts, and because line graphs are the most abstract form of graphing, they should not be introduced until the intermediate grades. Line graphs are especially valuable to show changes in temperature during the year, rainfall changes, population changes, or production changes (Figure 9-30).

As with bar graphs, you should formulate a good set of questions to guide children through the interpretation of pie or line graphs. A sample questioning sequence for the line graph might be: "What data does our graph summarize? What does it show? What is the average amount of rainfall for January? Which month receives the greatest amount of rainfall? The least? Do any months receive equal amounts of rainfall? Which month receives the most rainfall, March or May? During what months does the amount of rainfall gradually decrease? During what months do we see the steadiest rise in the amount of rainfall?"

TIME LINES.   A time line graphically represents a succession of historical events by dividing a unit into proportional segments showing important events that occurred in particular time periods. In the early primary grades, time charts might show events of the daily or weekly school schedule, important events in the community, major national observances, and personal experiences. An understanding of chronology can be developed in the early years by presenting children with large

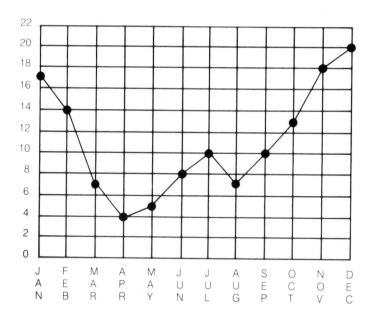

FIGURE 9–30

A Line Graph Showing Average Monthly Rainfall of a Tropical Rainforest

cards that illustrate steps of a familiar process in a jumbled sequence. The children must decide which card comes first, second, and so on, and hold the cards in front of themselves in proper sequence. Begin with a familiar series of events, such as the routine of a typical school day, and gradually apply the same teaching strategy to sequencing steps in a series of events in a social studies topic (Figure 9–31).

Constructing time lines is similar to constructing other semiabstract or abstract learning aids in that initial experiences should be as concrete as possible. A wise way to begin the study of chronology is to start with the children's own lives. You can prepare large cards (and add appropriate photos, if possible) with the labels "Birth," "Learn to Walk," "Go to School," "Enter Grade _____ ," "Graduate from

FIGURE 9–31

Sequencing Steps

High School." Take the children to the playground and assign one card to each child. The child holding the "Birth" card would be the starting point for the time line. The children can next suggest the age at which they began to walk. The child holding the "Learn to Walk" card should pace from the "Birth" point the number of steps as years from birth to walking. Use the same process for each of the other cards. Relationships between the distances can then be discussed. In the same way, you may wish to develop time concepts related to other key events, such as important inventions, famous explorers, changes in transportation, notable events in the community, and the like.

This procedure can also be useful in showing the sequential development of historical events. The children can first be presented with a random number of cards listing events of history. They can go to the playground, organize the cards in sequence, and walk off one step for each year between events. This practice is especially appropriate in the upper grades, since history facts are difficult for most primary children to understand. Transferring this practice into the classroom, then, you would use a similar procedure, but the children will soon realize that if they take one step for each year between events, they will soon run out of room and not be able to complete their task. You can then direct them toward discovering that a smaller unit of measure will be needed—perhaps one inch to represent a year.

When working on smaller-scale time lines in the classroom, you should emphasize exactness and consistency. An inexact or inconsistent scale distorts time relationships and hinders true conceptualizations of chronology.

The attractiveness of the time line is also a major factor in its effectiveness as a learning aid. Pictures and illustrations add to the charm of the time line and encourage children to use it as an organized frame of reference. Figure 9–32 shows a fairly even span of time between events. If the periods between historical events are not even, you will need to choose an illustration that is not symmetrical.

On time lines such as in Figure 9–33, groups of children can be given a set of cards identifying events from a current topic of study. Ask the children to look up

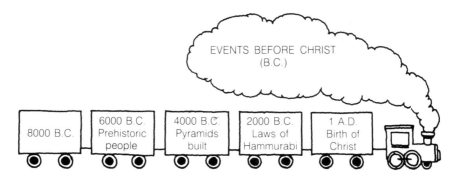

FIGURE 9–32
Organized Frame of Reference

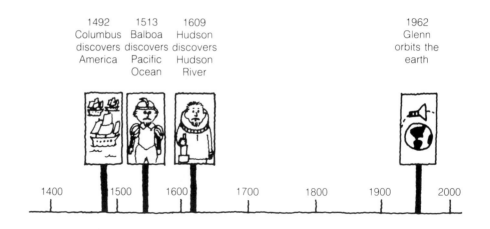

FIGURE 9–33
Group Work on Time Line

information about their events and draw an illustration about it. From there you can direct the children to find the date for each event and place their illustrations in chronological order on the time line. After the time line is constructed, you may want each group to share pertinent information about the different events with the rest of the class. By the time this project is completed, your class will have constructed a master guide of the major events under study and will have begun to develop a historical perspective of particular events.

SUMMARY

Maps, globes, tables, charts, and graphs are summary techniques for representing information in clear, concise, symbolic form. The primary characteristic of each system is a pattern of scale, color, or shape that comprises its symbol scheme. The ability to use a map, table, globe, chart, or graph rests solely on a child's ability to unlock that symbol scheme, much as success in conventional reading rests on an ability to unlock the symbol scheme of letters and words. Like conventional reading, the ability to read maps, tables, globes, charts, and graphs is comprised of many subskills that need to be taught in a developmental sequence so the children will become skillful in their use.

Developing map and globe skills depends on the child's ability to perceive representations of her environment. Piaget's work shows us that up to about seven or eight years of age, children may be limited in their ability to unlock the map and globe symbol scheme because of the characteristics of *egocentrism* and *conservation*. Because of these characteristics, children younger than eight years may need "readiness" activities to promote geographic understandings such as representation, physical features, and the earth.

As the children indicate an ability to advance to actual beginning map instruction, you need to plan a developmental program that will promote each of these map reading skills:

- Locating places
- Recognizing and expressing relative location
- Interpreting map symbols
- Developing a basic idea of relative size and scale
- Reading directions
- Understanding that the globe is the most accurate representation of the earth's surface

Planned instruction in these skills should offer *direct involvement* and *concrete experiences*, for when children experiment with challenging materials that stimulate mental processes they are best able to organize and integrate new information into existing mental structures.

Tables, graphs, and charts are comprehensive representations that allow students to gather information, visualize relationships, and make comparisons much more easily than through the use of narrative materials. Like conventional reading, these symbolic systems attain maximum usefulness when children become able to comprehend them on three levels: literal, inferential, and critical. As with map and globe instruction, children learn best about tables, charts, and graphs through direct, meaningful instruction and by becoming involved in situations in which they actually use the skills.

Each of the symbol schemes described in this chapter is an important part of the communication system of the social studies, and each requires a sound, developmental pattern of instruction.

ENDNOTES

1. Stephen M. Corey, "The Poor Scholar's Soliloquy," in *Open Sesame,* ed. Evelyn M. Carswell and Darrell L. Roubinek (Pacific Palisades, CA: Goodyear Publishing Company, Inc., 1974), pp. 55–56.

2. Alexander W. Siegel and Margaret Schadler, "The Development of Young Children's Spatial Representations of Their Classrooms," in *Contemporary Readings in Child Psychology,* 2nd ed.; ed. E. Mavis Hetherington and Ross D. Parke (New York: McGraw-Hill, 1981), pp. 170–76.

3. Ralph C. Preston and Wayne L. Herman, Jr., *Teaching Social Studies in the Elementary School* (New York: Holt, Rinehart and Winston, 1974), pp. 405–6.

10

Creative Arts in the Social Studies Classroom

KEY CONCEPTS

- [ ] *Understanding what is meant by "the arts" and how they contribute to the social studies curriculum*
- [ ] *Using the arts as a central organizer for planning a sequence of social studies instruction*
- [ ] *Encouraging children to use various types of creative expression to communicate what they learn in the social studies*
- [ ] *Appreciating the role of the arts in the process of learning and of self-expression*

> We turned our sixth-grade classroom into a Renoir Room! . . . Slowly but
> delightedly the students hung . . . fifty-four reproductions of Renoir
> paintings . . . on the four classroom walls.
>
> The purpose of this project was to have students enter the world of
> Renoir through the beauty of his work, to engage in independent research
> to discover the man Renoir, and to digest and share this newly found
> world with the rest of the school.[1]

In this classroom, children reproduce Renoir paintings, perform dramatic interpretations of Edna St. Vincent Millay, and move freely to Bartok sonatas. Through these great works, the children become emotionally involved with social studies subject matter. They enjoy dancing, singing, strumming guitars, painting, and sculpting. Is this meaty fare or is it a frill that school boards can snip in reaction to a "back-to-basics" trend or to shrinking school budgets?

Proponents argue that the arts belong in our schools because they make indispensable contributions to a child's total education. The arts help students improve the quality of their lives by challenging them to look at cultural beliefs, ideas, conditions, and problems in new ways. You need not be a professional musician, actor, or artist to present this segment of a culture's greatness to your students. You need only be aware of the beauty and excitement of the outside world and bring that world into your classroom. What are the arts? The arts umbrella covers dance, music, drama, drawing, painting, sculpture, creative writing, photography, video, and other visual arts (Table 10–1). The social studies classroom is an ideal context for integrating the arts, as King explains:

> Music, art, and literature know no national or cultural boundaries. The common expressions of human feeling found in these forms can be used effectively by the teacher to develop children's capacities to identify with other groups and other societies—indeed, the totality of mankind. . . .
>
> Aesthetic experiences, embodied in the arts and humanities, provide ways of giving the individual an opportunity to try on a situation—to know the logic and feeling of others—even though these others live thousands of miles away.[2]

The arts offer open-ended opportunities. They should build the risk-taking, do-it-yourself confidence that our future will demand. We must be aware of the value of the arts, especially as they can be used in the social studies program, and offer praise and reinforcement as the children allow their natural creative tendencies to flourish: "That's great. You used your own ideas!"

From infancy, children are excited by the sensory impressions they receive from their arts heritage. Songs, rhymes, fingerplays, and chants elicit enthusiastic responses from the very young. Stories, pictures, books, arts and crafts, television, radio, films, stage plays, puppets, video- and audiotapes, dance, and other forms

Special encouragement for this chapter was provided by Dr. Arthur Mark, Professor of Elementary Education at East Stroudsburg (PA) University.

TABLE 10–1
Arts in a Cultural Heritage

Arts Category	Popular Art Forms
Visual arts	Oil paintings, water colors, prints, sculpture, pottery, jewelry, architecture, furniture, crafts, landscaping, gardening, cartoons, film, television comics
Music	Classical, folk, ballads, rock and roll, country and western, show tunes, commercial jingles, ethnic styles, soul music, symphonies, ballet; musical instruments; dance (folk dance, contemporary, special cultural styles)
Literature	Myths, legends, folk tales, nursery rhymes, poetry, biographies, autobiographies, stories, informational books, drama

of creative expression add zest to childhood. Yet formal schooling often ignores the arts, and experiences in the creative fields are often limited to special, private training for but a few children. Children's arts experiences in school are usually limited to one or two classes a week with the art teacher and the music teacher. But children should understand that the arts reflect a culture, and one cannot fully *appreciate* the value of any art without some understanding of the cultural matrix from which it emerged. Conversely, one cannot fully appreciate a culture unless one respects and values the creative efforts of its individuals. Why wait until your children go to the art or music teacher to learn about the world's great creative artists? The social studies classroom is an ideal place to immerse children in the arts—greatness that is part of every culture.

The two most popular experiences with the arts in a social studies program involve (1) sharing the creative arts of various cultures and (2) providing for creative expression in the classroom.

SHARING CREATIVE ARTS OF CULTURES

The arts belong in our schools because they are serious business, not frills. Teachers must treat them as indispensable parts of education because they help children understand human civilizations through examination of creative outlets for thoughts, emotions, and aspirations.

One teacher took her class to an "Igbo Arts" exhibit of more than one hundred objects produced by the Igbo (or Ibo) people of southeastern Nigeria who, in 1967, attempted to secede from Nigeria and form their own Republic of Biafra. The objects in the exhibit included wooden totemic sculptures, pottery, textiles, examples of painting and body adornment, and a variety of masks. Wood predominated, as it does in most African art, but the exhibit included objects fashioned from bronze, iron, and ivory.

The purpose of the visit was to stimulate interest in the Igbo through the beauty of their creative work. The teacher's goal was achieved, as the students returned full of questions ripe for research and discovery: "Why did the Igbo make the small totemic figures? What were the purposes of the elaborate masks on display?" The children ventured into the world of the Igbo through intensive reading and research in the school library, newspapers, books at home, and other references including informational pamphlets from the exhibit.

A whole new world opened up to them through the arts—the children learned that the Igbo art form was a direct expression of their culture. For example, the small, wooden totemic figures (*ikenga*) symbolized traditionally masculine attributes such as strength, courage, and aggressiveness. These carved figures were kept in the men's meetinghouse. Among women, body jewelry such as ivory and brass anklets symbolized prestige and social satisfaction. The masks played a major role in the Igbo's masquerades, in which male performers acted out various aspects of their spiritual beliefs. Other art forms—sculpture, drama, dance, paintings, music, and costumes—were also used in masquerades.

The Igbo culture became more meaningful each day. Their rich creativity came alive in the classroom. After they had accumulated all their data, the children chose ways to share what they had found out. One group recreated jewelry for a mini-display; another made a model of an Igbo mask; a third dramatized an Igbo spiritual celebration; a fourth made a model *ikenga*. Through their expressive activities, the children became creators of original art forms that communicated the discoveries they made as members of a social group.

In this example, the study of the culture was not taught through the presentation of information that historians or anthropologists established about the life of the Igbo people. The teacher did not use the traditional practice of communicating information through assigned readings, film presentations, lectures, or student reports. Instead, she treated the study of the culture's arts as a process of inquiry. The children studied not only *what* the culture accomplished but also *how* historians or anthropologists arrive at their conclusions about a culture's character. This teacher frequently brought examples of the arts and crafts of different cultures as the children studied them so they could better understand people's beliefs, ideas, and problems.

Creative expression through the arts is also valuable in examining contemporary social and political conditions. For example, during the 1960s, Bob Dylan, Jimi Hendrix, Joan Baez, the Beatles, and other artists sought through their music to awaken America's conscience to the country's frustrations and failures. Presently, a new generation of musicians is displaying a level of political commitment and social concern unparalleled since that protest age. The causes have multiplied: Cyndi Lauper and Boy George sing for the victims of AIDS, Billy Joel sings to prevent teen suicide, Willie Nelson organizes a Farm Aid concert, and Bruce Springsteen tells of failed American dreams in his popular "Born in the USA" album. Springsteen, especially, has been a leader in the social concern movement. Unlike the often destructive protests of the 1960s, contemporary artists use television and marketing as tools to make their point. Bob Geldoff, for example, with Springsteen as a major force, organized the Live Aid concert in Philadelphia during the summer of 1985 to raise money for food for starving Africans. Because of his efforts, Geldoff had been nominated for a Nobel Peace Prize. Events like the Live Aid concert serve as an excellent "launching pad" for creating a study into the topic of "World Hunger." Some areas of research one might explore are:

What are people's nutritional requirements in different parts of the world? How are they alike or different from our own?

What is the agricultural picture in Russia, China, the United States, Africa, Egypt, or any other place?

What is the role of foreign aid in world hunger?

Does the United States have a hunger situation?

Should we pay farmers not to grow food that can otherwise be shipped as surplus to other countries?

What is the role of population growth in world hunger?

What will the world food situation be like in 150 years? What will happen (population growth, farming techniques, scientific breakthroughs, new forms of international governments) to make it that way?

What are the best ways to increase food productivity in developing countries?

What happens to food as it is readied for shipment from the United States and when it arrives at its destination?

What benefits do you suppose those who work to aid the world's hungry expect to receive?

People have sent messages to each other in many ways during the history of humanity; some in print, others in dance, and still more in music. Whatever the form, children must have opportunities to examine how creative ventures have been influenced by or have influenced human behavior at different times in different places.

If you fear that exposing children to history or to the study of a particular culture will fail because they are insecure in their knowledge of facts, or because the information seems irrelevant to the children's lives, or because they might become bored and reject the study completely, try something new. Work together with your children to *explore* a culture's music, graphic art, crafts, drama, dance, film, and creative writing. You will be amazed at the amount of information they discover and retain as well as at the interest and eagerness they bring to their work.

CREATIVE EXPRESSION IN THE CLASSROOM

Children's exposure to the arts should not stop with exploration. John Dewey said, "A beholder must create his own experience." This thesis has become a contemporary theme. Children need to express what they learn about people through as many avenues as possible, and the arts are the most accessible way. Isadora Duncan said, "If I could tell you what I mean, there would be no point in dancing."[3]

Albert Einstein once commented, "the gift of fantasy has meant more to me than my talent for absorbing positive knowledge."[4] A recent report, "Performing Together: The Arts in Education," states: "Studying the arts gives all students that gift. When they study drama, they can become someone else, if only for a few minutes. When they create a painting, they can see the world with fresh eyes. Research has shown that students who study the arts are also more likely to display originality and creativity in other subjects."[5] The report outlines several characteristics of a successful arts program, including incorporating arts activities into the regular classroom. For more information, write to Arts Alliance for Arts Education, 1801 North Moore Street, Arlington, VA 22209–9988.

It is impossible to present all the possibilities for arts usage in social studies programs, so we will discuss only some of the major areas we have not yet touched on. Chapter 5 also offers a number of suggestions for creative expression.

Art Activities

Painting or drawing provides children with ways of thinking through new concepts and combining them with already familiar ones. After a trip to a farm, for example, children's art would reflect a variety of expressions. Carol might draw the barn and silo in such detail that it would look as if she could still see it before her; John might paint the farmyard full of farm machinery; Marie's picture would reflect her growing interest in farm animals; Mark's drawing might show a determined rider sitting on a large horse, with the caption, "This is me leading the cows to pasture."

Prerequisite to any art work in the social studies is a stimulating learning experience that has special meaning for the child. A significant *intake* of ideas through direct experience or intensive research must occur before ideas develop to the point where they can be expressed effectively in some art medium. For example, one teacher planned a trip to the circus and felt that it was a wonderful experience for all of the children. Maurice, however, became terribly frightened of the clown, cried, thrashed about, and withdrew from participating in the rest of the trip. When the class returned to school and was asked to express the things they best remembered from the trip, Maurice withdrew even further and failed to respond at all. His fright caused a lack of understanding of the trip, and he was thus unable to express his ideas effectively; he had no experience from which to draw.

Additionally, children need an *assimilation* period before they become ready to express their thoughts. For example, a teacher asked his students to draw a picture depicting the high points of a famous person's life immediately after he had read the biography to them. The children produced inaccurate and substandard drawings. A major reason may have been that the teacher did not follow up the story with a discussion of major events to help the children organize their thoughts. The original idea was a good experience, but the teacher did not give his students a chance to sort out and put together ideas to the point of creative expression. For these two personalized reasons—intake and assimilation—art related to the social studies must be done on a relatively organized basis.

Materials for art activities in the social studies are virtually limitless. A creative teacher sees the possibilities in "junk" materials all around her—cloth, straw, seeds, gift wrap, leaves, sand. Uses of art in elementary school social studies are limited only by the vision and creativity of the teacher (Table 10–2). Keeping this thought in mind, consider some creative extensions of these art activities.

TABLE 10–2
Junk Art Materials for Use in Elementary School Social Studies Classrooms

Textured Materials

Fur scraps	Sandpaper	Feathers
Leather	Velvet	Cotton
Felt	Corduroy	Pipe cleaners
Burlap or sacking	Seeds	Acorns
Corrugated paper	Twigs	Shells
Egg carton dividers	Pebbles	Styrofoam
Carpet scraps	Dried flowers or weeds	

Patterned Materials

Wall paper samples	Linoleum scraps	Catalogs
Magazines	Patterned gift wrap	Greeting cards
Seasonal stickers	Candy bar wrappers	Stamps

Transparent and Semitransparent Materials

Net fruit sacks	Lace	Metal screening
Onion sacks	Plastic wrap	Colored cellophane
Crepe paper	Thin tissue paper	Paper lace doilies

Sparkling or Shiny Materials

Sequins	Ribbon	Christmas tinsel
Glitter	Seasonal wrapping paper	Mica snow
Aluminum foil	Paper from greeting cards	Metallic paper

Shapes

Buttons	Cork	Rubber bands
Drinking straws	Bottle caps	Toothpicks
Wooden applicators	Keys	Beads
Spools	Tongue depressors	Fluted candy cups
Scrap sponge	Cup cake cups	Gummed stickers
Paper clips	Heavy cotton rug yarn	String
Metal washers		Old jewelry

Scattering Materials

Sand	Tiny pebbles	Twigs
Sawdust	Wood shavings	Vermiculite
Yarn	Kitty litter	Colored aquarium gravel
		Eggshells

DIORAMAS.   A diorama is a three-dimensional model that depicts activities performed by people, animals, or objects. A cardboard box usually encloses the representation. Cut the lid from the box and paint the exterior or cover it with colored paper. Background scenery can be painted or cut from colored paper and pasted to the interior walls. People, animals, and other objects have a construction-paper tab at their base; this tab is folded and glued or stapled to the bottom of the box to keep the figure in place.

A variation of the diorama is the "peep show." Remove the lid from a cardboard box and place a mirror on the inside wall of one end. In the opposite end, punch a small hole. Construct the rest of the interior in the same way as the diorama. When you are finished, glue a sheet of translucent paper over the top of the box, thus making the scenery on the inside undistinguishable except through the peep hole. The effect is extraordinary.

MURALS.   In many social studies units, a mural can summarize a group's investigation or pull together the contributions of several groups into one expressive product for the entire class.

Research is the first step in constructing an authentic mural, so as to develop the necessary background information for planning a theme. Once the theme is chosen, a list of the significant, contributing ideas should be cooperatively developed. A large durable piece of wrapping paper is then laid on the floor of the classroom, and each committee is assigned a section of the mural. Each child on a committee is assigned to a portion of the mural and can make his at his own desk. Usually, individual contributions are made from paintings, sketches, cut paper, and similar art techniques. When the pupils finish, the sections are placed on the mural. When all of the pieces are in location, the teacher suggests the need for a background, usually a simple tempera-painted scene. When the background is complete, the children place their work back on the paper for gluing or pasting in final arrangement.

MOSAICS.   Begin a mosaic by having the children lightly draw their scenes on a nine-by-twelve-inch piece of construction paper. This will serve as a pattern for the mosaic work. Then use small pieces of colored paper, seeds, beans, rice, macaroni, eggshells, or other materials pasted on to form the mosaic pattern.

PRINTS.   Potatoes, erasers, wooden blocks, or linoleum can be used to make a printing surface. Begin by drawing a picture or design on a flat surface of the printing material. Use a knife or sharp cutting tool to cut away all background, leaving the design to stand out. Paint the design with tempera paint and stamp it on paper. These are possible printing activities:

Rolling pin printing: Rolling pins, cardboard tubing, or metal cans are equally effective. Glue yarn or string to the rolling pin so that it is strongly attached. Dip this printing tool into the paint and roll it over a surface.

Sponge printing: Dip various sponge pieces into paint and dab them onto a surface.

Button printing: Glue a variety of buttons to dowel sticks and use them for printing.

Food printing: Cut potatoes, green peppers, corn cobs, celery, apples, or other fruits or vegetables across the center to get a variety of natural printing stamps. Special designs can be cut into solid vegetables such as potatoes or carrots.

Clay printing: Make a design on a slab of clay using fingers or sticks; paint the raised surface and "print" by rubbing the back of the paper with a spoon.

Wet chalk print: Make a design with moist chalk, then place a piece of paper such as newsprint over the design and rub it to transfer.

Junk stuff: Use bottle caps, rulers, spool, corks, etc., to make a design or picture. Cover the object with tempera paint and press it on drawing paper.

Stenciling: Paint or color through the design cut into a piece of oaktag or other stiff paper.

Leaf print: Place a leaf under paper and rub the side of a crayon over the paper.

Potpourri: Use thread spools, hair curlers, cookie cutters, the round ends of paper towel rolls, forks, cotton balls, carpet scraps, bottle caps, and other common scraps to make printing tools.

COLLAGES. A collage is an arrangement of pictures or other materials. Abstract collages can be constructed by pasting pictures from newspapers or magazines within an outline in a free-form style. Realistic collages can be constructed by pasting scraps of materials in patterns. For example, a truck can be cut from construction paper, clouds can be made from chunks of cotton, foliage can be represented by green fabric, and a fence can be made from corrugated cardboard. Dried grass can be pasted in place to show a field. Encourage children to use their imaginations as much as possible while experimenting with collages, but they should not become so engrossed in novel materials that they forget the original purpose of the finished work.

ILLUSTRATIONS. Illustrating concepts related to field trips or research activities is probably the most popular art medium used in elementary social studies classrooms. Children may be asked to draw the details of the process involved in making linen from flax, to use crayon for indicating various areas on a state map, or to paint a picture of a landscape in the high Andes Mountains. Children like to illustrate group notebooks and decorative charts. There are literally hundreds of possibilities.

CUT PAPER. Construction paper can be bent, rolled, folded, or fringed to achieve highly interesting effects. A simple rolled paper cylinder can form the base for a totem pole. Additional paper cut into a variety of shapes can be pasted to the cylinder to provide more distinguishing features. Entire villages, cities, or farms can be made by arranging stand-up scenes: simply fold construction paper in half and cut an object as shown in Figure 10-1. This will produce an object that can stand upright because it is joined together at the top fold line. Color each object as required.

FIGURE 10–1
Cut Paper Design

TELEVISION.   Because children are highly motivated to watch television, they are also highly motivated to become "producers" of their own special shows. The shows can present information, summarize a research activity, or recall specifics of a field trip (Figure 10–2). The technique involves a small number of basic steps:

1. Cut a square hole into one side of a box and place circular wooden blocks along the side to give the box an appearance of a television set. Remove the back of the box.
2. Cut two round holes into the opposite sides of the box at the top and bottom. Make sure they are directly opposite each other.
3. Slide rollers through the box. (Paper towel rolls or wooden dowel rods work well.)
4. Section a long strip of wrapping paper into a series of nine-by-nine-inch squares.
5. Encourage the children to illustrate a series of pictures telling a story about a topic they are studying.
6. Prepare an oral description or dialogue for each picture.
7. Fasten each end of the wrapping paper to the rollers in the "television set."
8. Turn the rollers and watch the action on the screen. Narration can be provided by tape recording the story or by simply telling the story as the pictures appear.

FIGURE 10–2
Television for the Classroom

Construction Activities

Classrooms rarely contain *all* of the real materials children need for exploration or for expressing the relationships they are learning. Some items are not made commercially, some are not readily available, and some are too expensive. In these cases, you can capitalize on the children's natural interest in construction and invite them to *create* original representations of their learning discoveries. For decades, educators have been telling us that when children are able to take information, work with it, and represent it in their own way through construction-type activities, they bring meaning to their learning and become intrinsically motivated to learn even more.

In *construction activities*, children use tools and materials to represent real people, places, or things, while clarifying social studies concepts and related processes. These activities provide meaning through motivation and interest and give purpose to reading and research. To illustrate, let us assume that a fourth-grade class is involved in a study of Colonial living. The teacher may suggest that a group of students interested in Colonial housing construct a model log cabin. Several purposes for this activity may be apparent to you. The teacher's purpose, for instance, is to have the children conduct research and select the appropriate information to help them construct an accurate representation of a log cabin. This enriches concepts and develops understanding as the children engage in a purposeful, creative activity. The children's purpose may be to learn as much as they can about a log cabin to enable them to build a model they can show to their classmates as they explain how logs are fitted and held together, what types of materials were used for roofs, and so on.

The value of this type of expressive activity is not in the aesthetic or "gimmicky" quality of the finished product, but in the *process* that contributes to the final structure. All too often, teachers unknowingly lose sight of their original purpose for an activity and place undue emphasis on constructing an awesome or impressive model. Use construction activities only if they:

Serve to achieve meaningful purposes

Follow careful planning and thinking by the children

Clarify concepts and understandings

Lie within the children's ability levels

Result in somewhat authentic, but not awesome, models

As children mature, their need for accuracy in construction increases. Early primary-grade children, for example, are generally satisfied with a minimum of detail in the items they use in their play. An orange crate is a perfectly adequate automobile. Blocks and boxes are entirely acceptable as stores or buildings. More mature children are likely to require more realistic details in expressing their new ideas. They become more aware of detail and want to make their construction projects look as real as possible.

Guiding Art and Construction Activities

Your role in guiding art and construction activities involves two tasks: (1) arranging the environment with equipment and materials, and (2) supervising the work in a warm and friendly manner. While *arranging* the room for creative art activities, remember children grow best when they are allowed to explore freely and imaginatively in a stimulating and challenging setting. Have adequate space for working comfortably alone or in small groups and have materials and equipment easily accessible. Children must be unhurried and free to plan and carry out special projects in their own ways.

Guidelines to follow as you *supervise* the children during their independent creative art endeavors are to:

- Offer encouragement and praise to let them know how much you value their unique efforts. Do not pressure them to describe what they are doing—they may be merely exploring with the art media and may not be able to express anything in particular about their product. You may wish to comment about the color, shapes, sizes, or design of the product and show an interest in and appreciation of the work, but refrain from forcing conversation when none seems constructive.

- Avoid comments such as ''What is it?'' or ''What are you making?'' when children are engaging in media work. The children may well look at you blankly. Instead, use the open-ended request, ''Please tell me about your picture.'' Along the same line, never admonish children for their accidents when involved in constructive activity.

- Resist the use of patterns, outlines, or guides whenever possible. Of course, some special projects call for them, but excessive use limits the freedom of expression offered by unstructured art activity.

- Help children and encourage their efforts, but refrain from fulfilling requests such as, ''Will you draw a dog for me right here?'' Do not allow children to become dependent on you—encourage them to think about ways they can accomplish their goals by themselves. Requests for help usually come from a desire to produce a ''masterpiece'' to please the teacher or parent. Let children know that what they create should be pleasing to them, not to the teacher.

- Remember that your enthusiasm should extend to everyone. Emphasizing the work of only a few talented children will soon discourage the rest.

Creative Dramatics

A popular activity among all children, creative dramatics is considered a natural part of human growth. The wise teacher capitalizes on children's natural urge to dramatize adult life by making creative dramatics an integral part of social studies instruction.

Creative dramatics can benefit the social studies program in many ways. Children enjoy it. Being able to do something they like enhances their interest in learning. The program also provides a purpose for gathering information. Children often need additional information to accurately portray real-life circumstances in their dramatic representations. This spontaneous motivation for new information can be capitalized on to expand the child's knowledge of other people's characteristics and actions. Dramatics can build the child's sensitivity to others' feelings. By the time a player has decided which character he is, what decisions he must face, and why he behaves as he does, he has gained a great deal of insight into understanding people in unique situations. Putting on a play is also a valuable opportunity for group cooperation. Social acceptance is often an extremely valuable outcome, as children develop a common bond of respect for a job well done. Plays can also be used to evaluate concept attainment. The situations the children portray reflect their knowledge of related information.

Children need teacher help to effectively use creative dramatics in handling the increasingly difficult concepts about their world. Dramatic representation takes many forms, and children must be moved gradually from one form to another. Creative dramatics proceeds developmentally from the free-style play of preschool and kindergarten to the organized forms found in the upper primary and intermediate grades.

Dramatic play requires creative thinking when children enact roles or activities that are familiar to them. The process encourages growth in all areas of development:

- *Social:* sharing and planning with other children
- *Emotional:* savoring pleasurable experiences and expressing emotions such as anger, hostility, and aggression
- *Affective:* exhibiting likes and dislikes; exploring and expressing good and bad notions
- *Physical:* exercising muscular development and control
- *Cognitive:* expressing thoughts in play action (conceptual thought)
- *Creative:* bringing original thinking to the solution of problems

The dramatic play area is a popular setting for young children. Various props encourage children to experiment at being mothers, fathers, babies, community members, teachers, animals—the list is endless. Whatever the design of the dramatics area at any one time, the furniture and equipment should be child-size whenever possible. Many kindergarten classrooms contain a permanent housekeeping corner as well as a separate dramatic play corner that is changed periodically. The *housekeeping corner* generally includes a table and chairs; wooden kitchen equipment such as a stove, refrigerator, or sink; a wide selection of dolls; and cupboards containing cups, saucers, pots, spoons, pitchers, and so on. These materials do not need to be purchased—a little imagination turns orange crates into stoves or storage cabinets, and a little resourcefulness leads you to used and outgrown toys. The *dramatic play corner* offers children a wide variety of creative possibilities. Changeable items should be provided so that children can shift roles whenever they have the inclination. In this area children can explore people's lives in varying occupations and locations; they can use their equipment to pretend they are in many different places:

> *Ice cream store:* Ice cream scoops, empty ice cream containers, white aprons and caps, a table with chairs
>
> *Automobile repair shop:* Overalls, work caps, tools, hose for gasoline, miniature vehicles or crates to represent cars and trucks
>
> *Hamburger stand:* Aprons, caps, paper bags, napkins, fast-food containers, pad and pencil, cash register, play money, trays
>
> *Hospital:* Doctor bag, stethoscope, bandages, doctor or nurse uniforms, bed, crutches
>
> *Tailor shop:* Table, measuring tape, variety of cloth, scissors, needle, thread, dolls to be fitted with clothes
>
> *Beauty parlor:* Hair curlers, aprons, shampoo and makeup bottles, hair dryer, old electric shaver, mirror
>
> *Bakery:* Cookie cutters, bowls, baker's apron and cap, flour sacks, rolling pin, pie tins, cash register, toy money

Other creative possibilities for roleplaying include: shoe repair persons, launderers, jewelers, service station attendants, firefighters, police officers, factory workers, secretaries, farmers, barbers, postal workers, race car drivers, and the like. Children want and need to play with each other. For that reason, play is perhaps the most potent vehicle in kindergarten and early primary-grade classrooms for encouraging social growth. Do your best to ensure ample opportunities for free dramatic play. Provide plenty of resources and abundant space.

Your role during this early part of the creative dramatics sequence is mainly that of observer and arranger. You must know the developmental sequence of play and use it as an index for selecting equipment and materials. Basically, children of ages three to six prefer play situations centering around familiar, adult-living conditions in the home, school, neighborhood, and community. The opportunities for the child in an unstructured setting provide the readiness framework that will enable her to successfully participate in other forms of creative dramatics later on.

Piaget believes that the child does not move from unstructured play to directed, cooperative play until after the age of seven or eight. When this stage is attained, more direct guidance is required on the part of the teacher, and new dramatic opportunities can be offered in the intermediate grades.

PANTOMIME.   Children of all ages enjoy using bodily expressions to convey ideas without words, and this is a good technique for introducing creative dramatics to the social studies program. Pantomime offers opportunities to characterize actions and personalities without having to furnish dialogue.

Pantomime is a logical extension of dramatic play because it helps youngsters become more sensitive to what is around them. Before that happens, children must become aware of how they can express their emotions and ideas, best described as *sensitizing*. To begin, gather the children in a large circle and have them cover their eyes or close them while you come around the circle with various objects for them to touch, smell, hear, taste, and see. For example, you would say, ''Close your eyes and *touch* . . . a soft snuggly teddy bear . . . rough sandpaper . . . cold ice cube''; ''Close your eyes and *smell* . . . a fresh flower . . . a sour pickle . . . cinnamon''; ''Close your eyes and *listen* to . . . a sharp bell . . . a pencil tapping on the desk . . . paper being crumpled''; ''Close your eyes and *taste* (provide small samples) . . . sugar . . . salt . . . apple slice''; ''Look outside the room and *see* . . . far away mountains . . . a cloud castle . . . a green grass carpet.'' Then ask the children to close their eyes once again and *think about* the things you will say to them even though the real items will not be in the classroom: ''Close your eyes and touch . . . a hot stove; a sharp pin; a slimy jellyfish; a soft, furry kitten; a cold icicle;'' ''Close your eyes and smell . . . hot cookies straight from the oven; soiled diapers; crisp bacon frying in a pan; dirty old garbage cans.''

At this point you may want to say ''Freeze.'' This technique, introduced to me by E. Riley Holman, is a signal for the children to keep any expression frozen on their faces and to open their eyes. Ask them to examine each other's expressions and to discuss how we would all know we had just smelled something awful. Intermittently use the ''freeze'' technique so that children become aware of how their faces communicate ideas and emotions without using words. Some other examples: ''Close your eyes and *listen to* . . . your favorite popular tune; the crowd at the championship football game; a baby crying; chalk being scraped across the chalkboard; two cats fighting.'' ''Close your eyes and *taste* . . . onions; a glass of fresh orange juice; the first food you've seen in two days; pizza with your favorite topping; a sour lemon.'' ''Close your eyes and *see* . . . an old creaking house on a stormy night; two eyes looking back at you through the dark; a bright, colorful birthday package; a quiet beach with waves lapping the shore; a soft, gentle sunset.''

As you share these and other sensitizing cues with the children, discuss each effect with the ''freeze'' technique and let the children describe the feelings or ideas they encountered during the experience. After you've suggested five or six cues for each of the senses, invite the children to suggest their own. You will be surprised at the creative responses they offer.

After the children become comfortable in the sensitizing phase, encourage them to explore the possibilities of communicating ideas and emotions with other parts of their bodies; for example, with parts of the body:

Say with your finger, ''Come here.''

Say with your nose, ''I smell a skunk.''

Say with your eyes, ''You're hopeless.''

Say with your foot, ''I'm stuck!''

Say with your ear, ''I hear beautiful music.''

Say with your arms, "It's heavy."

Say with your hands, "Look at my acrobatic flea."

Then encourage them to communicate with the whole body:

You are now lifting the winning weight in the Olympics.

You are a peacock showing off for the people.

You are a tin soldier in Santa's toyshop.

You are a dish of Jello.

You are a caged monkey in the zoo.

You have scored the winning touchdown in a football game.

You are playing a musical instrument in a parade.

If the children do reasonably well with these easy pantomime situations, enjoy them, and indicate an interest for more, introduce more advanced situations. For the advanced situations, you may want to group the children so that each situation can be repeated and the different interpretations shared. But before you ask the children to work cooperatively in planning to pantomime a short scene, give them opportunities to work together in pairs. Pantomiming opposites is a good activity. Pairs of children act out contrasting words while others guess their meanings. You might use:

open and *close*	*stand* and *sit*
north and *south*	*hit* and *miss*
brave and *cowardly*	*cold* and *warm*
loud and *soft*	*in* and *out*
few and *many*	*follow* and *lead*
over and *under*	*sweet* and *sour*
crooked and *straight*	*left* and *right*
melt and *freeze*	*inhale* and *exhale*
dry and *wet*	*big* and *small*
serious and *funny*	*tight* and *loose*

Mirror images are popular and fun for actors of all ages. In a game called "copycats," two players face each other, one acting as the other's mirror image. Whatever the first person does, his image must reproduce precisely. With practice this can become a skilled performance, challenging to the players and fascinating to those watching. Greater awareness as well as the ability to work together develop in the process. Older groups may ask to repeat this exercise from time to time, realizing the possibilities for technical improvement.

From simpler exercises, you can work up to presenting pantomime scenes. Use your imagination to determine stimulating situations for pantomime in the social studies classroom. Here are some possibilities:

"What am I doing?" or *"Who am I?"* Many social studies concepts relate to people involved in making or doing something. Children enjoy imitating others' unique movements. They can be encouraged to portray activities of people in the unit under study and to challenge their classmates to guess who they are. Some suggestions: Pilgrims landing at Plymouth Rock, the first landing on the moon, Ben Franklin's kite flying experience, Henry Aaron's record-breaking home run, the type of work people do at home or in the community.

Shadow Plays. Put up a sheet at one end of the room with the light behind it. Have the children pantomime something behind the sheet. The magic quality of a silhouette never fails to stimulate an immediate desire to try out ideas. This particular activity, incidentally, is excellent for the timid child who feels less exposed behind a sheet than he does out in the open. Acting behind the sheet leads to inventiveness: what happens when the actor is close to the sheet? Far from it? Approaches or leaves it? How can a figure be exaggerated? Enlarged? How is humor obtained? Then try acting out appropriate scenes and stories in shadow.

Pantomiming Feelings. Along the way, feelings will enter the pantomimes. You may ask the class to discuss the feelings they experienced while playing out their roles or observing others in the pantomime situation. As time goes on, you can ask groups of children to create situations that illustrate specific moods or feelings:

You are a hungry baby. Show your feelings and how you respond to your parents as they feed you.

An important game is about to begin. Suddenly someone yells to you from the crowd, "Cheat! You cheated that time!"

A famous scientist is working on an experimental machine in which moods are rapidly changed. You volunteer to see how it works. Enter the machine and go from tired to energetic, happy to sad, hot to cold.

Your role in guiding social studies pantomimes begins with establishing a rich background of study trips, books, magazines, films, pictures, recordings, and other sources of information on which children build their pantomimes. After they share an experience, the children should discuss its characteristics and their feelings about the insights they gained. You may then divide the class into small groups and encourage each group to pantomime whatever they felt was their most meaningful recollection. Each group should then share their creative expression with the others, after which you should lead a follow-up discussion: "What persons are represented in the action? What helped you recognize them? Where do you think the action took place? What helped you know this? What do you think the people were talking about? What are some of the feelings you think the characters experienced? From what you know about the actual situation, do you think the actors accurately portrayed what really happened? What feelings did you have as you watched the action? What would you have done if you were any one of the characters in the same situation? Can you predict what might happen to the people after what was shown in the panto-mime?''

IMPROVISED SKITS.   A charming characteristic of young children is their ability to use their creative imaginations in improvisations, unplanned situations where dialogue is necessary and characterized by scenes involving *no* learned lines, *no* costumes, and *no* sophisticated scenery. But improvisations can be difficult if the children have not had a great deal of practice in pantomime. With practice and a thorough knowledge of the story situation, however, dialogue begins to flow, and children further their understanding of a social studies condition by describing its characters more completely.

Many of the classroom situations described as pantomiming activities are also suitable for improvisation experiences. The teacher should also begin the initial improvisation experiences with simple situations. As the children gain confidence, they can attempt more challenging material.

The following improvised skits may be done by various age groups in the social studies classroom:

Scenes depicting the past. Children can be encouraged to portray ''You Are There'' situations such as the assassination of Lincoln, the Boston Tea Party, the signing of the Declaration of Independence, and innumerable other events.

Scenes depicting the present. Children can depict news topics.

Scenes depicting the future. Children, given unfinished stories describing a real or hypothetical situation, continue the action and demonstrate what they think will happen. Teachers use unfinished stories about holidays, special events, special people, and unique situations and ask the children to suggest, through improvisation, how the story might end. In the same light, children may be asked to improvise a scene in which they speculate on the outcome of an ongoing current news topic. For example, suppose a recent newspaper article described a woman's attempt to change her name from Spellman to Spellperson because of the sexist overtones of Spell*man* (the name is fictitious but the event really happened). The article leaves off at the woman's plea before the judge but does not tell what the judge decided. Invite children to dramatize the situation by assuming the roles of judge, Ms. Spellman, her lawyer, or the witnesses and to speculate on what the eventual name change decision would be.

Scenes suggested by objects. Placed in a scene that has a few items frequently used by the early Indians of Mexico, children are asked to prepare a skit in which they dramatize the actual use of the items by the Indians.

Fanciful scenes. Children can be encouraged to alter scenes by ''hamming'' them up. For example, one group of children created a modern parody of *Jack and the Beanstalk* by having Jack play the role of the thirteen colonies and the giant play the role of Great Britain.

Elementary school children enjoy acting out such scenes and often repeat the scenes to communicate different interpretations of the related information, to switch roles, or to create new endings to open-ended situations. Youngsters easily fluctuate between worlds of fantasy (witness the number of children who have "imaginary" playmates) and reality, and pantomime and improvisation give them opportunities to enter and leave new and different worlds at will. Even though spontaneity appears to be strongest during kindergarten and into the early primary years and tapers off as children reach the later grades, a skillful teacher can bring it to the surface again in a relaxed, developmentally appropriate setting.

By mimicking words and actions as they have experienced them in other settings, children actually *feel* how tired the mail carrier becomes, how frustrated a teacher becomes when children become rowdy, or how elated a candidate is when he wins an important election victory. It is its power in helping children to empathize that makes dramatic experiences so valuable; children express and experience another person's viewpoint. This creative technique helps children understand people or events more fully.

PUPPETRY.   Puppets are effective tools in creative dramatics, especially with shy children, enabling them to talk for something other than themselves. Once they have acquired social studies background information through any learning experience, the children can represent what they have learned through a puppet presentation. In the kindergarten and early primary years, the puppet becomes an extension of the child's personality; the child often speaks for the puppet and for herself. The use of puppets is most often unplanned or unstructured at this level; the child will spontaneously choose a puppet, manipulate it, explore its properties, and create a short, unstructured scenario. Expecting anything but free expression from most younger children is unrealistic and may only hamper rather than enhance creativity.

As the children gain maturity, they will not only become more directed in their efforts, but will also take a great deal of interest and pride in constructing their own puppets. In social studies, for example, children can more realistically represent a historical event with puppetry; they may show a holiday celebration, a fable, a problem related to playground safety, or a recommended solution for ecological damage. Problem solving, research, group interaction, and creative writing, all within a democratic setting, contribute to the learning experience in ways that go far beyond the apparent value of the puppet as an artistic production.

The puppets in Figure 10–3 might be provided for children in an elementary school classroom.

1. *Sock puppets.* Take an old sock and turn it into an attractive hand puppet by sewing on buttons, yarn, and other materials.
2. *Box puppets.* Use an empty cereal box for this puppet. Cut the box along one long side and two short sides at its middle. The box should bend when you place your hand into each section. Draw a face on a piece of paper and cut it in half at the mouth. Glue the upper part of the face on the top half of the box and the lower part of the face on the bottom half. Operate the puppet by placing the hand in both halves of the box.

Sock Puppet

Box Puppet

Stick Puppet

Finger Puppets

Food Puppets

Paper Plate Puppets

Paper Bag Puppet

FIGURE 10-3

Sample Puppets

3. *Stick puppets.* Draw and color a figure or face on a piece of cardboard (or cut pictures from magazines) and glue them to tongue depressors or ice cream sticks. For a two-sided puppet, place faces with opposite expressions (but identical outlines) on each side of the stick.

4. *Finger puppets.* Draw a head on a piece of drawing paper and leave a tab at the bottom. Tape the tab around the index finger so it forms a tube.

5. *Food puppets.* Fruits or vegetables can be mounted on a stick and used much as stick puppets. Cloth or crepe paper can be used to make a ''skirt'' to cover the hand. Facial characteristics can be made from pins or cut with knives.

6. *Paper plate puppets*. Glue or tape decorated paper plates to coat hangers or wooden dowel rods, or staple two plates together so the child's hand can slide in between them.

7. *Paper bag puppets*. Draw a face on the bag, stuff it partially full with newspaper, and tie it at the bottom (leaving enough room to use as a grip). Add construction paper or yarn hair, ears, hat, etc.

Large cardboard containers, such as those used to pack appliances, make excellent puppet stages. Cut out an opening for the stage and decorate the side facing the audience. Children may kneel inside and hide themselves from view as they manipulate the puppets (Figure 10–4).

DRAMATIZATION. Older children may wish to put on a formal play with script, costumes, and scenery. If the children have had sufficient experience with pantomime and improvisation, the most effective type of formal play is one in which the children are responsible for most of the planning. Your role is to guide the students in formulating the different scenes. As the children plan their script, ask them, "What are the most important things to tell? What are the people really like? What kind of place do they live in? What do the people do to make them interesting? How will you stage your play?"

The dramatization can result from many of the same sources described for pantomime and improvisation. The students' concern for elaborate scenery and costumes should not take precedence over the concepts or ideas the play is designed to convey. Simple objects can effectively represent more intricate objects; for example, a mural or bulletin board design can serve as a backdrop; a branch in a big can filled with dirt makes an excellent tree or bush; the teacher's desk becomes a cave; chairs placed in a straight line can be seats on a train or airplane; a pencil can become a hand-held microphone.

SOCIODRAMA. Our examples of creative dramatics in the social studies classroom have dealt primarily with methods of summarizing or communicating highlights of learning experiences through pantomime, improvised skits, puppetry, or

Puppet Stage

Dowel for curtain

FIGURE 10–4
Puppet Stage

dramatization. Sociodrama is a specialized use of any of these techniques in a situation characterized by an affective, or human relations, dilemma. Children dramatize, unrehearsed, real problematical situations and offer suggestions for resolution through their dramatic interpretations. The topics should be fairly simple at first—schoolroom, playground, or cafeteria conflicts, for example. Later, children can play out problem situations they encounter in social studies class.

Leslie D. Zeleny names these steps for developing sociodramas in the elementary school classroom: identify the problem; assign roles; discuss the situation; and replay the situation.[6]

- *Identify the problem.* Through discussion and observation, you and the children identify problems that may be causing difficulties. For example, one young girl had been the target of ridicule in her classroom because she had recently tried out for her elementary school football team, exclusively the boys' property. However, the adults in charge of the football program would not allow a girl, however eager or talented, to participate in the traditionally male-dominated sport. The boys in the classroom were unrelenting in their demeaning comments and actions and soon the girl withdrew from other activities. The teacher felt the problem had reached such proportions that sociodrama would be the best way to alleviate it. Frank discussions of the problem situation were then initiated, and the children were asked to share their thoughts.

- *Assign the roles.* Tensions in social situations usually arise because people do not understand the motivations and feelings of those involved. Therefore, children should be encouraged to imagine what others would say and do in the problem situation. After the problem has been discussed and the principal roles identified, volunteers are chosen to spontaneously enact the problem in front of the class, acting as *they* would in the situation, not as they think the real characters would.

- *Discussion.* By analyzing the sociodrama, the class can easily grasp a more complete understanding of the problem. The teacher should guide discussion by directing questions such as these to the players and audience: "How did each of you feel in your role? Do you think the treatment was fair? Why do you think the girl was treated as she was? Do you think people were fair to her? Why?

- *Replay the situation.* At this point, the children may wish to replay the situation, to depict what they consider to be proper treatment or to suggest a fair solution to the problem. Replay may be done by the same group or by several different groups who may suggest alternative solutions. The various proposals can be discussed and a final solution decided upon.

Because sociodrama is an effective process for understanding feelings, some teachers extend its use from illustrating issues in the classroom to studying people's feelings as they face important decisions in contemporary life and throughout history. You can glean scenarios from newspaper stories, textbook readings, photographs or study prints, films, and the like. Some of the most popular of the commercially produced materials designed especially to encourage dramatic play with a focus on feelings are those of Fannie R. and George Shaftel.[7]

The major objective of the Shaftel sociodrama design is education for citizenship, using problem stories of day-to-day living that pose dilemmas of childhood in American culture. The intent is to help young people discover their own feelings, modes of action, and values, and learn to modify them objectively. Role playing and sociodrama are particularly appropriate to the young child's way of exploring ideas by playing characters and improvising action. In the Shaftels' program, for example, the children are given a situation where they find money on the classroom floor and must role play what they would do—return it to the owner or pocket it. Besides such contrived situations, the Shaftels also use a number of study prints to encourage children to act out their approach to the illustrated dilemma—should bystanders have a responsibility to stop a fight between a bully and an obviously smaller child?

LITERATURE

In many elementary school programs, children's literature is not a separate, distinct area of the curriculum. Although many educators argue that it deserves more attention, literature is commonly addressed only when it contributes to regular curricular areas such as social studies or reading. Literature is especially valuable to the social studies; as Elliot Eisner points out, this area of the arts gives children the opportunity to "play with images, ideas, and feelings, to be able to recognize and construct the multiple meaning of events, to perceive and conceive of things from various perspectives."[8] This philosophy pertains to all the arts, of course, but underscores the importance of using a wide variety of literary works to show the many ways people interact with each other and with their environment. Literature is a vital part of the cultural heritage and should be an inherent part of all social studies programs. We have covered the use of literature in Chapter 7; let us say only that by providing a wide range of pleasant experiences with literature in the social studies, teachers help children develop the feeling that "one good book leads to another." An interest in reading helps children discover how interesting it can be to express themselves in writing.

WRITTEN EXPRESSION

Learning to communicate thoughts and feelings through written expression is a significant event in each child's life. When we provide writing experiences in the social studies, we must be extremely aware of the degree to which we allow a child to pour out her ideas, experiences, or desires. The experience can be a happy, creative endeavor or it can be boredom and drudgery. Certainly you will spur the children to encounter the excitement of stretching their imaginations through the medium of original written expression. But to help children achieve full satisfaction from writing, you must guide and support them along the way. You have learned much of what you need to know about written expression in your language arts methods course, so we will concentrate on some forms of written expression that seem especially appropriate for the social studies classroom.

Creative Stories

Prerequisite to creative story writing is a rich, broad program in oral expression. Children's first story experiences are usually of the *language experience* type, in which children see the teacher write down their own words. When they begin to acquire handwriting skills and have been exposed to a variety of experiences, children become ready to reproduce all their interesting experiences in their own handwriting.

Children's first stories, therefore, are usually about something that has happened to them. Gradually, they call upon their inborn creative abilities and begin to write stories they "make up." On the first attempt to interest children in creative writing experiences, you cannot simply tell them to "be creative in writing this story"; you must furnish guidance and direction.

Begin by encouraging a great deal of focused informal conversation among the children. You might want to help children build a *descriptive vocabulary* for spring,

FIGURE 10–5
Picture Me

in which case you might ask the children to tell you "sights of spring," "sounds of spring," "smells of spring," and list the descriptive phrases on the board or chart paper. If you want to help children extend their *general vocabulary*, your task would be to structure oral activities in ways that help the children enjoy learning many different kinds of new words. The purpose of oral activity, then, is to introduce new words into the child's spoken vocabulary so they can call upon them to enrich the creative writing experience.

One teacher, realizing that her children were especially interested in knowing more about each other, began her creative writing program by passing out a sheet like the one illustrated in Figure 10–5. She invited the children to talk about themselves by filling in the blanks with words that could be funny or serious. The teacher read the lines and invited the children to offer descriptive words for the first line. Children initially offered colors, *blue, brown,* and *green,* but soon words like *pretty, big, shiny,* and *narrow* began to enter the activity. As the children offered each word, the teacher wrote it on the chalkboard for the children's use when they filled in each blank on their papers.

After this first creative writing activity, the teacher went on to enrich the children's language growth by providing a number of similar activities in other contexts. For example, she introduced *couplets* and *triplets* (two- or three-line rhymes) by first asking children to generate lists of words, for example, related to winter. Let us assume she asked the children to think of all the different things we see during winter. The children responded: "snow," "Christmas trees," "frost," "ice." The teacher then said she was going to try to make up a rhyme about winter and asked the children to use the words they had generated or to give another word to help her finish the rhyme:

> Winter is nice
> But don't slip on the _____ .

Eventually, she encouraged the children to make up their own wintertime couplets or triplets by thinking of the sights, smells, tastes, and feels of the season.

These are some of the language arts activities that might be used in the social studies program.

1. *Haiku.* This highly structured form of Japanese poetry consists of three lines of seventeen syllables—the first and third lines have five syllables each and the second line has seven. These poems usually describe nature and appeal to children of all ages.

   > The rain is falling.
   > Soon the flowers will burst out.
   > Spring is beautiful!

   Tankas are extensions of haikus; they add two lines of seven syllables to the haiku and contain a total of thirty-one syllables:

   > Big puffy white clouds
   > Floating across a blue sea.

A white castle there?
Maybe a giant white ship?
What do you want them to be?

2. *Endings.* Ask the children to write stories that *end* with a sentence you provide for them, such as:

I'll never do that again!
And that's how the state of Texas got longhorn cattle.
"Mrs. Jackson is right, Melissa. There is a city law against keeping a horse in your backyard."
And, even though Lake Michigan still faces other problems, fish are finding it a safe place to live again.
We held onto our lifeboats for what seemed like forever!

3. *Objects.* Bring in intriguing objects related to a topic of study and encourage children to write about them. Perhaps the children could pretend to be that object and describe a typical day as the object.

4. *Historical Transplants.* Describe the reactions of famous people of the past if they were to come back to life today. What do they see or experience that would make them happy? Unhappy? Afraid?

5. *Character Transplants.* Take someone who has assumed a strong stance on a particular issue (like Jane Fonda) and place him or her into a new situation—for example, as a Colonial housewife. Of course, the character's personality and attitudes must remain unchanged.

6. *Someone I Admire.* Invite the children to write about the most impressive character they ever met.

7. *Unusual Questions.* Put a series of unusual questions about a social studies topic on the board and invite the children to write about one:

What does Paul Revere's horse think of him?
What is it like being a skyscraper?
How would you like to yabber with a jackeroo?
How did bees get such small waists?

8. *Story Starters.* Provide beginnings to stories and ask the children to complete them. For example:

"The storm lasted two days and two nights. I never saw waves so high or the wind blow so hard. Our ship was thrown against huge rocks and was smashed to bits. We held onto our lifeboats for longer than I could remember and finally spotted some land. . ."

9. *Diaries.* Use popular situations (such as Columbus's journey to America) or famous personalities as a stimulus to write daily diary entries. For example, a diary can be used to extend the *story starter* in # 8:

"Day 10. Fresh water is disappearing. Captain Jones divided us into four groups. Each group was to go in a different direction to search for fresh water. In midafternoon the fourth group found a freshwater spring on the west side of the island."

10. *A-B-C Stories.* Use the names of personalities, places, events, or holidays as beginning letters for each line of a poem or story.

   A is for *apron*, which must be worn by the Amish women at all times.
   M is for *marry*. You cannot marry someone outside the Amish faith.
   I is for *isolated*. Amish keep apart from other people.
   S is for *shun*, to keep away from those who break Amish rules.
   H is for *hats*, which must be worn by men at all times (except in houses, churches, or schools).

11. *Cartoons.* Select comic page cartoon panels and white out the captions. Invite the children to create their own captions.

12. *Letters.* Children can utilize their letter writing skills in a variety of social studies situations:

   To say thank you to people involved in field trips or resource persons
   To companies, travel agencies, and the like to request information
   To personalities being studied—George Washington, Abraham Lincoln, Jefferson Davis, and so on
   To authors or publishers of books and magazines to complain or congratulate
   To invite people to visit the classroom
   To a sick classmate or one who has moved
   To children in other places (pen pals). These are some pen pal sources:

The Canadian Education Association 151 Bloor Street, West Toronto, Ontario M561V5, Canada	Student Letter Exchange R.F.D. No. 4 Waseca, MN 56093
League of Friendship, Inc. P.O. Box 509 Mt. Vernon, OH 43050	World Pen Pals 1690 Como Avenue St. Paul, MN 55108
The International Friendship League 40 Mt. Vernon Street Boston, MA 02108	Youth of All Nations 16 St. Luke's Place New York, NY 10014

13. *Biographies.* Children research and write biographies of people they have learned about during a particular topic of study. Also, "Made Up" biographies provide enjoyment and good motivation for reading.

14. *Editorials.* Encourage children to study editorials in newspapers and see how they reflect a writer's opinion. Compare editorials with the front page where stories report only the facts of an event. Ask the children to write editorials about a special contemporary or historical concern. One boy was concerned about his principal's decision to remove the restroom door as a measure to curb vandalism and expressed his feelings in the editorial shown in Figure 10–6. His friend, sharing the same feelings, offered to supply the accompanying political cartoon.

15. *Newspapers.* Children benefit most when their classroom newspaper is based on what they know about real newspapers. A trip to a newspaper publisher can help the children understand how newspapers are planned and produced.

"Are bathrooms private anymore

Mr. Towson has a great sence of hummer, his last joke was the funnyest of of all. "You better sit down for this Ready?" Okay - He took... you sure your ready for this... Well, he took the bathroom door off See! I told you should sit down. Now you propally think all the resonibillaty has gone to his head. Well for once I think he's absolutely almost right. Heres his side. Someone took three rolls of tolite paper in the toilet and flush it. It flooded the bathroom and the boys locker room. But taking the bathroom door off is to much. I mean you ever try and go in the bathroom with about 50 girls standing in front. But, there is a good part, the vandalism has gone down.
Now Mr. Towson has something to worry about that is weather the school board impeaches him and if the health board calls the school a health hazid.

Har! A littel town with a littel school has there own Watergate. I can see the head of linds now "First Princepal to be Impeached." I thought Mr. Towson is a nice guy (sometimes). But the health hazard is yet a nother thing. But don't worry Mr. Towson will figure out some and we hop bathrooms are still private

Chris

OH The Bathroom, first open Door on the right

FIGURE 10–6

Sample Editorial

Although newspaper publishers differ in organizational arrangements, some responsibilities of newspaper people can be simulated in the classroom; for example:

Publisher—owner or person who represents the owner; responsible for the overall operation of the newspaper. (The teacher usually assumes this position.)

Editors—responsible for several facets of newspaper production, such as deciding what goes into the newspaper, assigning reporters to cover events, determining where to position the stories, or writing their opinions of significant events (editorials).

Reporters—cover the stories; columns to which reporters can be assigned include class news, school news, local, state, national, and world news, sports, or special events; reporters can interview others as primary sources for gathering their news or use any secondary sources, such as radio, television, newspaper, or magazines.

Feature writers—produce special columns such as jokes and riddles, lost and found, a variation of Dear Abby, recipes, and so on.

Copy editors—read stories for mistakes and adjust length to meet space requirements.

After assigning several students to the news gathering and processing activities, you will want to get the rest of the class involved in these "behind the scenes" departments:

Production department—put pictures and stories together and get them ready for printing. (Children who know how to use the typewriter, or have a desire to learn, make special contributions here.)

Art department—create ads (with pictures) that highlight coming events, special sales, parent meetings, special assemblies, or other important school functions.

Mechanical department—run the ditto machine or copier, collate the newspaper pages, staple them, and get them ready for distribution.

Circulation department—deliver the newspaper to the principal, other teachers, and classmates.

By simulating a real newspaper, children bring more interest and excitement to their work. Be careful, though, to make sure that all children have an equal opportunity to assume as many different newspaper responsibilities as possible. Let them try the various jobs so they develop a complete understanding of the many duties performed on a real newspaper and enlarge their interests in the different areas. Figure 10–7 is an example of an elementary class's newspaper.

Reports

Children in the middle and upper elementary grades often work on independent research and inquiry activities, so they have many opportunities to write reports. In fact, most of their learning activities can result in some type of oral or written

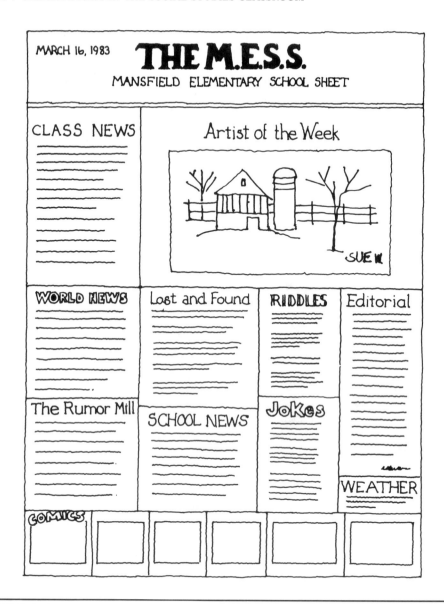

FIGURE 10–7

Newspaper (Adapted from a creative classroom newspaper program developed by Dr. John Heaps when he was a laboratory school teacher at Mansfield (PA) State College.)

report: research accounts based on readings, interviews, and experiments; or accounts of personal or class experiences such as field trips or polls. As with creative story writing, reports in the early primary grades are normally in the form of experience charts, but in the later grades, it is important to extend all the developing study skills while helping children locate information, select the most appropriate,

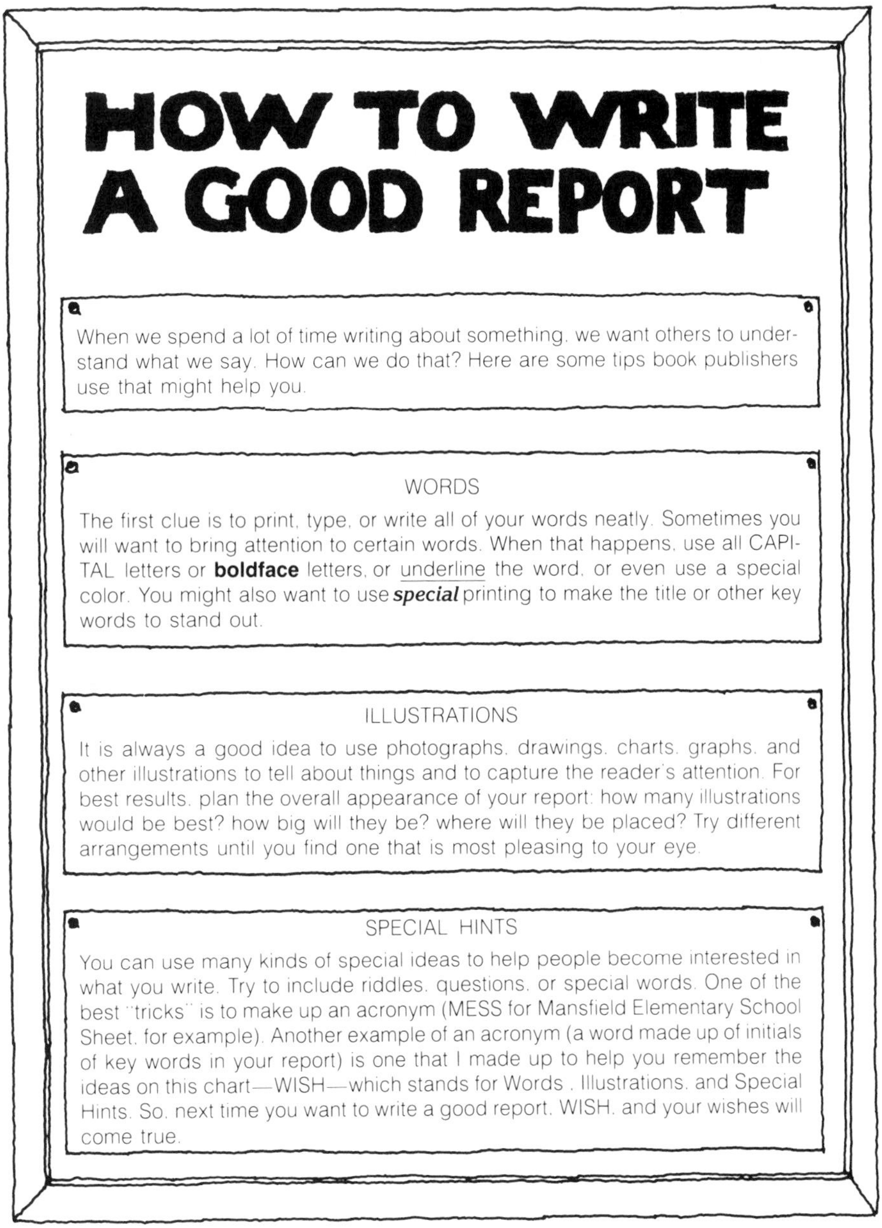

HOW TO WRITE A GOOD REPORT

When we spend a lot of time writing about something, we want others to understand what we say. How can we do that? Here are some tips book publishers use that might help you.

WORDS

The first clue is to print, type, or write all of your words neatly. Sometimes you will want to bring attention to certain words. When that happens, use all CAPITAL letters or **boldface** letters, or underline the word, or even use a special color. You might also want to use *special* printing to make the title or other key words to stand out.

ILLUSTRATIONS

It is always a good idea to use photographs, drawings, charts, graphs, and other illustrations to tell about things and to capture the reader's attention. For best results, plan the overall appearance of your report: how many illustrations would be best? how big will they be? where will they be placed? Try different arrangements until you find one that is most pleasing to your eye.

SPECIAL HINTS

You can use many kinds of special ideas to help people become interested in what you write. Try to include riddles, questions, or special words. One of the best "tricks" is to make up an acronym (MESS for Mansfield Elementary School Sheet, for example). Another example of an acronym (a word made up of initials of key words in your report) is one that I made up to help you remember the ideas on this chart—WISH—which stands for Words, Illustrations, and Special Hints. So, next time you want to write a good report, WISH, and your wishes will come true.

FIGURE 10–8

Special Hints for Writing a Good Report

and organize it into a comprehensive written account. By the time children reach the upper grades, they sould be able to write reports that exhibit these basic skills:

Determining appropriate sources of information

Searching for the main idea in specific reading materials

Deciding what facts are important

Organizing the selected information into a readable and understandable report (without *copying* from a resource)

Figure 10–8 illustrates some of the considerations children should keep in mind as they prepare written reports. You may want to prepare guidelines in chart or bulletin board form so the children can refer to it when needed.

MUSIC

To develop a musical segment of your social studies program, consider the dimensions and directions organized by Alexander Frazier in Table 10–3.

In the social studies program, we do not formally teach Orff, Suzuki, or any of the other approaches employed by music teachers. Melody and rhythm as they express people's values and feelings, however, are an excellent vehicle (along with the other arts) for understanding and expressing aspects of a culture that cannot be effectively communicated in any other way:

> People have sent messages across distances by pounding on drums. People have marched off to war to stirring music and down the aisle to the joyous strains of a wedding march. People—great crowds of people—have raised their voices in national anthems. People have sung work songs or chants to keep their work rhythm straight as they pulled in nets or pried rails back into line. People have sung songs of worship in camp meetings and cathedrals, and they have celebrated harvests with festive dances. People have expressed their grief in tender ballads and their love in songs and dances both tender and gay. People have delighted in playacting that brought song and dance to the stage. They have been eager everywhere to listen to good music sung and played for itself alone. Wherever and whenever possible, people have gained satisfaction and joy in making music for themselves and for others.[9]

How can children be helped to understand all of this? Certainly, they must have experiences with many kinds of music. The primary aim is not to develop musical talent, but to think of music as an enjoyable art form and as a means of self-expression. Music and associated movements or dance can be used in the social studies program to enhance understandings of other cultures and for creative self-expression. Folk songs that reveal cultural or ethnic characteristics are a good example of the first use. But teachers cannot simply put a record on the record player and listen passively with the children. Elementary school children require more stimulation than that; they need a confident, expressive teacher who does not hesitate

TABLE 10–3
The Functions of Music

Function	Type of music	
	Vocal	*Instrumental*
Communicating (over distance)	Yodels	Drum messages
		Band music (at sports events)
Marching, parading	Marching songs	Marches: military, wedding, funeral, parade
Uniting together	War songs	Dances: tribal
	Patriotic songs	
Working	Work songs and chants	Recorded music in stores and factories
Worshiping	Masses	Processionals
	Oratorios	
	Hymns	
Celebrating, rejoicing	Victory hymns and chants	Victory dances
		Festival music
	Holiday songs	Folk dances
Grieving	Ballads	Funeral marches
	Lamentations	
Romancing, courting	Love songs	Dances of many kinds
Playacting	Opera	Incidental music for plays and background music for movies
	Operetta	
	Musical comedy	
Pleasing self and others, entertaining	Art songs, popular songs	Chamber music
		Ballet
	Choral works	Symphonies
		Solo works of many kinds

From Alexander Frazier, *Values* (Boston: Houghton Mifflin, 1980). Reprinted by permission.

to get up and begin to dance. A folk dance, for example, encourages vigorous participation while helping children acquire individual responses to a creative art form.

A folk dance is a model the children must copy, and some teachers prefer not to use a patterned experience initially. Instead, they prefer to stimulate free movement during the first creative movement activities. Eastern and African music are outstanding sources for individual responses. The teacher encourages children to move according to how the music makes them feel. If the children seem self-conscious at first, try using colorful scarves, streamers, or balloons to start the dance activity. These accessories divert attention from the children and help minimize self-consciousness.

Both planned dance experiences and free movement activities are delightful activities to draw upon. They can be further enhanced by inviting resource people into the classroom to share their talents with the children or by allowing children to use musical instruments during the activity. Whatever the situation, combining musical experiences with other parts of the social studies program demonstrates to children that music is an integral part of all people's lives rather than a form of expression for only a talented few.

SUMMARY

Children wonder about many different things in the social studies, including many kinds of artistic expression, and teachers must provide a balance between content and experience. Children need, of course, to learn about Stephen Foster or Beethoven, but they are more motivated to learn if they can dance or sing. They must encounter art products of different cultures and be encouraged to let their own creative talents spill out—by illustrating a poem they have written or dramatizing jobs they have observed during a trip to a department store. Children can learn to write, paint, sing, or dance without learning about Picasso, Mark Twain, or Marian Anderson, but to really learn about and appreciate the arts, both content and experience are necessary.

Perhaps no area of the elementary school curriculum is so well matched to the normal creative tendencies of childhood as the social studies. So the social studies program should provide many experiences in the creative arts, including those that fall into these two broad categories: (1) sharing the creative arts of various cultures, and (2) providing for children's creative arts expression within the classroom.

By sharing the creative arts of various cultures, teachers help children understand and appreciate a society's imagination and enthusiasm, for it is through the arts that a people's triumphs and failures are most vividly portrayed.

Children's exposure to the arts should not stop with exploration; they also need to creatively express what they learn. Among the many creative opportunities in the social studies program are:

- Art activities—dioramas, murals, mosaics, prints, collages, illustrations, television
- Construction activities
- Creative dramatics—dramatic play, pantomime, improvised skits, puppetry
- Literature
- Written expression—creative stories, reports
- Music

The arts provide a valuable source of new information about people and a good base for inquiry learning. In the process, the children not only learn content, but broaden their understandings to a culture's "feeling dimension." As children express themselves through the arts, they not only present ideas vividly and forcefully, but they tap the natural tendency to share with others through creative expression.

ENDNOTES

1. Albert Cullum, *Push Back the Desks* (New York: Citation Press, 1967), pp. 52–53.

2. Edith W. King, *The World: Context for Teaching in the Elementary School* (Dubuque, IA: William C. Brown, 1971), pp. 5–6.

3. Patricia McCormack, "Are School Art Courses a Frill or a Staple?" (West Chester, PA: *Daily Local News*, Wednesday, November 13, 1985), p. A15.

4. Patricia McCormack, "Are School Art Courses a Frill or a Staple?" p. A15.

5. "Performing Together: The Arts in Education." (Arlington, VA: Arts Alliance for Arts Education, 1985).

6. Leslie D. Zeleny, "How to Use Sociodrama," in *How to Do It Series*, no. 20 (Washington, DC: National Council for the Social Studies, 1964), pp. 4–5.

7. Fannie R. Shaftel and George Shaftel, *Role Playing and Social Values* (Englewood Cliffs, NJ: Prentice-Hall, 1967).

8. Elliot Eisner, *The Arts, Human Development, and Education* (Berkeley, CA: McCutcheon Publishing, 1976), p. vii ff.

9. Alexander Frazier, *Values* (Boston: Houghton Mifflin, 1980), p. 141.

Planning Lessons and Units

KEY CONCEPTS

☐ *Using a recommended format for constructing long- and short-term social studies teaching plans*

☐ *Selecting a topic and organizing the most suitable teaching strategies*

☐ *Understanding and using various methods for evaluating instructional objectives*

☐ *Identifying physical and mental impairments found among elementary school pupils and devising ways to adapt teaching strategies to these special conditions*

Teaching is an art form and the lesson plan is its working sketch. As the goal of art is unity, it is unity that becomes the key to effective lesson planning. Whether the impression to be conveyed is an emotional or an intellectual one, it must be a unified impression. Any effective lecture or inquiry lesson has a totality of its own which is the result of its unity. Most beginning teachers and not a few veterans collapse in hopelessly fragmented lessons . . . [ending] with . . . bewildered students . . . asking themselves, after thirty minutes of holding forth, "So what?" . . . After twenty-five years of attending classes and ten years of watching colleagues teach, I can still count on one hand the number of teachers whose classroom presentation reflected some notion of unit.[1]

It is exciting for all beginning teachers to plan and present a lesson to a group of children for the very first time. As with any creative endeavor, teachers go about the task of planning in many different ways. Some writers have favorite pens and writing pads without which they cannot function; some artists must have their palettes arranged just so; actors or actresses must have a perfect emotional climate. Just as each of these settings depends on individual "mystique," so does the creative art of teaching. I cannot handle in this book the many subtle virtuosities that will influence your teaching of fourth-grade social studies, but I can help you maximize your flexibility so that you can become one of those teachers who operates effectively in many styles. Then you will be able to react to a teaching situation with a style that is appropriate rather than because it is the only one you know.

Figure 11–1 illustrates my conceptualization of available teaching options. I specify four not because they are universally accepted or because they are the only styles; they are merely a convenient way of thinking about all the different facets of social studies instruction. Good teachers usually intermix the components of each style into a personalized teaching strategy.

We have discussed the basic characteristics of each of these styles throughout this text. Your success in teaching will depend on two factors: (1) awareness of your role as prescribed by a particular teaching model; and (2) willingness to carry out

FIGURE 11–1

Instructional Patterns

that role with insight and enthusiasm. Although there are differences among teaching models, all have certain principles in common:

- Individual differences among children must be recognized and accounted for.
- Instructional needs can be met most effectively if they are accurately identified and matched with appropriate teaching resources and strategies.
- Children must be motivated to learn before one can expect success with any model.
- You must provide appropriate activities and materials that lead to successful challenges.
- Children can experience success if the teacher presents instructional activities in such a way that they make sense to the children.

UNIT PLANS

As Kellum says, facilitating children's learning in the social studies is largely a matter of organizing and manipulating the environment so that all learning experiences are characterized by some degree of *unity*. If we do not systematically plan what we offer to the children, we risk having random and chaotic lessons that cause children to wonder what they are supposed to be learning. Traditionally, social studies teachers have organized instruction in the form of long-term plans called *units*.

Most teachers develop units around chapters in social studies textbooks. Because the children's textbooks are accompanied by extensive teacher's guides, they are handy sources upon which to build instructional sequences. As teachers gain experience, however, they often find that the textbook does not suit all children in all instances. These teachers may center their programs around the content or concepts of the textbook and use many of the suggestions in the teacher's guide, but personalize these components to achieve more self-directed learning and creativity.

Choosing a Topic

Unit plans begin with a teacher's desire to pursue a topic in an organized way. Choosing a topic calls for answering the question, "Where do I want to go?" For that reason, deciding upon a topic for a social studies unit is much like planning a vacation—both processes involve similar logical thinking patterns.

Assume that it is the beginning of spring break and you and a group of friends have the opportunity to visit one of four possible vacation spots: Bermuda, Paris, Florida, or Vail, Colorado. This kind of decision would most probably involve much discussion of the merits of each place, since "individual differences" are sure to influence your final decision. For example, if no one is a skier, you would certainly rule out Vail. If most individuals were interested in swimming, sunning, or some other aspect of the state of Florida, that might be the best location for a successful vacation.

Regardless, the decision involves a great deal of careful deliberation before eventually taking a direction. Planning a teaching topic is a similar process. You do not simply choose a topic out of the air and use it; you must consider the talents and interests of each child in your classroom. Therefore, just as you and your friends can choose from among several vacation spots, you can choose from among hundreds, or perhaps thousands, of topics for your program and suit them to the needs and interests of your children. This is only a small sampling of possible social studies topics:

Cities, Towns, Suburbs	We Have Many Wants and Needs
Consumer Concerns	England and Her American Colonies
Weather and Climate	Settlers Move Westward
Understanding Myself	Civil War Divides a Nation
A Nation of Immigrants	Old and New in Japan
Practicing Map and Globe Skills	A Trip Through China
The United States Government	Transportation
Tundra Regions	Canada: Neighbors to the North
The Philippine People	Explorers and Discoverers
Protecting our Wildlife	Deciduous Forest Regions
Community Workers	Women Work for Equal Rights
Games Around the World	Our Country
Family Groups	How are Human Beings Alike and Different?
How are Laws Made?	
We Have Beliefs	Religions of the World
The Pollution of Our Environment	War and its Influence on Change
	Canals and Early Railroads
A War for Independence	The Importance of Culture

Although many teachers have complete freedom to choose topics for their classrooms, others are bound by recommendations from one or several different sources, including the most frequent sources—textbooks and districtwide curriculum guides. Check your college curriculum library for textbooks or curriculum guides for a grade level you might teach. Inspect the contents to analyze the various topics offered to teachers as directions for study. Some school districts demand that teachers sequentially cover each topic from either the curriculum guide or the textbook while others encourage teachers to choose topics. Some districts want a coordinated schoolwide program where all teachers are aware of each other's responsibilities; others value a program that responds to children's fluctuating needs and interests. If you are free to choose topics, you must determine whether a topic you are considering is suitable for the children. These guidelines will help you evaluate a topic:

1. Is it suited to the developmental level of the children?
2. Will the children find the topic interesting?
3. Do the children have the necessary background of experiences to cope with the skills and concepts involved in this new topic?
4. Is the topic relevant and realistic in terms of the contemporary world?
5. Is the topic significant enough to warrant classroom time and effort?
6. Are adequate materials available for the children?
7. Are adequate teaching resources available (films, art supplies, recordings)?
8. Will continuity of experiences before and after study be considered?

Choosing a topic for study is an involved, time-consuming procedure. Certain responsibilities of a new job may prevent you from giving the time and effort necessary to independently choose and carry out plans for a topic of instruction. Hanna, Potter, and Reynolds suggest an advantage of using preprepared curricula for beginning teachers:

> The choice for a beginning teacher is difficult. He will have problems of organization and must familiarize himself with many things before a suitable [topic] for his class may be chosen and initiated. In these cases, the principal, the curriculum coordinator, or the supervisor serve as integrating agents. Conferences on the choice of a [topic] for a particular group should be planned before school opens or early in the year . . . . If children are encouraged to continue with (their) interests until the teacher has had time to become acquainted with his group, leads for guiding the children into the selection of a new [topic] are usually perceived. The values of a curriculum framework for new teachers are evident. If a curriculum organization has been developed for a school, the choice can be made within the established framework with confidence and assurance. The fact that the framework has been built upon a careful study of the needs and interests of children means that the unit selected is considered . . . to be of value to children.[2]

Considering this argument, some school districts suggest that beginning teachers use a textbook or curriculum guide, but encourage them to gradually supplement strategies to meet special needs and interests. Regardless, you must choose to some degree from among the topics available for your social studies programs. Suppose that you and your friends chose Florida as your vacation spot for spring break; in short, you answered the question, "Where do we want to go?" just as you will when you must choose a social studies topic for your children.

Suppose you choose as a unit topic *Explorers to the New World*. This title is fine, but it fails to inform anyone of the direction in which you intend to guide the unit. For that reason, and to help you organize your planning, it is best to write a brief, descriptive paragraph indicating the emphasis of the unit. This statement of unit emphasis was written for a fifth-grade unit on Explorers to the New World:

By 1620, the desire to find better routes for trade and travel brought explorers from European nations to the shores of the New World. Eventually, many considered this new land a place for freedom and opportunity. Settlers came from Europe and made their new homes along the eastern shore. Soon these people faced major decisions regarding their welfare and order. The kinds of decisions these brave settlers faced and the methods they used to make them forged the mold of a great new nation.

The next task the teacher faces in unit planning is choosing and organizing the content. Probably the most popular method of doing so is the *conceptual* approach, which includes three main steps: selecting generalizations, identifying main ideas, and choosing what basic information to present.

Selecting Generalizations

The teacher must first research the unit topic to become familiar with the possible content from which to develop generalizations. Remember that generalizations are broad statements containing two or more concepts from the social sciences that serve as subject matter organizers. Generalizations should be broad enough to establish a focus for the unit, but should not be limited to spelling out the exact subject matter. Two teachers chose these generalizations for a unit based on the same theme:

TEACHER #1, "EXPLORERS TO THE NEW WORLD"

Generalizations

1. People with strong *convictions* frequently band together to seek a new environment. (Sociology)

2. All societies make laws that *govern* their members' behaviors. (Political Science)

3. Nearly all human beings have *special skills* and *capabilities* that make valuable contributions to a culture. (Anthropology)

TEACHER #2, "EXPLORERS TO THE NEW WORLD"

Generalizations

1. *Geographic factors* and *natural resources* influence what jobs people do. (Geography)

2. The *economy* of a country is based on its available *resources*. (Economics)

3. Humanity's struggle for *freedom* has been expressed in different ways throughout history. (History)

From these two examples, we can make several important points:

- Generalizations are based upon the social science disciplines.

- The generalizations are so broad that they might be used with almost any unit dealing with almost any societal or cultural group (American Indians, Japanese, Latin Americans).

- Although both teachers chose completely different generalizations to direct and organize their units, one cannot say that chances for success in one unit will be greater than that of the other. Both teachers determined what was best for their students' interests and needs at the time.

Identifying Main Ideas

The second step for the teacher is to identify two to five main ideas directly related to the unit topic to support each generalization. Teacher #1, for example, chose these main ideas:

Generalization 1: People with strong convictions frequently band together to seek a new environment.

Main Ideas:
1. The desire for better trade routes brought explorers from many nations to the New World.
2. The early colonists established colonies in the New World for many different reasons.

Generalization 2: All societies make laws governing their members' behaviors.

Main Ideas:
1. The Pilgrims established a form of government to please the majority.
2. Many outstanding leaders influenced the government of the people.

Generalization 3: Nearly all human beings have special skills and capabilities that make valuable contributions to a culture.

Main Ideas:
1. The Pilgrims endured because they were able to develop survival skills in a new environment.
2. The Pilgrims worked together and contributed special skills to the improvement of their communities.

Notice that each of the main ideas relates more specifically to the topic under study and focuses the subject matter of the unit more narrowly. The teacher can now select specific content for a logical instructional sequence.

Choosing Basic Information

The third step in planning a unit is to select the basic information needed to develop and deepen the child's thinking about the concepts, generalizations, and main ideas. Each of the larger ideas must be based on sound, well-organized information. Identifying information brings the content into final focus and prevents instruction from wandering in many different directions. Teacher #1 might select this information for her first generalization:

Generalization 1: People with strong convictions frequently band together to seek a new environment.

Main Idea 1: The desire for better trade routes brought explorers from many nations to the New World.

Information:

1. Spain's desire to find an all water route to the East Indies brought Columbus to the New World in 1492.

2. John Cabot claimed North America for England as he led the first English voyage to the New World in 1497.

3. Jacques Cartier claimed portions of North America for France as he sailed up the St. Lawrence River to seek an all water route to the East.

4. Henry Hudson explored parts of North America as he sought a Northwest Passage to the East.

Main Idea 2: The early colonists established colonies in the New World for many different reasons.

Information:

1. Pilgrims and French Huguenots left their countries because they wanted religious freedom.

2. Colonists from several nations came to the New World to establish trade.

3. Many adventurers came to the New World with hopes of finding gold and other riches.

4. Some settlers came to the New World in hopes of finding good farm land.

As you can see from the examples for each step, it is best to organize the material in outline form that suits your personal style.

Selecting Appropriate Objectives

Choosing a title for a unit provides us with an organizing framework. After we establish our major direction, we must develop objectives—"What do we want to accomplish?" *Objectives* are statements that identify *what* you want your children to accomplish from the planned sequence of instruction, and keep the instructional sequence from wandering aimlessly.

As we observed in Chapter 1, social studies objectives fall into three categories: (1) knowledge, (2) skills, and (3) values. Each category is important, but cannot be equally emphasized during all topics of study because your chief concern during some topics may be values, as in "Understanding Myself"; skills, as in "Practicing Map and Globe Skills"; or knowledge, in "How are Laws Made?" Some units, of course, lend themselves to development of all three categories, such as "Understanding Others."

These are examples of general objectives for the unit, "Explorers to the New World."

1. Children will understand why settlers came to the New World (knowledge and understanding)

2. Children will understand how the early settlers adapted to the environment (knowledge and understanding)

3. Children will be aware of the problems of establishing new communities (knowledge and understanding)

4. Children will use reference materials independently as they seek information (skills)

5. Children will work harmoniously with others as they complete group projects (skills)

6. Children will appreciate the contributions of hard work and loyalty to the growth and development of a nation (attitudes and values)

Remember two important points when you write your unit objectives:

1. State objectives in terms of the *children*. An inappropriate objective would be one that describes the behavior of the teacher; for example, *The teacher will furnish the children with information about early settlers of America*. When you identify objectives, your statements must describe what you want the *children* to accomplish; *your* expectations, of course, are to make sure the objectives are realized.

2. List only a few objectives. One problem characteristic of many beginning teachers is to state *too many* objectives. You can expect a topic of study in the primary grades to last for one to two weeks, and in the upper grades from two to three weeks. That time limitation restricts you to choosing only objectives that appear most desirable. It is usually appropriate to list from four to seven or eight objectives for any topic of study.

Some educators criticize unit objectives for being stated too generally to have real meaning. For example, an objective such as "The children will understand that our ancestors were early settlers of America" lacks focus. For that reason, these educators prefer to state objectives in terms of direct, observable behaviors, called *behavioral objectives*. Behavioral objectives identify the specific behaviors children will demonstrate as they progress through the learning activities you plan. Behavioral objectives are comprised of three parts: (1) identifying the input process; (2) describing what the student is to do; and (3) stating the minimum acceptable level of performance

Behavioral objectives frequently give specificity to broader objectives. For example, a general objective might be "The children will understand that our ancestors were early settlers of America." Specific behavioral objectives for this general objective might include: (1) "After viewing a film dealing with the living conditions in England (*input*), the children will be able to write (*what the children are to do*) five reasons why the English came to America (*level of performance*)"; and (2) "After reading five pages in the social studies textbook, the children will draw a picture illustrating the one condition that would make them leave England if they lived there at the time.''

You should state at least *one* specific behavioral objective for each general objective. Proponents of behavioral objectives feel they provide more direction to a unit because each general objective must be examined in greater depth. Depending on the philosophy of a school system, objectives need not always be stated in behavioral terms, but when you want to write a behavioral objective, you will find that certain words or phrases cue in its three parts. To cue in the *input process*, these typical phrases would help:

- After interviewing ten classmates. . . .
- Given an encyclopedia. . . .
- After examining the globe. . . .
- After listening to a taped interview. . . .
- Given five unrelated objects from Brazil. . . .

These phrases alert you to the *observable performance* (what the child is to do):

- . . .the child will write. . . .
- . . .the children will organize. . . .
- . . .the children will compute. . . .
- . . .the children will read aloud. . . .
- . . .the children will list. . . .

Phrases like these cue in the desired *level of performance*:

- . . .five ways to measure the height of a tree.
- . . .a paragraph of five sentences.
- . . .within ten minutes.
- . . .with eighty percent accuracy.
- . . .a minimum of three things they love to do.

Test your ability to identify behavioral objectives by examining this list of five objectives.

1. The children will really understand the concept of exploration after they read five pages from their textbook.
2. Given a scrambled list of capital cities and states, the children will match each capital and its corresponding state with one hundred percent accuracy.
3. After reading a biography of any famous explorer, the children will write a paragraph of nine or ten sentences describing at least two major events in the person's life.

4. To gain insight into the lives of the Pennsylvania Dutch.

5. Other than watching television, the children will write all of the things they could think of doing on a Saturday morning.

Discuss with your classmates the reasons for your choices. I have selected statements 2 and 3 as behavioral objectives. Statement 1 lacks mention of observable performance and level of performance; statement 4 does not include input process, observable performance, or level of performance; and statement 5 does not specify the input process. Do you agree with me? Try rewriting each nonbehavioral objective to make it a behavioral objective.

Learning Activities

Goals or objectives for a unit provide us with direction; they give us *reasons* for pursuing a topic and describe the *outcomes* we wish to attain. For that reason, the types of learning experiences we provide for the children should be closely allied with the stated objectives. Using our trip to Florida as an illustrative example, we must ask ourselves the question, "Now that we've determined *where* we're going and *what* we want to do when we get there, *how* can we get there most efficiently?" We can examine all the possibilities: airplane, boat, car, bus, motorcycle, pogo stick, balloon. Choices are numerous and varied—some are ridiculous selections and would never allow us to satisfy our objectives; others are more realistic and reasonably suited to helping us accomplish our goals. A pogo stick would be useless in relation to the objective of getting to Florida as quickly as possible, but how would our attitudes change if we chose to "break the *Guiness Book of World Records* entry for the longest trip by pogo stick?" Likewise, learning activities that appear appropriate for one set of objectives may be totally useless in accomplishing another set. Too often, activities are chosen because they are "cute" or "gimmicky" and not because they have been identified as the best strategy for accomplishing particular objectives.

What should your children experience and what is your role in that setting? If-then statements will help you choose classroom learning activities. For example:

If we want to provide a quick general overview of events leading to exploration of America, *then* a common textbook reading assignment could be used.

If we want the children to acquire skills of effective problem solving, *then* they should examine town records and conduct interviews to produce a "living history" of their old community.

If we want the children to share their feelings about the accomplishments of the early explorers, *then* small discussion groups operating in an open, trusting environment could be appropriate.

Social studies educators classify learning activities or resources in many ways. Some classify those that are best for the *introductory phases* of unit development (pictures, map study, exhibits) and those that are best for the *developmental phases* (reading, writing, interviewing). Some label activities that are best for *research* (using references, collecting), and others as best for *expression* (murals, music). Still others classify resources or activities under labels such as *dramatics, audiovisual, oral expression,* and so on. A major fault with labeling activities or resources this way is that many are multipurpose. For example, a resource such as a movie can be shown as a *launching activity* at the beginning of a unit to create interest and enthusiasm as well as a common background of knowledge. Or, it may be a *developmental activity* when shown as a source of information. The movie could also be a *culminating activity* if it were shown to summarize main ideas at the end of the unit. Despite the limitations of categorizing activities, we will discuss unit activities as launching activities, developmental activities, and culminating activities.

LAUNCHING ACTIVITIES.   Launching activities are stimulating experiences provided during the first day or two of a unit to arouse curiosity in the topic, introduce the topic to the children, and provide a common experience from which all the children can draw. Usually, you will want to arrange the environment during the launching phase so as to give the children exposure to the topic. Some teachers provide books, pictures, models, realia, clothing, and other items for the children to explore and manipulate. As the children make comments and ask questions of each other, the teacher notes which might be elaborated during a subsequent discussion period. Other teachers may not plan an extensive launching activity; they may simply show a film, read a story, take a field trip, or play a recording. Regardless, your concern is to establish interest, help the children relate the new material to previous experiences, and provide direction for subsequent learning.

DEVELOPMENTAL ACTIVITIES.   After the introductory or interest-generating phase, you will begin appropriate activities for achieving the unit objectives. Know what learning experiences your new class has had prior to entering your classroom. If they had been accustomed to problem-centered learning and group work, you can move on from there. If they have only used a basic textbook with very little enrichment work, you should not plan for great changes during the first few weeks of school. Young children need the security of familiar experiences. Judge where the children are and move them cautiously to where you want them to be. A continuum of teaching methodologies commonly employed during the developmental phase of units is illustrated in Figure 11–2.

After you determine the level of the children's experience, start your instructional pattern there and move the students step by step toward the point you want them to reach.

CULMINATING ACTIVITIES.   Although units are usually planned for periods of two weeks or more, a unit should end when the children's interest begins to wane. Culminating activities bring a smooth conclusion to the study and pull together the learnings gained through various activities. The culmination might be an assembly program to which all parents are invited; completing a map or mural; presenting a play; or visiting a historical site. Whatever you choose, all culminating activities should help children come to conclusions, draw generalizations, evaluate progress, and suggest areas for further study.

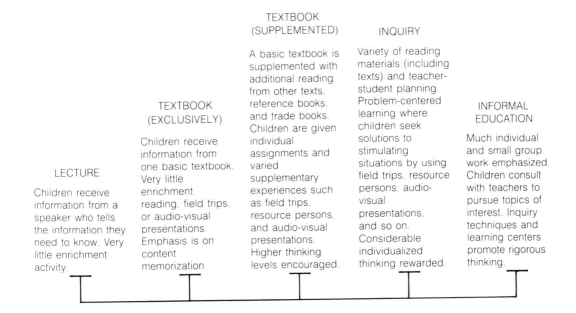

TEXTBOOK
(SUPPLEMENTED)   INQUIRY

A basic textbook is   Variety of reading
supplemented with   materials (including
additional reading   texts) and teacher-
from other texts,   student planning.
reference books,   Problem-centered
TEXTBOOK   and trade books.   learning where   INFORMAL
(EXCLUSIVELY)   Children are given   children seek   EDUCATION
                       individual   solutions to
Children receive   assignments and   stimulating   Much individual
information from   varied   situations by using   and small group
one basic textbook.   supplementary   field trips, resource   work emphasized.
LECTURE   Very little   experiences such   persons, audio-   Children consult
                   enrichment   as field trips,   visual   with teachers to
Children receive   reading, field trips, resource persons,   presentations,   pursue topics of
information from a or audio-visual   and audio-visual   and so on.   interest. Inquiry
speaker who tells presentations.   presentations.   Considerable   techniques and
the information they Emphasis is on   Higher thinking   individualized   learning centers
need to know. Very content   levels encouraged.   thinking rewarded.   promote rigorous
little enrichment memorization.   thinking.
activity.

FIGURE 11–2

A Continuum of Teaching Methodologies Commonly Found in Elementary Social Studies Classrooms

Not all units need to end with a culminating activity. Sometimes the unit that follows is such a natural transition that neither a culminating activity for the first unit nor an introductory experience for the second is necessary. If one unit deals with personal growth, perhaps "Belonging to Groups," stressing the interdependence between individuals and their groups, and the next unit, "Being Yourself," stresses the importance of uniqueness, the continuity need not be broken in the transition from one unit to the other. You will soon learn to judge whether to end a unit with a culminating activity.

You must carefully arrange the three major categories of activities, because each activity flows from preceding experiences and furnishes the foundation for those that follow. Arranging a meaningful sequence is like putting together a puzzle (Figure 11–3). Some teachers fit the pieces together by moving from the specific to the general, as illustrated in the teacher-directed sequence in Figure 11–4. These program designs demand a carefully planned beginning sequence, since all subsequent higher-level thought is based on clear understanding of the topic. The teacher thus deliberately controls learning experiences and sequences them to lead children in a cumulative way to eventual mastery of the whole. This list of activities illustrates how one teacher sequenced instruction for a unit on "Ecology: Save Our Earth."

Activity One. The class will view a film describing various conditions of ecological abuse: acid rain, chemical and sewage pollution, nuclear waste disposal, stripping

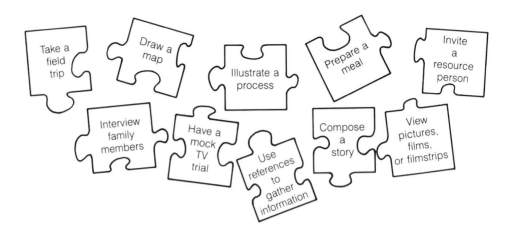

FIGURE 11-3

Putting Together the Pieces of a Unit

of forests, toxic pesticides, and other examples of environmental disregard. Following the film, a Taba concept-formation strategy will be implemented as a discussion guide.

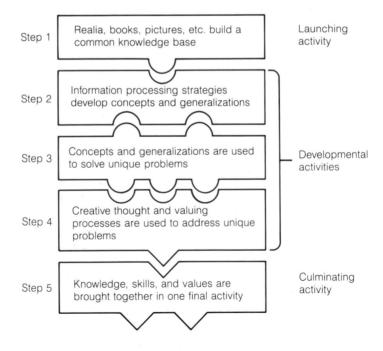

FIGURE 11-4

One Method of Organizing Lessons within a Unit

Activity Two. Review the findings of Activity One. Divide the class into several small groups and ask each group to draw a poster depicting one of the conditions described in the film. Ask each group to explain its poster and display them all on a large bulletin board labeled "Ecology: Save Our Earth."

Activity Three. Invite a senior citizen to speak to the class about changes in the local environment during his lifetime. Discuss the effects of these changes on soil, animals, water, and people.

Activity Four. Ask groups to plan their own "before and after" albums by drawing illustrations of the ideas shared in Activity Three and putting them together in a booklet. As an extension, ask them to illustrate a scene depicting an ecological condition in the year 2100 if current habits do not change.

Activity Five. Today the class will participate in an ecology field trip to a nearby woodland area recently cited in the newspaper as particularly subject to ecological abuse. Ask the children to each remember two glaring examples of ecological abuse they encounter.

Activity Six. Discuss the field trip, including "What did we see at the woodland? What did we learn? How did you feel about what you saw?"

Ask the children to share the two examples of ecological abuse they found and to think about what can be done to eliminate them.

Activity Seven. Review the conditions uncovered during Activities Five and Six. Create committees for dealing with the problems.

Activity Eight. Students do an independent study of what can be done to solve the problems at hand. Encourage them to make proposals for improving the situations.

Activity Nine. Groups organize an action plan for their unique problems. Possibilities include letter writing campaigns, circulating a petition, conducting observations of other sites, writing a letter to the editor of a local newspaper, or organizing a clean-up campaign.

Now let us look at a few of the characteristics of units that avoid predetermined content and activities. Although almost all involve some predetermined processes, they deviate from the premise that learning is necessarily best accomplished as a step by step progression of activities. Self-directed learning units, for example, provide a common experience for children during the launching phase, but instead of merely establishing a unified background of knowledge, they create interest or pose problems that will stimulate independent data collection. The launching, developmental, and culminating activities of a self-directed unit are described in Figure 11–5.

The self-directed program begins with a set of unresolved problems and encourages children to uncover their own data in seeking solutions. The teacher provides guidance throughout the process, but assumes that because the children have selected their own areas of study, their motivation to learn will be much greater than if the content were predetermined. We can illustrate the progression of events in

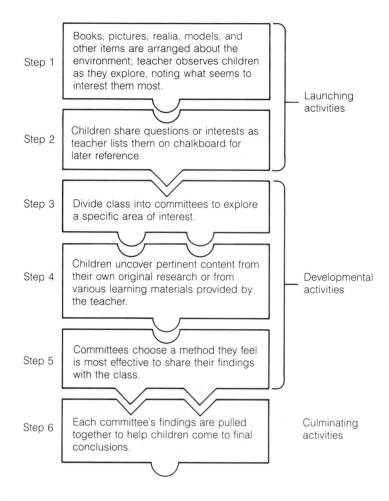

Step 1   Books, pictures, realia, models, and other items are arranged about the environment; teacher observes children as they explore, noting what seems to interest them most.

Step 2   Children share questions or interests as teacher lists them on chalkboard for later reference.

Launching activities

Step 3   Divide class into committees to explore a specific area of interest.

Step 4   Children uncover pertinent content from their own original research or from various learning materials provided by the teacher.

Developmental activities

Step 5   Committees choose a method they feel is most effective to share their findings with the class.

Step 6   Each committee's findings are pulled together to help children come to final conclusions.

Culminating activities

FIGURE 11–5

An Optional System of Organizing Lessons within a Unit

this approach by referring to the ecology sequence. The teacher who is interested in personalized, self-directed learning could use the same sequence but eliminate activities One through Four. This teacher would not consider it efficient to take time to teach specific concepts if she is promoting autonomy and personalized learning. You may wonder how you can be sure the children are learning important concepts through self-directed learning; in fact, you can't. Whenever you make choices in teaching styles, you make trade-offs. If you value self-directed learning, you must believe the children are capable of building their own conceptual structures and that whatever concepts they form are most meaningful because they grow from the children's own interests and thinking. But you cannot assume that all children will acquire a common set of specific, fundamental concepts. If you want to be sure the students develop a particular set of concepts, then the best approach is to structure the learning experiences until they acquire those concepts. *Self-directed* and *directed learning* are both good teaching practices, but they have somewhat contrasting purposes.

LESSON PLANS

A well-planned lesson, like the unit, shows *unity*. A unified lesson incorporates three areas: (1) objectives (2) methods and materials, and (3) evaluation.

Objectives tell the teacher's purpose for the daily lesson. Usually, the teacher develops one, two, or three lesson plans to teach or reinforce one of the long-range objectives from the unit plan. You will often have to clarify your thinking by stating specific behavioral objectives for each long-term objective.

The *methods and materials* section of the plan outlines the procedure a teacher expects to follow to meet the lesson objectives and lists the teaching materials she will use. This section should fall into three parts:

1. A good beginning, in which you arouse curiosity and stimulate the imagination
2. An effective learning situation (for which you should always have a "contingency plan" in case a learning activity falls flat)
3. An effective finale that achieves some sort of intellectual or aesthetic closure

The *evaluation section* states how you will determine the success of the lesson. This section reveals to what extent the objectives were accomplished and what points need to be reemphasized or reinforced.

We will look at a sample lesson plan. For each unit of study, you will need ten to fifteen specific daily plans. Beginning teachers should always write out lesson plans in detail—it helps them organize their thoughts and points out possible weaknesses. Daily lesson plans help us find specific ways to accomplish our stated unit goals.

LESSON PLAN

   I. Unit Objective

     The children will understand why settlers came to the New World.

  II. Behavioral Objectives

     Based on data from a film, the children will identify at least five significant events in the life of any single explorer to the New World.

 III. Methods and Materials

    1. Show the film *Explorers to the New World*.

    2. Hold a brief discussion to summarize major points of the film.

    3. Divide the class into six equal groups, each group representing a prominent early explorer depicted in the film.

4. Call attention to a display entitled "Explorer Hall of Fame." Relate the various halls of fame (baseball, football, rock and roll, etc.) to this hall of fame and inform the children that each group's explorer has been voted into the "Explorer Hall of Fame."

5. Pass out appropriate work materials and have the children prepare a large illustration of their explorer for the hall of fame. Each group will then write a brief biographical description containing at least five significant events in the life of their explorer on a large piece of paper shaped like a plaque.

6. Display the illustrations and plaques in the "Explorer Hall of Fame" and tape record each group's presentation of the accompanying biographical sketch.

7. Play back the entire tape for the class, other classes, or for a parent's night project.

IV. Evaluation

1. Observing the children working in groups.

2. Examining the illustrations.

3. Listening for at least five significant events in the life of the assigned explorers.

Evaluation

We always judge our experiences according to how they fulfill our original expectations or objectives. In the same way, you should constantly examine your unit objectives to judge whether or not they are being accomplished. Before we discuss the various processes of evaluation, however, let us look at what evaluation is. *Evaluation* is any *formal* or *informal* process by which teachers gather and analyze pupil data for the purpose of determining whether changes should be made in a program to more adequately meet unique individual or group needs and interests.

In the past, evaluation involved administering paper-pencil tests. That was fine in the days when command of information was the exclusive social studies goal. On an Indiana statewide test given to all eighth graders in 1887, each student had to score an average of seventy-five on each part without falling below sixty on any subject to qualify for an eighth-grade diploma. These were some of the geography questions:

1. Name the capitals of Germany, Norway, Canada, Kansas, North Carolina.

2. Through what waters would you pass on a voyage by water from Duluth to Panama?

3. What is the Gulf Stream? What effect has it on the climate of Europe?

These are examples of the history questions:

1. Describe the character and purposes of the settlers of Virginia and Georgia. Give names, locations, and dates of their early settlements.

2. Explain nullification, and relate the events connected with that doctrine in our history.

3. Give a brief sketch of the history of Indiana (or your own state).

Evaluation in the past meant that a child's performance on such a test determined his success as far as the social studies curriculum was concerned. When we use the term *evaluation* today, we still focus on a type of value judgment. Because children have uncanny insight into our behaviors and beliefs, the value judgments we make about them have great power. If we, the teachers, believe something about the child, then it must be so! In using factual tests exclusively as an evaluative instrument, we unwittingly help children develop certain beliefs about themselves: "I got the lowest score on the test. That makes me the dumbest kid in class." "I'm going to fail social studies this time. I tried hard, too. I guess I'll never be a good student." "I got a 60 on my last social studies test. I hate that subject!" Our judgments are so crucial in establishing the sense of self that will accompany the youngster into adulthood that we must never confine ourselves to one—perhaps negative—evaluative technique.

Despite their limitations, tests as an evaluative instrument in the social studies curriculum should be used judiciously in conjunction with other procedures. Other evaluative tools help us see that evaluation is an integral part of the learning process. They help us measure growth along each of the social studies objectives—knowledge, skills, and values. Sound evaluation begins with an examination of stated objectives:

■ *Knowledge objectives.* How can we measure learning of facts and concepts?

■ *Skills objectives.* What evidence exists as to the child's ability to gather worthwhile information, work with others in a group, solve problems, and perform other tasks necessary for effective classroom performance?

■ *Values objectives.* How have the children's attitudes and appreciations changed as a result of studying a topic?

By continually examining each category, we are able to judge whether children are progressing satisfactorily toward our objectives. If we find they are not, we may have to reteach certain concepts or provide additional experiences. Figure 11–6 illustrates how the process of evaluation is ongoing. While tests typically measure only how much a child has learned, we have other concerns about how well our objectives are being met.

TEACHER OBSERVATION. Simply watching the children during the social studies class period is perhaps the most popular technique for evaluating knowledge, skills, and attitudes. Information gathered during observations is normally kept for future reference. Teachers often record short but detailed comments on 5″ × 8″ index cards, describing the child's behavior in a variety of situations. These cards are referred to as *anecdotal records* on which you can record any behavior you feel is significant, but not your interpretation of that behavior. For example, a teacher

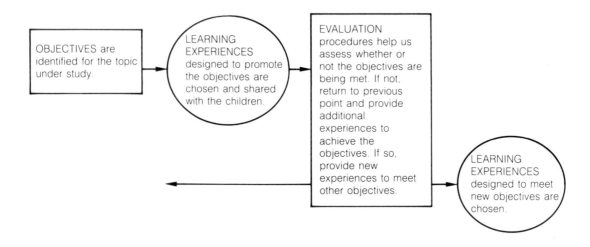

FIGURE 11–6

Process of Evaluation

made this comment about Arnie and placed it in his permanent file to follow him around during each successive year of schooling: "Arnie created a disruption with his social studies' group today by refusing to share a library book with Arlene. His social skills are much below those of the other first graders and will certainly cause him problems as he enters the higher grades." By recording your opinion, especially in reacting to some negative aspect of a child's behavior, you run the risk of stigmatizing that youngster for the rest of his school years. If you *must* enter negative observations, make every effort to balance them with positive comments so that future teachers will be aware of the child's strengths as well as weaknesses. An anecdotal record card might take this form:

Name ____Florence K.____   Grade ___3___

Monday   (10–18–86)

    Worked for 20 minutes alone in the map learning center. Florence can now recognize basic primary-grade map symbols. She still becomes upset, though, when participating in reading related projects.

Wednesday   (11–19–86)

    Florence worked at solitary activities again today. She threw a tantrum when asked to share her materials with others. She appears reluctant to work with others or share her possessions with them.

    Normally, anecdotal records are kept only for those few children who need careful observation for some specific reason, as in the case of Florence's persistently immature social behavior. When you need to record more routine observations, *check-lists* are particularly useful. Checklists focus on many areas of development and can be filled out much more quickly than anecdotal records:

Name of Student: ___Oliver T.___   Yes   No

Knows where to locate information
Assists co-workers when needed
Follows group-established rules
Does fair share of group work
Respects group decisions
Shares materials willingly
Returns materials when finished

WORK SAMPLES.   Many elementary school teachers maintain folders of work samples for each child taken periodically—weekly, biweekly, or monthly—through-out the year. This accumulated work provides an idea of how well a child is progress-ing and what steps might be necessary to reinforce areas of need. The samples are especially useful for sharing with parents during regularly scheduled parent-teacher conferences. Keeping samples of written reports, artwork, and checklists of study skills or other evaluative information for extended periods of time gives us an indi-cation of a child's growth in the program.

GROUP DISCUSSION.   Group techniques were described in detail in Chap-ter 4. In addition to the normal class opportunities available in the social studies classroom, group discussion can be an important evaluative tool in a variety of situa-tions: to follow up a major class activity such as a field trip, a school service project, or a dramatization; to evaluate group reports, unit projects, and creative dramatics activities; to find out how to improve small group endeavors; to evaluate class be-havior in social situations, such as at a school assembly, in the lunchroom, or on the playground; and to work out some classroom human relations problem.

SELF-EVALUATION.   Student checklists, a less frequently used evaluation, are constructed from teacher-pupil planned standards. We are often surprised at chil-dren's reactions when they are given an opportunity to evaluate themselves and let you know whether or not your activities are pleasing or interesting. You can often get feedback like this when you informally ask questions such as, "What did you think of Officer Lincoln's visit to our classroom today? What did you enjoy most (least) about social studies class this morning? Show me what you mean about how the project can be improved."

Teachers sometimes use self-evaluation checklists so children can indicate their feelings about a particular social studies learning activity, as in this example:

Circle the number that shows how strongly you feel.

1. Amount of learning in my committee project

   1   2   3   4   5
   Little   Great

2. Value of what was learned

    1   2   3   4   5
    Little   Great

3. Amount of effort I supplied in my committee

    1   2   3   4   5
    Little   Great

4. How hard our committee worked

    1   2   3   4   5
    Little   Great

5. Additional comments:

TEACHER-MADE TESTS.   Classroom tests measure factual learnings from a unit of instruction. Although they may be used with some success in the primary grades, they are more effective with intermediate- and upper-grade students. Regardless of the form your test takes, the *reason* for giving a test is to evaluate the change demonstrated by the children from the beginning of the unit to the end. For that reason, do not try to "stump" the children by putting in questions unrelated to your emphasis in class or to the unit objectives. Be sure you measure what you want to measure; test scores not only reflect the children's progress but your teaching effectiveness as well. Types of items for tests are these:

Arrange steps in a process

Match events or people and dates

Supply key words missing in statements

Match vocabulary and definitions

Support true-false answers with relevant data

Answer questions from maps, charts, or graphs

Select the most appropriate answer from a list

Although attitudes and values are not as easy to evaluate on teacher-made tests as are factual details, Chase and John suggest several types of questions:

1. To select, from a teacher-prepared dialogue, comments that reveal desirable or undesirable attitudes.
2. To respond, yes or no, to questions that ask, "Do you think. . .?"
3. To respond to a list of statements of belief, feeling, or opinion by indicating degree—always, sometimes, never.
4. To respond to statements that imply prejudice, or lack of prejudice, by indicating statement of agreement—I agree, I disagree, I am uncertain.
5. To match attitudes with likely resultant actions.
6. To state what one liked best about the unit of work being developed.

7. To give opinions about described situations that reveal the attitudes of the characters.

8. To give reasons to support the action that should be taken in a described problem situation.

9. To write an ending to a story that describes a problem situation.

10. To complete an unfinished sentence, such as, "Our unit of work has changed my ideas about. . . ."[3]

In choosing a combination of evaluation approaches, ask yourself, "Do tests provide the bulk of my evaluative data?" If so. . .

- Do I label children on the basis of test results?
- Do I inform children of the results?
- Are the children afraid of the tests?
- Do I identify special talents of children who do poorly on the tests?
- Do the tests influence the relationship between the children and me?
- Do the tests reflect upon my teaching effectiveness?
- Are my objectives for instruction too narrow?

Regarding other areas of evaluation, you must also ask yourself:

- Are skills and attitudes being evaluated along with knowledge and concepts?
- Do my evaluation procedures have an impact on my planning and selection of learning activities and materials?
- Do I encourage the children to express their own feelings regarding the social studies learning experiences?
- Do I encourage student feedback about their own progress?
- Other than report cards, how do I share the results of my evaluation with parents?

So, evaluation in the social studies should be a continuous process and a key component in the teaching-learning process. Seek to design creative, integrated forms of evaluation as you assess both the children's progress and the effectiveness of your teaching strategies. Use these guidelines to develop evaluation procedures for your social studies program:

Think of evaluation as a continuous process and not as an end-product.

Develop cooperative standards with the children before each unit begins.

Encourage self-evaluation by every child or committee.

Be concerned with individual growth, and do not compare children to other members of the class.

Use a variety of evaluation techniques.

The following evaluation techniques were chosen for the unit "Explorers to the New World":

1. The teacher will conduct careful observations of committee members' general work habits as they engage in all phases of unit development. She will record observations on a checklist of appropriate behaviors.
2. Through pupil-teacher discussion, the teacher will evaluate research effort and presentation.
3. The teacher will keep individual folders of representative work samples for comparisons.
4. A short paper-and-pencil test will evaluate mastery of content and development of attitudes.

References

The final section of a unit plan should be a comprehensive list of books, magazines, films, slides, pictures, stories, games, and other resources that contribute to the learning experiences. The reference list, although initially time-consuming, is valuable for gathering and organizing materials when you use the unit again.

ADAPTING INSTRUCTIONAL TECHNIQUES

The Handicapped

"There are more than eight million handicapped children in the United States today, and the special educational needs of these children are not being met. More than one-half do not receive appropriate services . . . and one million are excluded entirely from the public school system."—Introduction to PL 94–142 (1975)

The *Education for All Handicapped Children Act* (Public Law 94–142) was passed by Congress and signed into law by President Gerald R. Ford on November 29, 1975. PL 94–142 is primarily a funding bill offering fiscal support to the states in return for their compliance to its provisions. The law, implemented in steps over a five-year period, required that by September 1, 1980, each state must provide a free, appropriate public education for every handicapped child between the ages of three and twenty-one years.

The law affects all schools and calls for educating handicapped children in "the least restrictive environment," often requiring regular classroom teachers to accommodate handicapped children in their classrooms. Therefore, the money provided through PL 94–142 is made available to help schools make needed changes for these children and provide in-service training so that regular classroom teachers can more effectively integrate children with special needs into the established classroom routine. Moving handicapped children from a special setting into regular classes for their education is called *mainstreaming*. Although PL 94–142 calls for educating youngsters in "the least restrictive environment," it does not specify that such an environment be the regular classroom. Mainstreaming became the accepted practice for implementing PL 94–142 through the efforts of the Council for Exceptional Children (CEC), which identified the regular classroom as the most appropriate educational setting for all children, exceptional and nonexceptional. Underlying this philosophy is a recognition that when handicapped and nonhandicapped children learn, grow, and play together, they develop the sensitivities and understandings necessary for creating interpersonal relationships.

You should know as much as possible about PL 94–142 because as more and more handicapped children become integrated into the regular classroom, your entire program, including social studies instruction, will most likely need to be adjusted to provide appropriate experiences for all. A number of teaching competencies are necessary to make those adjustments; those that follow are specified by the Commonwealth of Pennsylvania from *Guidelines for the Preparation of Teachers in Compliance with U.S. Public Law 94–142*, Pennsylvania Department of Education, 1980. Does your state have a similar listing?

The prospective teacher will:

1. Understand the legal basis for educating students with handicaps in the least restrictive environment.
2. Understand the implications which handicapping conditions have for the learning process.
3. Recognize students who may be in need of special services.
4. Make use of appropriate resource and support services.
5. Confer with and report to parents on educational programs for students with handicaps.
6. Facilitate the social acceptance of persons with handicaps by encouraging positive interpersonal relationships.
7. Use individual, group, and classroom management techniques for effective accommodation of students with handicaps.
8. Assess the educational needs of students with handicaps.
9. Modify instructional strategies to provide for the individual needs of students with handicaps.
10. Evaluate classroom progress of students with handicaps.

SPECIAL HANDICAPS. Elementary school teachers agree that every child is unique and special. For that reason, all of education should be *special education*, and all educational practices should be directed toward meeting each individual's unique needs. Some children, however, have mental or physical difficulties that cause them to differ markedly in behaviors or characteristics from the typical child at a particular age level.

Mentally Retarded Children. Mental retardation has been defined differently by educators throughout the years, most commonly by an IQ score below seventy-five or eighty. Many professionals today, however, question this classification based solely on IQ scores, and federal regulations prohibit educational placement decisions (placement in special education classes) solely on the basis of a single test of intelligence. Thus, you should be aware of alternative methods of determining the extent of mental retardation:

> Observe the child for characteristics or behaviors that are obviously immature for his chronological age.
>
> Examine the child's cumulative records for information regarding the development of such skills as crawling, creeping, walking, and talking.
>
> Evaluate the child's ability to remember things over a period of time.
>
> Check the child's attention span and frustration level.
>
> Examine the child's ability to get along with others and determine whether he is accepted or rejected by his peers.
>
> Observe the child's interest in books or other learning-related materials.

The severity of mental retardation varies widely, from the mildly retarded youngster who fits well into the normal daily routine to the severely retarded child who needs special care and understanding. You will normally have little difficulty absorbing the mentally retarded child into the classroom or providing special educational services if you follow these recommendations:

1. Initiate a systematic procedure for determining the child's level of development and plan a step-by-step program in which the child can experience repeated success.

2. Use as many direct experiences as possible.

3. Use manipulative, real learning materials so the child can experience as many sensory modalities as possible (hearing, seeing, touching, tasting, and smelling) in his learning. Don't rely on talking to the child!

4. Plan for patient repetition because the mentally retarded child needs more time than his normal counterpart to grasp ideas—be tolerant and understanding.

5. Provide constant reinforcement through reward and praise for each accomplishment.

6. Provide many opportunities for the child to speak. Piaget, Chomsky, and others describe the interrelated development of language and intelligence and emphasize the importance of language as an evolving process of intelligence.

7. Encourage the child to persist and let him know that you like him and want to help him.

8. Be consistent in your behavior. Mentally retarded children become anxious and frustrated when their authority figure fluctuates in behavior patterns.

9. Respond to the child's questions and comments. The mentally retarded youngster will feel better about himself if he knows his questions and comments are sincerely accepted by his teacher.

10. Be sure to avoid comparisons with the normal children in your classroom and eliminate a competitive climate. Help the child adjust to regular routines and get along with the other children.

Hearing Impaired Children. Although total deafness is relatively rare in classrooms (only 4 percent of all hearing problems result in deafness), mild or moderate hearing problems appear about as often as any other handicap. The degrees of handicap are based on the extent of hearing loss as measured in *decibels* (db), standard units for measuring the volume of sound. A loss of 40 db or more usually indicates an impairment by which children have difficulty hearing a person speak in a normal tone.

Although physical examinations and parental observations uncover some cases of hearing difficulty before the child comes to school, many mild or moderate hearing problems remain undiscovered until a child enters the classroom. Symptoms of hearing difficulties include:

Reluctance to speak; very loud, very soft, or very slow speech; poor articulation (forming of words or speech sounds)

Unresponsiveness when spoken to; may often ask "Huh?" or "What?"

Watching the speaker's face while the speaker is talking

Cocking or turning the head toward a speaker

Difficulty maintaining attention when spoken to

Complaining about earaches or demonstrating actions that indicate pain in the ear

In keeping with the spirit of PL 94–142, you are not only responsible for helping identify youngsters with hearing impairments but for planning programs that provide least restrictive environments for them. This need not be threatening; as R. A. Stassen points out, "Of all handicapped pupils, those with amplifiable hearing losses are among the most potentially teachable."[4] Your classroom setting should be the same for children with impaired hearing as it is for everyone else, except for the following recommendations:

1. Develop an attitude of readiness to listen. Use special signals to remind the child that you are about to speak. Encourage him to let you know when he's ready to listen to you.

2. Use the voice to get the child's attention. Say the child's name when you wish to talk to him. Tapping him on the shoulder and similar measures only bring unnecessary attention to the child's handicap.

3. Keep within close range when speaking. Turn toward the child so he can see your face. It helps him to be able to interpret your lip movements as well as your facial expressions.

4. Use a normal conversational tone of voice. Speak in short sentences with a clear voice. Clarity is much more important than loudness; increasing your volume only singles out the handicapped child and labels him as "different." Besides, clear speech is much easier to lip-read than is exaggerated speech.

5. Serve as a good speech model. Avoid overuse of gestures or exaggerated lip movements or facial expressions. Children benefit from observing normal speech behavior.

6. Use frequent repetition. Talk to the hearing impaired child and repeat your words when it seems necessary. If you create an accepting environment, the child will feel free to let you know when your words need to be repeated.

7. Encourage parents to expand your work in the home; their cooperation is essential to the success of any school program, but especially when special measures have been instituted to compensate for hearing handicaps.

8. Develop a favorable attitude toward the child. The single most important variable in working with the hearing impaired is an understanding teacher. You should treat the child as an able individual and be empathetic (not sympathetic) with his condition. Overprotection is unnecessary; except for these few recommendations, they need to be treated like others in your room.

Deaf children, of course, present a different situation from those who have some degree of hearing. The ultimate goal, again, is to integrate the children into the regular classroom, but they are unlikely to make a good adjustment unless at least *some* communicative speech patterns have been developed in the home or in special school settings before the child comes to the regular classroom. Northcott believes integrating the deaf into the regular classroom is not appropriate if these conditions are present:

1. **The hearing loss was recently diagnosed and there has been no parent guidance to ensure transfer and maintenance of educational gains through home stimulation, and**

2. **The child is not yet aware that his hearing aid brings in meaningful environmental sounds, including speech, or that he must look at faces to gain understanding from moving lips and facial expression.**[5]

If it has been determined that the deaf child can be mainstreamed, he must be placed in a situation where he can gain optimum benefit from his experience. This means that the major goal of his early experiences should be *socialization*. Once the socialization process has begun and the deaf child indicates an interest in formal learning, you may wish to contact hearing specialists or other resource persons for suggestions of supplementary teaching materials. Use special materials or methods within the context of the regular classroom whenever possible so that the deaf child is generally treated like any other.

Children with hearing problems are able to feel good about themselves and can gain from the educational setting if they are integrated with normally hearing children. You must match their unique needs to your program's resources. Except for following the special recommendations, the hearing impaired child should be treated like any other in your classroom.

Visually Impaired Children. Like the hearing impaired, the visually impaired child is most often normal in all other areas of development, so he needs much the same kind of educational environment as the normally sighted child.

Visually impaired children are usually classified into two categories: the partially sighted and the blind. Partially sighted children are those whose field is 20/200 (that is, they can see at 20 feet what a normally sighted person can see at 200 feet) or better in the corrected better eye, but not greater than 20/70. Blind children have a 20/200 field of vision or less vision in the corrected better eye.

Children with visual impairments exhibit distinct symptoms that you should be constantly alert to:

Crossed eyes (strabismus)

Involuntary, rapid movements of the eyeballs (nystagmus)

Squinting

Rubbing the eyes

Crusts, sties, or swollen lids

Reddened or watery eyes

Tilting the head to one side

Pupils of uneven size

Sensitivity to light

Awkwardness in eye-hand coordination (in puzzles, dressing, and so on)

Facial distortions while doing close work

Avoiding tasks that require good vision

Complaints of pain in the eyes, headaches, dizziness, or nausea following close work

Lack of interest in normally appealing visual experiences

Tendency to regularly confuse letters, words, or numerals: *6* and *9, d* and *b,* or *bad* and *dad.*[6]

You must follow a number of special practices with visually impaired children:

1. Arrange your furniture and other classroom materials so that the visually impaired child is able to move freely and safely.

2. Use your voice to tell the child what is going on. You or another child can verbalize aspects of meaningful experiences.

3. Encourage the child to explore with the other senses. A cow's cold, wet nose or the smell of freshly cut hay are only vague concepts until real sensory experiences add to their meaning.

4. Give the child opportunities to help others during group situations or projects; the visually impaired youngster is often on the "receiving end" rather than the "giving end" of human interaction.

5. Be a good language model for the child. Talk directly to the youngster and often explain what the other children are doing. Encourage the other youngsters to do the same.

6. Encourage the child to verbalize her needs. Let her know that people are sensitive to her requests.

7. Praise the child for each success.

8. Work with specialists who may be able to give you activities for encouraging growth of other senses.

With certain limitations, visually handicapped youngsters—like children with normal eyesight—should be provided with an environment in which they can explore, discover, and manipulate. You must respond to the children's interests and lead them to master special skills and abilities. When a blind child trusts a teacher in such a setting, he becomes able to move more confidently toward autonomy and increased skill.

In addition to the recommended teaching practices, you might contact a teacher or supervisor who has had special training in the field for other suggestions. Close cooperation among resource people, the classroom teacher, and parents can lead to special practices and procedures that will make the visually handicapped youngster's adjustment to the regular classroom successful.

Physically Handicapped Children. Some children are born with a physical handicap; others acquire it after birth. The type and degree of each child's physical problem require the teacher to make appropriate adjustments in the regular classroom. Since the special skills required to work with the wide range of physical disorders are too broad for this text, we will just list the physical handicaps that most commonly appear in elementary school children. They are cerebral palsy, epilepsy, spina bifida, amputation, and paralysis.

Obviously, your chief role is to be aware of these conditions and try as hard as possible to design programs to fit the physically handicapped. Be especially mindful that physically handicapped children suffer from many disadvantages brought about by their condition. Dorothy Rogers explains:

> Physically handicapped children experience many disadvantages. For one thing, their developmental progress suffers, leaving them out of step with children of the same age.
>
> A child lacking motor skills rarely plays an important role among peers. Activities are restricted, so one child grows envious, resentful, and withdrawn—sustained only by the successes of fantasy. Another may become anxious and angry, engaging in offensive aggression. Afterward he feels guilty, but his efforts to "make up" are rebuffed. Still another child may, either consciously or unconsciously, use her handicap to gain selfish ends. In any case, her mood and attitude may make her such poor company that she becomes more rejected still—a vicious cycle. . . .
>
> The handicapped child also suffers simply by being a child. Children are frequently insensitive to the feelings of less favored persons. They can be bru-

tally frank, causing deep wounds. In one case, a lame child was called "Crip." In another instance, children mimicked a boy with a cleft palate, taking no pains to remove themselves from his hearing. . . .

The handicapped also suffer from societal attitudes toward them. While ostensibly heeding their welfare, people often feel pity or repulsion—or even an unconscious resentment that such people must be provided for. The handicapped, in turn, come to expect society's negative attitudes toward them, and they often acquire deep-seated inferiority complexes. Despite intermittent struggles, the majority are unhappy and often doomed to social isolation.[7]

You need to make the physically handicapped child comfortable, but be careful not to be overly helpful or to communicate pity. These children have had therapy that encourages self-help and positive self-concept. Your role is to build on this foundation by providing an accepting environment of warmth and tolerance. Kirk explains how the previous therapy received by the child can be supported and extended within the regular classroom setting:

1. Develop motor abilities in the child through special materials, special aids and supports for mobility, and through special methods provided by the physiotherapist, the occupational therapist, and the special teacher. In the school situation the teacher is the coordinator of the program even though specific prescriptions are given by the attending pediatrician or orthopedic specialist.
2. Develop language and speech, especially in the cerebral-palsied child, since this is one area where the majority are retarded or defective. This includes the ability to perceive oral language and to express it, to perceive visual stimuli and interpret them, and to express oneself in motor terms. The latter includes both speech and gestures. This phase of the child's development is assisted by a speech correctionist, the parents, and the special teacher.
3. Develop in the child the psychological factors of visual and auditory perception, discrimination, memory, and other factors considered intellectual. These functions are best developed through the school program which includes language usage, listening, planning, problem solving, dramatization, imagination and creative expression (through art and music media), creative rhythms, visual and auditory memory and discrimination, and perception.
4. Develop social and emotional adequacy in the child at home and in the school by providing him with opportunities for acquiring emotional security, belongingness, and independence. The school situation is probably superior to the home in not overprotecting the child and in giving him opportunities to do things himself. The environment of the school which includes other children of the same age gives the child an opportunity to learn to interact with others, to share, and to cooperate. It offers him examples of activities which he can imitate, and at the same time the protection and help which he needs when he really needs it.[8]

Learning to overcome physical problems at an early age in a regular classroom setting helps a child accept the handicap.

Planning an Instructional Design

PL 94–142 mandated that schools develop an Individualized Educational Program (IEP) for every child mainstreamed into the regular classroom. The IEP is a written statement developed jointly by a qualified school official, the child's teacher, the child's parents or guardian, and, if possible, the child. The written statement must include:

1. Analysis of the child's present achievement level
2. Listing of long- and short-range goals
3. Statement of specific services that will be provided to help the child reach the goals
4. Indication of the extent to which the child will become involved in regular school programs
5. Schedule for evaluating the progress experienced with the IEP and recommendations for revisions

Mainstreaming

Since our mission in social studies education is equal opportunity for all, the concept of mainstreaming physically and mentally handicapped children should be met enthusiastically. In mainstreaming children, we build on all we know about the importance of the elementary school years to all aspects of the child's development.

View the child as a whole child with strengths as well as weaknesses. Avoid looking at the handicapped youngster as an "epileptic" or "mentally retarded," but just as a child.

Learn all you can about the mainstreamed child's specific disability. Become aware of therapy techniques and technical terminology.

Involve parents in dealing with their child both in the school and at home. They should learn what you are doing in school so that your practices can be reinforced and extended in the home.

Maximize interactions between the handicapped and nonhandicapped children. Give simple explanations about a child's handicap, when needed. Youngsters are curious; they want to know about a new child and will be satisfied by an open, honest explanation. ("Jeannie's legs don't work well so she needs a wheelchair.") Read books or tell stories about children with differences. Encourage the handicapped child to share strong capabilities. For example, the wheelchair-bound youngster can help another child in a project that demands manual dexterity and soon gain that child's appreciation for outstanding manual skill.

Individualize your program. Start where the child is and plan a sequential program to encourage him to build one skill upon another. Build on continuous success.

Make appropriate spatial and environmental changes in and around the school. It may be necessary to build ramps for physically handicapped youngsters or to put grab bars in the bathrooms.

Take special in-service training through workshops or seminars. Keep up on the current principles and practices of mainstreaming.

Mainstreaming requires changes in attitudes, behaviors, and teaching style. Since you will be part of this movement, you must gain the skills and attitudes necessary to help children function effectively in society despite a handicap. What better place to start this process than in a social studies classroom?

THE GIFTED

Exceptionally talented or intelligent children were given little attention in our schools until the 1970s. To single out and provide special classroom instruction for these youngsters was considered elitist, somewhat un-American. Why, people asked, should we channel extra money and resources toward these youngsters' education when others, particularly the handicapped, needed them so much more? We began to realize, however, that our concern for so-called un-American schooling was paradoxical. We realized our schools were, in most instances, meeting the needs of handicapped learners but failing to meet the unique needs of gifted students. In effect, the gifted were prevented from having an opportunity to reach *their* fullest potential.

At the same time, educators began searching for the characteristics to describe gifted students and for the most suitable classroom experiences for them. We consider gifted children those who are exceptionally intelligent, creative, or talented in some special way, such as in music, art, or even sports. Originally, though, giftedness was defined primarily in terms of rank on a standardized intelligence test, most frequently the Binet scale. Some specialists identified those with IQ scores of 120 or more as gifted because they made up only 10 percent of the population. Others suggested a 130 IQ score because only 2.27 percent had scores that high; still others suggested an IQ score of 140 or over because it would restrict giftedness to a group of only 0.5 percent of the total population. Since IQ tests are somewhat inaccurate in these upper ranges, however, psychologists and educators searched for other definitions of giftedness. Eventually, Martinson suggested a well-rounded, practical definition:

1. A score in the top 3% for the child's ethnic or cultural group or an individual intelligence test (a score of 130 or better for white, native-born Americans).
2. The results of a teacher's observation. Walton found that when teachers were asked the following questions, they were often able to select gifted individuals from their classroom: Who learns easily and rapidly? Who uses a lot of common sense and practical knowledge? Who retains easily what he or she has heard?

Who knows about many things of which other children are unaware? Who uses a large number of words easily and accurately? Who recognizes relations and comprehends meanings? Who is alert, keenly observant, responds quickly?

3. Previous accomplishments in an area of special talent. Experts in the field are usually called in to judge the quality of a child's artistic, musical, dramatic, or other creative talent.

4. Creativity test scores. Not all children with high IQs are necessarily the most creative individuals. Tests of creativity may help identify gifted youngsters normally not selected by standard IQ measures.[9]

You face a special challenge with a gifted child in your classroom. Although we are still groping for suitable curriculum methods and activities to meet their special needs, these are suggestions for adapting typical social studies activities for the gifted child:

Choose material that meets their intellectual needs. Reading material, for example, may be at least two grade levels higher than the rest of the class.

Allow gifted children to work at an accelerated pace. They may feel bored or apathetic if you force them to work at the same pace as the other children.

Allow them time to independently pursue projects that interest them.

If computers are available, encourage the gifted child to change programs or design new programs.

Be aware of the special social needs of gifted learners. Because they are gifted or talented in one area does not necessarily mean they are exceptional in all areas of development. Help them participate with both older playmates and children their own age.

Keep a positive outlook. It is common to feel inadequate around such children when they ask questions you cannot answer or point out mistakes. Avoid feeling resentment and alienation.

Release the child to special classes that are often directed by teachers with special training for working with the gifted.

Every gifted child presents a unique challenge. Whatever strategy you use to meet their needs, your major responsibility is to prevent boredom.

SUMMARY

Effective teachers of elementary school social studies are good decision makers. They examine the recommendations of experts in the field, weigh the consequences of each, and settle on a program that is compatible with their philosophies and the group or individual needs of the children. Nothing is as exciting and rewarding as watching children react positively to a dynamic program that grows and develops under your guidance. Every paycheck or outstanding evaluation from your supervisor pales in comparison to the feeling on the last day of the school year when a tearful group of youngsters says to you, "We don't want to leave. School was so much fun this year!"

To help in your decision making, consider this summary:

Philosophy—How do I view the development of children? What theory best explains the process of learning?

Objectives—What are the needs of the children? What do I hope to achieve? What is expected of the children at this stage of development?

Curriculum—What is my role? The children's role? What materials and activities will I use? How will I arrange the classroom? How will I schedule daily activities?

Evaluation—To what extent did my planned sequence of instruction achieve its objectives? How favorably did my children compare to others? How should I adapt my instruction to meet the results of evaluation?

Individualization—What range of backgrounds and experiences do my children have? Interests? Motivation? Intelligence? Physical capabilities? Language facility? Reading ability?

Plan your program to fit your children's needs. No single chapter can give you a complete idea of the innumerable factors that influence your planning. If you truly want to be a successful teacher, you must build an awareness and sensitivity to the *real world* of children, one that includes careful, day-by-day observation and evaluation to serve as a basis for effective lessons and units.

ENDNOTES

1. David F. Kellum, "Presenting Subject Matter," in *Teaching Is . . .*, ed. Merrill Harmin and Tom Gregory (Chicago: Science Research Associates, 1974), pp. 47–48.

2. Lavonne A. Hanna, Gladys L. Potter, and Robert W. Reynolds, *Dynamic Elementary Social Studies: Unit Teaching* (New York: Holt, Rinehart and Winston, 1973), p. 80.

3. Linwood Chase and Martha Tyler John, *A Guide for the Elementary Social Studies Teacher* (Boston: Allyn and Bacon, 1972), pp. 243–44.

4. R. A. Stassen, "I Have One In My Class Who's Wearing Hearing Aids!" in *The Hearing Impaired Child in a Regular Classroom: Preschool, Elementary, and Secondary Years*, ed. W. H. Northcott (Washington, DC: Alexander Graham Bell Association for the Deaf, 1973), p. 3.

5. W. H. Northcott, "Candidate for Integration: A Hearing Impaired Child in a Regular Nursery School," *Young Children* 25, no. 6 (September 1970): 368.

6. List generated from material in Dorothy Rogers, *Child Psychology*, 2nd ed. (Belmont, CA: Wadsworth, 1977) and Samuel A. Kirk, *Educating Exceptional Children*, 2nd ed. (Boston: Houghton-Mifflin, 1972).

7. Dorothy Rogers, *Child Psychology*, 2nd ed. (Belmont Calif.: Wadsworth, 1977), pp. 94–95.

8. Samuel A. Kirk, *Educating Exceptional Children,* 2nd ed. (Boston: Houghton-Mifflin, 1972), pp. 258–59.

9. R. A. Martinson, "Children With Superior Cognitive Abilities," in *Exceptional Children in the Schools: Special Education in Transition,* ed. L. M. Dunn (New York: Holt, Rinehart and Winston, 1973), pp. 580–84.

Index

About the Author

 George W. Maxim is a professor in the Department of Childhood Studies and Reading at West Chester University in Pennsylvania, specializing in social studies and early childhood education methods courses. He is an experienced teacher, holding positions at both the elementary and nursery school levels. He has received the Certificate of Excellence in Teaching from the Pennsylvania Department of Education and the Certificate for Outstanding Contributions in Teaching and Research from the Pennsylvania Association of Private Academic Schools. An active member of the National Council for the Social Studies, he has served on the Educational Publishing Advisory Committee and has chaired the Early Childhood/Elementary Advisory Committee. Dr. Maxim has written several articles on social studies education as well as an early childhood college text, *The Very Young* (Wadsworth, 1980). *Social Studies and the Elementary School Child,* Third Edition, reflects Dr. Maxim's belief that social studies teaching is a critical career because it prepares young children to become responsible, informed citizens as adults.

WE VALUE YOUR OPINION—PLEASE SHARE IT WITH US

Merrill Publishing and our authors are most interested in your reactions to this textbook. Did it serve you well in the course? If it did, what aspects of the text were most helpful? If not, what didn't you like about it? Your comments will help us to write and develop better textbooks. We value your opinions and thank you for your help.

Text Title _____ Edition _____

Author(s) _____

Your Name (optional) _____

Address _____

City _____ State _____ Zip _____

School _____

Course Title _____

Instructor's Name _____

Your Major _____

Your Class Rank _____ Freshman _____ Sophomore _____ Junior _____ Senior

_____ Graduate Student

Were you required to take this course? _____ Required _____ Elective

Length of Course? _____ Quarter _____ Semester

1. Overall, how does this text compare to other texts you've used?

_____ Superior _____ Better Than Most _____ Average _____ Poor

2. Please rate the text in the following areas:

	Superior	Better Than Most	Average	Poor
Author's Writing Style	_____	_____	_____	_____
Readability	_____	_____	_____	_____
Organization	_____	_____	_____	_____
Accuracy	_____	_____	_____	_____
Layout and Design	_____	_____	_____	_____
Illustrations/Photos/Tables	_____	_____	_____	_____
Examples	_____	_____	_____	_____
Problems/Exercises	_____	_____	_____	_____
Topic Selection	_____	_____	_____	_____
Currentness of Coverage	_____	_____	_____	_____
Explanation of Difficult Concepts	_____	_____	_____	_____
Match-up with Course Coverage	_____	_____	_____	_____
Applications to Real Life	_____	_____	_____	_____

3. Circle those chapters you especially liked:
   1   2   3   4   5   6   7   8   9   11
   What was your favorite chapter? _____
   Comments:

4. Circle those chapters you liked least:
   1   2   3   4   5   6   7   8   9   11
   What was your least favorite chapter? _____
   Comments:

5. List any chapters your instructor did not assign. _____

6. What topics did your instructor discuss that were not covered in the text? _____

   _____

7. Were you required to buy this book? _____ Yes _____ No

   Did you buy this book new or used? _____ New _____ Used

   If used, how much did you pay? _____

   Do you plan to keep or sell this book? _____ Keep _____ Sell

   If you plan to sell the book, how much do you expect to receive? _____

   Should the instructor continue to assign this book? _____ Yes _____ No

8. Please list any other learning materials you purchased to help you in this course (e.g., study guide, lab manual).

   _____

9. What did you like most about this text? _____

   _____

10. What did you like least about this text? _____

    _____

11. General comments:

    May we quote you in our advertising? _____ Yes _____ No

    Please mail to: Boyd Lane
                      College Division, Research Department
                      Box 508
                      1300 Alum Creek Drive
                      Columbus, Ohio 43216

    Thank you!